The Art of the Character

Highlights from the Glenn Close Costume Collection

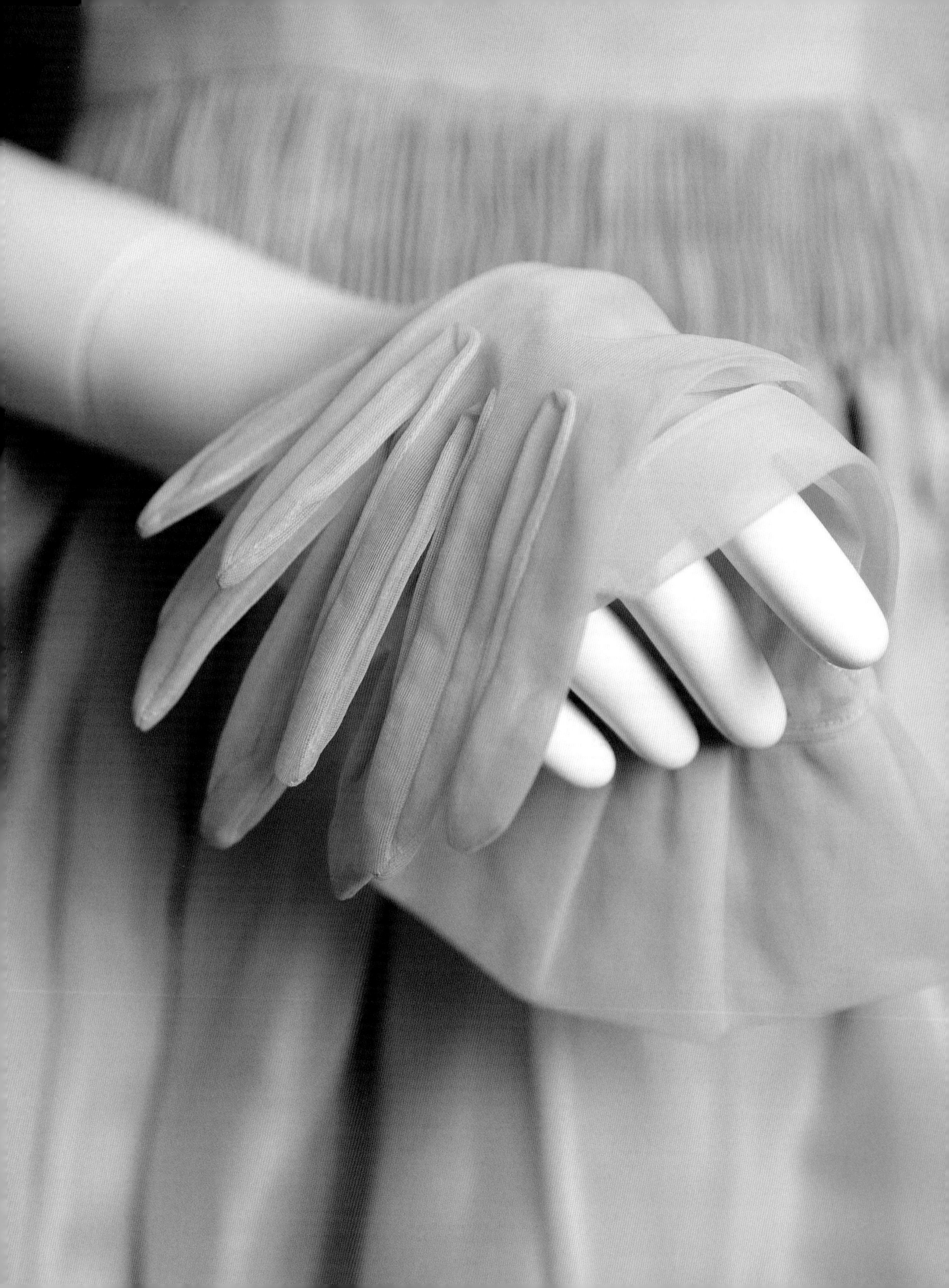

The Art of the Character

Highlights from the Glenn Close Costume Collection

Kelly Gallett Richardson and Galina Olmsted

with Heather Akou, Jennifer E. Maher, Heather Milam, and Linda Pisano

Sidney and Lois Eskenazi Museum of Art, Indiana University
in association with Scala Arts Publishers, Inc.

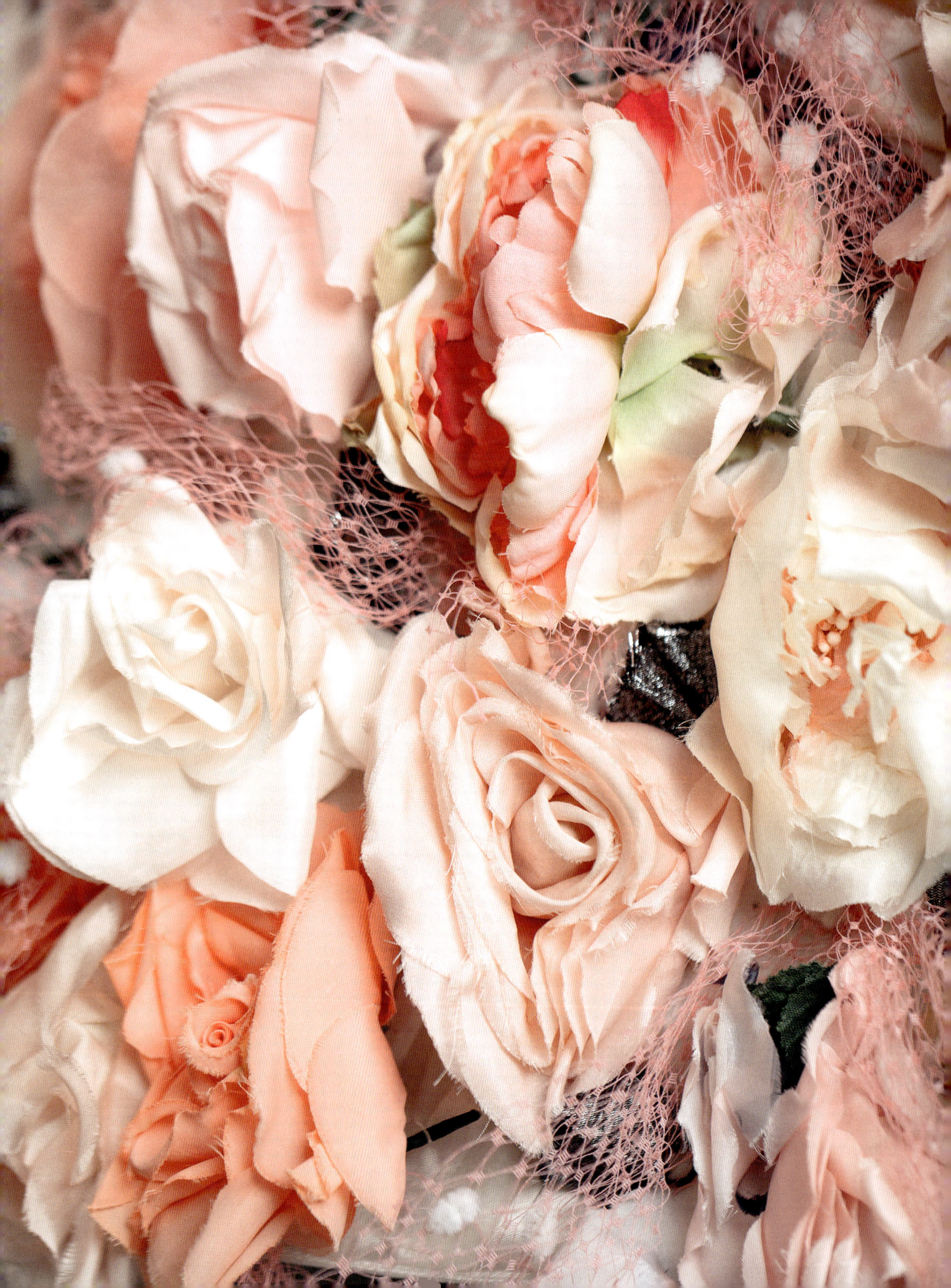

Contents

Director's Foreword

We are proud to copresent *The Art of the Character: Highlights from the Glenn Close Costume Collection*, an exhibition and catalogue that offers unprecedented insight into the high art of costuming, which enabled a phenomenally gifted actor to transform herself into her most memorable roles. A seven-time Academy Award-nominated and three-time Emmy and Tony award-winning actor, Glenn Close's success is in part the result of her deep and ongoing collaborations with brilliant designers, including Anthony Powell (*101* and *102 Dalmatians*), Ann Roth (*The Stepford Wives*), and James Acheson (*Dangerous Liaisons*), as well as her appreciation for the artistry and highly skilled handcraft of makers such as Barbara Matera and Katherine Marshall.

Glenn Close has intentionally collected her costumes from the outset of her career to the present day, a testament to her commitment to documenting the creative process and to preserving these unique creations for the study and enjoyment of future generations of actors, designers, and makers. Her generous donation of more than eight hundred costumes and other items to the Elizabeth Sage Historic Costume Collection in the Sidney and Lois Eskenazi School of Art, Architecture + Design at Indiana University in 2017 provides an indispensable resource for students and faculty that enhances learning in a variety of studies, but especially theater, merchandising, and design.

Indiana University is home to many astonishing cultural resources, among them the Sidney and Lois Eskenazi Museum of Art and the Sidney and Lois Eskenazi School of Art, Architecture + Design. We are forever grateful to Sidney and Lois Eskenazi, generous benefactors after whom the museum and school are named. Distinguished by its superb collection and its recently renovated building designed by I. M. Pei, the Eskenazi Museum of Art is honored to partner with the Sage Collection to present an exhibition that exemplifies the diversity and excellence of cross-disciplinary opportunities at a world-class university.

We are grateful to the staff of the Eskenazi Museum of Art and the Sage Collection for working so effectively together to produce this exhibition and catalogue. It is extraordinary to think that most of this work was accomplished during a worldwide pandemic. We particularly recognize the efforts of curatorial project leaders Kelly Gallett Richardson, Curator of the Sage Collection, and Galina Olmsted, Assistant Curator of European and American Art at the Eskenazi Museum of Art. Their careful shepherding of this landmark project has ensured its success. Mariah R. Keller, the museum's Director of Creative Services, provided expert oversight of the catalogue's production. We are also grateful to the other contributors—Heather Akou, Associate Professor of Fashion Design and Director, Sage Collection; Jennifer E. Maher, Clinical Associate Professor, Department of Gender Studies; Heather Milam, Professor of Practice, Department of Theatre, Drama, and Contemporary Dance; and Linda Pisano, Professor and Chair, Department of Theatre, Drama, and Contemporary Dance. The breadth and depth of expertise at the university is evident in the pages that follow.

This project would not have been possible without the passionate support of Indiana University's First Lady, Laurie Burns McRobbie. Her initial embrace of the idea to welcome the Glenn Close Costume Collection to the university and her unwavering enthusiasm and support of the exhibition and catalogue were instrumental to the project's success. We are grateful for her unstinting leadership and counsel.

We also want to acknowledge and thank designer James Nadeaux, who generously advised us and provided additional insight into the creative process. His open-minded and lively spirit helped move this project forward.

Generous support for the exhibition and catalogue was provided in part by the Indiana University Foundation Well House Society, Women's Philanthropy Leadership Council, Kimberly and John Simpson, and Office of the Bicentennial at Indiana University. We deeply appreciate their help in making this exhibition and catalogue a reality.

Finally, we want to express our deepest appreciation to Glenn Close for the transformational gift of her costume collection and her enthusiastic embrace of this project. *The Art of the Character* is just a taste of what her collection means to our university community and beyond. We trust that she feels that her lovingly and thoughtfully assembled collection of costumes has found a good home at Indiana University.

Peg Faimon
Founding Dean
Sidney and Lois Eskenazi School of Art, Architecture + Design
Indiana University

David A. Brenneman
Wilma E. Kelley Director
Sidney and Lois Eskenazi Museum of Art
Indiana University

Acknowledgments

The Art of the Character: Highlights from the Glenn Close Costume Collection has been many years in the making, and we would like to extend our gratitude to all those who helped bring this project to life. First and foremost, we want to thank David Brenneman, the Wilma E. Kelley Director of the Sidney and Lois Eskenazi Museum of Art, Indiana University (IU), and Peg Faimon, Founding Dean of the Sidney and Lois Eskenazi School of Art, Architecture + Design, IU, for their support. This project's success is also due to the generosity and steadfast support of IU's First Lady, Laurie Burns McRobbie, and we are grateful for her counsel and leadership in moving the exhibition and catalogue forward. We also thank designer James Nadeaux, whose expertise, advice, and guidance were invaluable. Our appreciation also extends to Bernice Pescosolido, Distinguished Professor of Sociology at IU, whose relationship with Glenn Close led to talks about her costumes, and Kathleen L. Rowold, Professor Emeritus and Former Director of the Elizabeth Sage Historic Costume Collection (Sage Collection), whose leadership and determination made Close's offered gift a reality.

Our research into the designers and makers was assisted by Holly Poe Durbin, Michael Lewis, Marilyn Lintel, Danielle Milton, Hannah Sorkin, and Wendy Watts, and we thank them for their help in highlighting the artists who brought Close's characters to life. For their insightful contributions to the catalogue, we are grateful to Heather Akou, Associate Professor of Fashion Design and Director, Sage Collection; Jennifer E. Maher, Clinical Associate Professor, Department of Gender Studies; and Heather Milam, Professor of Practice, and Linda Pisano, Professor and Chair, Department of Theatre, Drama, and Contemporary Dance.

The dedicated and talented staff at the Eskenazi Museum of Art and the Sage Collection devoted a great deal of time and effort to the exhibition and catalogue, much of which was accomplished during an unusually challenging time when both institutions were closed because of a global pandemic. The following colleagues provided research assistance, cleared image rights, managed the logistics of mounting an exhibition, raised funds, edited texts, managed publicity, photographed costumes, and much more—at the Eskenazi Museum: Anita Bracalente, Registrar; Joii Cooper, Assistant Director of Donor Relations and Stewardship; Heidi Davis-Soylu, Patricia and Joel Meier Chair of Education; Carol Dell, Director of Administration; Lasserina Dowell, Associate Director of Development; Mariah R. Keller, Director of Creative Services; Shanti Knight, Photographer; Maggie Kroh, Assistant to the Director; Kristin Londergan, Marketing and Communications Coordinator; Christopher Myers-Nunn, Andrew W. Mellon and Anthony J. Moravec University Experiences Manager; Pete Nelson, Chief Preparator; Erin Ryan, Tour and Docent Experiences Manager; Laura Scheper, Interpretation and Public Experiences Manager; Cassi Tucker, Manager of Museum Technology; Richard Valdez, Finance Manager; Jessie Waymire, Graphic Designer; and Patricia Winterton, Director of Development; and at the Sage Collection: Emily Rosolowski, Collections Assistant.

At IU, we also received important assistance from Madi Bell, MFA candidate in Costume Technology; Doug Booher, Executive Director of University Events; Lynn Burgin,

Executive Assistant to the Dean of the Eskenazi School of Art, Architecture + Design; Deb Christiansen, Executive Director of Academics, Eskenazi School of Art, Architecture + Design, and Senior Lecturer, Fashion Design; Heather Dies, Director of Development, Office of the Provost and Executive Vice President; Haley Garl Hatton, Assistant to the First Lady; Paula Jenkins, Vice President of Development, Bloomington, IU Foundation; Heather Kogge, Director of Development and Alumni Engagement, Eskenazi School of Art, Architecture + Design; Beth Maben and Emily Meier, alumnae, Fashion Design; Vaughn Nuest, Head of Auxiliary Library Facilities Management Services; Helene O'Leary, Assistant Provost for Strategic Campus Advancement; Bryan Orthel, Area Coordinator and Associate Professor, Interior Design; John Wilhite, Assistant Vice President for Real Estate, Personal Property, and Insurance, IU Foundation; and the students enrolled in F402: Collections Management for Historic Costume and Textiles (spring 2020).

We are also grateful to Andrea Felder, Permissions and Reproduction Services, The New York Public Library; Susan Lennon, Alamy; Robert Neuman, Professor of Art History, Florida State University; Katie Salzmann, Lead Archivist, Wittliff Collections, Texas State University; Petra Slinkard, The Nancy B. Putnam Curator of Fashion and Textiles, Peabody Essex Museum; and Emily Stamey, Curator of Exhibitions, Weatherspoon Art Museum, University of North Carolina Greensboro, for their assistance with research and images for this project. Our thanks also to Anna Powell Denton for her beautiful photography.

It has also been a privilege to work with the enthusiastic and capable staff at Scala Arts Publishers on the production of this publication: Jennifer Norman and Claire Young, as well as designer Antonio Alcalá of Studio A and copyeditor Magda Nakassis.

Our thanks to Nancy Evans, Executive Assistant to Glenn Close, and Allison Palmero, former Assistant to Ms. Close, for their help in arranging schedules and gathering images for the catalogue.

Much gratitude must be extended to the many talented designers and makers whose craft is the subject of this project. We are delighted to shine the spotlight on James Acheson, Consolata Boyle, Alexandra Byrne, Pierre-Yves Gayraud, Judianna Makovsky, Ellen Mirojnick, Anthony Powell, and Van Broughton Ramsey. Thanks especially to Ann Roth for her thoughtful afterword to this book.

For their support of the exhibition and catalogue, we thank the IU Foundation Well House Society, Women's Philanthropy Leadership Council, Kimberly and John Simpson, and Office of the Bicentennial at IU. In addition, we thank Daniel Smith, President and CEO, IU Foundation; and Kelly Kish, Director, Office of the Bicentennial.

Finally, we are deeply grateful to Glenn Close, both for the gift of her collection to the university and her enthusiastic, unwavering support of this project. Her commitment to celebrating the designers and makers who bring her characters to life is at the heart of this exhibition and catalogue.

Kelly Gallett Richardson
Curator, Sage Collection
Sidney and Lois Eskenazi School of Art, Architecture + Design
Indiana University

Galina Olmsted
Assistant Curator of European and American Art
Sidney and Lois Eskenazi Museum of Art
Indiana University

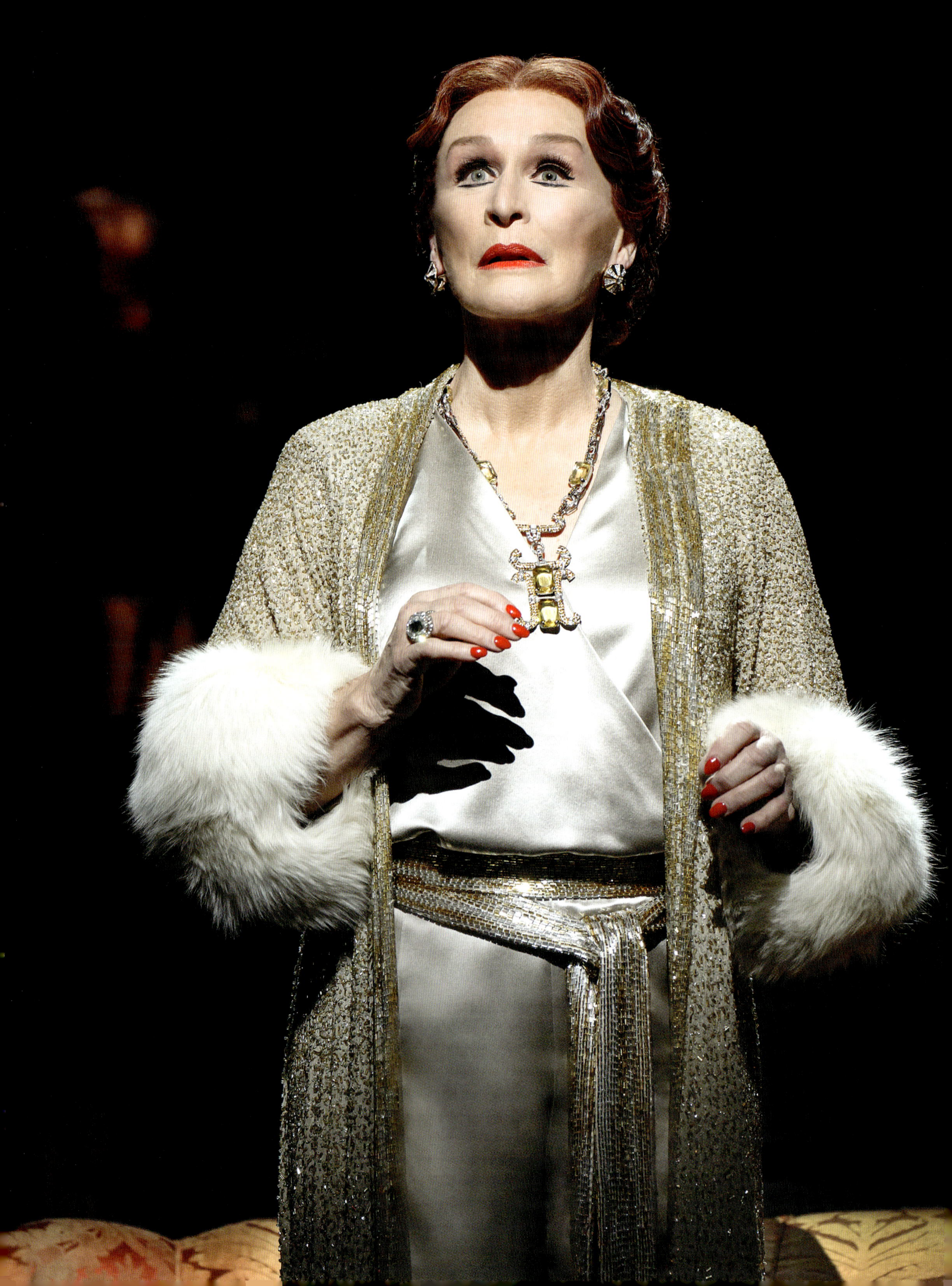

Interview with Glenn Close

Laurie Burns McRobbie
First Lady
Indiana University

April 22, 2020

LBM: What motivated you to start collecting your costumes? And was it a particular production that sparked your interest in collecting the costumes you were wearing?

GC: Unfortunately, I only started collecting after my first movie—*The World According To Garp*. I'd had some wonderful costumes onstage before that. I was motivated to start collecting because my costumes were such a vital part of whatever character I had created. As I have gained a deeper knowledge and respect for my craft over the years, I have found that the careful, assiduous collaboration with my costume designer is as important, really, to any rehearsal process or collaboration with my directors. My first movie costumes were designed by Ann Roth and built by Barbara Matera, at Barbara's atelier in New York City. I was told that usually, after a production has run its course, film and theater companies sell the costumes to costume houses, where they get rented out, reworked, and often ripped apart. I equated that with the obliteration of the characters whom I had come to love and for whom those costumes had been created—the obliteration of examples of the high art of costume design. I simply didn't want my costumes to end up on a rag heap, so I started collecting.

LBM: And can you say more about what it is about the costume that informs the character? Or maybe it's the other way around, but what is that relationship?

GC: Well, a costume will inform how that character presents herself to the world. That costume will inform how you move physically, because of the shoes, the underpinnings, the weight and texture of the fabrics, and how long or short the skirt is. I just had this thought: I was brought up by a wonderful woman who was probably the most un-materialistic person I will ever meet in my life—my mother. She had a real Yankee sensibility, which was basically: buy something of value and wear it until it's worn out. We didn't go shopping for fun. Malls were never a part of our life. We would go shopping to get new dresses for Easter and for Christmas. And usually, I was expected to wear the same piece of clothing after my sister outgrew hers.

LBM: I had an older sister, too.

GC: So I think I know more about creating the wardrobe for a character than I do about creating a wardrobe for myself. I'm not a shopper. I hate shopping. I would be happy to go around in blue jeans or a comfortable uniform my entire life. For me, it's a real effort to get all dolled up for a red-carpet event. It is not what I would ever choose to do for fun. Other people love it and I can certainly understand that, but I realize now that my appreciation for costumes has been in the context of a given character I'm being asked to portray—not ever for myself. So maybe I wanted to collect because I am more interested in and engaged in creating a wardrobe for a character than I would ever be for myself. My first movie character

OPPOSITE
Glenn Close as Norma Desmond in *Sunset Boulevard*, 2017

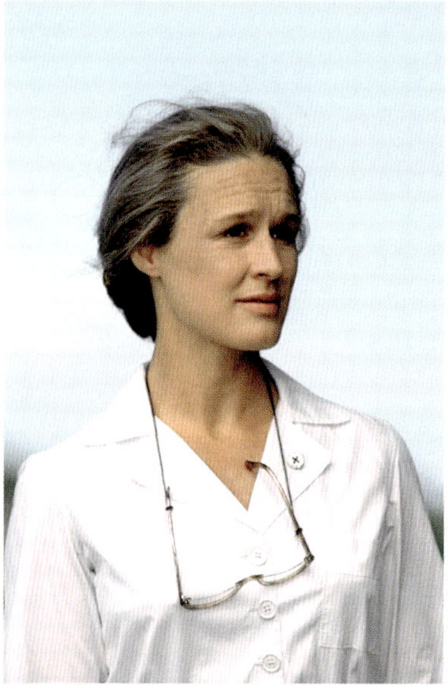

Glenn Close as Jenny Fields in *The World According to Garp*, 1982

was Jenny Fields in *The World According to Garp*. Her uniform was how she presented herself to the world. It was a starched, white nurse's uniform and white, low-heeled, old lady shoes. That is all Jenny ever wore. Ann Roth designed a beautiful, classic, long, navy blue, wool coat that Jenny wore when she needed to—you could still wear it today. Jenny's back was as straight as my Connecticut Yankee grandmother's. I was helped in maintaining that posture by an old-fashioned girdle, with garters attached that held up my white stockings.

LBM: Oh, like a hook deal?

GC: You know those girdles that were like huge, wide rubber bands around your waist and thighs. My underpinnings for Jenny were what women usually wore, including a bullet bra—the kind made famous by Madonna. And so that was it. Jenny had her armor underneath her uniform. That was my first movie character and that uniform was her image, her persona.

LBM: I don't know if I ever told you this, but of all the amazing pieces in your costume collection, I think that nurse's uniform is, well, I guess it's my favorite. Not because it's necessarily the most beautiful, but because I have a vivid recollection of that movie. I loved the book and I thought the movie was just an excellent retelling of that whole story. Obviously it wasn't the same as the book, but it was its own thing. And Jenny Fields, I loved her.

GC: That's why it will be fun for your students because that costume was custom-made, evident in the details—the buttons and the lovely little detail around the waist. This was in the early eighties, and I remember being gobsmacked to hear that those uniforms cost five hundred dollars apiece. That was expensive!

LBM: Oh, that's a lot.

GC: Parts of those uniforms were hand-stitched. As simple as that uniform looked, every detail was thought-out. You could never buy a uniform like that off the rack. It would be interesting to get Ann Roth to come in and tell you about it.

LBM: When you were talking about your mother, I wondered, did she teach you to sew?

GC: No. I wish. My mom knew how to knit, but she started knitting a sweater for my older sister and finally finished it for my younger sister—eight years later!

LBM: Because it took her that long?

GC: Yeah, she would get distracted. But I remember loving the sound of the clicking needles.

LBM: I love that. So when you sign on to a role, do you already have an image of what the character will look like? What the character's dress will look like? And do you have a designer in mind? Can you influence the choice of designer for the character's costume?

GC: Now I can. When I started out, I couldn't. Designers, throughout my career, have been as important as directors, because I do not necessarily have an image of what a character should look like. I could never have shopped for Alex Forrest in *Fatal Attraction*! I mean, I would not know where to start. But what the designer, Ellen Mirojnick, brought to that role—the black leather coat, the seductive dress at the cocktail party, the white dress in the final fight—was an enormous inspiration. So Ellen's work was an incalculable gift. Alex Forrest's wardrobe is everything to that character. Sometimes, if you're really in tune with the designer, a piece of your personal wardrobe may end up in a movie. For example, there is a coat that I wore in the subway scene in *Fatal Attraction*. It's a heavy, knitted gray coat that I had bought for myself. I still have it. It's a fabulous coat, with huge shoulders. Ellen saw it and suggested it for the subway scene, and it was perfect. Another example is the coat that Jenny Fields wears over her uniform in an early scene at Steering School. It's an Irish tweed houndstooth coat that, at the time of filming, was already about thirty years old. It's one of my treasured possessions and indestructible. It had come from a little shop that one of mom's friends once had in Greenwich, Connecticut. It has raglan sleeves, so you can fit anything under it. Ann Roth saw it on me and fell in love with it, so I wore it in the movie. It got a new lining out of the experience.

Anthony Powell, Shoes (Cruella De Vil, *101 Dalmatians*), 1996, Manolo Blahnik, Leather, metal, GC 2017.2.2 AB

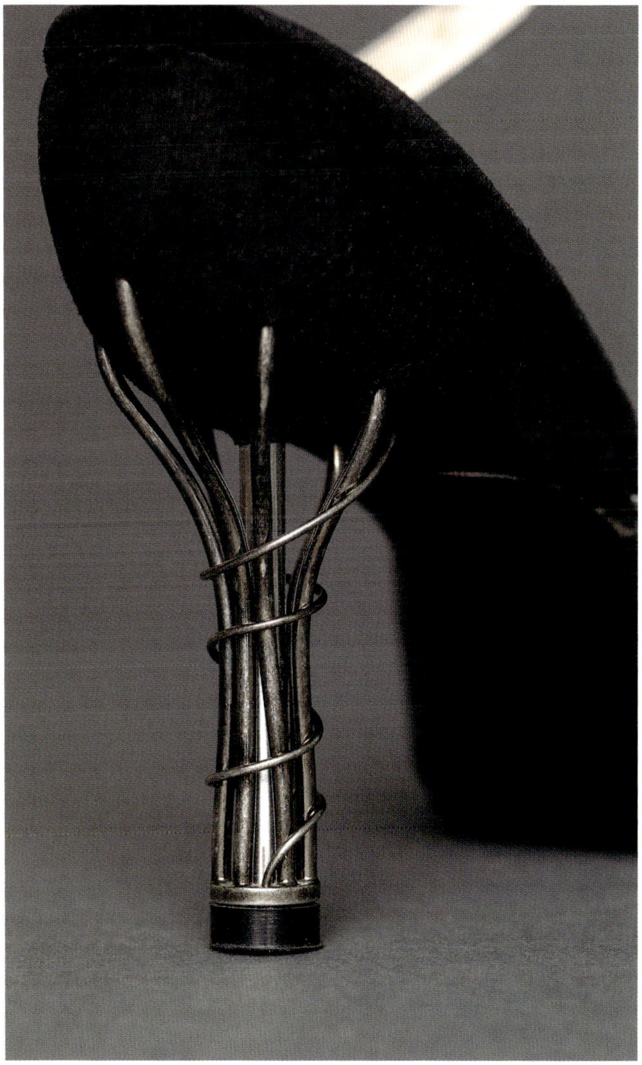

LBM: A bonus!

GC: Yes.

LBM: You obviously have a very close collaborative relationship with the designers. As you said, they are as important to you as your collaborations with a director. Can you talk more about some of those long-term collaborations? Ann Roth, who you've worked with multiple times, or Anthony Powell. What have those long-term collaborations been like? How have they developed?

GC: I think the long-term collaborations exist because of a deep respect for someone's talent and the challenge their work represents—you can be very challenged by a costume. Ann Roth and Anthony Powell challenged me all the time. People should really understand the importance of designers like Ann Roth and Anthony Powell. Look at their incredible résumés!

Anthony and I did *Sunset* [*Boulevard*] first and then [*101*] *Dalmatians*. He'd come up with these incredible designs. For example, there is a pair of shoes—they are in the collection—that I wore when you first see Cruella [De Vil] in *101*. When she steps out of the car, you see her foot sheathed in these challenging, high-heeled shoes. Literally, each heel is made out of a single nail! Those were beyond, but the design was so fabulous I couldn't say, "Anthony, are you kidding me?" On a movie set, you spend hours in shoes and have to command your brain to not pay attention to the pain. When Anthony proposed a challenging design, he'd say, "Oh, I know you can pull this off. I know you can do this." And, because I love a challenge and love the effect, there was no way I would refuse to wear what he was proposing! We both knew the nail shoes were perfectly spectacular. You would never know, when you see me walk down the runway, early in *101 Dalmatians*, that my feet were on fire. And he did it to me over and over again. I mean, I had long, heavy furs that I had to know how to use and move in. And it's something that's very important, I think, for an actor. You have to wear the costume. The costume can't wear you. You have to move in it like it is second nature or else the costume will be a distraction from the action. But anyway, I was hugely—thrillingly—challenged by Anthony's costumes. Another one that I found challenging was an Anthony design for *Sunset Boulevard*—the zebra-print kimono which I wore at the top of the second act, when I had to run down a long set of stairs. The kimono is constructed out of hand-painted, weightless silk. It was a challenge because its lightness made it hard to manage, plus it had long, trailing sleeves that tried to kill me. Every performance I had to tame that zebra, had to make my entrance look effortless and graceful, to be aware of what the sleeves and the fabric were doing with every step. I never did fall.

LBM: So, did you ever push back?

GC: Oh yes.

LBM: And were you successful?

GC: No!

LBM: Were you able to say no?

GC: Sure, but he usually won because he had a brilliant piece of costuming and he knew how ready and able I was to figure out how to make it work. In theater, it's all in real time—if you fall down the stairs, you fall down the stairs. Wearing the costumes in *101 Dalmatians*—I spent hours in them—meant that I couldn't sit down because the corset was so tight. I was much thinner then, but when Jim Nadeaux put me in that corset, my waist had to be twenty-one inches and the corset had to be in exactly the right place or I would literally faint. So we carefully placed it correctly, then Jim would pull it in, measure my waist, and slip the costume on. But that's what you're living in for sometimes up to twelve hours, with a lunch break, during which I would disrobe and loosen the corset. On set, I had to have a leaning board, which means that rather than sitting down, you lean against a board, with an angled rest for your feet. I still have the pair of platform boots with five-inch-thick soles that I wore when my feet were not on camera. I actually wore them to the Oscars one year and had a ball because my feet didn't hurt. One suffers because high heels elongate the figure to lovely effect, so you grin and bear it. I don't wear torturous shoes anymore. Can't do it.

LBM: It's true. When I think about stage performances, when the character kneels down and has to get up again, I wonder how they keep from tripping on their costume. And the fact that the actor can negotiate that becomes part of what you're seeing onstage. It becomes

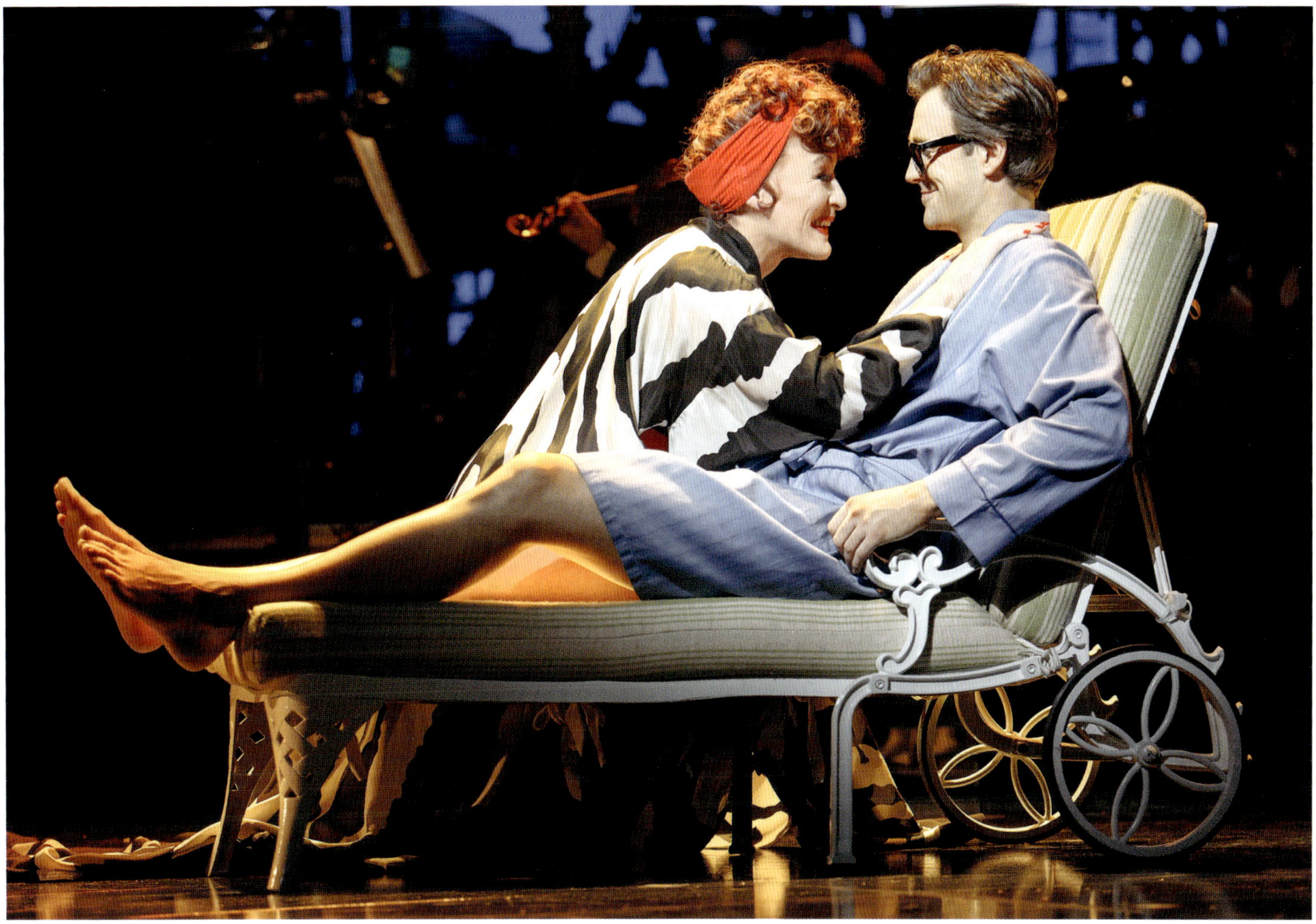

Glenn Close as Norma Desmond, *Sunset Boulevard*, 2017

part of how you trust that character. I can see why you would adapt yourself to what the designer wants. You have to. The character has to be able to manage this.

GC: Yes. Another reason why I have my collection is that costume designers have to contend with how a costume moves through light. You have to know how the director of photography is going to light a film or how the lighting designer is going to light the play. What gels they're going to use. Will this blue hat look green? How will this fabric move through light and shadow? So the knowledge is all-encompassing. The finished costume must define and serve a particular character, in a particular scene, as that character moves through space and light. Designers have to know how to achieve the effect they want. So, ideally, they must be equal collaborators with the director, as well as the set and lighting designers.

LBM: And sound, too, I imagine, because some fabrics are going to be audible when they move.

GC: Well, in the collection is the glass-beaded ensemble that Norma Desmond wore in the Joan of Arc scene [in *Sunset Boulevard*]. And as I came down the stairs, the audience could hear the sound of the heavy beads, dragging over and dropping from stair to stair. My entrance had a sound and that sound added tremendously to the atmosphere of the scene.

Anthony Powell made by Barbara Matera Ltd. and Woody Shelp, Beaded Jumpsuit and Coat (Norma Desmond, *Sunset Boulevard*), 1994, Silk, glass beads, fox fur, GC 2017.253.1–.2

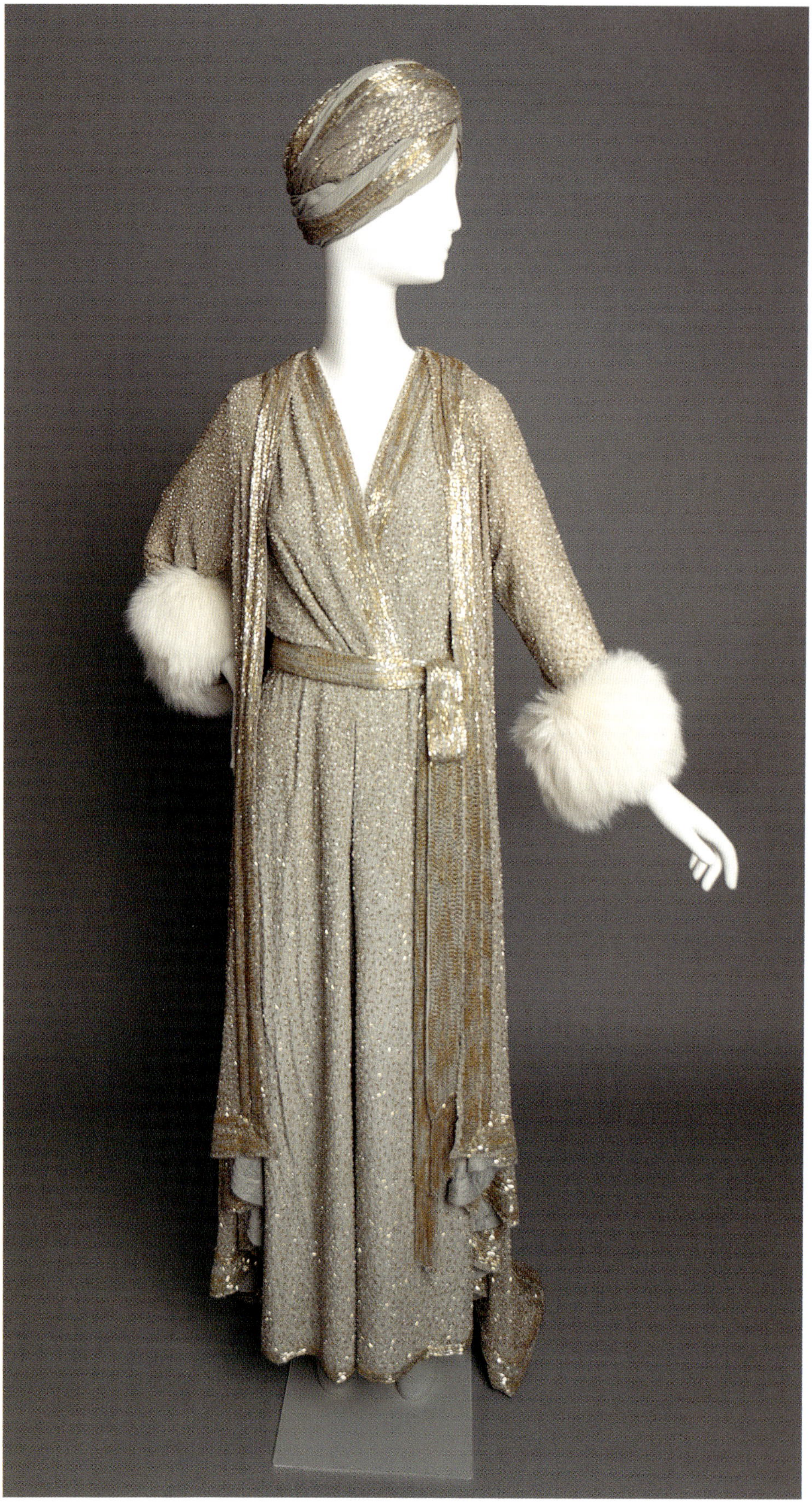

LBM: Have you seen technology affect costume design and construction over the span of your career?

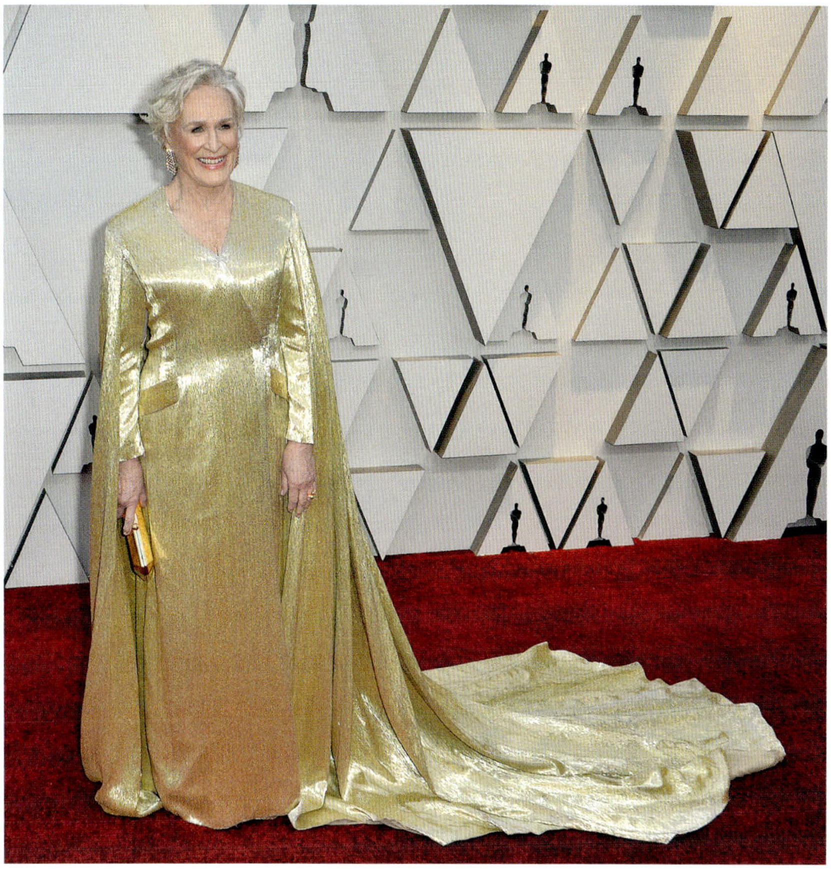

Glenn Close in a custom hand-beaded Carolina Herrera gown at the 91st Academy Awards, 2019. This gown, along with other personal appearance pieces, is included in the Glenn Close Costume Collection.

GC: Two ways, I guess. The *Sunset Boulevard* and *Dalmatians* costumes were all made by hand. All the beading was done by hand, in New York, at the Barbara Matera costume shop. Now, that kind of work is sent to India where it's usually done by machines. People rarely do that kind of handwork in the United States for costumes anymore. It's too expensive. That is a big difference. Even the magnificent, beaded gold dress that was made for me by Wes Gordon at Carolina Herrera, for the 2019 Oscars, was beaded in India. The fabric was beaded, by hand, at the best beading company there, but it would have been impossible to do that kind of beading by hand in the United States. When Jim Nadeaux saw it, he practically fainted. He told me that, because it was hand-beaded, if a thread breaks, literally thousands of beads won't end up on the floor and you can re-bead the repairs without threatening whole swatches of the fabric.

I learned about another new kind of technology when I played the Nova Prime, commander of the Nova Corps, in *Marvel Studios' Guardians of the Galaxy*. Alexandra Byrne, the costume designer, had found the fabric she wanted for the Nova Corps uniforms in China. It had the qualities of a thin neoprene—like a wet suit. But, Alexandra wanted the fabric to have more structure, so in her brilliance, she decided to bond two layers of the same fabric in order to achieve her desired effect. The beautifully structural uniform is made out of a fabric created by the designer—two bonded layers of synthetic fabric. It didn't exist before. It was invented for *Guardians of the Galaxy*. If you feel that fabric, it has the same feel as a wet suit. Its density means it keeps its structure through movement. Alexandra could have done one layer, but she did two. I found that really fascinating. But, in the fittings, I felt sorry for the tailor, who needed real muscle in order to manipulate the challenging fabric!

LBM: Your character was a commander, right? So the costume had the look of armor. I think that was partly what she was going for. You think somehow you can get away with something a little less elaborate if it's just on film, but they're really doing it so that, as you say, everything else has to interact with that piece.

GC: Yes, who would have thought to do it? "Yes, I love this, but let's bond it." Wow.

LBM: So I assume that designers, like artists across the spectrum, like architects, have all transitioned to versions of computer-aided design. Have you been able to see any of that process as they're creating costumes now?

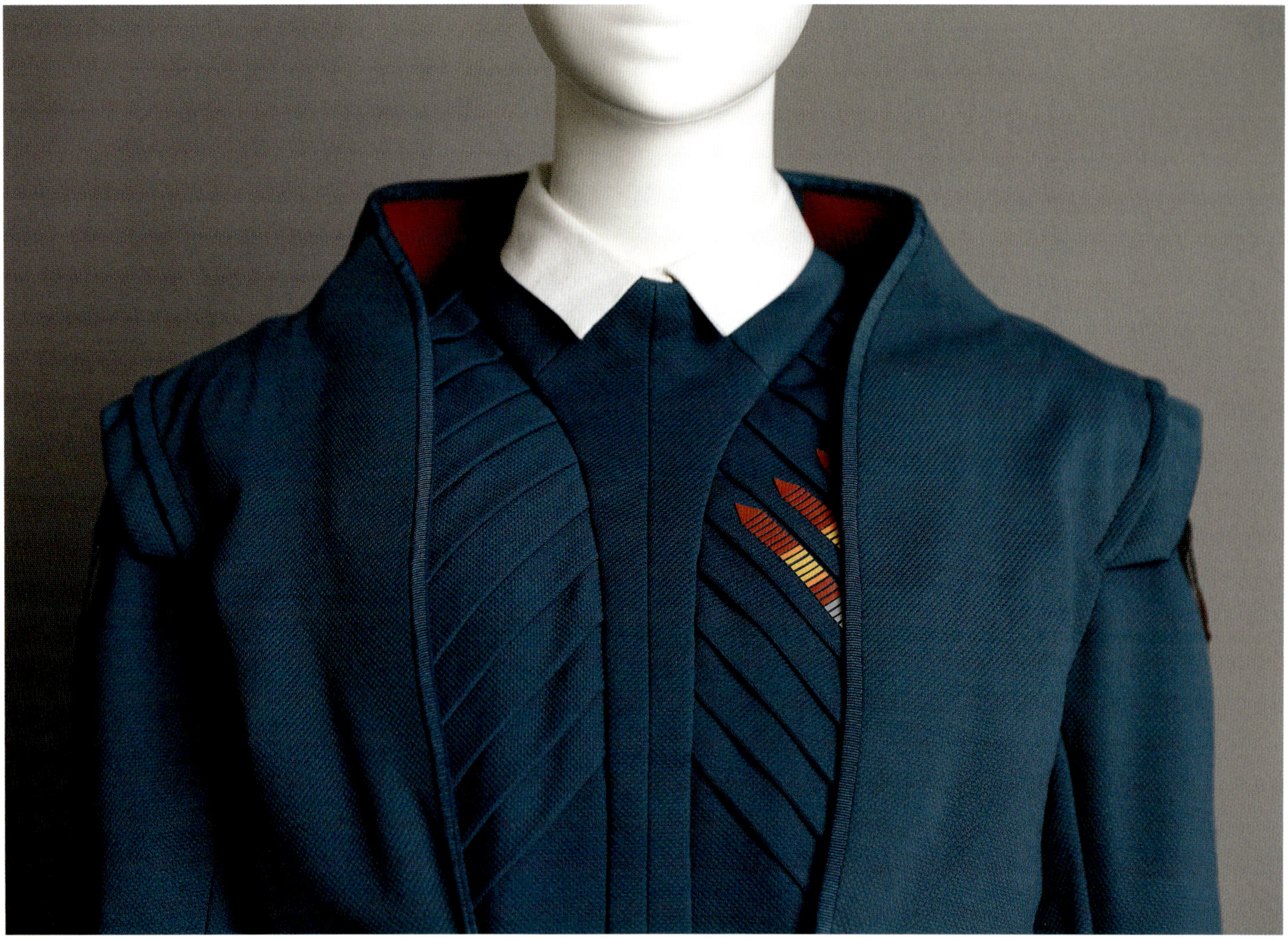

Alexandra Byrne, Nova Prime Uniform (Nova Prime, *Marvel Studios' Guardians of the Galaxy*), 2014, Polyester, spandex, rubber, linen, GC 2017.345.1-.4, .6

GC: I haven't. All the designers I've worked with start with a sketch. It's the first thing they show their directors. Actors first see the sketches and swatches of proposed fabrics. For me, that has always been the beginning of any collaboration—a discussion about the actual design and the fabrics. You see the design and feel the fabric and the fun begins. And what's fabulous about the process is what somebody like Barbara Matera does with that sketch, the designer's original inspiration. After the fabrics have been decided on, it is really up to the person who's interpreting that drawing to create a costume that is a manifestation of the initial inspiration. And that's something to witness. It is a huge privilege because you're standing there, you're the mannequin, and they know how to fabricate it and they want—like an actor—to fulfill what the designer envisions, tempered by the director's input. The person in whose studio the costume is built wants to fulfill the vision of the designer. And how they do that, with the designer, is the heart of the process. So all those costumes are the result of vigorous collaborations. I remember the incredible coat of silk roses from *102 Dalmatians*. Barbara was the one who ultimately decided which roses would go where—with Anthony's blessing—and, for some of the other *Dalmatians* costumes, where the feathers would go and all that. So she had a great eye and she knew how to create a designer's vision with fabric, beads, paillettes, feathers, and thread.

LBM: You've said this to me many times: clothes are made; costumes are built. So the builder is really part of the design process, too. Does that remain the case today, even though some of the construction of costumes is probably being outsourced or done by machine?

GC: Well, Jim Nadeaux was on a movie where he had to practically redo all the costumes for one of the stars because they were so badly constructed. Anthony Powell and Ann Roth knew what good hands they were in with Barbara Matera, who was one of the greats because she came from this point of view: my ladies are in the back room and we are going to make this happen. And Barbara had Woody Shelp, a legendary milliner, working in her shop. Most of the hats in my collection are Woody Shelp hats. A final fitting was a wonderful ceremony of sorts. I was the mannequin and the underpinnings would go on and be inspected, then the costume would be carefully carried in from the sewing room and put on me. Everyone—Barbara and her assistant, Anthony and his assistant, and sometimes the woman who had been in charge of the workshop—everyone was completely focused on the costume, slowly circling, making sure it was perfect. Then came the moment when Barbara would ask, "Is Woody ready?" And Woody would come in, carrying the hat as if it were the crown jewels on a velvet pillow—the final *pièce de résistance*. And Woody would carefully place one of his exquisite creations on my head just so and there I'd be, standing in the middle of the circle of collaborators, all of us looking at my reflection in the big mirrors, the room filled with a palpable thrill of accomplishment—the finished costume.

LBM: So you've played a lot of really strong female characters over the years. I mean, just starting with Jenny Fields, and that's not even counting your stage roles before that and obviously since. Can you talk about how their costumes contributed to your way of interpreting their strength and who they were as women?

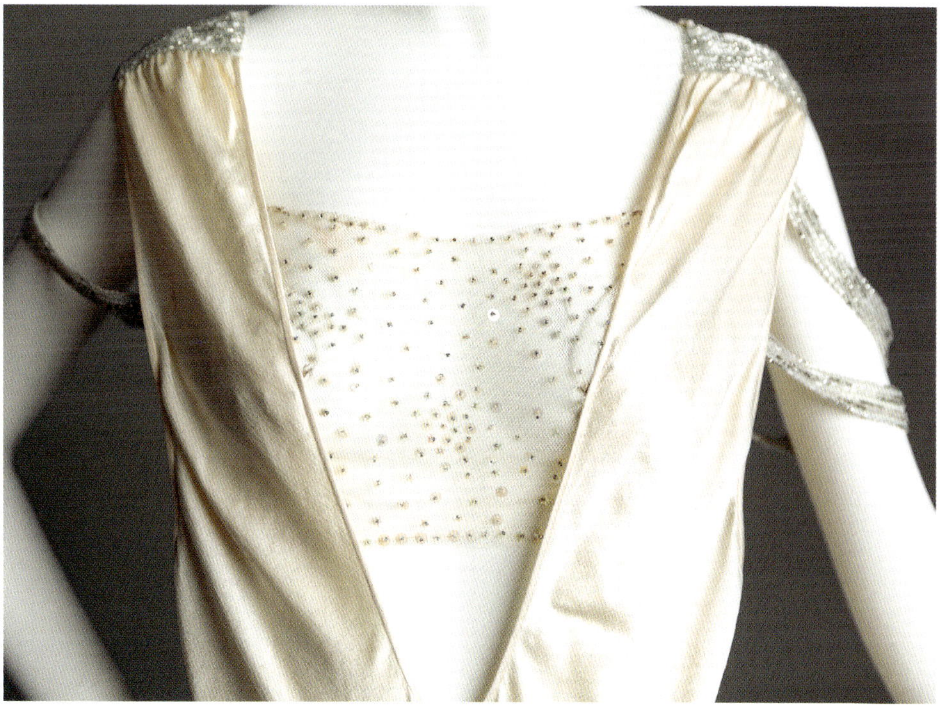

Ann Roth made by Barbara Matera Ltd., Evening Gown (Jan/Maxie, *Maxie*), 1985, Silk, glass beads, plastic sequins, GC 2017.94.1

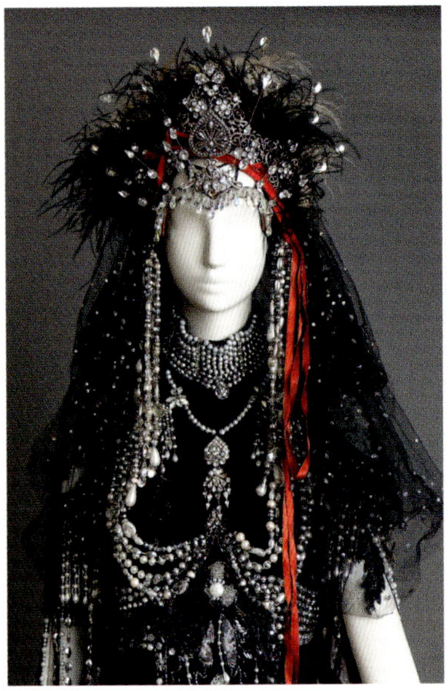

Anthony Powell made by Barbara Matera Ltd./Woody Shelp, Headdress (Norma Desmond, *Sunset Boulevard*), 1994/2017, Silk, lurex, glass beads, faux pearls, feathers, vintage cotton lace, vintage brooches, GC 2017.260.1-.3

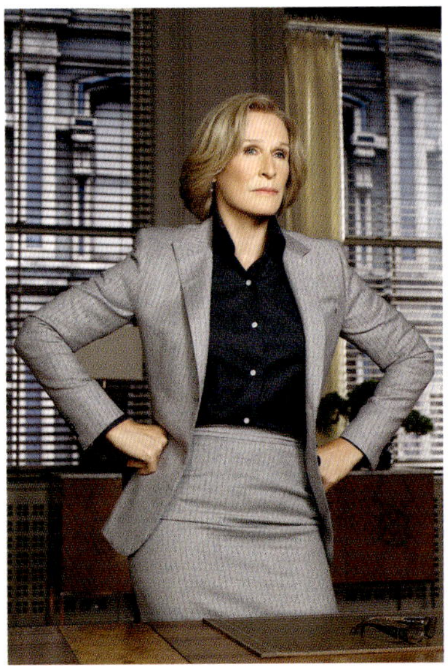

Glenn Close as Patty Hewes in *Damages*, 2009

GC: Well, take Patty Hewes from *Damages*. I don't know how many pieces I have from her wardrobe. Frank Fleming was the designer. We had a lot of discussion about it. My feeling was that she wasn't a woman who would ever go shopping for herself, that she would have a personal shopper, that she basically had a uniform that she felt comfortable and powerful in. She had a lot of beautiful suits, most of them designed by Domenico Vacca and Armani. In the first three years of that show, I had some incredible clothes. Patty's shirts had stiff, rather big collars which, on a man, would be finished with a tie. But Patty's shirts were open at the neck, with no ties—a deconstructed power suit. It was her saying to the men she confronted, "I'm just as powerful as you, but am more comfortable." Her wardrobe was calculated but not self-conscious. Her shoes were high, expensive, and sexy. They looked good when she crossed her legs. After she put on her beautifully constructed suits and killer shoes in the morning, she didn't give a second thought to what she was wearing. My Domenico Vacca shirts were very expensive. For the last two seasons of *Damages*, Frank had a shirtmaker in LA make all my shirts. In the collection, they are the shirts with "GC" or "Glenn Close" in their collars. At home, Patty Hewes wore soft cashmere sweaters and comfortable, unstructured pants.

For *Dangerous Liaisons*, both corsets are in the collection. The blue corset is worn bare in places from my everyday use during filming. Of course, the corset was incredibly important as far as movement and class. Aristocratic women didn't get into their confining corsets until the afternoon, and we know why—because the corsets were challenging to wear. That's why the chaise longue was invented. During the day, an aristocratic woman could receive people in her boudoir, dressed in a comfortable negligee or a morning dress, until she had to get into proper court dress, later in the day.

I love the beginning of *Dangerous Liaisons* because it shows, literally, that the process of getting dressed for court society was like putting on armor for a battle. You see the Marquise de Merteuil's corset being tightened and Vicomte de Valmont's wig being put on. Both are going into an ongoing battle of the sexes. Although [Pierre Choderlos de] Laclos wrote the novel *Dangerous Liaisons* right before the French Revolution, the movie is set during the reign of Louis XV, arguably the most refined era of the eighteenth century. Two of my costumes, designed by the brilliant James Acheson, were inspired by gowns worn in famous portraits of Louis XV's mistress, Madame de Pompadour. As the movie progressed, Stephen Frears, our director, got more and more into the faces, which made Jim Acheson despair because he had a beautiful hem or a wonderful pair of shoes that he wanted the audience to see. In a shot, at the beginning of the movie, in which I'm sitting at my dressing table, my legs are crossed in a rather awkward way. That is because Jim had come up to me and whispered, "Can you make sure that the shoes get in the scene?" He got an Oscar for his costumes, so I guess I was right to show the shoes. But to address your question, the costumes totally informed the way I moved. I wanted to look as if I were gliding when I walked, playing against the tight corset. Merteuil is a proud aristocrat and should radiate elegance, class, and control.

LBM: Very much in control.

GC: Yes, to lose control was to lose power.

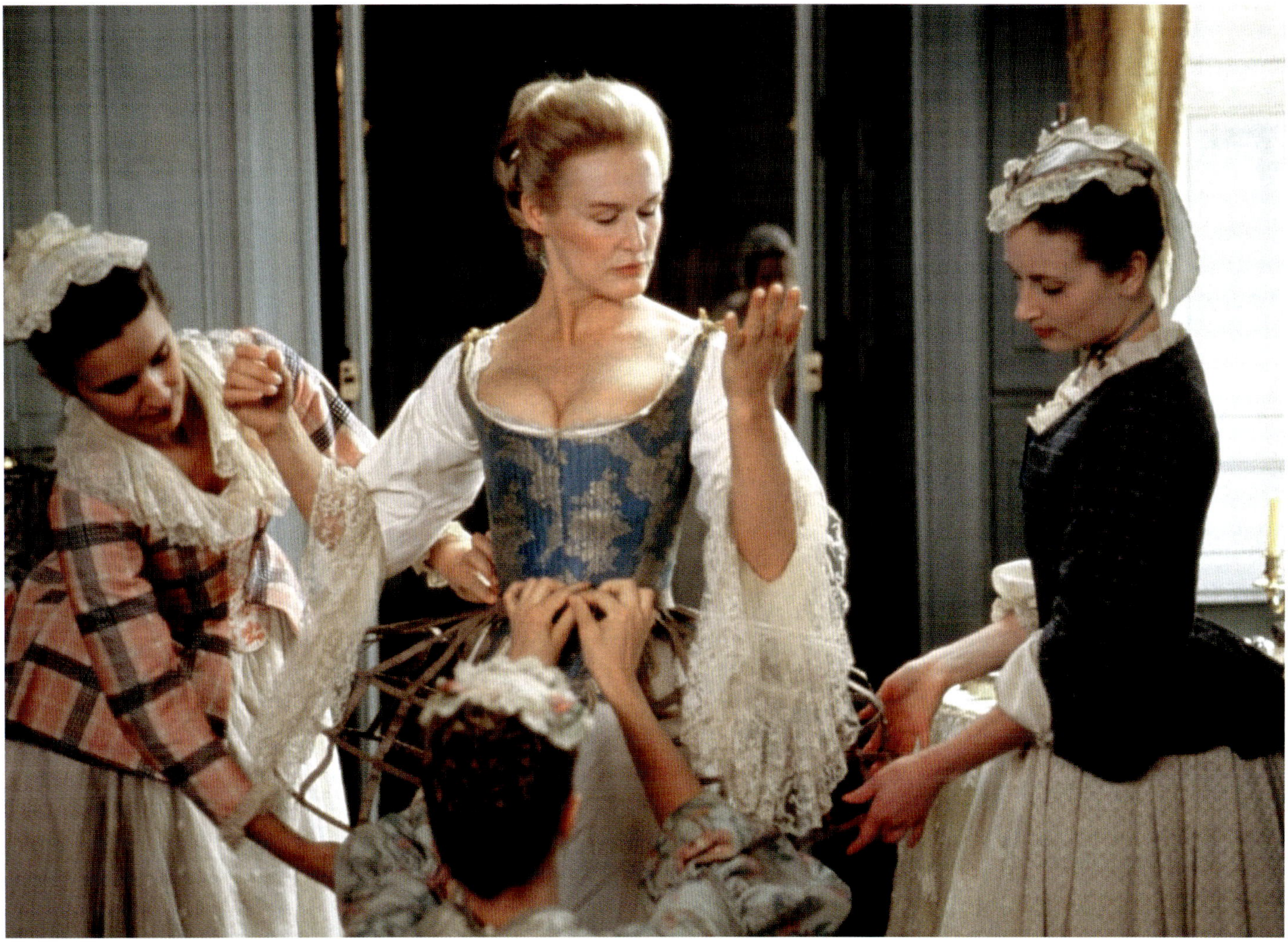

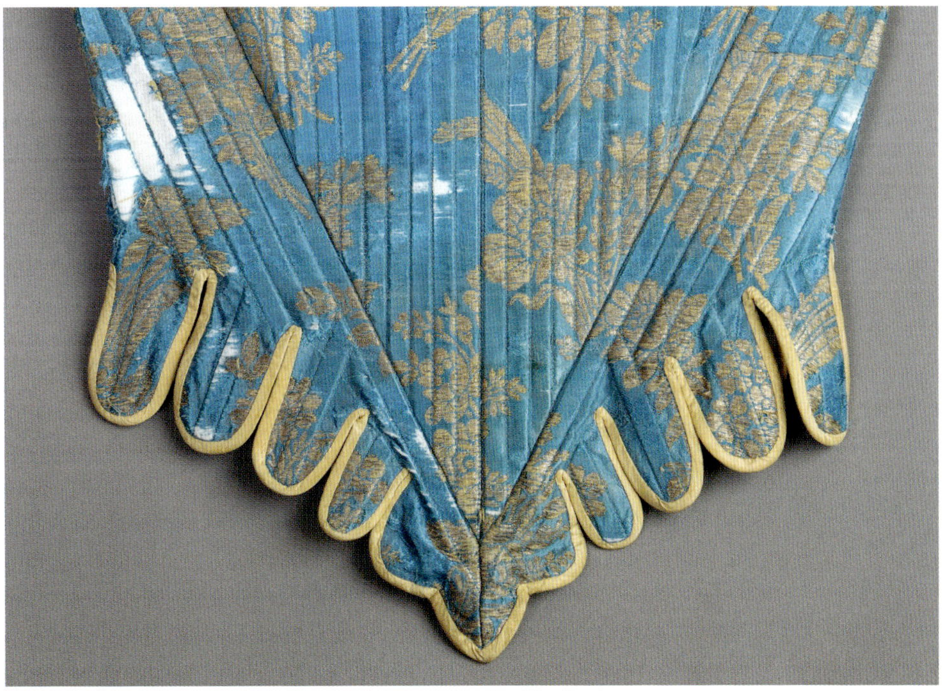

Glenn Close as the Marquise de Merteuil in *Dangerous Liaisons*, 1988

James Acheson made by Annie Hadley, Corset (Marquise de Merteuil, *Dangerous Liaisons*), 1988, Silk, metallic thread, GC 2017.50.2

LBM: What about a movie that no one has seen yet? *Hillbilly Elegy*. For some reason when I was thinking about this question today, I was thinking of your character in that movie.

GC: Mamaw.

LBM: And that costume is a T-shirt, right?

GC: Men's jeans and men's T-shirts, mainly, yes. Virginia Johnson, our costume designer, did a beautiful job in capturing the essence of Mamaw.

LBM: For some reason that one is sticking in my mind. It must have been something you said about it. Obviously, the costume was very much a part of her, of her social class. What she could afford to wear, but also what allowed her to do what she did.

GC: She probably could afford to wear other things, but she chose to wear rather ungainly, comfortable clothes. The great thing was we had quite a few pictures of Mamaw, and I met with some of her family. I was able to ask them: How did she sit? How did she hold her cigarette? How did she change the chemistry of a room when she entered? And I basically decided to embrace all that they told me. She would sit in a certain way in those blue jeans, so we worked hard on coming up with the right heft and weight for my stomach padding, which informed how I sat. I'm not a tall woman, but Mamaw was tall—she was probably about five feet seven—with big, expressive hands. We also padded my breasts so that they wouldn't be lost in the big T-shirts. That, of course, also informed how I moved. Her shoes were beaten-up, old Reeboks—I loved them because they were so comfortable! We shot in Atlanta over the summer, so I sweated a lot in my padding, but I loved getting into those costumes every day. I loved every T-shirt Virginia gave me. I loved Mamaw.

LBM: Obviously you do research into each character, and part of that is understanding how they dress, how they walk. Have you had other experiences where you've been able to talk to contemporaries of that character? Or, like in the case of Mamaw, family members who knew that person or who knew someone that they were modeled after? How much of that is research into how they dressed, how they put their shoes on, how they walked in those shoes?

GC: When appropriate, and when possible. For *Serving in Silence*, Margarethe Cammermeyer was on the set. The person I was playing was right there, and I loved that. She taught me how to salute. She was a model soldier. I mean, she was deeply military. So that informed me all the time. I asked her many questions. But her whole demeanor was something that I tried to assimilate. Her straight back, her love and respect for the military, for what it meant to be a soldier. Her posture and her uniform were impeccable.

When I did Sunny von Bülow in *Reversal of Fortune*, I wished I'd had a chance to talk to people who knew her, but her family and friends, understandably so, were incredibly protective of her. When we shot that film, Sunny was still in a coma in Columbia Presbyterian

Hospital, surrounded by her Persian carpets and flowers. I think that script was written very much from a male point of view. One comment I heard was that she walked like a dancer because she had taken dancing, and that she was rather shy. With Sunny, I was very aware of working in the dark as far as details of her character were concerned. I know being better informed would have certainly affected how I played her.

LBM: The scene in which you wore a gorgeous pink dress has always stuck in my mind.

GC: With the tiger.

LBM: The tiger! That's probably why I'm remembering it. Here's this incredibly wealthy

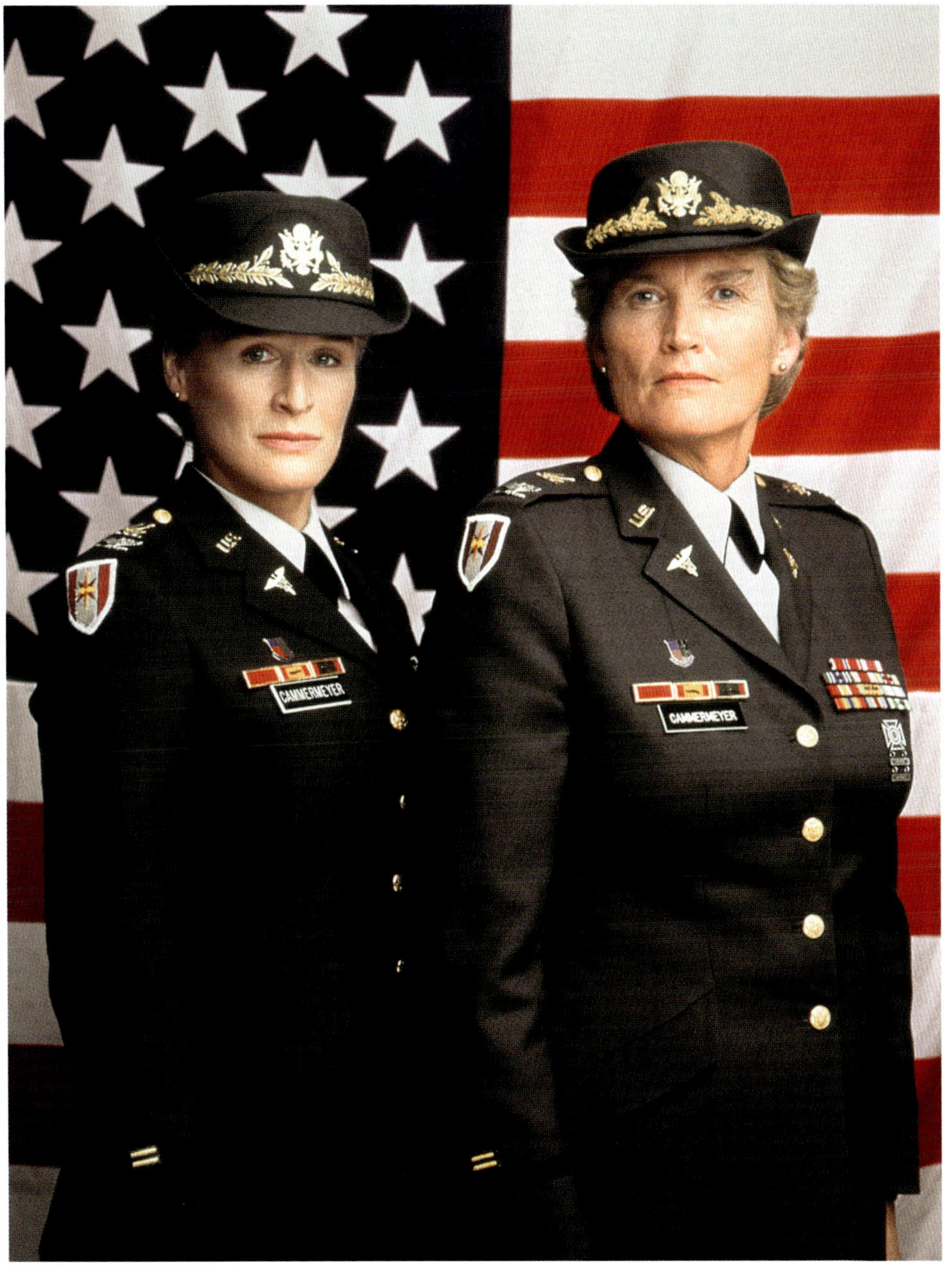

Glenn Close and Margarethe Cammermeyer from the television movie *Serving in Silence*, 1995

woman who could do anything she wants, seemingly apart from the crowd, being very quiet and by herself. But you do get that sense—she's an introverted character. We have that dress in the collection. It is so striking.

GC: Yes, off the shoulder, designed by the great Judianna Makovsky.

LBM: It is something else. So I have to ask you about *Albert Nobbs* because, of course, costume was certainly important, maybe even more important, in that film because it was part of how you transformed into a man. So is that an example of when you did think about how to dress beforehand as you were collaborating with the designer? That may be a simplistic question because obviously you're not going to dress like a woman, but like a man.

GC: I had thought about it a lot! First of all, we had the inspired costume designer Pierre-Yves Gayraud. The other day, Rodrigo García, who directed *Albert Nobbs*, sent a picture of me at Angels costume house in London when we first put on Albert's clothes. I always wanted

Glenn Close as Sunny von Bülow and Jeremy Irons as Claus von Bülow. *Reversal of Fortune*, 1990.

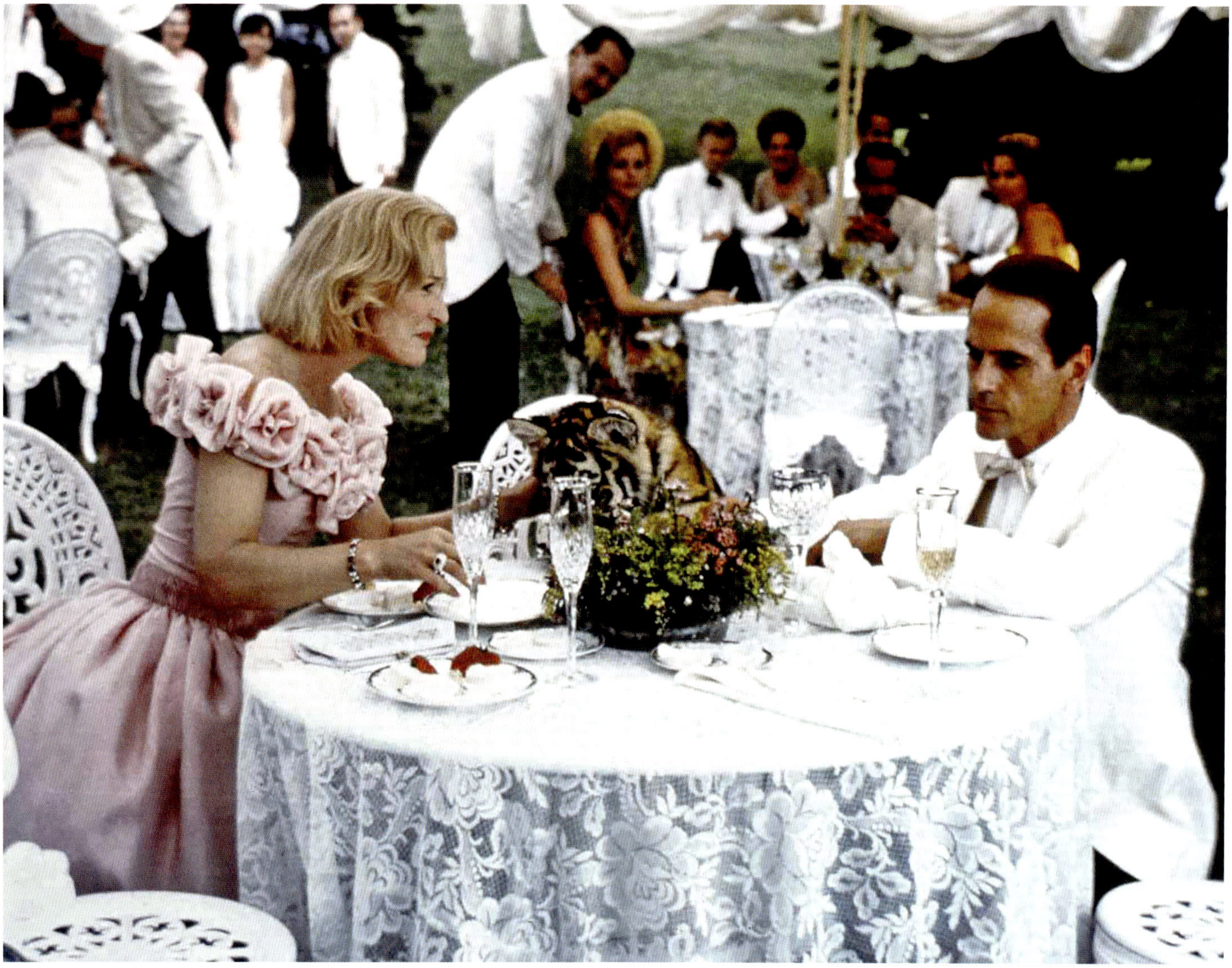

Albert to have a kind of Chaplinesque quality to her. I studied Charlie Chaplin's "Little Tramp" movies, and his pants were usually baggy. So I experimented to see what is more heartbreaking—shorter pants or longer pants. Because Albert is a woman who exists in secondhand, men's clothes. She couldn't go to a tailor and get a properly fitted suit because she couldn't give away her true identity. So, I came to the conclusion that pants that were too long, like Charlie Chaplin's "Little Tramp," made her seem more fragile and clownish. And the shoes—I wanted those to be big, like men's shoes, and weighted to inform how I walked. A lot of shoes from that period had steel in the soles or toes, so the period shoes I found worked well. It was subtle. They don't look like clown shoes, but they are too big for Albert. The suit, shoes, shirt, vest, tie, and hat that I wore in that movie came from the vast archive at Angels costume house in London and they're all real period pieces. As far as her butler's costume is concerned, the only thing that Pierre-Yves built was the corset that Albert wears to flatten her breasts. That's a wonderful piece of design. It looks like a torture instrument because that's basically what it is. I put that on every day and it really informed everything.

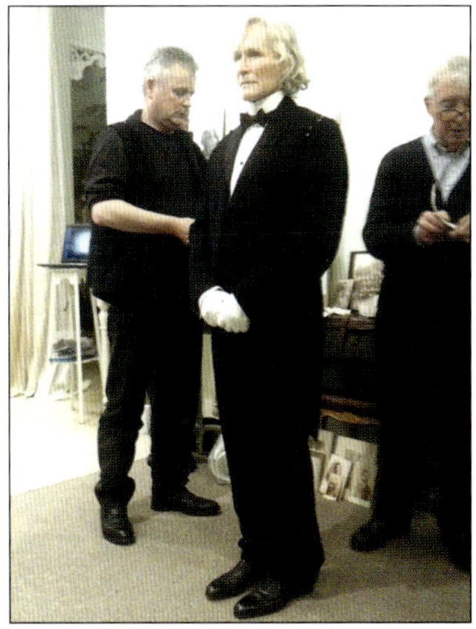

Glenn Close being fited for *Albert Nobbs* at Angels Costumes, London

LBM: I imagine it would change your breathing, too.

GC: Well, the tight ones change how you place your breath. But that one wasn't as restrictive as the ones for *Dangerous Liaisons* or certainly the *Dalmatians* movies. It was kind of mentally restrictive because none of the characters in the movie knew that I was wearing something underneath my suit that was keeping me from being who I really was. So, to me, it was a crucial, psychological piece of costuming.

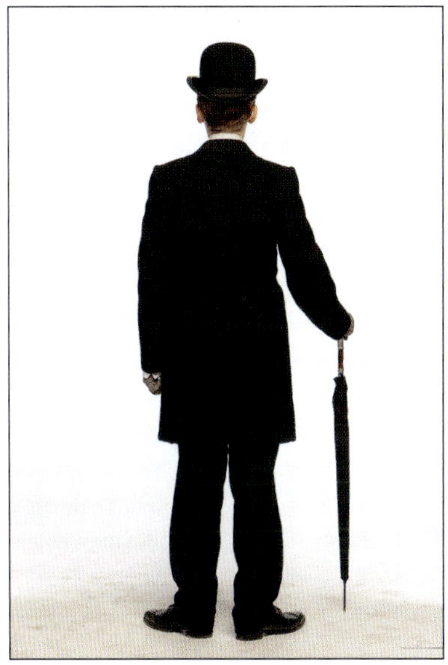

Glenn Close as *Albert Nobbs*, 2011

LBM: Does it change how you talk? Does it change the quality of your voice or is that really something you can control?

GC: I pitched my voice lower as Albert because I think she would have had to do that in life. The corset did not affect that.

LBM: What about the use of prosthetics? I mean, you needed them in *Albert Nobbs* and I think you've had them in other roles. How do prosthetics affect your acting as well as your interpretation of a character?

GC: Well, I've played a number of characters that didn't reveal themselves until I was in full drag: Norma Desmond and Cruella—even though I didn't have prosthetics for those two characters—Albert and Mamaw. It starts in the hair and makeup trailer. Matthew Mungle designed the nose and the ears for both Albert Nobbs and Mamaw. I had seen Nicole Kidman in *The Hours* playing Virginia Woolf and all I could think about was, "There's Nicole Kidman with a fake nose." For me, it was incredibly distracting. So, I didn't want that to be the case in *Albert Nobbs*. I always knew that whatever we did to my face had to be very subtle. I wanted prosthetics to help me remove myself from myself and help the audience forget that it was Glenn Close. That kind of subtlety is the kind of challenge Matthew loves. He eventually got an Oscar nomination for the work he did for both me and Janet McTeer. For me, he made my earlobes bigger, changed the tip of my

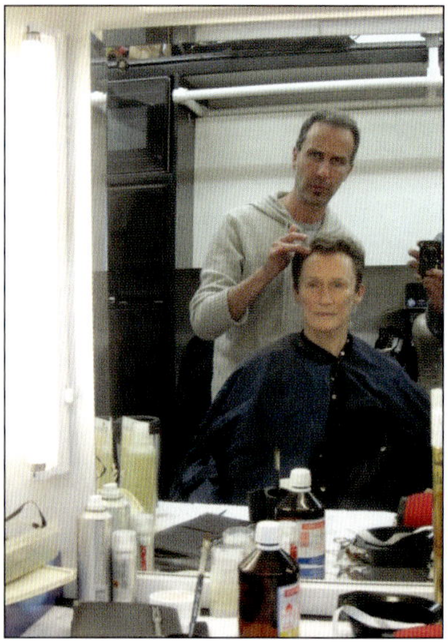

Martial Corneville and Glenn Close on the set of *Albert Nobbs*

nose, and made a plumper that went under my lower lip. Plumpers change the shape of your mouth. Martial Corneville, in my opinion the greatest wigmaker in the world and a longtime friend, made a genius wig for Albert. Nothing is harder to craft than a short wig with believable texture and movement. Martial is the master and he, too, was nominated for an Oscar for his work in *Albert Nobbs*. There was a moment, after the prosthetics had been applied and after Martial had put on my wig, when I would look in the mirror and say, "There's Albert. There she is." I specifically wanted to use prosthetics for Mamaw because she was so completely different from me and I didn't want to distract myself with the knowledge that I was "in" my own face. I could not attempt to step into Mamaw's shoes if she looked like me. So we experimented. Matthew came to my house and made a mold of my nose and my ears. Mamaw had very big ears and big earlobes. Ron Howard, our director, was skeptical at first because he was worried that applying the prosthetics would take too much time every morning, an important factor to consider given a challenging shooting schedule. When the day came for the on-camera hair, makeup, and costume tests down in Atlanta, my team was ready. Martial had made a fabulous wig mirroring Mamaw's hair, kind of frizzy, like a bad perm that is growing out. I got into the face, the wig, the jeans, T-shirt, and sneakers. I walked on set, with a cigarette hanging out of my mouth, and people didn't know it was me. They literally didn't know it was me! It was so cool. I don't think that would have happened without the subtle, beautiful work of Matthew and, again, the mastery of Martial. I loved that character. It was about being able to use my imagination. It helps when you have great costumes and makeup.

LBM: To see and feel something completely different?

GC: Yes.

LBM: So switching gears a little bit again—is there a costume designer you have not worked with but with whom you really hope to have the chance?

GC: I'd love to work with Alexandra Byrne again. I'd love to work with Sandy Powell. I first was made aware of her work in *Orlando*, the movie with Tilda Swinton that was based on the Virginia Woolf book. She also did the costumes for Cate Blanchett in *Carol*.

LBM: Oh, right, incredible. Amazing movie. So I have a question that I hope will cue up some funny stories because I know there's one that Jim Nadeaux told me about *Sunset Boulevard*, but this is really a question about getting into costume onstage. So when you're getting into costume, you've got to hit your mark, right? And you've got to do a costume change. So are there any stories about having to make those costume changes and how that figured into your experiences?

GC: Well that's a crucial aspect of costume design for theater—how to make quick changes possible. There is evidence of some hair-raising, quick changes in some of the costumes in the collection. In *Sunset Boulevard*, we had a seventeen-second complete costume change, wig to hat included. That takes expertise on every level. All of Norma Desmond's necklaces, for example, have Velcro clasps. And I've had several quick change close calls. I'm sure Jim told the story of when I couldn't get into a pant leg! It was a really quick costume change for a number in *Sunset Boulevard* called "The Lady's Paying." I had to come back onstage after a rather short musical intro. I ran offstage, leapt out of a gown, and could not get my leg into the pants of the next costume! The orchestra was playing the intro over and over again. Jim was assisting my then dresser and he just took the pant leg and ripped it open. It had somehow gotten sewn shut. Jim became my dresser after that. For the quickest, most difficult quick changes, you may have as many as four people working with you offstage. It's like a military operation. Everybody has crucially precise tasks. I have to know what height and angle to put my arms so a dresser can slip on a jacket. When to lift up my feet to change shoes. When to turn around. When I did *Sunset* in London in 2016, we used my original costumes. I took the team of dressers and we drilled the quick changes. "Let's do it again . . . do it again, and again." "You need to hold that up a little bit higher." "Should my arm be straight or do you want it slightly bent?" We went through the change until the moves were second nature. But if a dresser doesn't hold the skirt correctly or if the hat doesn't come on at the right time, we had rehearsed it enough for me to still make my entrance, on cue and in character.

LBM: Just keeping your cool when you've got to do it.

GC: During a quick change, my mind clicks into a pause mode. You have to be in the right emotional moment when you come on, even though you've had this frenzy of a seventeen-second costume change. Phew!

LBM: Yeah. I remember when I was in sixth grade, my class performed a parody of *Cinderella*. And I got cast as Cinderella. I had a dress for the ball scene, and during the big production with the parents and the whole bit, the zipper broke on this dress! I still have this memory of thinking, "I have to go out there." So I walked out with my back to the audience and I did the whole scene looking out the window with my back to the audience, and somehow

Anthony Powell made by Martin Adams, Necklace, (Norma Desmond, *Sunset Boulevard*), 1994/2017, Metal, magnets, cotton, GC 2017.349.2

Anthony Powell made by Barbara Matera Ltd., Quick-change rigging detail on final look (Norma Desmond, *Sunset Boulevard*), 1994/2017, Silk, glass beads, rhinestones, metal, GC 2017.260.1–.3

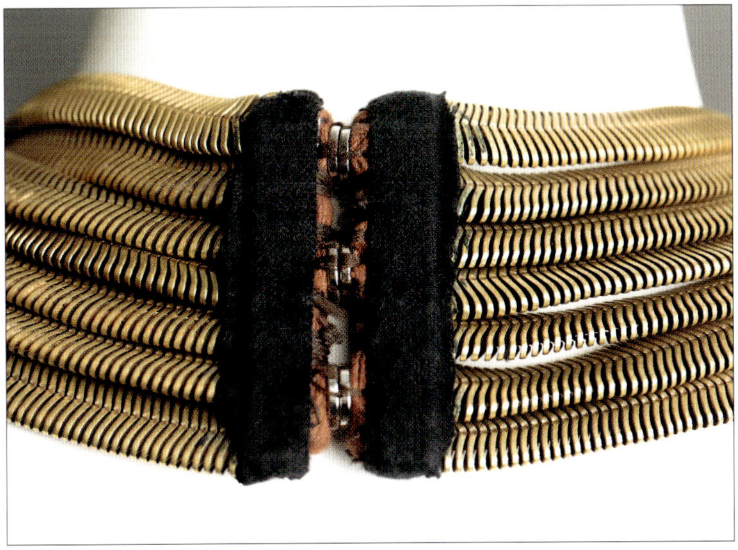

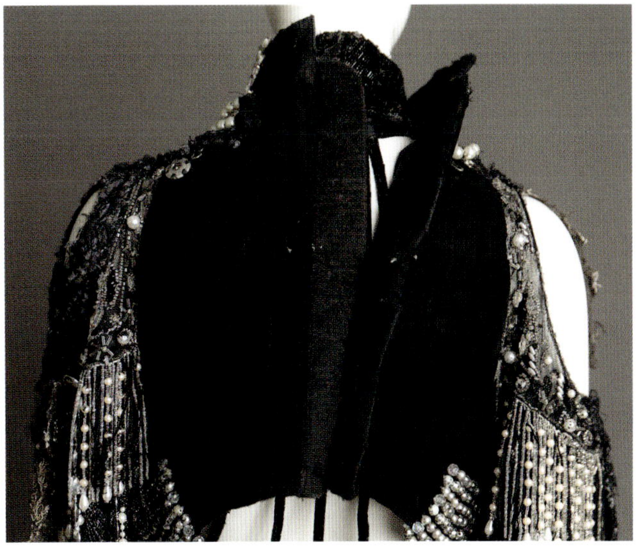

I managed to keep the dress on. So, I always appreciated the story Jim Nadeaux told about the reverse zipper.

GC: Oh, that was genius! He came up with the idea of putting a zipper in upside down for one of my crazy quick changes. If a zipper jams, you're toast! Jim sewed a zipper upside down in a jacket. It was an incredible solution—zipping up instead of down. That's where he's such a phenomenal problem solver. That same thing that happened to you happened to me in *Barnum*. I had a quick change getting into a fabulous apricot gown. I had a new dresser and she didn't get it done up on time, so I had to do the whole number with the entire back of my costume open. No one ever noticed. It's kind of amazing what an audience will not notice if you just act like it's normal. But that number in *Barnum* was a little too . . . airy!

LBM: So you've talked a bit about your couture for the Oscars and Golden Globes. And I think I remember you mentioning in an earlier conversation that the red carpet itself has evolved. How much of it now turns to what people are wearing? That's obviously affected what you wear, culminating in this unbelievable gown, really, that you wore for the last Oscars. Can you talk a bit about that from the standpoint of those awards ceremonies and what you've seen over the span of your career in terms of why and how the red carpet has changed?

GC: I think Alec Baldwin made a comment that the red carpet used to be just a way to get into the event. Now, it is the event. In LA, at the opening for *Garp* in 1982, John Lithgow and I just wore our street clothes, something out of our own closets! That would never happen now, unless somebody has an amazing closet. Someday, I really want to wear fancy pajamas on the red carpet! At the last, big *Vanity Fair* after-the-Oscars party, Melissa McCarthy and her husband, Ben, showed up in tracksuits and sneakers and everyone was green with envy. But, yeah, it has gotten to be a huge media frenzy. Some stars change dresses three times in the evening. They'll arrive in one dress, then at another party they'll be wearing something else, and at another party they're in something else yet again. They get paid to wear those dresses. It is a way for a designer to ensure that the actors wear their dresses, which, if they do, can be hugely lucrative. Otherwise, they make something, at considerable expense, not knowing if and where a star may choose to wear it. The last time I needed a dress for the Oscars was the first time I had choices from multiple designers. I had multiple fittings, not knowing what I would ultimately choose to wear. For many years, I wore Armani or Geoffrey Beene. And I have worn wonderful gowns by Zac Posen. These designers, and their exquisitely gifted teams, always knew that they were my first and only choice because it seemed fair to me. It made me feel uncomfortable to have multiple designers waiting—having done all this beautiful, costly work—to find out, usually at the last minute, whether you're actually going to wear their creation or not. So, I am probably going back to one designer for super-special events. And I've never been paid to wear a designer's clothes. It's been offered, but I haven't taken it. It is annoying to be made to feel that you have to make some sort of fashion statement. I hope I'll get on the best-dressed lists and be photographed a lot because it is the only way I can pay back a designer's generosity. I'm not a fashion model and I find it hard to imagine that people care about what I wear. So to be put in competition because of what

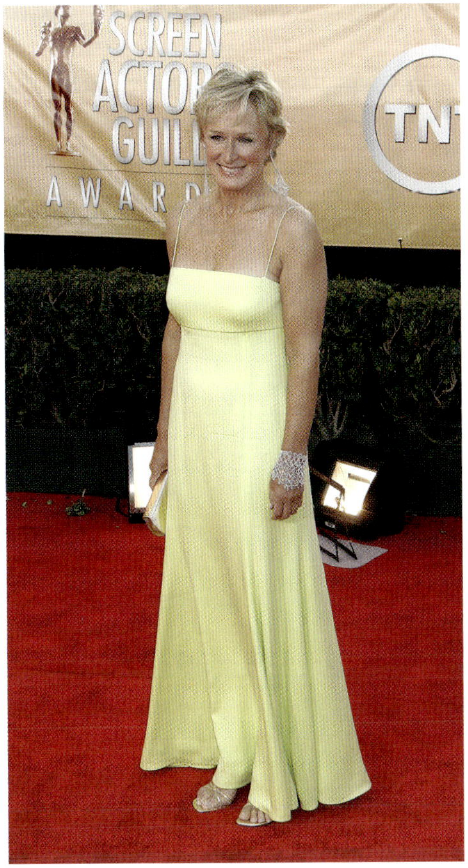

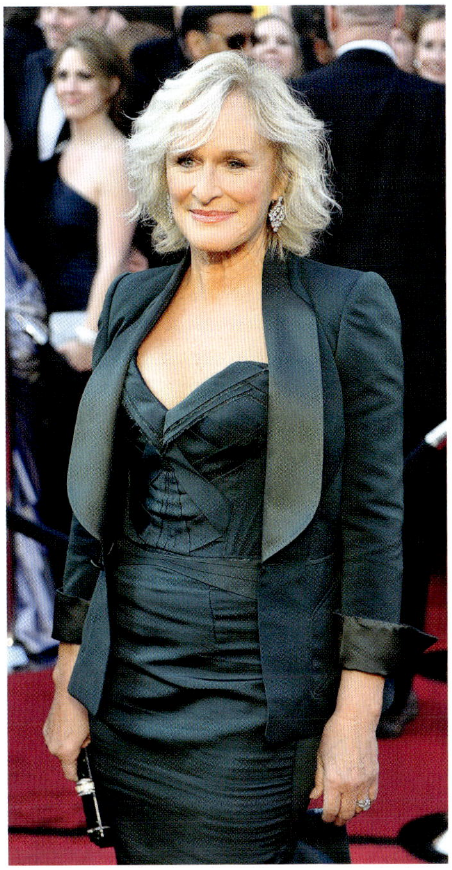

Glenn Close in Armani at the 2005 Screen Actors Guild Awards

Glenn Close in Zac Posen at the 84th Annual Academy Awards, 2012. Close purposefully selected this tailored jacket worn over her evening gown in celebration of her character, Albert Nobbs, for which she received a Best Actress nomination. These gowns are part of the Glenn Close Costume Collection.

I'm wearing on the red carpet is something I don't appreciate. There is enough competition in my profession as it is!

I have had a wonderful, long-term relationship with Giorgio Armani. I loved his early designs, all those classic suits, because they made me feel comfortable and effortlessly chic. I felt I could be me in an Armani design. I wore the clothes; the clothes didn't wear me. And I never needed jewelry. My mother had a couple of pieces of jewelry, but she was basically an unadorned woman. And I, too, have always thought of myself as an unadorned woman. I don't like gobbing myself up with a bunch of jewelry. Accessories terrify me! It takes a lot of time and focus. Men just get into their tuxedos. While women . . . a lot of energy is expended. I'd much rather be spending my energy on something else. Having said that, I don't want to sound ungrateful because I have worn beautiful pieces and I am eternally grateful for the exciting collaborations I've have with brilliant designers.

LBM: So, what led you to Indiana University and the Sage Collection as the repository for your collection?

GC: It started with Bring Change to Mind, the organization that I cofounded to fight stigma around mental illness. On campus, you have a world-class authority on stigma, suicide, social connectivity, and mental health: Bernice Pescosolido, Distinguished Professor of Sociology at IU. I learned of Bernice when I was putting together our scientific advisory board. I called her out of the blue and we talked about starting a Bring Change to Mind club at IU. I went to Indiana because Bernice had given her freshman class the task of creating campaigns about some aspect of mental illness and stigma. And she invited Pamela Harrington, our executive director, and me to come and judge the student campaign presentations. They were all well-dressed and had set up their pitches at various stations. It was thrilling. They came up with wonderful ideas. And I've always loved the idea of the Midwest. My best friend is from Iowa and I think of the Midwest as being open, generous, and down-to-earth. That's what I think of when I think of people from the Midwest. There are so many people in my profession who grew up there. I love Thomas Hart Benton and your campus is full of his murals. I love the fact that a lot of the buildings are made of earthy limestone. It just seems so strong and unfussy. It has gravitas and a kind of unselfconscious beauty. But, the absolute deciding factor was that there is no other educational institution in the country that has the kind of archival facilities for costumes that you have. I don't think even the new Academy Museum [of Motion Pictures] has that kind of state-of-the-art facility for costumes. So when I saw the building where my collection would be housed, at a great educational institution, where my costumes will be used to educate and inspire, my decision became a no-brainer.

LBM: Yeah, and they are. Well, I think those are some of the many things we're all very proud of, starting with Bernice. And it's always critical to get outside endorsements. I grew up in the Midwest. I've always lived here. So I know that tendency to sort of "hide our light under a bushel," that kind of mentality. You know, don't brag. As a consequence, I think a lot of things that are really world-class get overlooked.

GC: One of the reasons I'm so excited is because people in the arts, and in a lot of other fields, tend to concentrate on the coasts. So, to have my collection in the heartland, both figuratively and metaphorically, means a lot to me.

Glenn Close with students in Bring Change to Mind's Undergrad Program at Indiana University, Bloomington

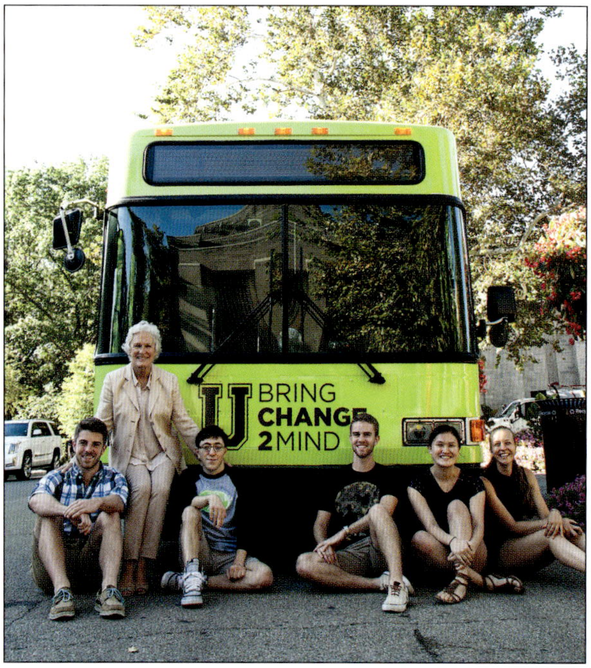

LBM: That's wonderful.

GC: You also have a superb museum and it's very exciting that the first, major exhibition of my costumes will be there.

LBM: The Eskenazi Museum of Art is an incredible place. Even during the time that I've been here, since Michael [McRobbie]'s been president, more and more spaces have been created for showing all the fantastic art. I meant to ask: Do you have an all-time favorite costume?

GC: What I call the "firebird costume" by Anthony—the red costume that Cruella wore in the dinner scene in *102 Dalmatians*. It is a phenomenal, gobsmacking costume. So, I guess that is, theatrically speaking, probably my favorite. One of my other favorites is the navy blue suit that Ann Roth designed for *Jagged Edge*, in which I played a lawyer, in the mid-eighties. It was a navy-blue suit with a white silk blouse. I remember hearing, at the time, that no one had done a movie with a woman lawyer in the lead,

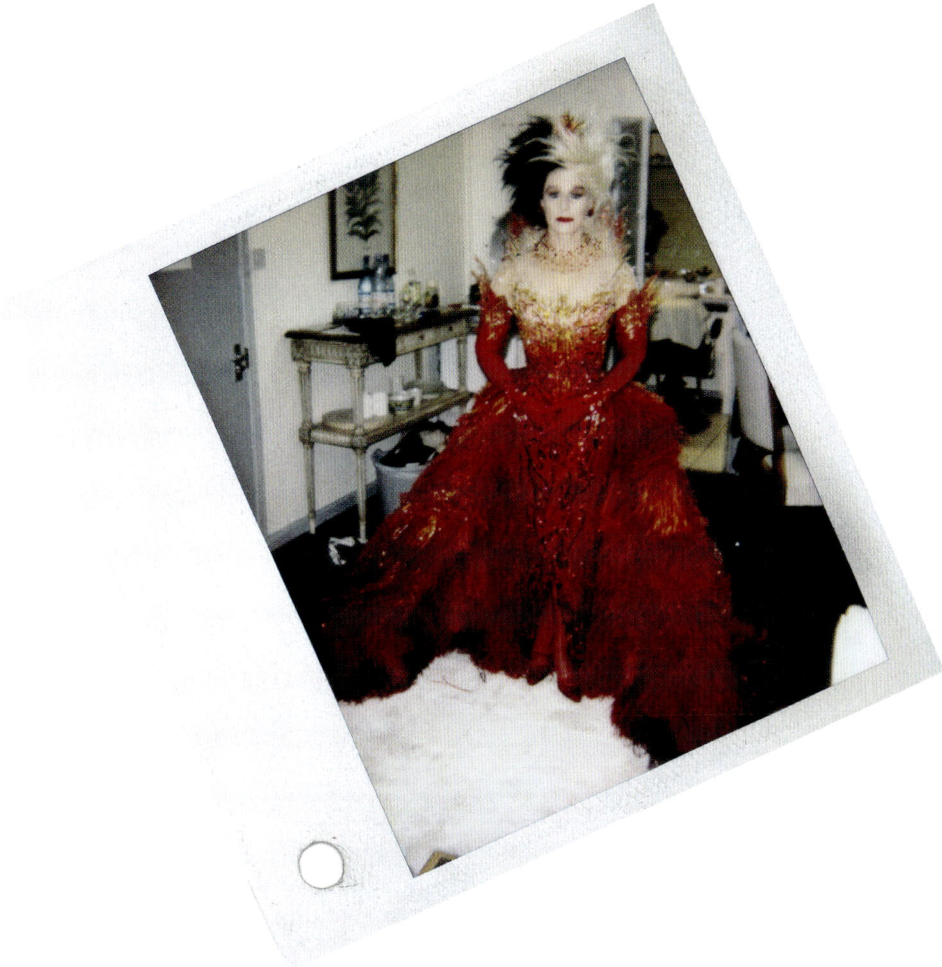

Glenn Close in Flame Dress,
102 Dalmatians (2000).
Used by permission from Disney Enterprises, Inc.

yet *Jagged Edge* was a big success for Columbia Pictures. Not long after, *L.A. Law* came on television, and Susan Dey's character had a suit exactly like my navy-blue suit in *Jagged Edge*. The suits that Ann Roth designed for me in *Jagged Edge* were precursors to Patty Hewes's power suits.

LBM: Well, that was also a time when women were surging into law schools, medical schools, and the workforce. And really the whole modern era of women, working women. *Jagged Edge* was hugely influential. That's another movie where I remember thinking about what that character was wearing. So thinking about the exhibition as a whole, what do you want visitors to take away from seeing your collection? What do you want their experience to be?

GC: I'd like them to understand the connection between character and costume. I'd like them to be amazed by the artistry. And I would like them to gain an insight into the creative process, which is basically the thing that keeps any artist's soul alive—the actual process. I get emotional about that. All my costumes are the product of an informed, passionate collaboration. When we had a day of experimentation and collaboration about the hair and makeup for *Albert Nobbs*, a Texan, who had given us a lot of money, was there to observe.

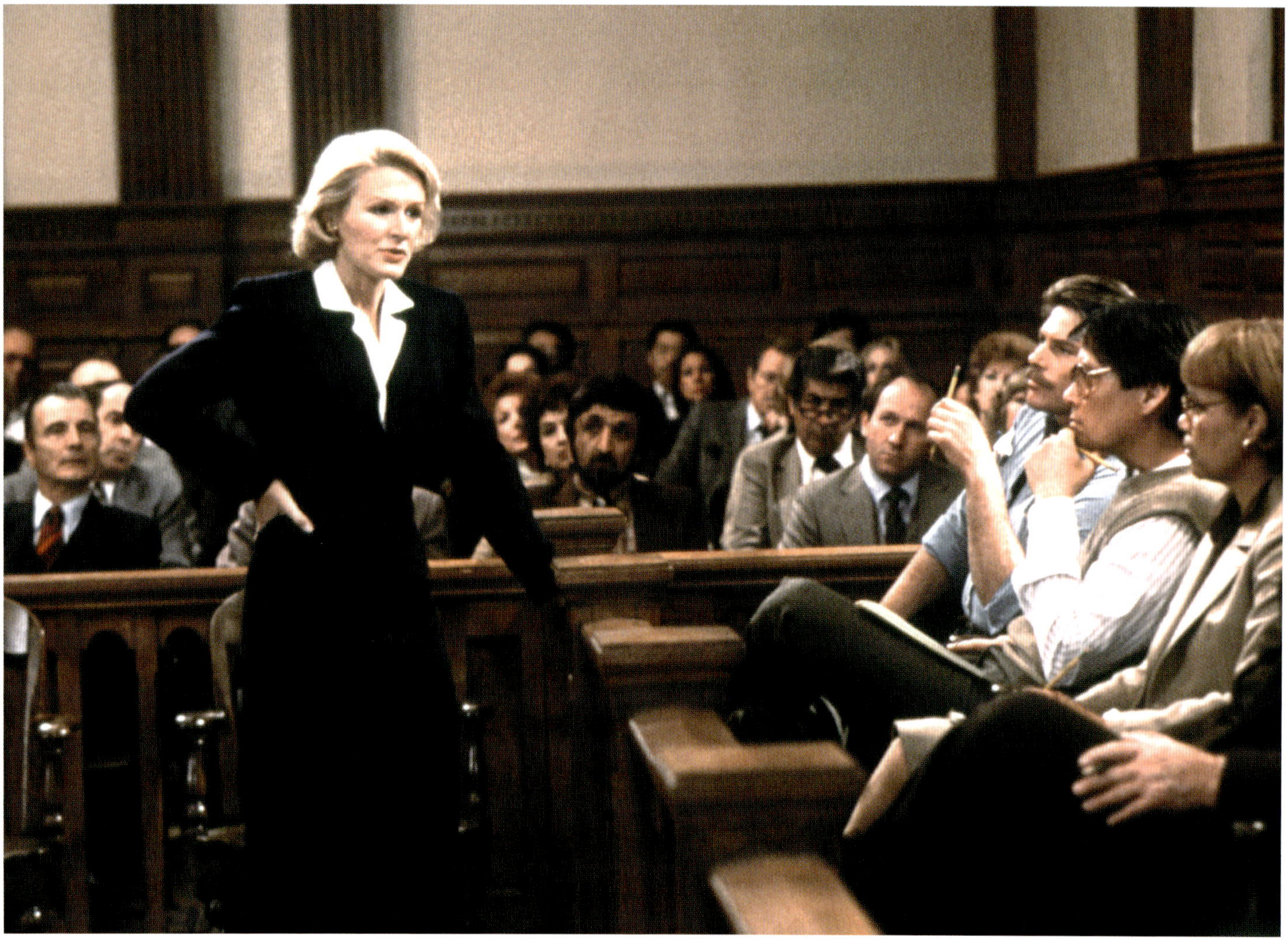

Glenn Close as Teddy Barnes, *Jagged Edge*, 1985

No money came from Hollywood for that movie. He was a billionaire real estate guy and I had been seated next to him at a dinner, in Dallas, where my fellow producers and I hoped to raise money. At one point he looked at me and said, "Well, I've made all the money I will ever need in the world. I've never been a part of a creative thing like this, so yeah, I'm in." And I said, "That's great, but I want you to see what we do." So he came to LA for that day of experimentation—six hours of Janet McTeer and I and the hair and makeup team trying on different hairstyles and shapes of noses and ears, refining the look for our two characters. "Is this what we want? . . . Her nose should look broken? . . . Her hair is too long," and so on. And at the end of the session, our Texan was absolutely astounded because he had never thought that that kind of thought, attention to detail, artistry, and egoless collaboration would go into the creation of a character on film. It was tremendously gratifying to see his reaction. He has a new respect, I'm sure to this day, for what we do. And people think, "Oh, celebrities, they're all spoiled people who are lucky to be where they are." I don't appreciate that. For me, it's not a complimentary thing to be called a celebrity because, to me, it means all image and no substance. But the people I know in my profession, actors as well as everyone who supports us, are there because of hard work and talent and sacrifice and vision and resilience. That's what my collection represents.

LBM: Well, I think it is even more appropriate that we are putting this exhibition in an art museum. And an art museum that is in the heart of a campus that values the arts and performance, and is a stone's throw away from wonderful performance venues that we are fortunate to have on this campus. And so the context will support that vision and the passion that you feel. The design of the exhibition will bring that out. There will also be opportunities to incorporate the exhibition into classes at the university. And we are hoping to do some IU Cinema retrospectives in conjunction with the exhibition.

GC: It's so exciting.

LBM: Thank you, Glenn. Thank you so much. I appreciate you and your collection. You've enhanced Indiana University with your collection and we are all very grateful to you.

GC: Well, I can't tell you what it means to me to know that it's in such wonderful hands.

LBM: We'll keep taking good care of it.

GC: And you will be getting Mamaw's very elegant costumes. She certainly had some great T- shirts—little kittens, the American flag.

LBM: I'm sure we can fit in a few more T-shirts. We will be very happy to have those in the collection, too. Thanks very much.

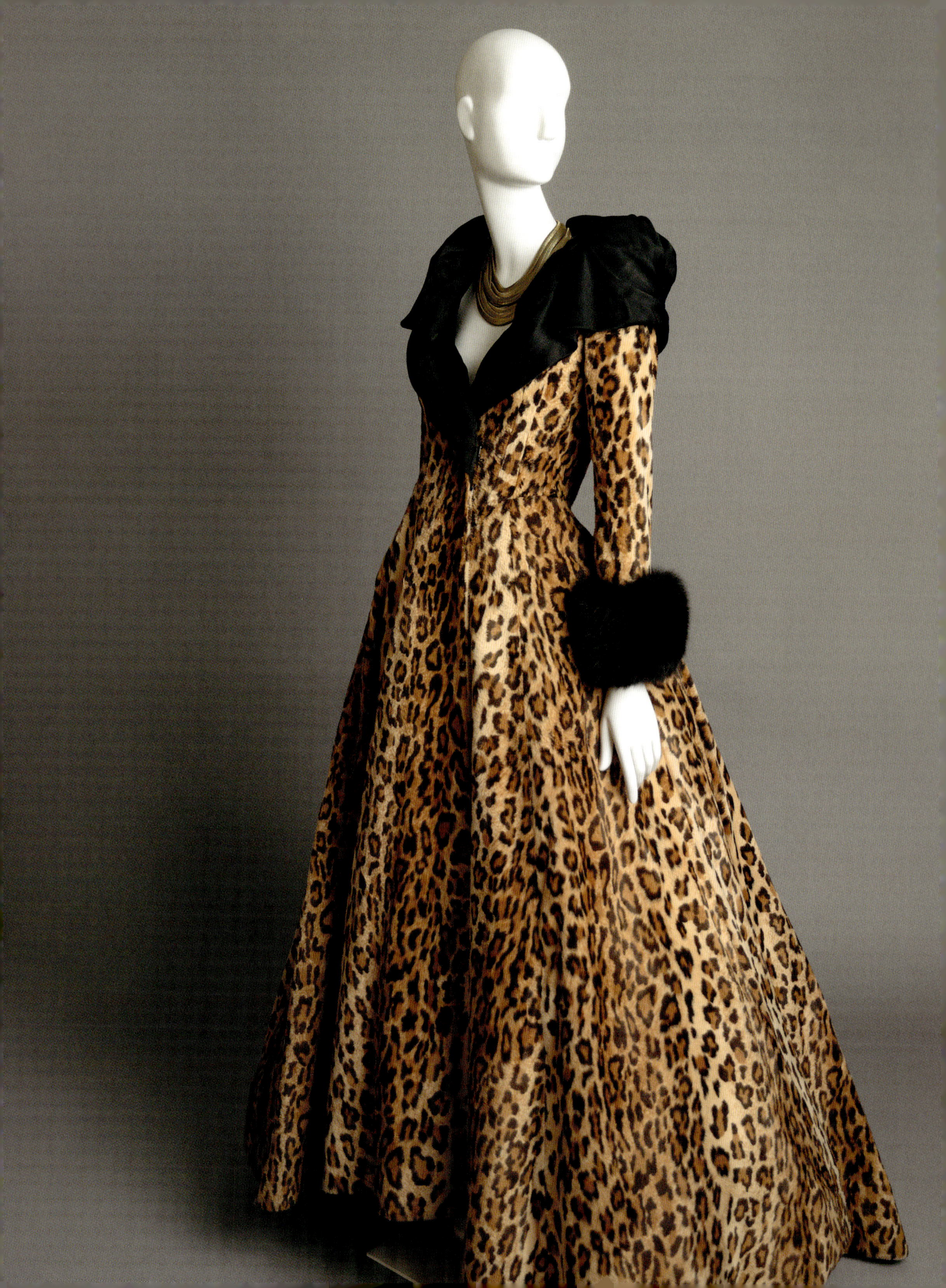

Bringing Fantasies to Life

Heather Milam

Focusing on the skilled artisans who create costumes and who help bring life to these garments will illuminate the process and people behind the Glenn Close Costume Collection. The making of clothing or costumes can be a mysterious thing to the majority of people. Most do not wonder about the different hands that created a pattern or chose a fabric. They may know the name of the designer or the place they purchased a piece of clothing, but often there is not a curiosity about the people, places, and workrooms that a garment has traversed before it arrives on the shelves. However, after examining some of the iconic pieces in the Glenn Close Costume Collection, I am drawn to honor and elaborate on the making process and the people behind the magic.

Having worked in the costume-making business for twenty-five years, I have spent a lot of time wondering about how garments are made. I am also intrigued by the process of creating characters for the stage and screen through costume design and construction. Admittedly, I have sat through boring meetings or church services staring at an interesting garment in my line of sight, deconstructing its three-dimensional form into what the two-dimensional pattern pieces might be—or making mental note of an interesting detail, embellishment, or fabric manipulation. I look at well-made garments and want to take them apart and dissect them to see what is on the inside. I *know* this is not how all people spend their odd hours, but because of the beauty in construction found in the Glenn Close Costume Collection, I would like to take you through my journey with costumes and highlight some of the "interesting to me" bits and pieces.

The costume-making industry is largely an apprenticeship-based training. I first interned at Barbara Matera Ltd., a shop featured in this essay, in the mid-1990s and learning from master patternmakers there directed the trajectory of my career. There are certainly academic programs that focus on costume production, but even when you attend a graduate school for costume technology, it should be done with the intent to learn from a particular person who can pass down their body of knowledge. Looking toward legacy, it is important to me to highlight the people who had an impact on these costumes. Many of the film costumes or red-carpet event pieces are gorgeous, well-made garments, purchased from upscale fashion designers or custom made from an haute couture studio; the labels inside some of these costumes are name brands that can be found and purchased in a store. Costume designers often use a combination of acquisition avenues—such as build, buy, borrow, or rent—to

OPPOSITE
Anthony Powell made by Barbara Matera Ltd. and Martin Adams, Leopard Coatdress (Norma Desmond, *Sunset Boulevard*), 1994/2017, Synthetic fur, silk, mink fur, nylon, metal, GC 2017.349.1–.2

The process of making a costume for the production of *The Heiress* (dir. D. McFadden), Indiana University 2018.

RIGHT
Costume design for the main character, Catherine Sloper, by Jason Orlenko, 2018.

FAR RIGHT
In collaboration with the designer, the draper and a team of makers prepare a mock-up of the costume. These mock ups are usually made of inexpensive materials, such as muslin or calico. This stage gives the designer, makers and the actor an opportunity to make modifications and adjustments.

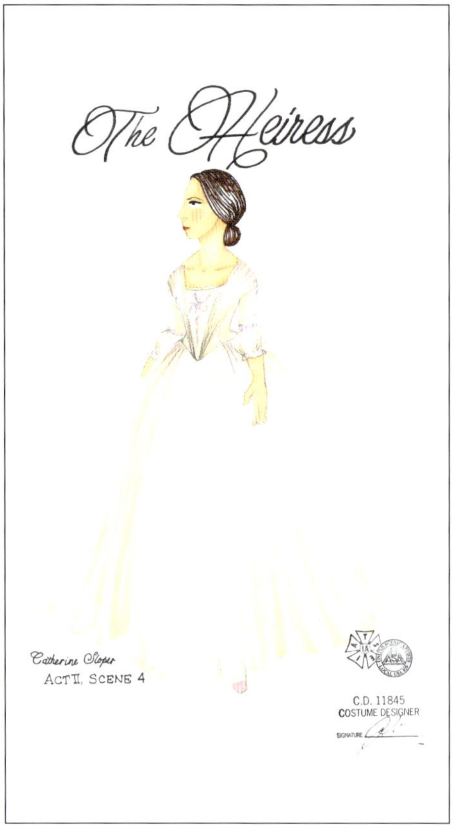

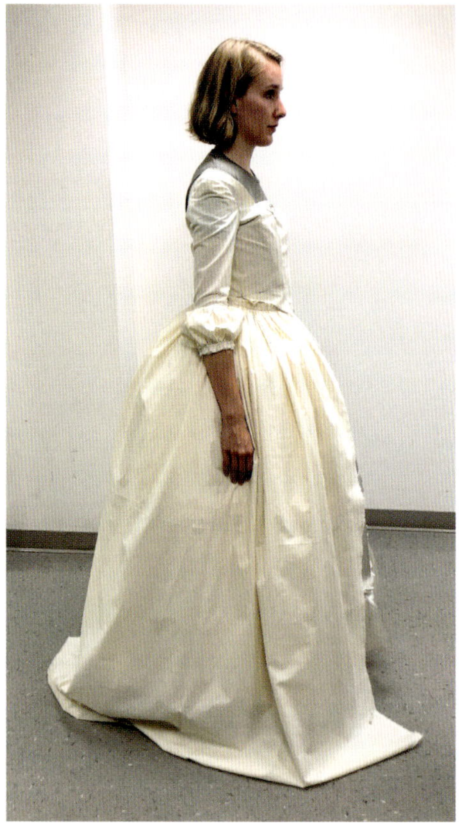

RIGHT
The actor Glynnis Marcelle models the near-finished gown during the final fitting.

FAR RIGHT
The bodice on a form after final fitting, before finish. At this stage, necessary adjustments are made and if required, embellishments are added.

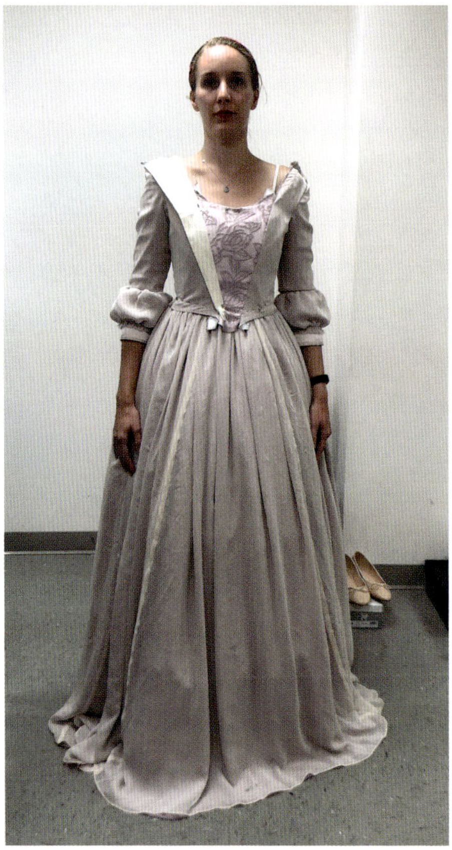

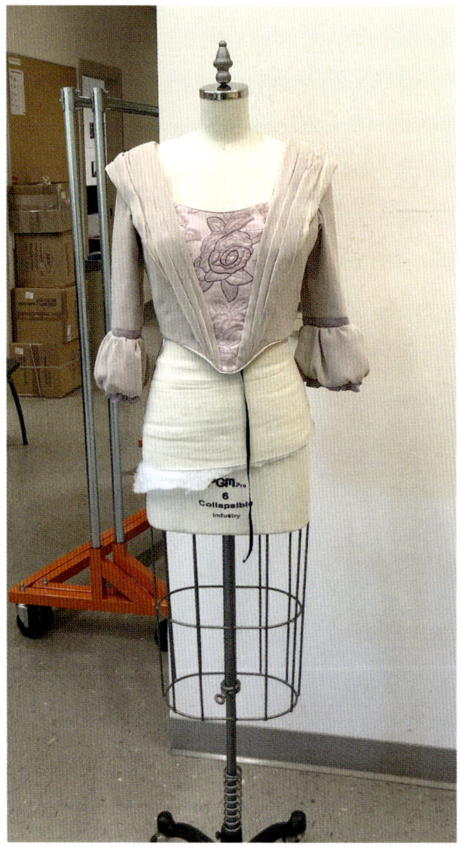

fill in the wardrobe of a character. Some of the obviously made costumes without designer or costume shop labels were most likely made by costume shops owned by producers or movie studios, likely on the West Coast or at Angels Costumes in London.

As a start, I will outline a very broad description of how costumes are made. E. Shura Pollatsek spells it out in the introduction of her book, *Unbuttoned: The Art and Artists of Theatrical Costume Design*: "Making custom clothing for the stage can seem magical. It is just as magical as the way flour and yeast, when combined with the right amount of elbow grease, become a delicious, crusty loaf of bread. Most people do not see the planning and time that the transformation of fabric into wearable art entails."[1] The book describes the specific ways in which costume making is different from mass-market fashion production. Almost every item for theater or film is created as a one-off, or something that is specifically made for one person to wear to one event. Mass-market fashion works for a broad audience—not an individual. Costumes are developed and constructed much in the same way that haute couture clothing is conceived. Each costume is created with one person in mind, evaluating their measurements and body structure specifically for the creation of individual patterns. The challenges and problem-solving are specific to the event it is being created for. Stage productions often have very specific needs, such as quick change rigging—tricks that allow for costumes to go on or come off quickly in the dark, often in seconds. This may involve unusual snap placement, zippers, magnets, or (my least favorite option) Velcro.

Glynnis Marcelle as Catherine Sloper in *The Heiress* at Indiana University. The final costume is a culmination of the designer's vision and technical expertise of the draper and makers. The costume is carefully constructed to be durable enough to withstand the rigors of a theatrical production with several costume changes.

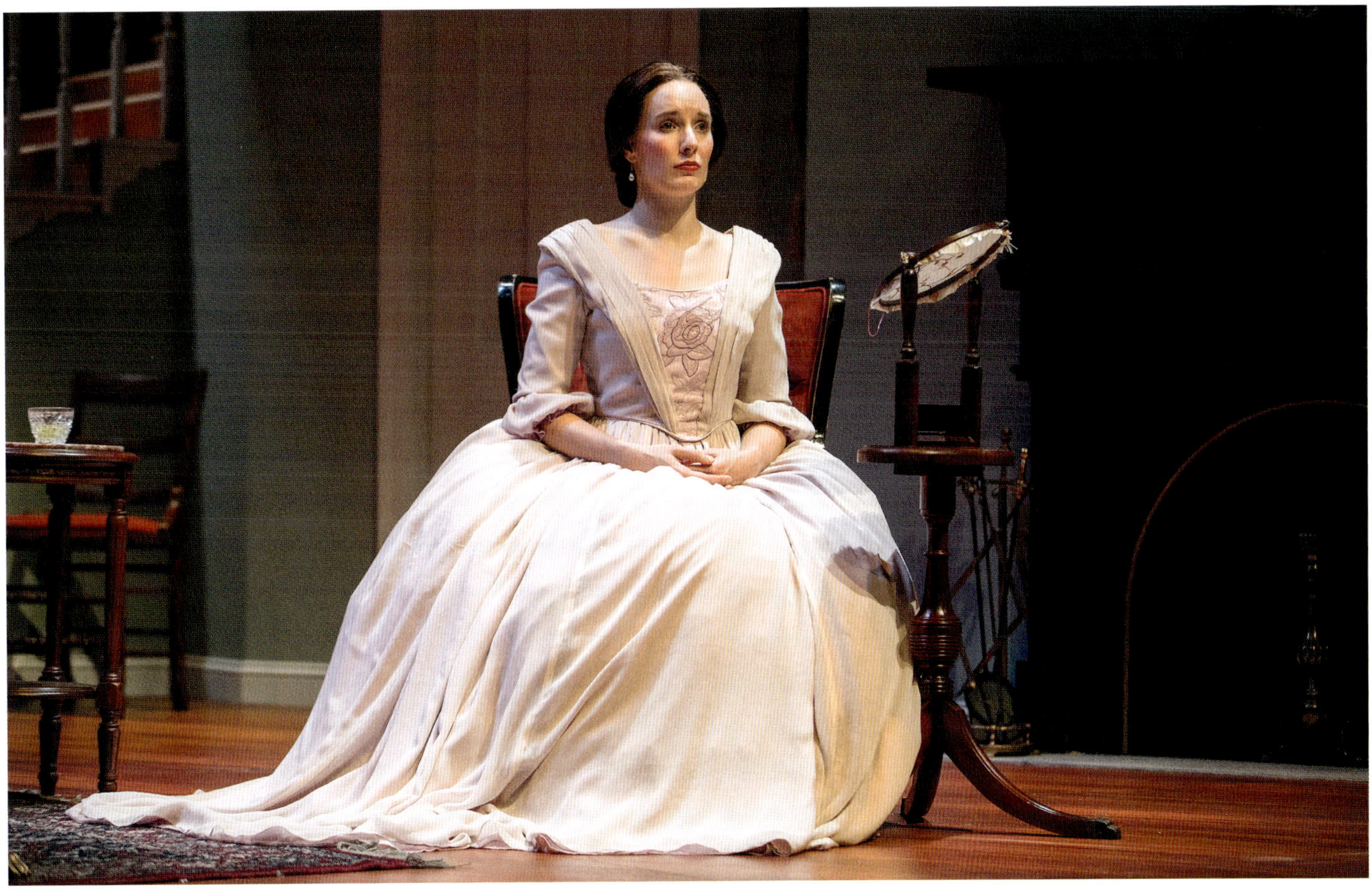

Costume shops specialize in the construction of costumes designed and rendered by costume designers. This process is referred to in several different ways: constructing, making, or building. It is essentially the transformation of a two-dimensional rendering, a painting or drawing from the costume designer, into a three-dimensional costume for a specific person embodying a specific character. This customized process requires skilled artisans who are trained in the patterning, draping, and making of clothes. In most costume shops, there are many people who create each costume. In the shops examined through this collection, they primarily work in teams of artists and makers. The teams are made up of drapers, first hands, dressmakers, and hand finishers. The shop also employs tailors, craftspeople, and beaders, as well as having a shopping department. Each member of the team brings their own expertise and knowledge and they work together to create the finished product.

The draper leads the team of makers. A draper begins the process after conversations with the designer. Collaboration between the draper and the designer is regular and constant. It is the draper's responsibility to think through how each piece is made and how it will be finished in order to create the costume as it is designed. They often begin by finding a dress form that is similar in size and shape to the actor being costumed. Working in this three-dimensional way is called draping. The other process often used by drapers is flat patterning, which uses measurements and formulas to draft a pattern directly onto paper. For draping, muslin is usually pinned to the dress form to create shapes that can be used together to create the style, shape, and fit for the costume pieces. At this stage, the draper is figuring out all of the details: seam placement, fabric fullness, contour, and how to fit and finish each piece. The draper usually has an assistant or first hand working with them to turn the drape into custom paper patterns, and then they make a mock-up. The mock-up is the first iteration of the pattern developed in fabric. It is usually made from a plain, easy to handle and inexpensive like muslin. The mock-up is fit on the actor to make sure that all of the choices and patterns work. It is also an opportunity for the actor to assess whether the costume allows them to physically perform onstage or on camera, as well as allowing the designer to see the three-dimensional garment. This is a low-risk fitting; many changes can be made since the final fabric has not been marked, cut, beaded, or embellished.

One aspect of collaboration that is vitally important to this process is the choosing of fabric. Fabric is the artistic medium of costumes. The fabric must be able to do what is needed: it has to stand up to what the costume is required to do and last as long as the show will run. Sometimes designers come to the conversation having already chosen fabric, or sometimes they have drawn the costume but wait for the shopping department to bring them options—often in the form of swatches—that meet the needs of the costume and are available for purchase in the required amount. Shoppers work in collaboration with designers, drapers, fabric store owners, and shop purchasing managers. Being a shopper in a big city is an exhausting job, walking all over the fashion district every day in search of fabric, trims, buttons, and more.

In an article published in *Theatre Design & Technology*, "The History of the Broadway Costume Business," Triffin and Gregory D. L. Morris cover in detail how commercial costume shops in New York City emerged from the uniform and costume rental market: "Through the post-war era costumes made for Broadway were generally of two types: the industrial builds of the big rental operations, and the gossamer creations of the *je suis artiste*

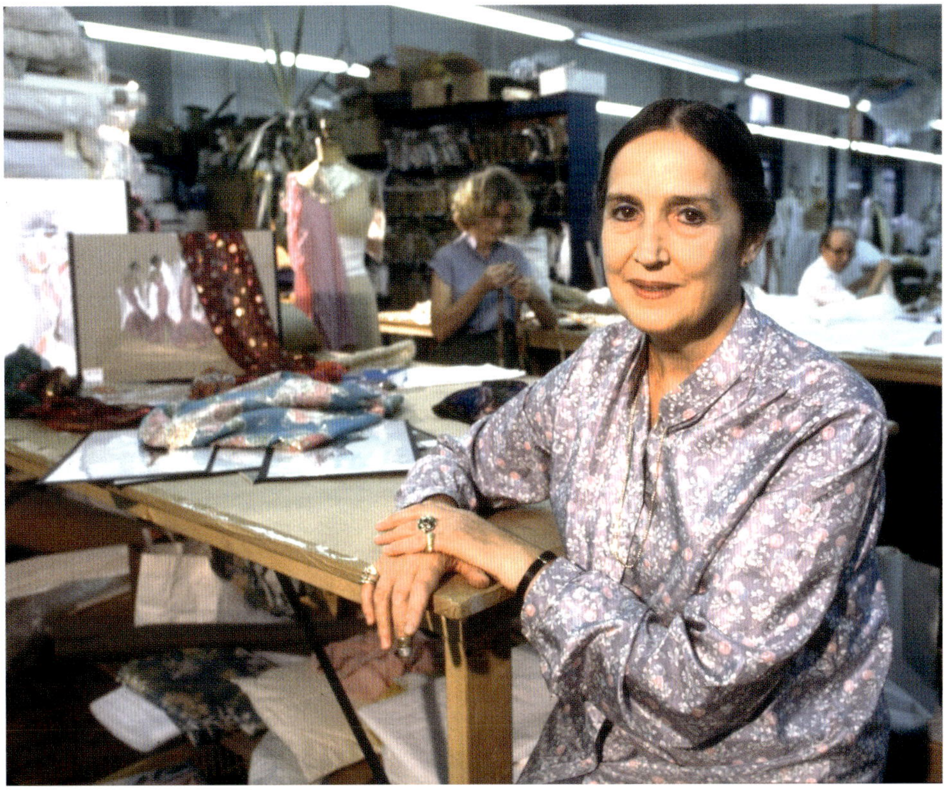

Publicity photo of theatrical costume maker Barbara Matera in her workshop, New York, 1981

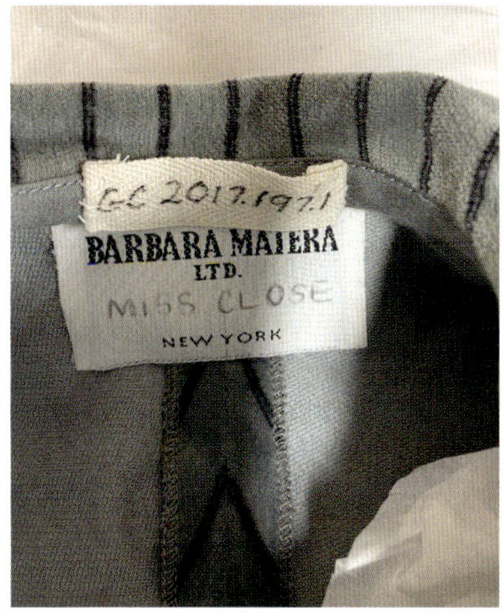

Barbara Matera "Miss Close" label.

Continentals."[2] The article interestingly traces a line from the first shops, by whom, and for whom they were run, to the "British Invasion" of designers and makers coming to New York. This history points toward Ray Diffen as having a great influence over the refined commercial shops of today: "Ray Diffen was the first to bring the European method of studying historic garments, and combine that with couture technology."[3] In 1958 Diffen sponsored Barbara Matera (then Gray) to come to New York from England. She worked for Ray Diffen Stage Clothes (RDSC) for several years before splitting off with her husband Arthur to start Barbara Matera Ltd.

Katherine Marshall, with whom I spoke at length about the Glenn Close Costume Collection, joined Barbara Matera Ltd. in 1978 and stayed until 2000, when she opened her own costume shop, Tricorne. "Kathy is wonderfully adept at making clothes look like they have been thought about and then done once, rather than messed about with," says designer Desmond Heeley. "Kathy is plumb sensible with charm to spare. Her shop is very calm, and bright. . . . Kathy has the best of Barbara in her bones."[4] Marshall's shop is still very much in demand and in fact she worked on the 2017 revival of *Sunset Boulevard* on Broadway.

All of this background set the stage for a discussion of the makers of these fantastic costumes. The costumes are made of beautiful material—beaded, feathered, sequined, and ultimately iconic. Within the collection, there are historical, fantastic, and "regular" clothes as costumes. For the costume maker, it is inspirational: legends in their field have had their hands inside these pieces. Many of the costumes made in these renowned shops are couture finished inside. The costume studio label that is most represented in the Glenn Close Costume Collection is Barbara Matera Ltd., with eleven examples from shows or events beginning in 1982. Other New York City costume shop labels include Eric Winterling,

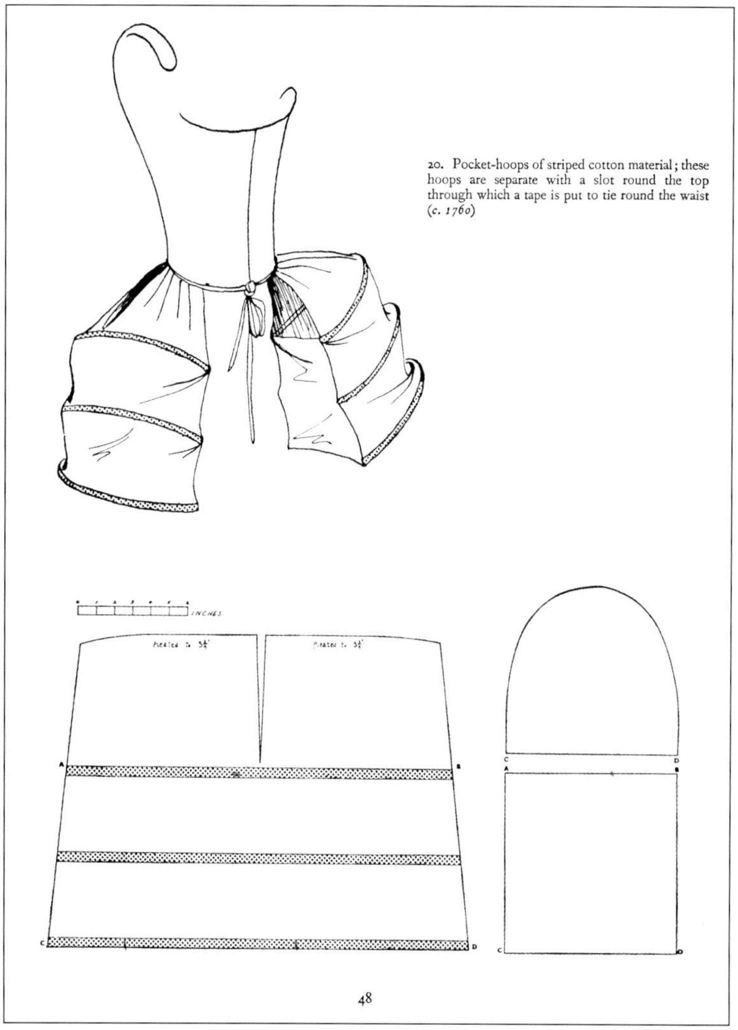

Norah Waugh, Pocket hoops pattern from *Corsets and Crinolines* (1954), page 48

Inc., and Studio Rouge, and there are also pieces from Angels Costumes in London.

The first costume made at Matera's was a garment for *Barnum* (1980) by designer Theoni Aldredge. In 1982 they made a nurse's costume for *The World According to Garp*, designed by Ann Roth, followed by designs from Anthony Powell for Norma Desmond in the original 1994 *Sunset Boulevard* and Cruella De Vil in *101 Dalmatians* and *102 Dalmatians* (1996 and 2000).

Interviews with Polly Kinney, Eleanor Wolfe, and Katherine Marshall (who worked at Barbara Matera Ltd. from 1985 to 2011, 1991 to 2007, and 1978 to 2000, respectively) allowed me to speak with some of the lead drapers from Matera's shop. I also had the privilege of interviewing Eric Winterling. These talented drapers had a hand in developing the patterns and overseeing the construction of some of the costumes in this collection. The drapers from Matera's spoke of a very special relationship between Barbara and Anthony Powell—how they shared an unspoken understanding of what the other wanted or was thinking, which allowed their interactions to be fluid and magical. I think that is why the *Sunset Boulevard* and *Dalmatians* costumes are so impressive. Marshall reported that Powell had an excellent knowledge and understanding of fabric and often came to the shop with specific fabrics already chosen or purchased. That is not always the case with designers—many hope for the shopping department to discover some hidden gem.

In their collaboration, the costume designer provides a rendering or sketch, some research, and other pertinent information, and drapers interpret these details in a number of different ways. It is common for drapers aiming to achieve historical silhouettes to reference texts by fashion historians, such as pattern books based on extant garments. For example, Marshall adapted a corset pattern found in her copy of *Corsets and Crinolines* for two of Glenn Close's costumes. Norah Waugh's 1954 publication includes a number of historical corset patterns, one of which Marshall developed for *The Ballad of Lucy Whipple* (2001), later modifying it for *102 Dalmatians*. Similarly, the functional panniers used in *Dangerous Liaisons* (1988) are closely inspired by the pocket hoops pattern in figure 20 of *Corsets and Crinolines* (left).

The theatrical costumes for *Sunset Boulevard* are iconic and the detail is incomparable. These costumes truly shape the impression that the character of Norma Desmond makes on the Minskoff Theatre audience. This is a large proscenium theater that seats 1,696 patrons. The costumes are for the people in the front row of the orchestra as well as the last row of the mezzanine. Anthony Powell designed costumes that did this extraordinarily well. The silhouettes are striking, the glamour is exaggerated, and the detail is both in the small things as well as the large visual picture. The fabrics chosen are stunning and the embellishments (beading and embroidery) heighten simple, elegant choices. The interesting details that make theatrical costumes different from mainstream fashion, or even most film costumes, are in the level of problem-solving in relation to getting it on and off. For a character such as Norma Desmond, you "exit stage left" and then within minutes must do a costume change, including wigs, hats, jewelry, and shoes. Preparing garments to quickly come off or go on involves swift change rigging, as mentioned earlier. The item must still look sumptuous or like any other normal dress, but it must be able to function as the script dictates. Another special consideration for big Broadway hits is that the same design will need to be custom made for any actor replacements, understudies, or national tours. The considerable amount of time that is put into the premiere costume has as much to do with the actor and how to optimize the garment. This might mean finessing the proportion or moving a seam to get the balance just so. Then the same team must take the measurements of the next actor and rebalance the design to maintain consistency and honor the original, creating the same character on a new body.

Matera's made another fantastic set of costumes for the character Cruella De Vil in *101* and *102 Dalmatians*. Marshall was kind enough to share a set of renderings from Powell that show all *102* costume designs on one plate. The costumes were intricately designed, from the most internal layer touching the skin to the last feather on the top of her hat. The incredible transformation that Glenn Close achieved through the collaboration of Powell

Anthony Powell, Costume sketches for *102 Dalmatians*. © Disney

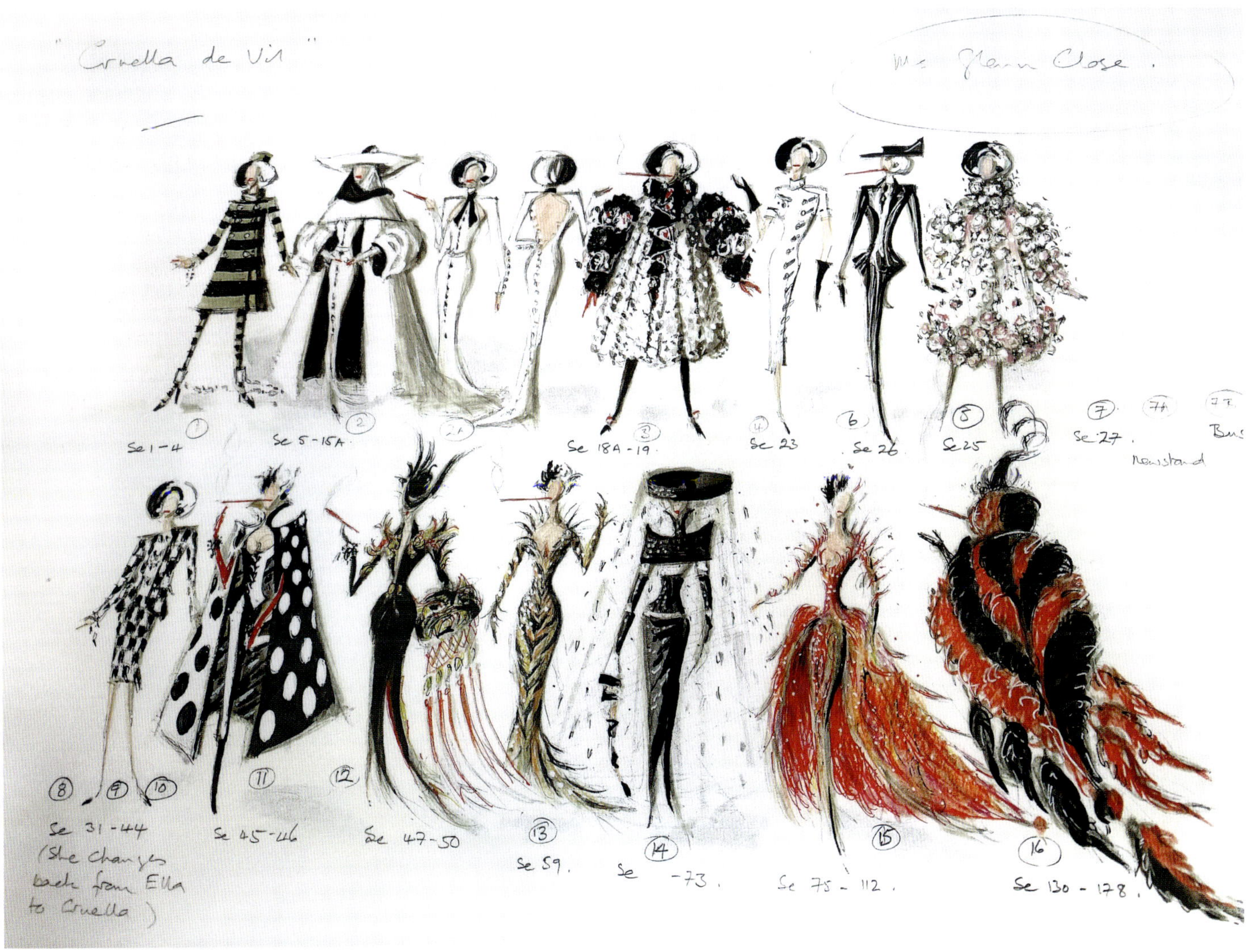

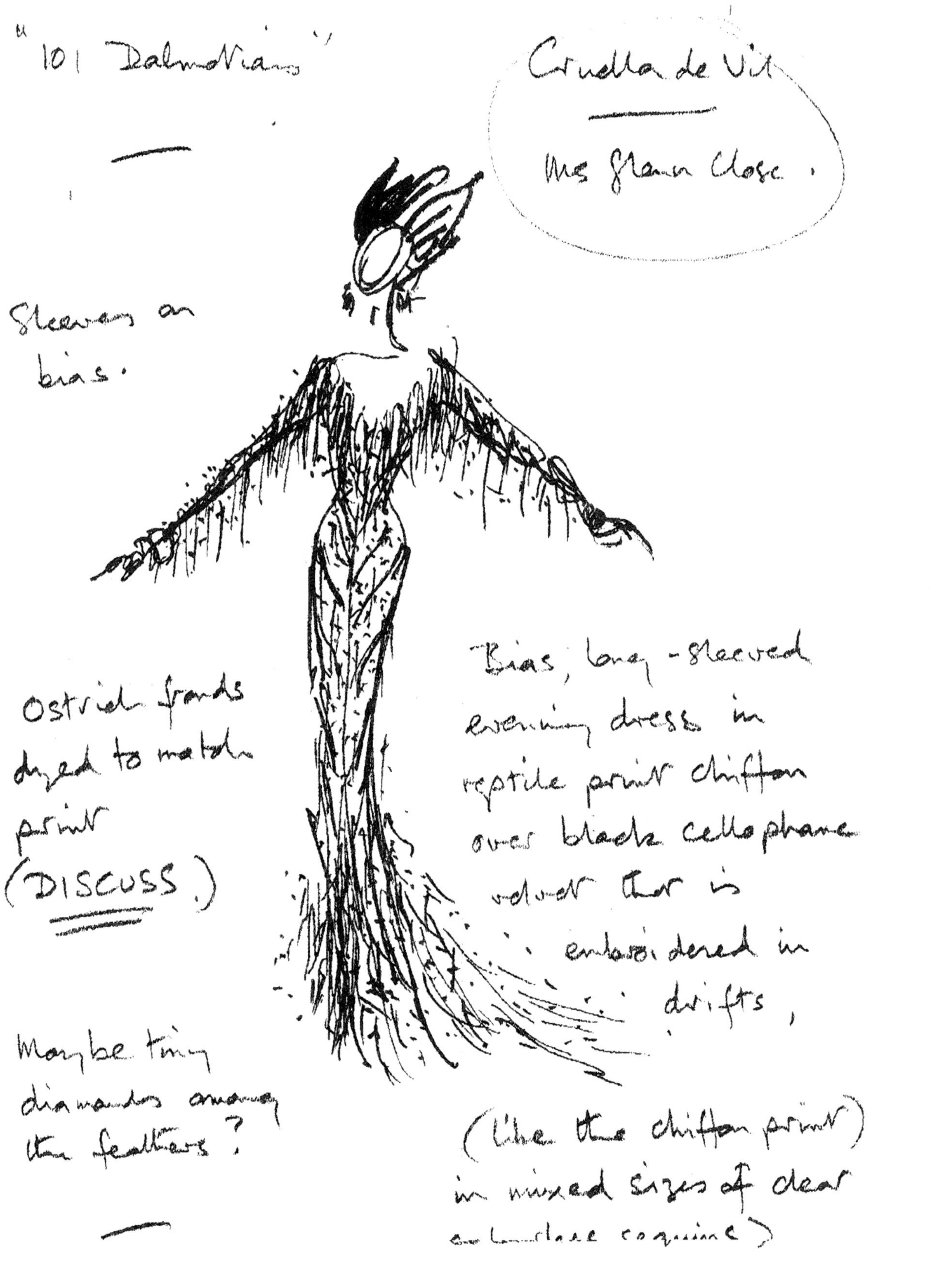
"101 Dalmatians"
Cruella de Vil
Ms Glenn Close.
Sleeves on bias.
Ostrich fronds dyed to match print (DISCUSS)
Maybe tiny diamonds among the feathers?
Bias, long-sleeved evening dress in reptile print chiffon over black cellophane velvet that is embroidered in drifts,
(like the chiffon print) in mixed sizes of clear colourless sequins)

and Matera's was the most exciting I have ever witnessed. As a young costume maker, I was awestruck as Close, after her final fitting, fully dressed in shoes, wig, hat, and long cigarette, came through Matera's and thanked every person working in the shop for their contribution. It was a moment that filled me with pride for what I made, as well as wonder that such a talented actor so appreciated our part in her transformation. It is a memory I will always cherish.

Polly Kinney, a lead bead designer, spoke with me about the nuance and extravagance that many of the *Dalmatians* costumes have. Eleanor Wolfe shared with me a black-and-white fax that Powell sent to Matera's, sketching the bias-cut sleeves and clear sequins scattered over the dress. This subtle use of sequins gives an unexpected shimmer as the actor moves. The notes that the designer included on the sketch illuminate the importance of fine details. Powell writes, "Bias, long-sleeved evening dress in reptile print chiffon over black cellophane velvet that is embroidered in drifts (like the chiffon print in mixed sizes of clear sequins). . . . Ostrich fronds dyed to match print (DISCUSS). Maybe tiny diamonds among the feathers?" These very specific conversation points show how Powell processed and shared his ideas, as well as his willingness and interest in discussing these issues with the makers. Kinney also discussed the heavily encrusted dragon beading on the back of Cruella De Vil's black coat in *102 Dalmatians*. She was very proud of the design and beading decisions for that piece, and yet the beaded detail is never seen in the movie.

Wolfe also shared with me several pages of notes on the flame dress for *102 Dalmatians*. It is a spectacular glory of undulating flames, with sparkles and an amazing collar of standing wisps. Wolfe kept her notes about construction decisions, her to-do list as the draper leading the team, a sleeve detail sketched by Powell, and pictures of the dress on a form before it left the shop. The notebook pages and pencil marks in light script would not be of visual interest to most people. However, when diving into the making of these costumes, it is exactly the level of detail I hoped for. Through these notes, I learned that the dress pattern was marked on organza and the stitchers applied flames in slightly overlapping, graduated colors of tulle and crystal sheer, with the largest flames at the hem. The colors are undulating purple, red, orange, and gold. There are beads, sequins, and stretch net on the bodice, and horsehair and Rigilene (flexible plastic boning) give the skirt structure and body. The dress as a whole picture, as well as the intricate details, is a costume masterpiece.

Other costumes from *Dalmatians* were made by Katherine Marshall's team. She is a genius as a draper and a lovely person to work for and with. Her costumes have an elegant flair and a refined finish. In our interview, Marshall began with an acknowledgement of Glenn Close and why this collection is so amazing, especially for students of costumes. She said, "That's a phenomenal thing about her [Close] that she does actually appreciate and recognize the making process." Marshall worked on the very first pieces that came into Matera's for Close. She started on *Barnum* in 1980, followed by *The World According to Garp* in 1982. Marshall was initially unfamiliar with the story of *Garp*, but she proceeded to read the novel and became very excited to have a part in the production.

Marshall continues to make the most exquisite costumes. She has an ability to develop trusting relationships with designers and actors, and an artist's hand at refining the patterns and costume construction choices. She spoke at length about some of the *Sunset Boulevard* costumes, as she worked on the originals at Matera's and the 2017 revival at Tricorne. She

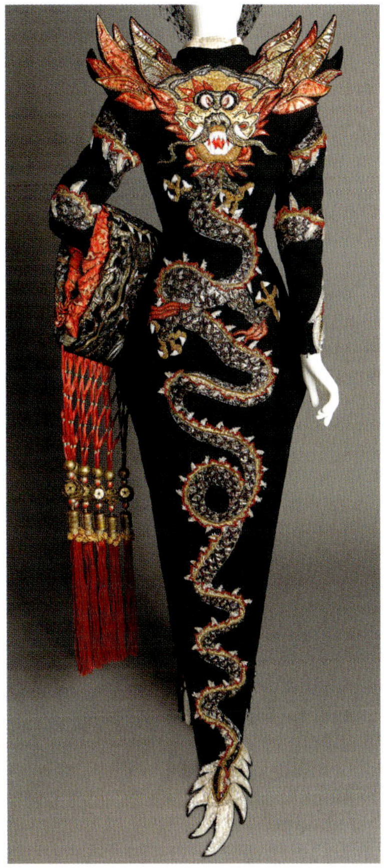

Anthony Powell made by Barbara Matera Ltd., Back of Dragon Ensemble (Cruella De Vil/Ella, *102 Dalmatians*), 2000, Wool, silk, polyester, metal, glass beads, glass stones, plastic sequins, feathers, GC 2017.13.1-.3, .7-.8

OPPOSITE
Anthony Powell, Annotated sketch for Python Dress from *101 Dalmatians*, 1995. © Disney

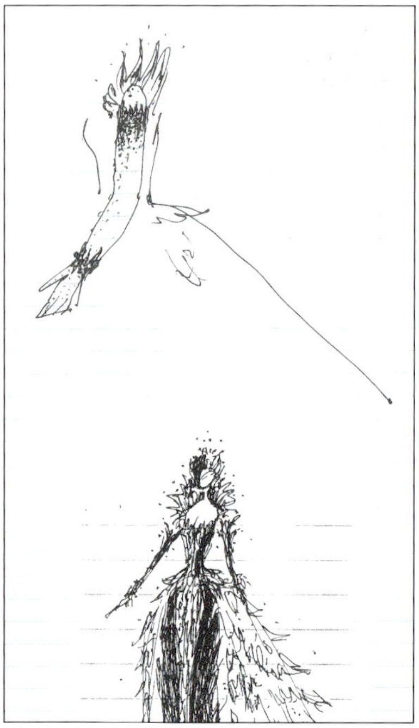

ABOVE
Barbara Matera Ltd., Workroom sketch for Flame/Firebird Dress sleeve from *102 Dalmatians* with detail by Anthony Powell. © Disney

RIGHT
Thank you letter from Anthony Powell to staff at Barbara Matera Ltd.

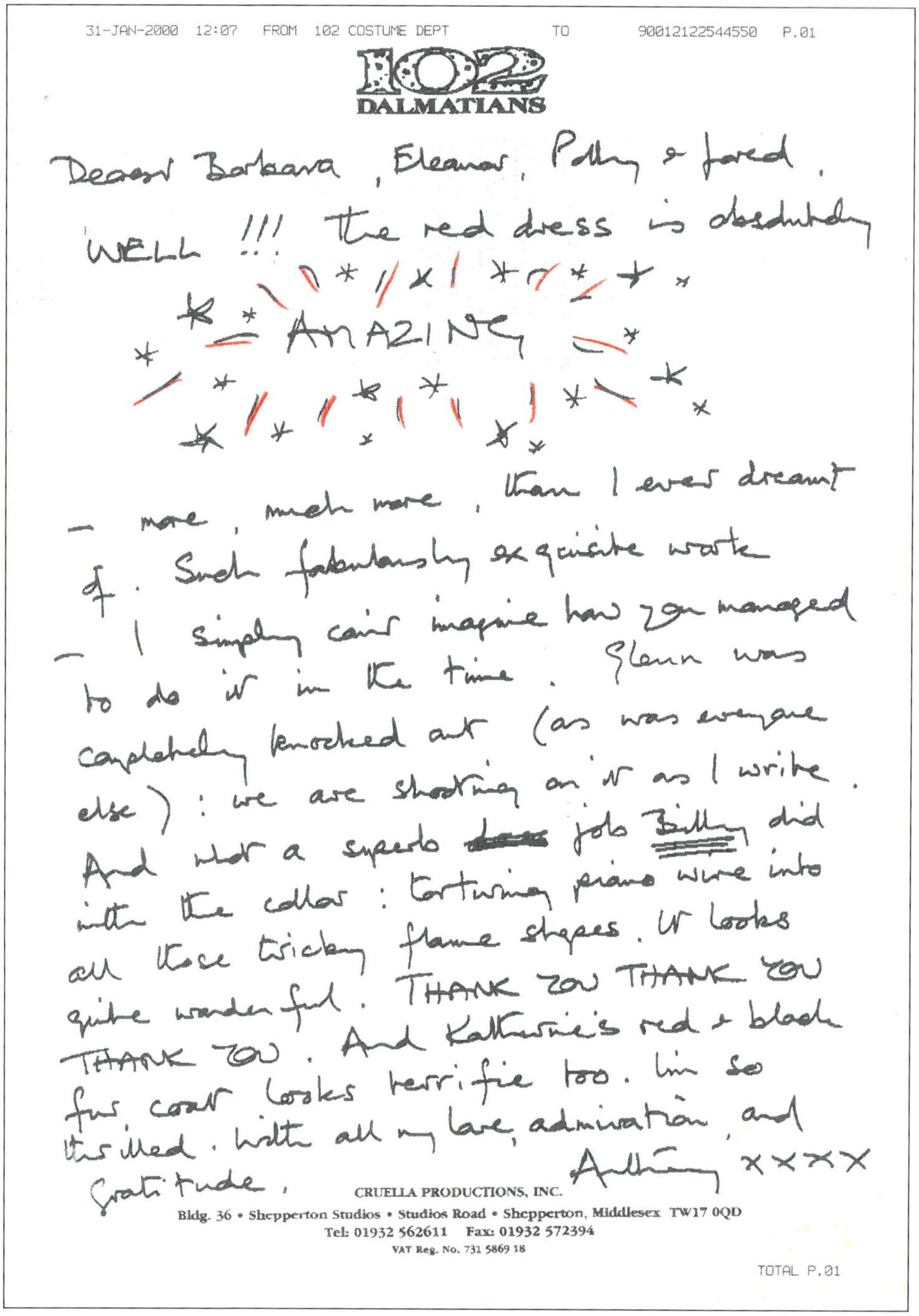

31-JAN-2000 12:07 FROM 102 COSTUME DEPT TO 90012122544550 P.01

102 DALMATIANS

Dearest Barbara, Eleanor, Polly & Jared.

WELL !!! The red dress is absolutely AMAZING – more, much more, than I ever dreamt of. Such fabulously exquisite work – I simply can't imagine how you managed to do it in the time. Glenn was completely knocked out (as was everyone else): we are shooting on it as I write. And what a superb job Billy did with the collar: torturing piano wire into all those tricky flame shapes. It looks quite wonderful. THANK YOU THANK YOU THANK YOU. And Katherine's red & black fur coat looks terrific too. I'm so thrilled. With all my love, admiration, and gratitude,

Anthony xxxx

CRUELLA PRODUCTIONS, INC.
Bldg. 36 • Shepperton Studios • Studios Road • Shepperton, Middlesex TW17 0QD
Tel: 01932 562611 Fax: 01932 572394
VAT Reg. No. 731 5869 18

TOTAL P.01

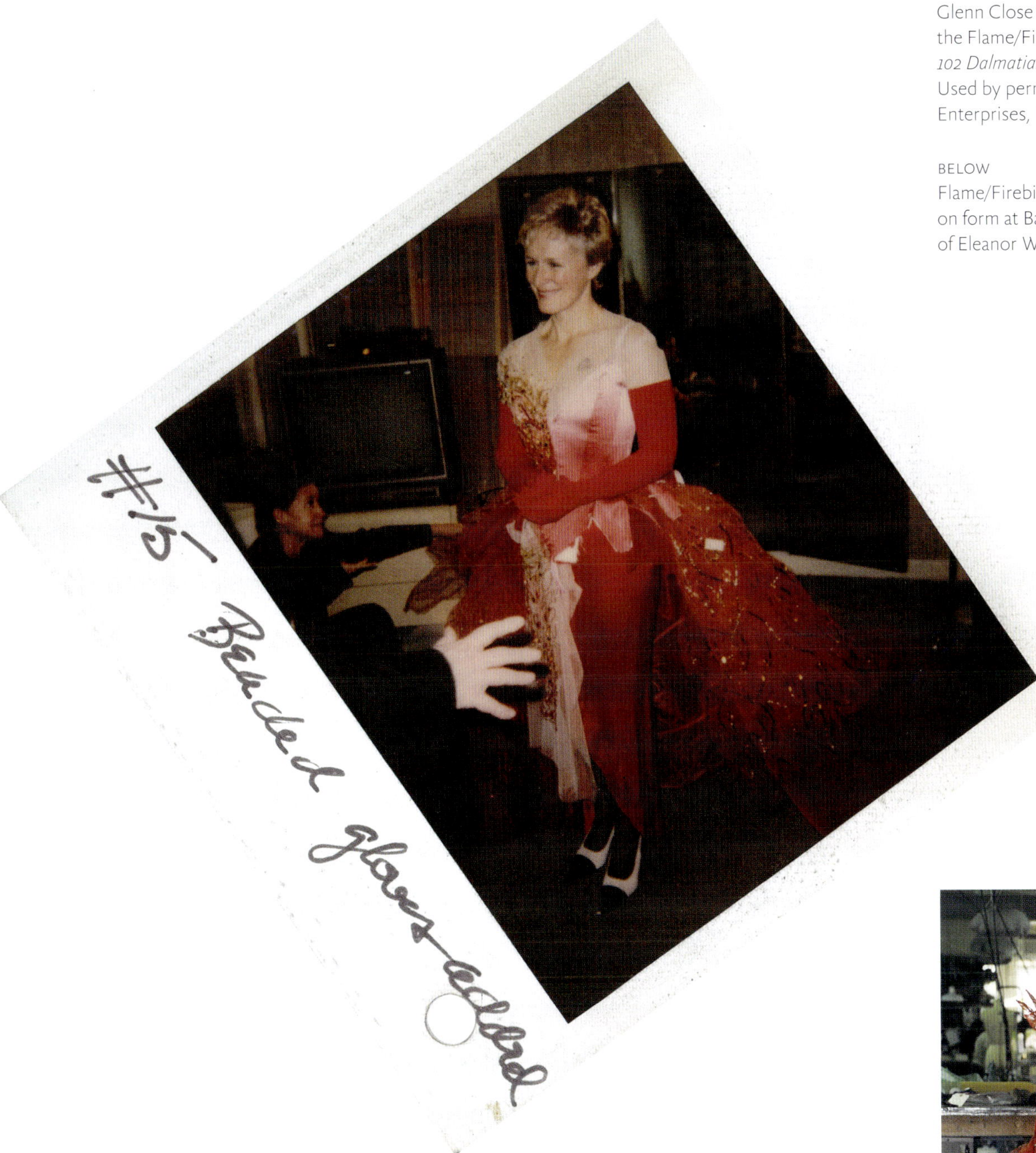

LEFT
Glenn Close in her first fitting for the Flame/Firebird Dress from *102 Dalmatians* at Barbara Matera Ltd. Used by permission from Disney Enterprises, Inc.

BELOW
Flame/Firebird Dress from *102 Dalmatians* on form at Barbara Matera Ltd. (Courtesy of Eleanor Wolfe)

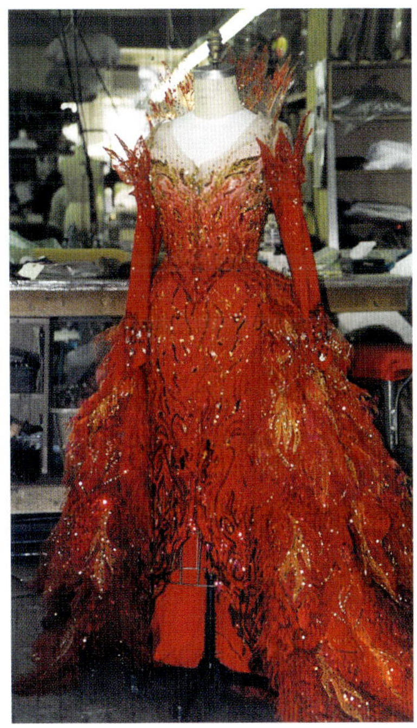

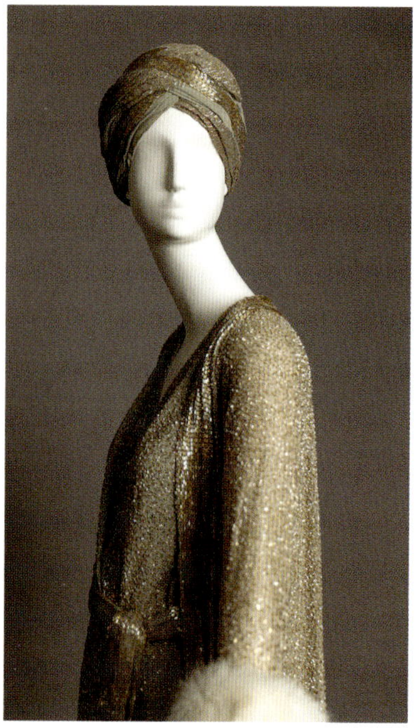

Anthony Powell made by Barbara Matera Ltd. and Woody Shelp, Beaded Pajamas and Robe (Norma Desmond, *Sunset Boulevard*), 1994/2017, Silk, glass beads, fox fur, GC 2017.253.1-.4

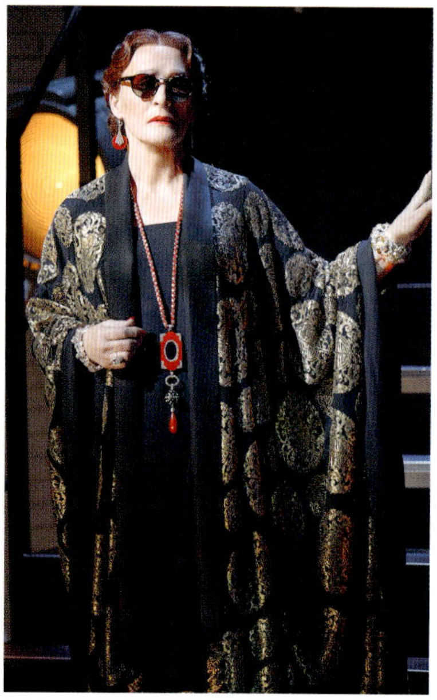

Glenn Close as Norma Desmond in *Sunset Boulevard*, 2017

recalls very specific costume moments that she experienced while watching *Sunset Boulevard* on Broadway. Specifically, she talked about the heavy, fully beaded jumpsuit and jacket that audibly swished and hit each step as Norma Desmond descended the sweeping staircase. This staircase also featured in a memory of the floating gold medallion kimono, which fluttered and billowed behind Close in her descent. Marshall recalled the weight of the leopard-print dress—how heavy the fabric was. The dress always surprised her with its weight because it did not look as though it should be that heavy, but between the fabric choice and structure underneath, there was no way to avoid it. Anthony Powell was the designer for both *Sunset Boulevard* and *Dalmatians*. Marshall said that he "is so unique because he has such a clear vision about where he is going. He knew what he wanted or what he was looking for. He understood fabric."

Some of the most interesting costumes that Marshall made in the Glenn Close Costume Collection are for the *Dalmatians* movies. Many were featured in magazines, newspapers, and advertisements. Cruella's very first costume, as she emerges from her luxury Panther DeVille vehicle, was made by Marshall's team. This "simple" black suit has hand-stitched, bugle-bead pinstripes on the jacket and skirt, with fantastic, structured shoulder wings. Paired with beautiful stiletto shoes, the costume has an immediate visual impact, helping to define the character. Cruella's negligee, with its long, feathered sleeves, was also constructed by Marshall's team; the feathers haunted their tables for months after the garment shipped out.

In *102 Dalmatians*, Marshall worked on the transformation of the houndstooth suits. She believes, although I could not confirm, that the original fabric was solid, plain black wool and that the houndstooth pattern was applied and emphasized with embroidery beading decoration. In regard to fabric, she discussed the nun's dress as being soft and supple, and therefore difficult to hide the firm structure of the corsetry beneath. She also remembers the large number of buttons on that dress. This subdued costume is a fine example of the mastery of Marshall's draping. It does nothing obvious or flashy, but the exquisite fit hugs the form perfectly so that the impact is solid, simple, and functional.

Examining the making of these costumes has been an honor and a privilege. Looking at the process of costume making shed a bit of light on the extremely talented pool of people who work on film, television, and theater costumes. Their art is showcased by gifted actors on stage and screen, in the designs drawn or painted by costume designers and with the intricate detailing of patterns and construction by costume shops. It is with humble appreciation that I recognize the individuals who took the time to speak with me and share tidbits of memories, photographs, and notes related to costumes in this collection. My thanks to Katherine Marshall of Tricorne, Eleanor Wolfe at Miami City Ballet, Polly Kinney of Polly Kinney Beading, and Eric Winterling of Eric Winterling, Inc.

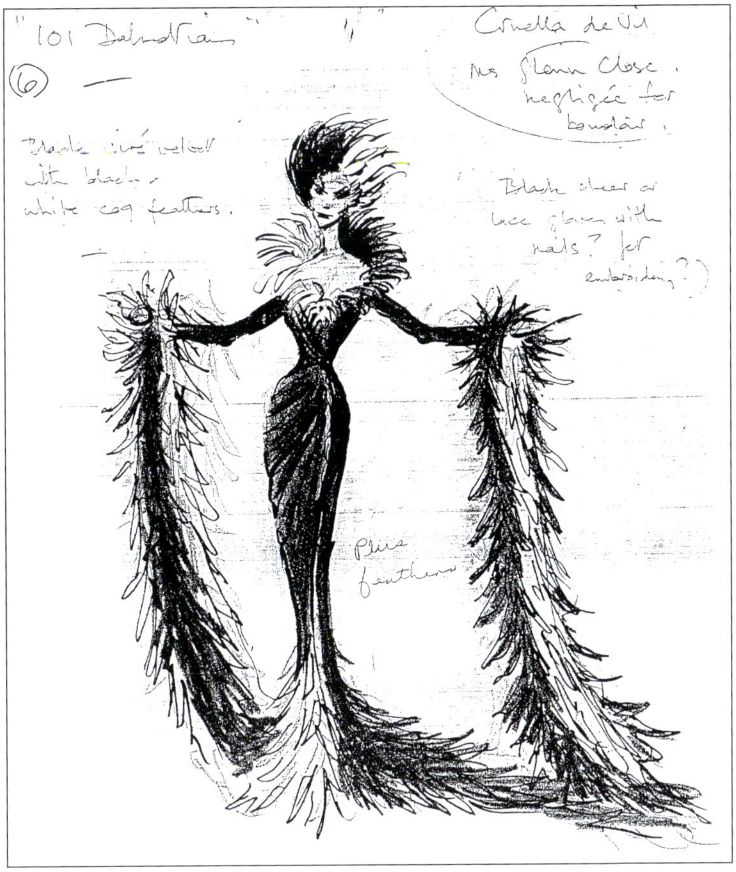

Anthony Powell, Annotated sketch for black and white feathered negligee from *101 Dalmatians*, 1995. © Disney

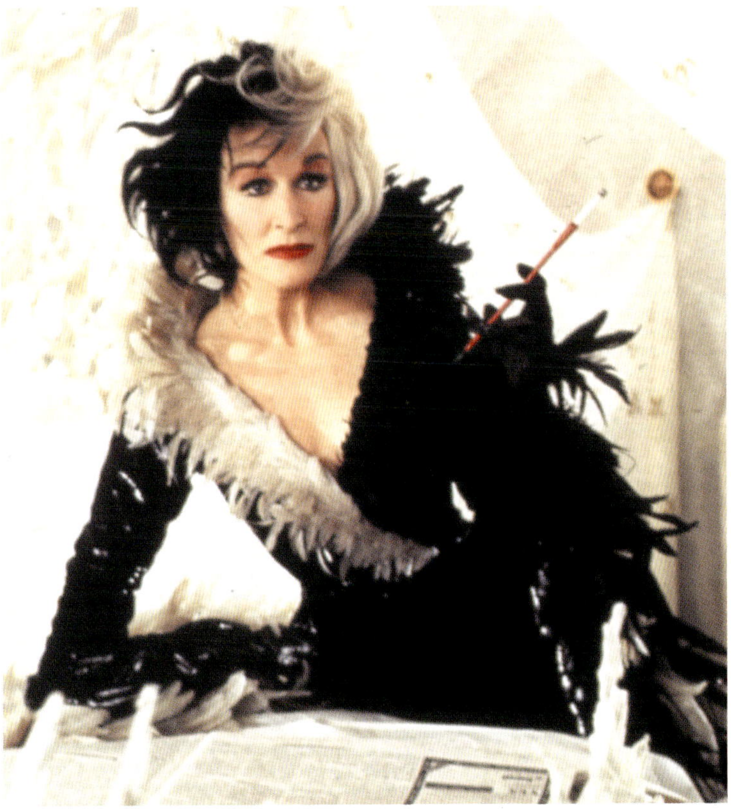

Glenn Close as Cruella De Vil from *101 Dalmatians*, 1996. © Disney

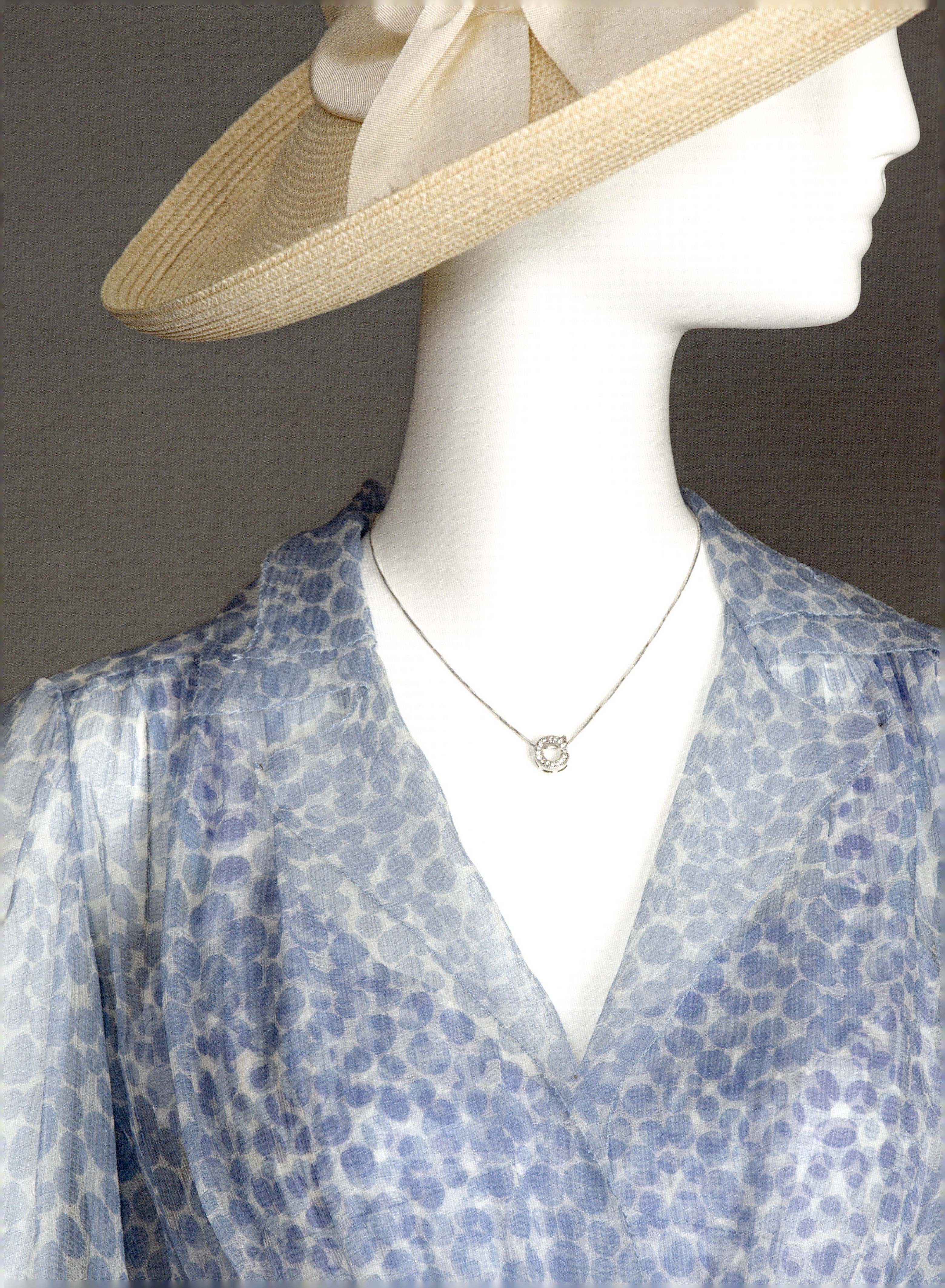

Fashioning Intra-Feminine Fascination

Jennifer E. Maher

The first time I met Glenn Close was in the fall of 2018, while I was teaching a class at Indiana University (IU) on "Feminism and the Body." OK, so it wasn't actually *her* I was meeting—it was her jacket. But, as her work and this collection attest, the seams between selfhood and self-*fashioning* can delightfully unravel.

"[Female stars] are 'made up,' in the immediate sense that the images, rather than the women, are put together, constructed, even fabricated or falsified in the sense that we might say a story is made up if it is a fiction."
—Annette Kuhn[1]

"I can write an article about shoes I've worn."
—Glenn Close[2]

That semester, in a windowless basement classroom, tucked low into the modernist limestone of Ballantine Hall, the eminently patient staff of the Sage Collection would don white cotton gloves and lay out a series of curated artifacts for my class each week. I designed my section of "Feminism and the Body" to illustrate how feminist theory might be written and read through clothing—for instance, during week one we looked at how an alumna's donation of a Frye boot and embroidered jeans might literally embody key texts from the campus women's liberation movement of the 1970s. I never told my students what the object would be beforehand, hoping to generate in them a series of rapid and emotive responses tying the material (a piece of clothing) to the discursive (an essay they had read that week). Dramatizing the ways in which the somatic and the theoretical coalesce is, of course, a fundamental tenet of costume on-screen. Though I was not aware of it at the time, my pedagogy called upon the ethos of the grande dame of costume design, Edith Head, winner of eight Academy Awards from 1949 to 1973 (and forever Pixar-immortalized as Edna Mode in *The Incredibles*). Of the function of dress in film, she famously claimed that "costume should carry enough information about a character so that the audience could tell something about them if the sound went out in the theater."[3]

Though the college classroom is not a theater by any stretch of the imagination, cinema's approach to the female body has long been a fraught topic for academic feminists. Beginning with the work of Laura Mulvey, in her widely taught and cited 1975 essay "Visual Pleasure and Narrative Cinema," feminist film theory examines how mainstream film elicits an imaginary masculine "spectator" from its audience, one whose "male gaze" (no matter the gender identity of the actual bodies in the movie theater seats) replicates and instantiates the feminine with passivity, objectification, and (in Mulvey's terms) "to-be-looked-at-ness."[4] And while cinema did not invent the objectification of women—Mulvey also draws on John Berger's theories of post-Renaissance fine art and portraiture in his work *Ways of Seeing*—film technology works particularly well as an advanced representation system illustrating "patterns of fascination already at work within the individual subject" while "reflect[ing] the psychical obsessions of the society which produced it."[5] In other words, feminist film theory provides us with a means to unpack how cinematic pleasure draws upon deeply embedded

OPPOSITE
Ann Roth (American)
Eric Winterling Inc.
Claire Wellington
The Stepford Wives, 2004
Silk
GC 2017.296.1-.3, .5

cultural beliefs about gender, which, combined with the camera's skill at initiating processes of voyeurism and fetishization, (re)affirm woman *as* image and man as "bearer of the look."[6] Female spectators are trained to gain pleasure from cinema in only two ways: (1) By temporarily identifying with the (almost always, in classical Hollywood) male lead, through whose eyes they see the action, via his point of view shots; and (2) Through a masochistic pleasure in identifying with their own objectification through the figure of the female star. Quoting Berger, Mulvey emphasizes this process as it occurs on-screen and in everyday life:

One might simplify this by saying: men act and women appear. Men look at women. Women watch themselves being looked at. This determines not only most relations between men and women but also the relation of women to themselves. The surveyor of woman in herself is male: the surveyed female. Thus she turns herself into an object—and most particularly an object of vision: a sight.[7]

The penultimate example of this process, for Mulvey, is Alfred Hitchcock's *Vertigo* (1958), whose relentless point of view shots and mystery narrative impel the audience to identify with "Scottie" Ferguson (Jimmy Stewart) as he becomes increasingly obsessed with the enigmatic Madeleine Elster (Kim Novak). Scottie literally turns Madeleine into a fetish by reconstructing her makeup, hairstyle, and clothing. One of the most famous scenes of fashion in film occurs when Scottie takes Madeleine to a department store, relentlessly in search of a gray skirt and jacket combo in the particular shade he requires her to wear.[8]

At around the same time that Mulvey's critique of cinema was gaining traction, popular second-wave feminism was making similar accusations against the veritable synecdoche of female oppression: the fashion industry. Fashion and self-decoration, in this view, was servitude to a tacit yet ubiquitous demand to monitor and maintain women's appearance for the pleasure of men. Robin Morgan, an organizer of the infamous Miss America protest in 1968,[9] put it plainly: to be truly free, women cannot continue to be "enslaved by ludicrous beauty standards that we ourselves are conditioned to take seriously."[10] For many American second-wave feminists like Morgan, the oft-quoted line from Simone de Beauvoir's *The Second Sex* (1949), that "one is not born a woman, but becomes one,"[11] was less a call to creative self-fashioning than blanket evidence of gender oppression writ large upon the female body. Articles of clothing such as girdles and high heels, for instance, were seen not only to hinder women's literal ability to move through space, but also to hijack their consciousness to the point where their full and effective participation in the social and political world was correspondingly hobbled. Fashion theorist Jane Gaines summarizes this position on fashion and femininity when she writes, "costume may disguise the [female] body, deform it, or follow its curves; [but it] ultimately 'puts it on display.'"[12] And while feminism called on women to abandon their excessive investment in appearance as false consciousness, mainstream culture continued to devalue fashion in general, dismissing any psychic investment in it as a trite and hopelessly *feminine* preoccupation. So while women were called on by feminism to abandon an allegedly time-consuming investment in appearance, they were also, and paradoxically, told that this investment was shallow and ephemeral. Like the archetypal female spectator, it was assumed that consumers of fashion participate in their own objectification, trapped in a binary where the hard and fast oppositions of feminine adornment and feminist agency construct a rhetorical corset of impeded selfhood.

Or do they?

We need look no further than Close's discussion of her work with costume designer Anthony Powell on *Sunset Boulevard* (1994), *101 Dalmatians* (1996), and *102 Dalmatians* (2000) to trouble this binary of oppression versus agency:

[He] took pleasure with torturing me with shoes . . . He knew if it was a challenge, I would take it up. The first scene when Cruella [De Vil] comes in '101' when she walks down the ramp; those shoes had heels that were actual nails. They were so painful that it probably gave me my performance. That's why Cruella is angry all of the time—her feet are killing her.[13]

Thus, just as gender itself is situated in social processes and shaped through performance, so too are we coming to realize that clothing, as a textual and material system, generates its own sorts of performances of self. This kind of "psychic intimacy between wearer and garment"[14] is evident here when Close discusses walking (probably slightly less than) a mile in Cruella's shoes. Her intimate engagement with character through materiality serves as an example of what Karen Barad calls an "entanglement with matter," a reworking of the animate and the inanimate.[15] I would argue that Close's physical and psychic entanglement here literally *animates* a live-action film based on an animated character, creating a performance of volitional and defiant forbearance beyond the kind of wholly objectified femininity articulated in early feminist film theory.

And while Cruella's over-the-top outfits may seem a one-off, she is not the only character in Close's sartorial oeuvre to a deliberately exaggerate (and thus call into question) conventional femininity. Cruella's high-powered passion for fur, organza, ostrich feathers, silk roses, and even bubble wrap most certainly serves as foil to maternal and conventionally feminine Anita, a designer and would-be protégée working in Cruella's fashion house, with her tidy hair, blazers, and imminent motherhood. In some ways, Cruella is a dragged-up,

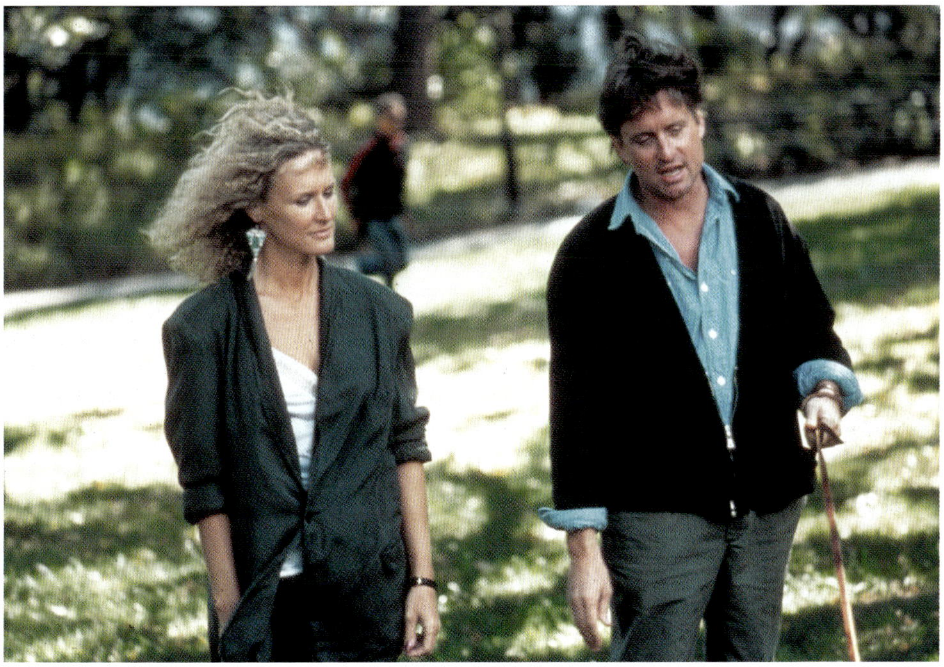

Glenn Close and Michael Douglas in *Fatal Attraction*, 1987

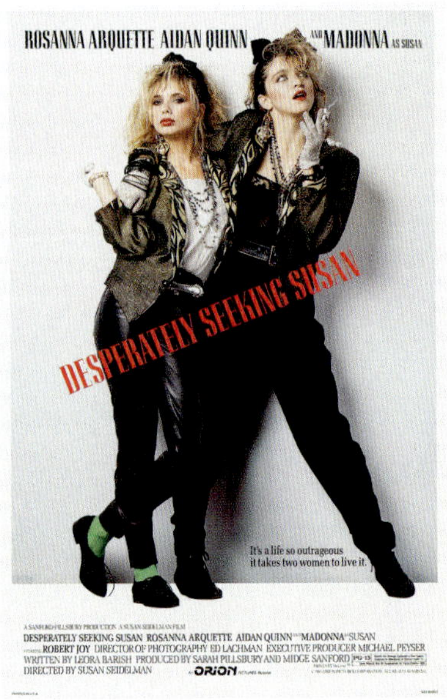

Rosanna Arquette and Madonna in *Desperately Seeking Susan*, 1985

played-for-laughs version of the wild-haired (albeit short-lived) resistance of Alex Forrest in *Fatal Attraction* (1987), whose assault on feminine decorum, selflessness, and male privilege leaves the audience on the edge of their seats until her rival, Beth Gallagher, a khaki-slacked, stay-at-home mother and wife, shoots her dead in the bathtub. Testament to Close's performance, while Alex is vanquished in the end, her character as a pop culture marvel is not. While *Fatal Attraction* has been overanalyzed into near banality as the filmic apotheosis of the 1980s feminist backlash,[16] the sheer audacity of Close's performance, despite her stated distaste for the ending, lives on. As recently as 2014, twenty-seven years after the film was screened, *Grazia* magazine offers us a chance to relive the leather jacket in my opening, with the headline "Why Glenn Close in Fatal Attraction Is Our Unexpected Style Icon," continuing, "You may not remember her name (Alexander Forrest, FYI) but you'll certainly remember a 1987 cinematic Glenn Close's power blazers."[17] The slippage between Glenn Close (whose name the reader, it is implied, will certainly know) and Alex Forrest (whose name must be supplied) attests to how Close's corporeal transformation for the role exemplifies what Gaines calls the "star style": "a direct and intimate link to the body and the consciousness of the female spectator."[18]

This sort of "intimate link" between the ostensibly female readers of *Grazia* and Glenn Close also typifies a specifically feminine form of fandom and admiration neglected in early feminist film theory and later described by Jackie Stacey in her essay "Desperately Seeking Difference," in which she argues in favor of female spectatorial pleasure beyond the masochism of the "male gaze."[19] Her reading of the films *Desperately Seeking Susan* (1985) and *All About Eve* (1950) illustrates a phenomenon which she labels "'intra-feminine' fascination . . . forms of otherness between women . . . which are not merely reducible to sexual difference."[20] While this form of enthrallment *can* be sexual (in the case of the lesbian/queer spectator), it does not have to be, as Stacey sees the relationships between the films' stars—Rosanna Arquette (Roberta) and Madonna (Susan), and Bette Davis (Margo) and Anne Baker

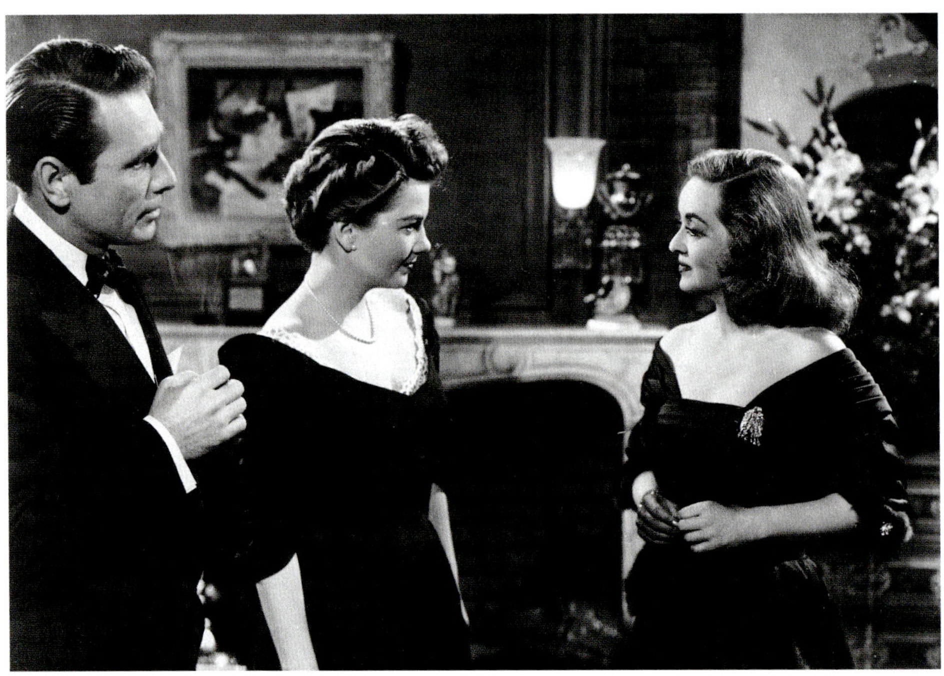

Gary Merrill, Anne Baxter, and Bette Davis in *All About Eve*, 1950

(Eve)—as collapsing the differences between a female object of desire and a female subject of that desire. Thus, Stacey argues that the films narrativize a particular pleasure in female spectatorship beyond Mulvey's oppressor/oppressed model.

What Stacey does *not* talk about in great depth in her essay though, is the role clothing plays in both of the films. In *All About Eve*, Margo and Eve are frequently dressed alike, in dark dresses with lace collars or sheer inlays around the shoulders; in one scene, Eve even goes as far as altering Margo's dress to fit her. Despite the studied innocence of her dialogue, even if the sound in the movie theatre went out, these costume choices clue the audience in to Eve's manipulative character thanks to Edith Head (and Charles LeMaire)'s costume design. Similarly, thirty-five years later, *Desperately Seeking Susan* presents Madonna at the pinnacle of her stylistic iconicity through the character of Susan, who fascinates as much through her personal style as her personality. Roberta (as stand-in for the female spectator) trails Madonna/Susan through crowded New York streets—not unlike Scottie tailing Madeleine in *Vertigo*—to a thrift store, where she buys Susan's previously owned gold pyramid embroidered jean jacket, later copying her hairstyle and overall look to the point where she is visually mistaken for her. This imitation-as-flattery move, not unlike young "Madonna wannabes" of the 1980s, sets the mistaken identity plot in motion, one that ends much more happily for Susan than it does for Margo.

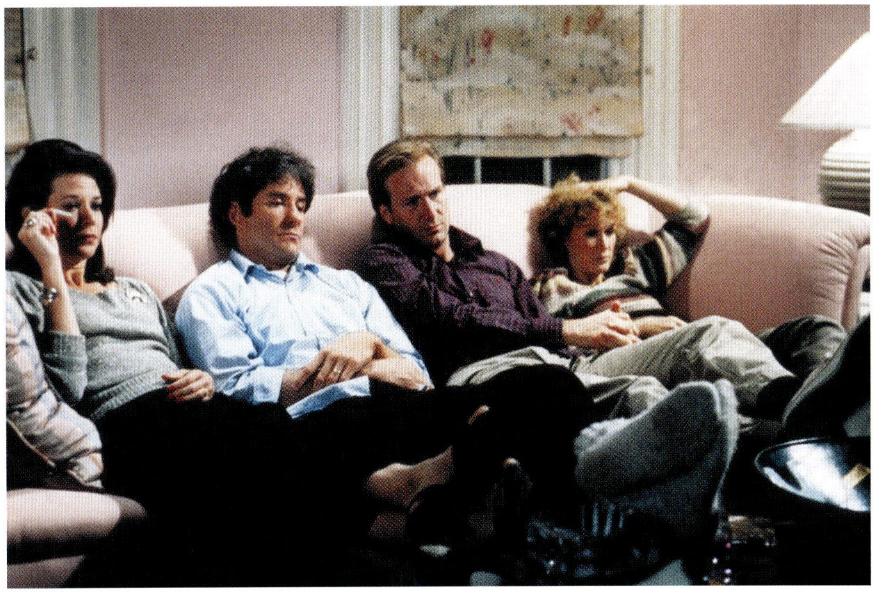

JoBeth Williams, Kevin Kline, William Hurt, and Glenn Close in *The Big Chill*, 1983

I would argue that clothing's ability to play such a pivotal role in agentic self-fashioning for all kinds of feminine "roles" (real-life and on screen) testifies to the fact that fashion is more than simple accommodation to objectified femininity. Taken as a whole, Glenn Close's costumed characters, like Susan and Eve, are *not* simply masochistic objects of a "male gaze," but rather bear the mark of their wearer as an eminently self-aware construct. In Close's own words, "My collaborations with anyone who designs my costumes are as important to me as my collaborations with a writer or director—sometimes even more so."[21] The nipped-in waist of Alex Forrest's black leather jacket; the dejected, fraying pinstripe of Albert Nobbs's vest, worn over a cream-colored corset; the buttoned-in certainty of Jenny Fields's nurse's uniform (*The World According to Garp*, 1982), the high-camp performance of Norma Desmond, with her "turban, scarves, and florid gowns in black, white, and shades of gold" (*Sunset Boulevard*, 1994);[22] the formfitting work suits of Teddy Barnes (*Jagged Edge*, 1985); the striped, popped-collar shirts of Patty Hewes (*Damages*, 2007–12); the cozy, earth mother sweater of Sarah Cooper (*The Big Chill*, 1983)—all of them *embody* a range of gendered archetypes that destabilize, rather than simply idealize, the feminine self. Clothing does not just make the man; it makes a protagonist. And as Close's career and the Glenn Close Costume Collection attest, it also "makes" for award-winning actors, who reward us all with riveting examples of how to be a central character in your own life, even when (and especially if) your shoes hurt.

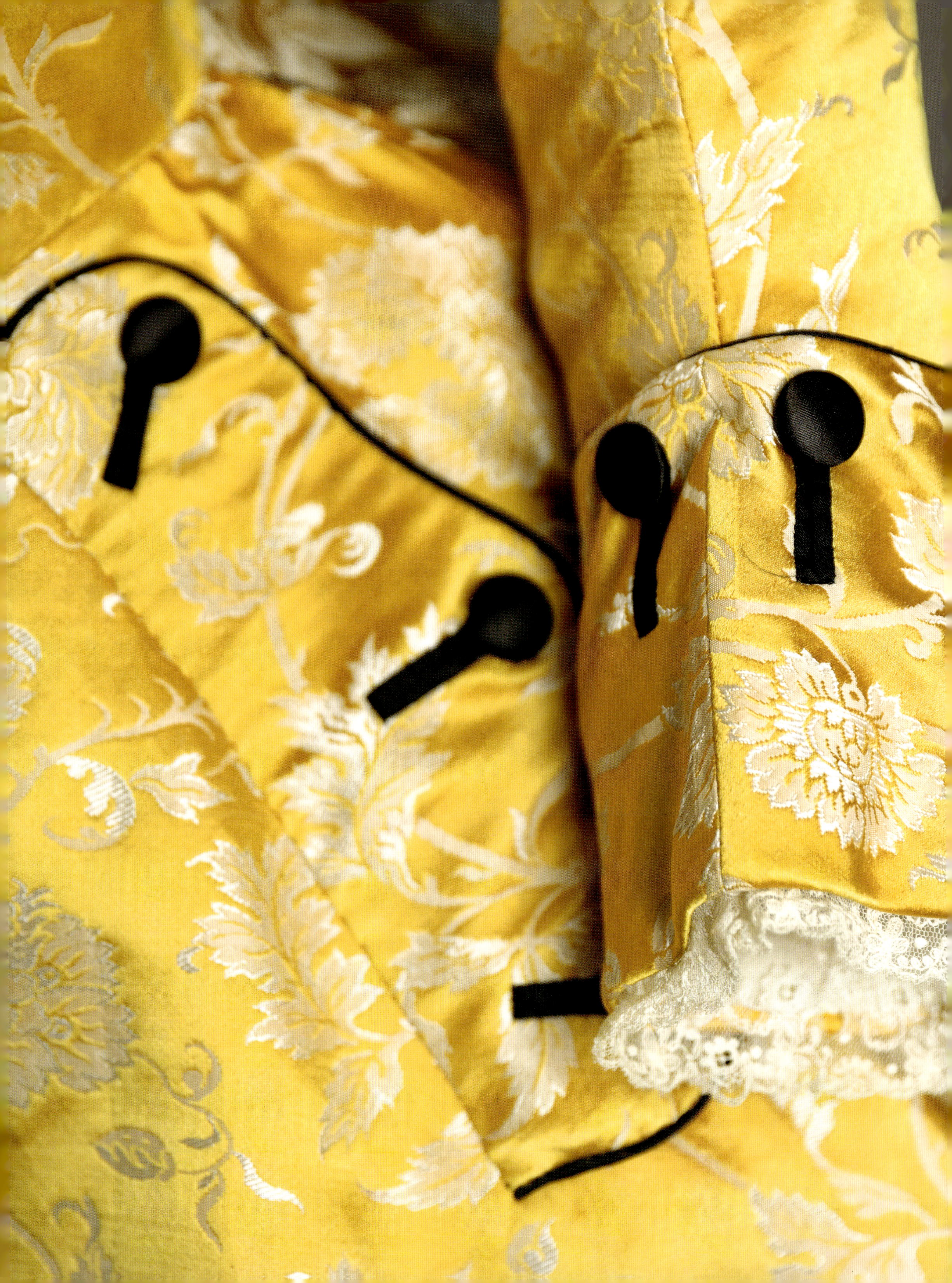

Telling History through Costumes

Heather Akou

Wearing costumes is an essential part of being an actor, but what happens when the production is finished? Actors move on and so do the costumes. They might be altered for another production (especially in theater), auctioned off, sold to a professional costume supply company, donated to a secondhand shop, or even discarded. In some cases, actors keep parts of their favorite costumes as souvenirs. In a 2018 interview on *Jimmy Kimmel Live!*, Chris Hemsworth—who played Thor in a series of films for Marvel Studios—admitted that he kept five of his character's hammers as mementos.[1] In the academic realm of dress studies, this kind of object would be viewed as an accessory or a handheld body supplement. In the realm of professional acting, Thor's hammer is called a prop.

Since costumes and props are usually owned by the production company, actors are not routinely allowed to keep what they want. At the beginning of her career, Glenn Close made an unusual move: she decided that she wanted to keep most of her costumes and accessories (shoes, hats, jewelry, etc.) and began to formally include that request in her contracts with theater companies and film studios. With that fateful decision, Close launched what has become one of the most extraordinary costume collections in the world, spanning her career of more than four decades. As the collection grew, she moved it to a storage facility and hired professional staff to catalogue, box, and maintain it.

THE SAGE COLLECTION

In 2017 Close donated her collection to the Elizabeth Sage Historic Costume Collection (Sage Collection) at Indiana University, pledging to add new costumes from new productions.[2] Historically, the word "costume" was used to mean "a style of dress" from a distinct time, location, and/or group of people. This is what the collection's founder, Elizabeth Sage, had in mind in 1913 when she began collecting examples of historic clothing and accessories to show in her classes.[3] (Sage was Indiana University's first professor of textiles and clothing and a pioneer in the study of historic fashion.) Today, English speakers are more likely to think of Halloween, Hollywood, and cosplay[4] when they hear about "costume." Sage is not the only fashion collection that also includes performance costumes. The Costume Institute in New York (now part of the Metropolitan Museum of Art) started in 1937 as a collection of theater costumes. Kent State University collects costumes from actor Katharine Hepburn;

OPPOSITE
James Acheson (English)
Annie Hadley
Marquise de Merteuil
Dangerous Liaisons, 1988
Silk, cotton

Texas State University has an archive of costumes and documents from the television production of *Lonesome Dove* (1989). The Victoria and Albert Museum in London has thousands of performance costumes from a variety of time periods and genres (theater, opera, dance, cabaret, etc.). The Smithsonian also holds some iconic pieces, such as a pair of ruby slippers worn by Dorothy Gale (Judy Garland) in *The Wizard of Oz* (1939) and a waitress uniform worn by Leticia Musgrove (Halle Berry) in *Monster's Ball* (2001). Only one other museum is known to have a comprehensive collection of costumes from a single, contemporary actor—the Harry Ransom Center at the University of Texas at Austin, which has "scripts, notes, costumes, and props" from throughout Robert De Niro's lengthy and distinguished career.

Like the rest of the Sage Collection, the Glenn Close Costume Collection is used for research, teaching, and exhibitions. Seeing (and ideally feeling) objects in person is a very humanizing and intimate experience. All conscious human beings dress their bodies[5]—we wear garments, style our hair, wash and decorate our skin—so on a human level, we can instantly relate to clothing (even a costume) that has been worn by another person; engaging with the item of dress makes that person's experience real in a way that just reading or talking about it does not. For a course in fashion design on "aesthetics,"[6] I asked groups of my students to watch one of Close's films and examine some of her costumes. The group that watched *Fatal Attraction* (1987) was struck by the importance of color in developing the characters (Alex Forrest wears mostly white and black, oscillating between innocent and threatening), but also how clothing that looks white on acetate film appears ivory in person. Students who watched one of their childhood favorites, *101 Dalmatians* (1996), were astonished by the materials and high-quality construction methods used by costume makers in Barbara Matera's workshop. To students living in a time when being a vegetarian is normal and wearing fur is unusual, the weight and texture of animal fur feels "evil." As an advocate for animal rights in real life, Close may have used the furs in these costumes to help her embody the evilness of Cruella De Vil for the sake of the film.

CLOTHING AND BODIES

Typically, when clothing enters a museum collection, it is never worn again. For conservation purposes, this is crucial. Our clothing takes a lot of strain from wearing and washing: threads break, seams burst, prints wear off, embellishments get damaged, and fabrics wear thin. Our bodies leave sweat, oils, and traces of soap, perfume, and deodorant. Even the gentlest handling is a risk.[7]

For the purposes of research and teaching, this reality creates an unfortunate gap between seeing and understanding. Clothing is made to be felt and, above all, to be worn. It shapes and reflects the bodies of the people who wear it, but no two bodies are ever exactly the same. We can look at a piece of clothing hanging in a closet or lying flat on a table as if it were a piece of art; however we cannot fully understand it as a two-dimensional object. In exhibitions we use dress forms and mannequins to suggest the body and give the clothing a three-dimensional shape; even this is not a perfect solution. Mannequins do not have the same colors and textures as human bodies. Mannequins are never uncomfortable in their clothes. They do not breathe, get injured, make gestures, gain or lose weight, or grow old. They were originally designed to display ready-to-wear clothing in retail shops, not to complement works of art.

When we look at exhibitions of costume and fashion, it is easy to forget the range of bodies that can inhabit clothing. Fashion magazines are dominated by tall, thin, young women with white teeth, clear skin, and no evidence of disability. They are mostly white and mostly heterosexual; they wear lavish clothing that only the global upper class can afford. Exhibitions can be more inclusive, but they are still constrained by what museum patrons want to see, by what donors are willing to give or lend, and by the cost of customizing mannequins to fit diverse body shapes. Ella Fitzgerald, for example, was not a fashion model. In order to exhibit two of the stunning dresses that she wore during performances, Sage Collection staff had to pad dress forms to her measurements. Used by fashion designers (and design students) to create new garments, dress forms come in a larger range of sizes than mannequins, but lack arms, legs, and heads. The Costume Institute at the Met has begun using 3D scanning and printing to make custom forms that can be used to both store and exhibit clothing.[8]

Over the course of her career, Glenn Close has maintained a remarkably consistent size and shape, but she has also played an extraordinary range of characters. Having begun her career in the theater, her first role for film (*The World According to Garp* [1982]) was Jenny Fields, a young woman who becomes a mother, grandmother, feminist, and political activist. The opening is set in the 1940s, when Jenny is a nurse taking care of a critically wounded soldier. For most of the film, she wears a nurse's uniform from the mid-twentieth century: a crisp, white, calf-length dress that buttons down the front; white lace-up shoes with modest heels; and a heavily starched white cap. Jenny is warm and nurturing. Her clothing conveys that she is a respected professional, but the style is also practical for the hard work of nursing. White cotton can be sterilized and bleached; short hems and minimal undergarments allowed nurses to move easily. Although the label is from Barbara Matera and not a uniform manufacturer,[9] Jenny Fields's uniform was an accurate portrayal of the character's time, place, and occupation.

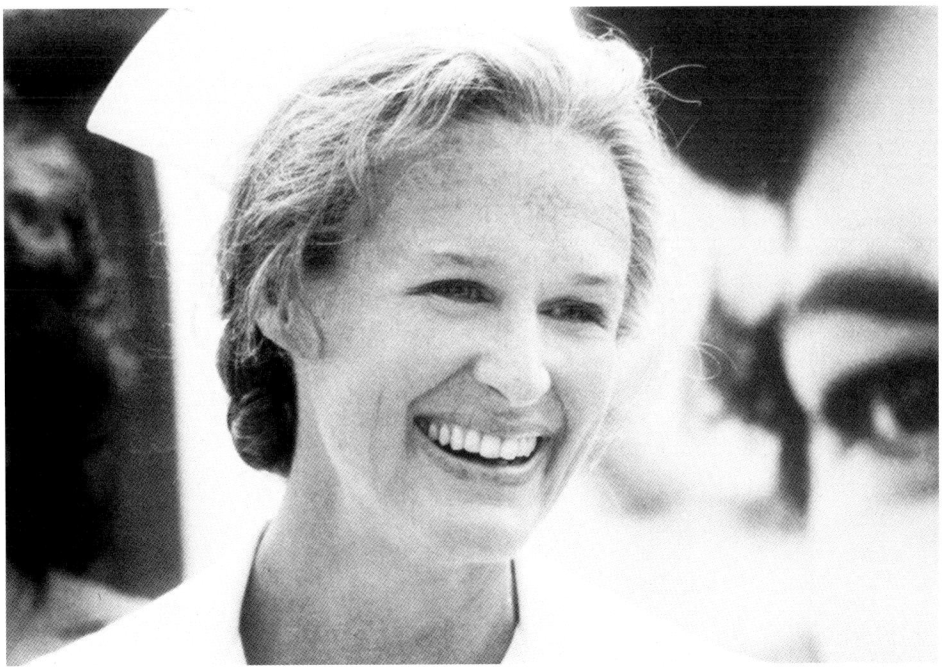

Glenn Close as Jenny Fields in *The World According to Garp*, 1982

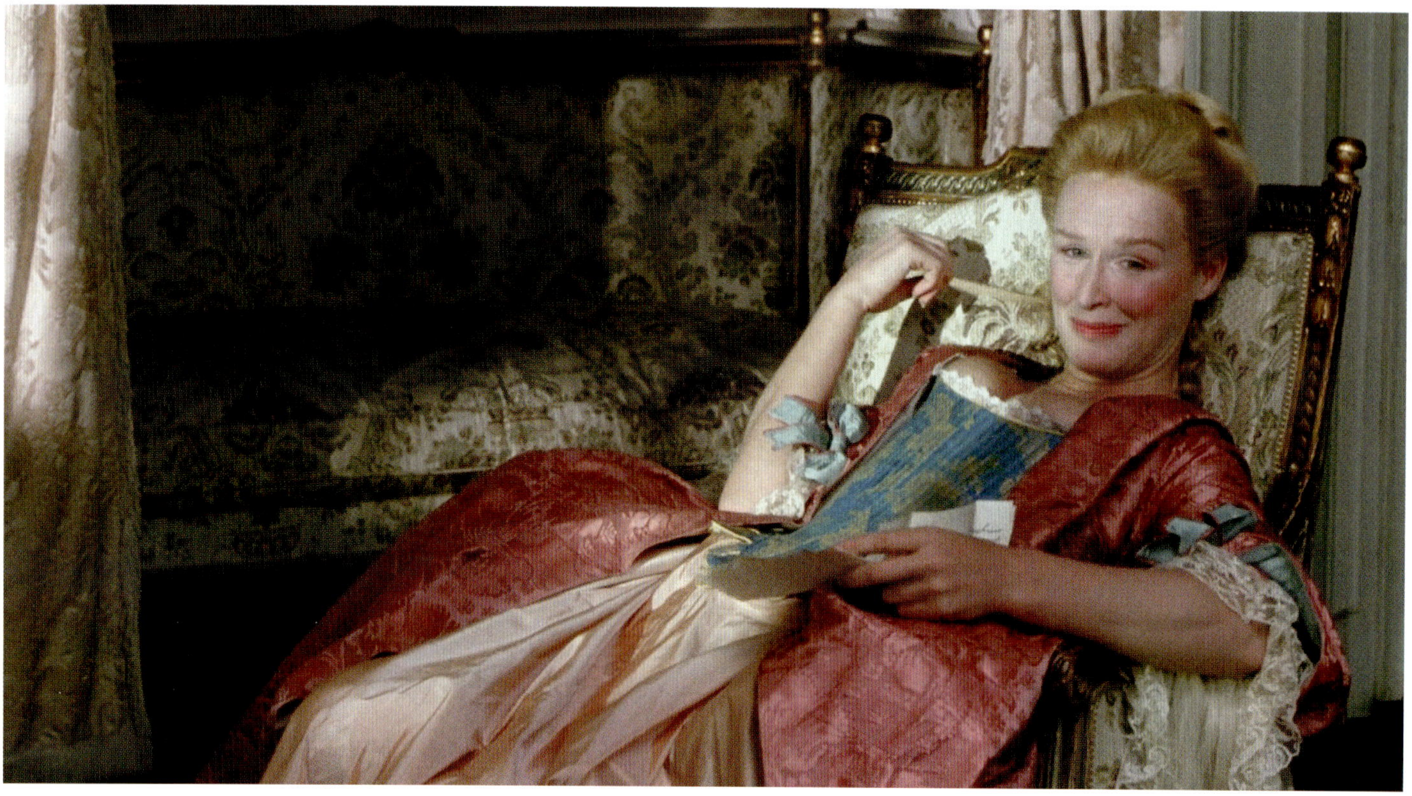

Glenn Close as the Marquise de Merteuil in *Dangerous Liaisons*, 1987

Just a few years later, Glenn Close played a very different character, the Marquise de Merteuil, in *Dangerous Liaisons* (1988). The film, based on a novel written in the eighteenth century, is set in France in the same period. As a wealthy and powerful woman, the Marquise de Merteuil appears in a variety of richly ornamented (and often brightly colored) floor-length gowns, accessorized with lavish wigs, hats, footwear, and jewelry. Corsets push up her breasts and minimize her waist, while cage-like underskirts called panniers hide her legs and dramatically exaggerate the lower half of her body. Like real women in that time period, Close was restricted in her movements by the elaborate clothing and the corsets made it difficult to breathe; she was often on the verge of fainting during the production. The Marquise is a woman of leisure, but she is literally and symbolically caged. As a result, she plays cruel and manipulative games with her peers. Although a small amount of eighteenth-century clothing still exists in museums, it is invaluable for scholars to see on film (in live action) how these styles of dress impacted the body.

FASHION HISTORY AND COSTUMES

While fictional films are not obligated to be realistic, directors and costume designers conduct research to make sets convincing—considering physical locations, exteriors, interiors, and of course the clothing of the people who inhabit them. Glenn Close has performed twice as Albert Nobbs on the stage (1982) and on film (2011). "Albert" is a woman disguising herself as a man in order to work as a servant—a job that was open to women in Dublin in the late nineteenth century, but that paid better (and was more respectable) for men. Having survived a terrible childhood, Albert is alone in the world, doing her best to protect and support herself. Like real people who wore the clothing of another gender—out of economic necessity or as an expression of their gender and/or sexual identity—it would have been dangerous for Albert to reveal her identity. She would have undoubtedly lost her job, but also might have been raped, injured, or even killed by someone furious about the deception.

Because of this history, scholars know little about the embodied experience of cross-dressing or being transgender (even today). In the film, Albert wears a high corset that flattens her chest. Where did she get it? Did she adapt an existing garment or make it from scratch? In a very memorable scene, a "man" that Albert has encountered reveals that she is also a biological woman, baring her chest to reveal her sizable breasts. Hubert binds her chest with woven cloth and wears oversize jackets that make her look barrel-chested—a style of dress that would have been realistic for a tall, overweight man. Albert and Hubert are not drag kings (women performing as men for entertainment). Their costumes show us two plausible and different ways that a woman in Dublin in the nineteenth century might have created a male persona that would convince most people in daily life.

Conversely, fashion historians and the general public know plenty about the dress of middle- to upper-class women in the early 1960s—a hyperfeminine and conformist time period associated with sweater sets, floral prints, pearls, pastels, and bouffant hairstyles (exemplified by icons like Audrey Hepburn, Elizabeth Taylor, and Jacqueline Kennedy). In 2004 Close played Claire Wellington in *The Stepford Wives*, a film based on a well-known, science-fiction book published by Ira Levin in 1972. Both take place in a small town in Connecticut that is filled with beautiful women who turn out to be robots. Judging from the

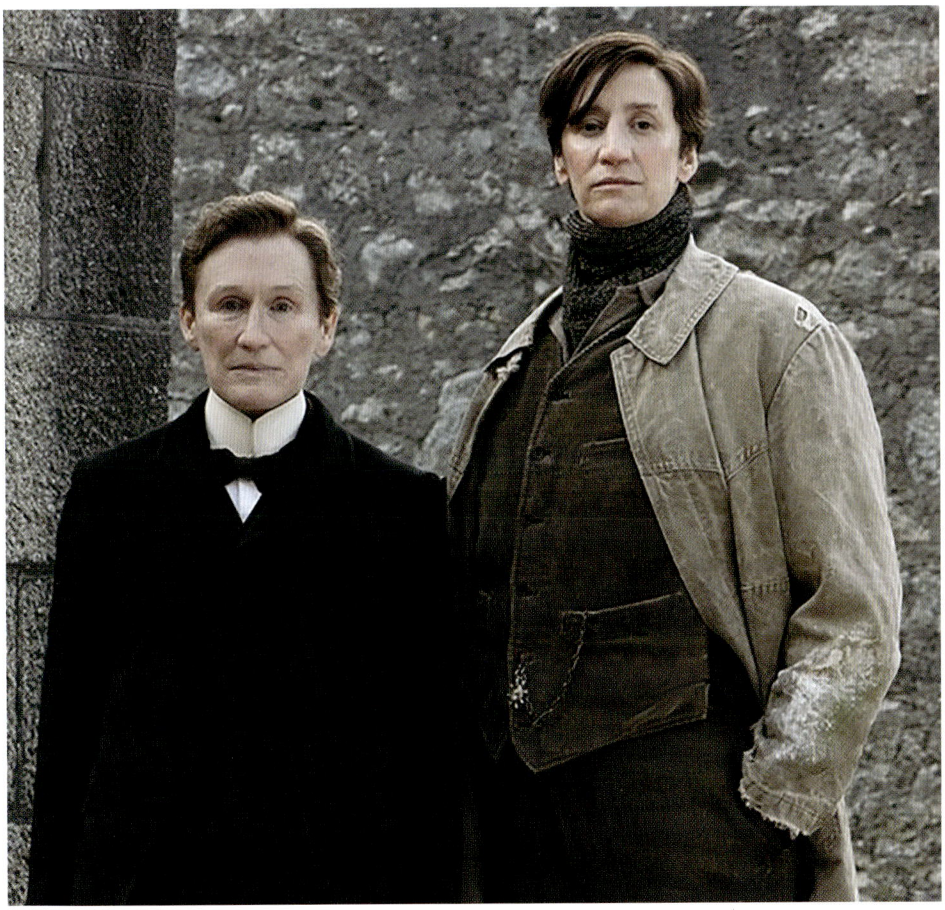

Glenn Close as Albert Nobbs and Janet McTeer as Hubert Page in *Albert Nobbs*, 2011

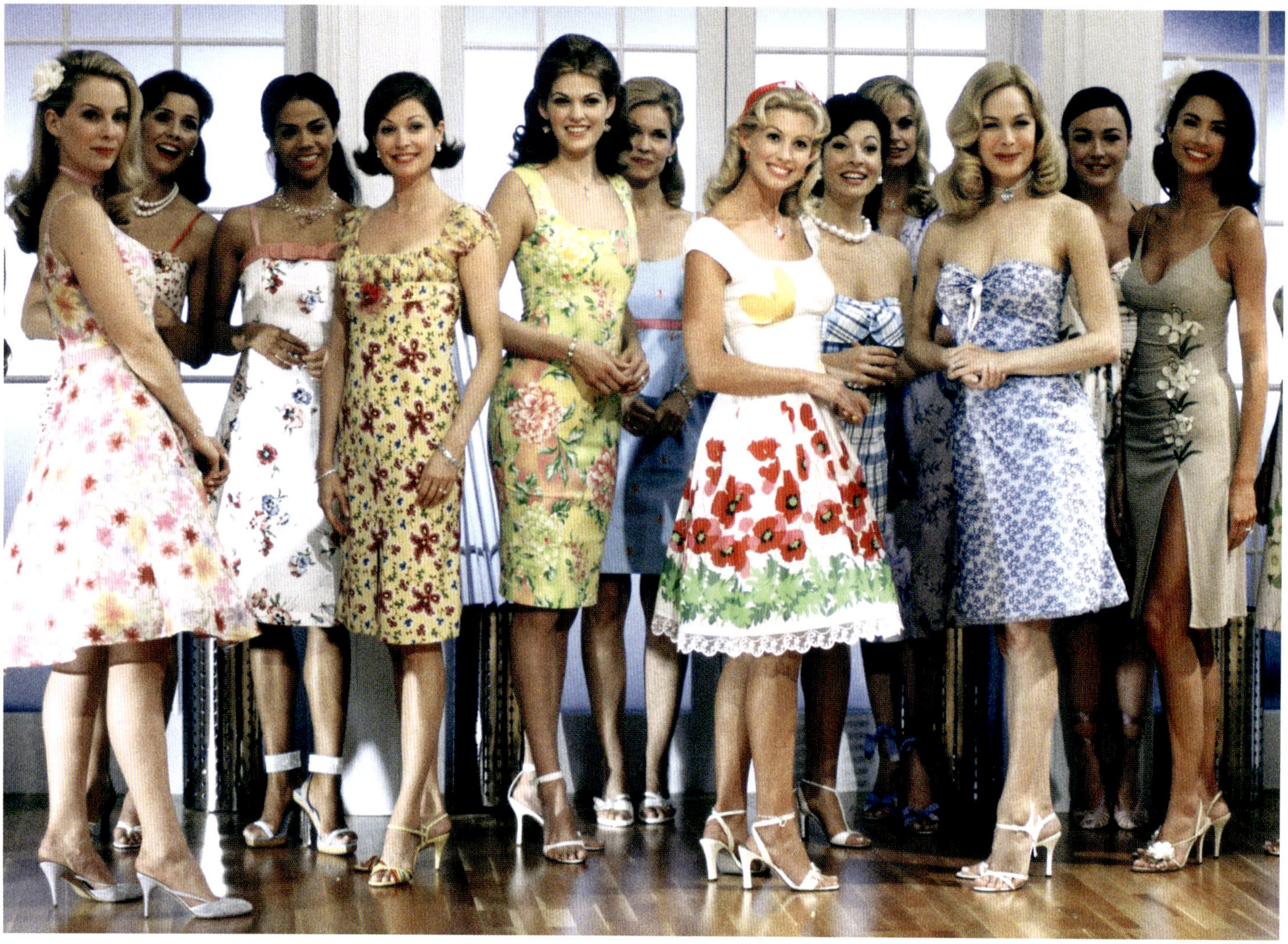

Women of Stepford from *The Stepford Wives*, 2004

Glenn Close as Claire Wellington leading "Claireobics" in *The Stepford Wives*, 2004

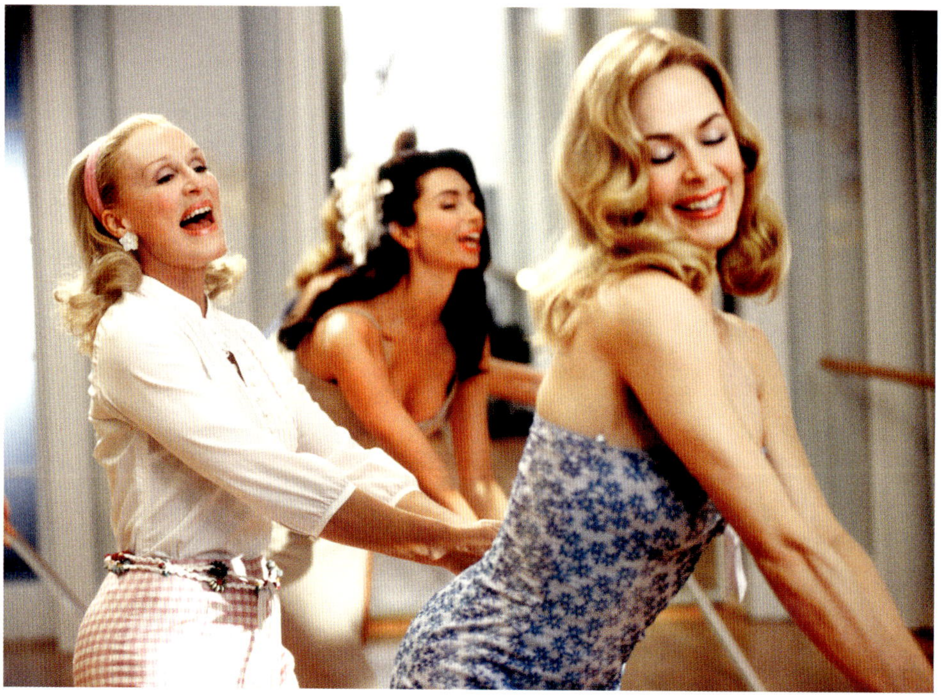

opening and closing scenes, the time period of the twenty-first-century film version is contemporary, yet the women of Stepford are dressed as if they are still living in the 1960s. The main character (Joanna Eberhart) does not suspect at first that anyone is a robot. However, their distinctive style of dress gives her an immediate impression—Stepford is not a place that welcomes individuality or diversity. In one amusing scene, Claire leads a modified aerobics class called "Claireobics" while wearing a white blouse and pink gingham capris, accessorized with a pink headband, mother-of-pearl earrings, high heels from Tod's, and a handbag from Kate Spade (two contemporary luxury brands). In an interview for the *New York Times*, costume designer Ann Roth noted the importance of dress in establishing the characters. "I wanted the audience to look at the women and think 'where did she get those clothes, that face, those toenails . . . ?' I wanted not smart, not hip, nothing that vaguely said TriBeCa or SoHo or the Lower East Side or Paris."[10] The Sage Collection has many similar examples of historic clothing and accessories worn by real middle- to upper-class women in the United States in the 1960s.

MORE THAN CLOTHING

In real life, women typically combine and recombine their clothing and accessories. Because of this, most donations come to the Sage Collection in pieces: a wedding dress without any undergarments, a box of jewelry without the clothing it accessorized. An exhibition requires some careful matching to form "complete outfits" and fill in the missing pieces. Photographs and documents (catalogues, diary entries, dress codes, etc.) can be invaluable, if they exist.

In films and theater productions, characters appear for limited amounts of time and have clear outfits (often for practical reasons, like helping dressers make quick transitions between scenes). Many of the costumes that Close collected have at least some of the matching accessories. For example, in a scene in *Fatal Attraction* where Alex Forrest and Dan Gallagher (Michael Douglas) are eating in a restaurant, Close wears an ivory suit. Although her shoes were hidden under the table and her earrings were barely visible through her hair, they were important clues about her character—gold snakeskin pumps and gold snakes for the earrings.[11] In *102 Dalmatians* (2000), Cruella De Vil appears in court wearing a striped prison uniform with macramé buttons and a hand-beaded prisoner identification number (comically, number 6660), but her accessories are even more over-the-top: a matching hat and gloves, enormous pearl earrings, striped high heels, and lavishly ornamented handcuffs

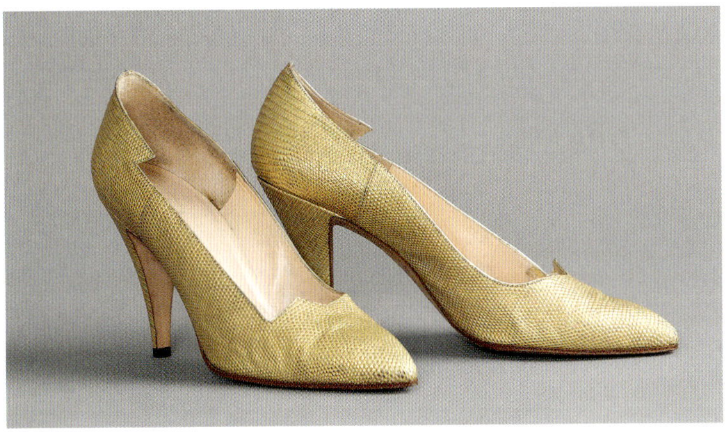

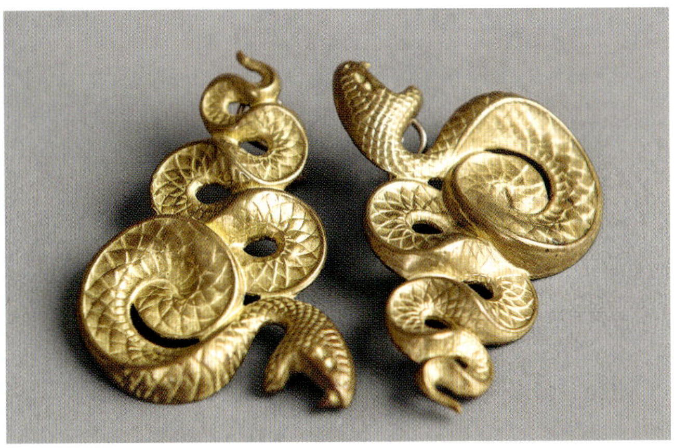

Ellen Mirojnick, Snakeskin Pumps (Alex Forrest, *Fatal Attraction*), 1985, Snakeskin, leather, GC 2017.58.2 AB

Ellen Mirojnick, Snake Earrings (Alex Forrest, *Fatal Attraction*), 1985, Metal, GC 2017.65.1 AB

Anthony Powell made by Barbara Matera Ltd. and Woody Shelp, Prison Coatdress (Cruella De Vil/Ella, *102 Dalmatians*), 2000, Linen, silk, cotton, glass beads, GC 2017.10.1–.2, .4

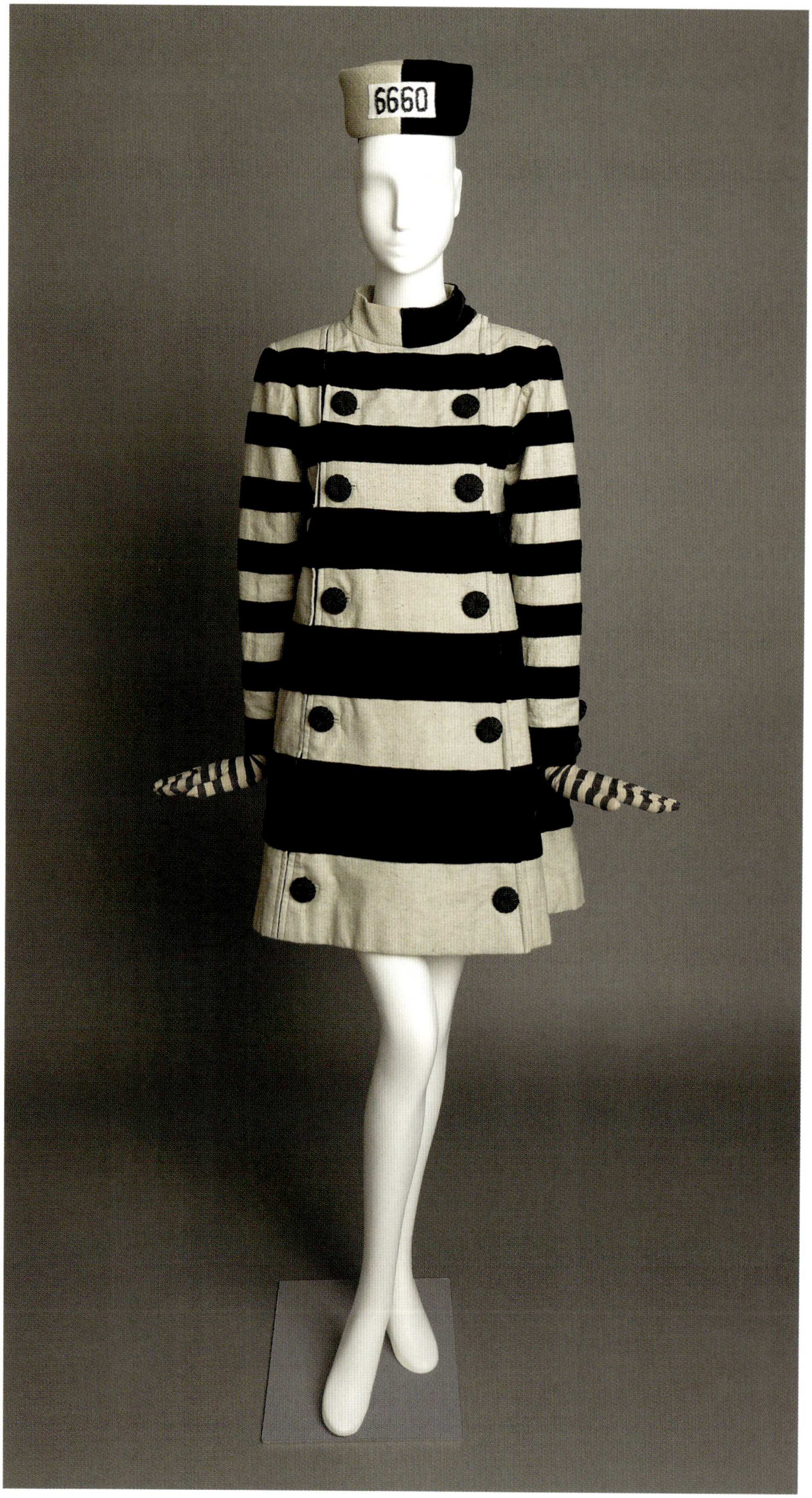

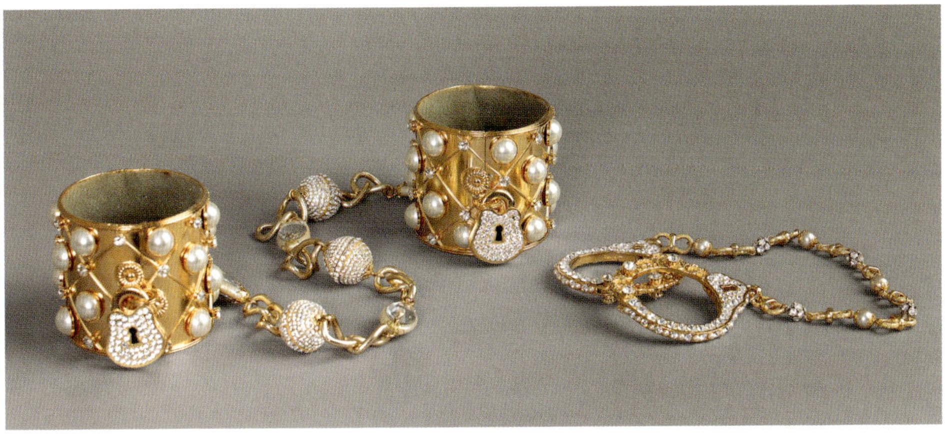

LEFT
Anthony Powell made by Martin Adams, Handcuffs and Shackles (Cruella De Vil/ Ella, *102 Dalmatians*), 2000, Metal, rhinestones, faux pearls, GC 2017.10.7–.8

BELOW
Glenn Close as Albert Nobbs from *Albert Nobbs*, 2011

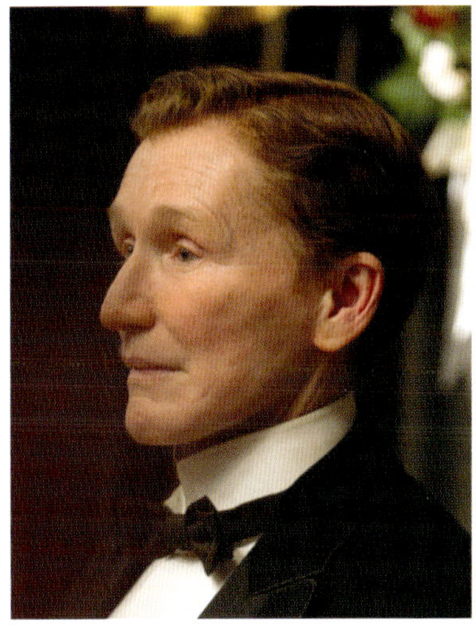

and shackles. She is not an ordinary prisoner, but a fashion icon. Custom made by Woody Shelp (hat), Martin Adams (jewelry), and Barbara Matera (dress), the complete outfit tells a rich story about the character and about the talented individuals who designed, made, and embodied the costume.

For the film version of *Albert Nobbs*, Close decided that she would only act in the film if her appearance could be disguised: she wanted the audience to focus on the character, not on Glenn Close. To accomplish that goal, makeup artist Matthew Mungle developed prosthetic tips for her nose and ears and temporary veneers for her teeth. Unusually, Close kept some examples of these pieces for her collection. This film is an outstanding example of how a skilled makeup artist can transform a character's appearance instead of relying on postproduction editing (CGI). Although the film did not win any Academy Awards, Close and Janet McTeer (Hubert) were nominated along with Martial Corneville (Close's wig artist) and the film's makeup team.

CONCLUSION

Until further research can be conducted, it is difficult to anticipate the many and varied ways that the invaluable Glenn Close Costume Collection will influence the study of costumes and fashion history. For my own research on the history of prison uniforms and their intersections with popular culture in the United States,[12] I was delighted to discover that we have one authentic example in the Sage Collection—an orange jumpsuit manufactured by Bob Barker,[13] which Close wore in *Cookie's Fortune* (1999). There will undoubtedly be more fascinating discoveries in the decades—and even centuries—to come.

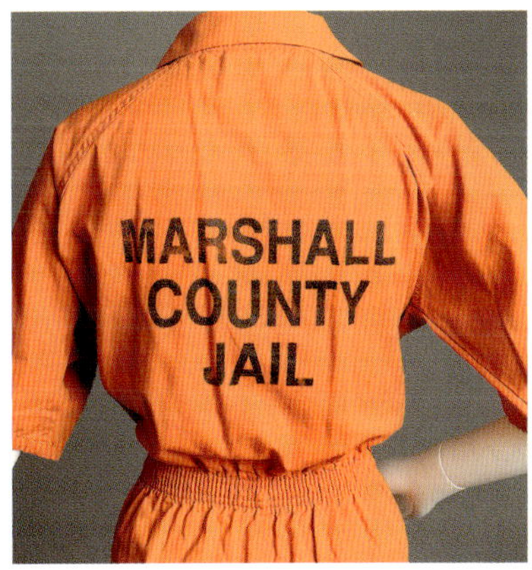

Dona Granata made by Bob Barker, Prison Uniform (Camille Dixon, *Cookie's Fortune*), 1999, Cotton, polyester, GC 2017.44.1

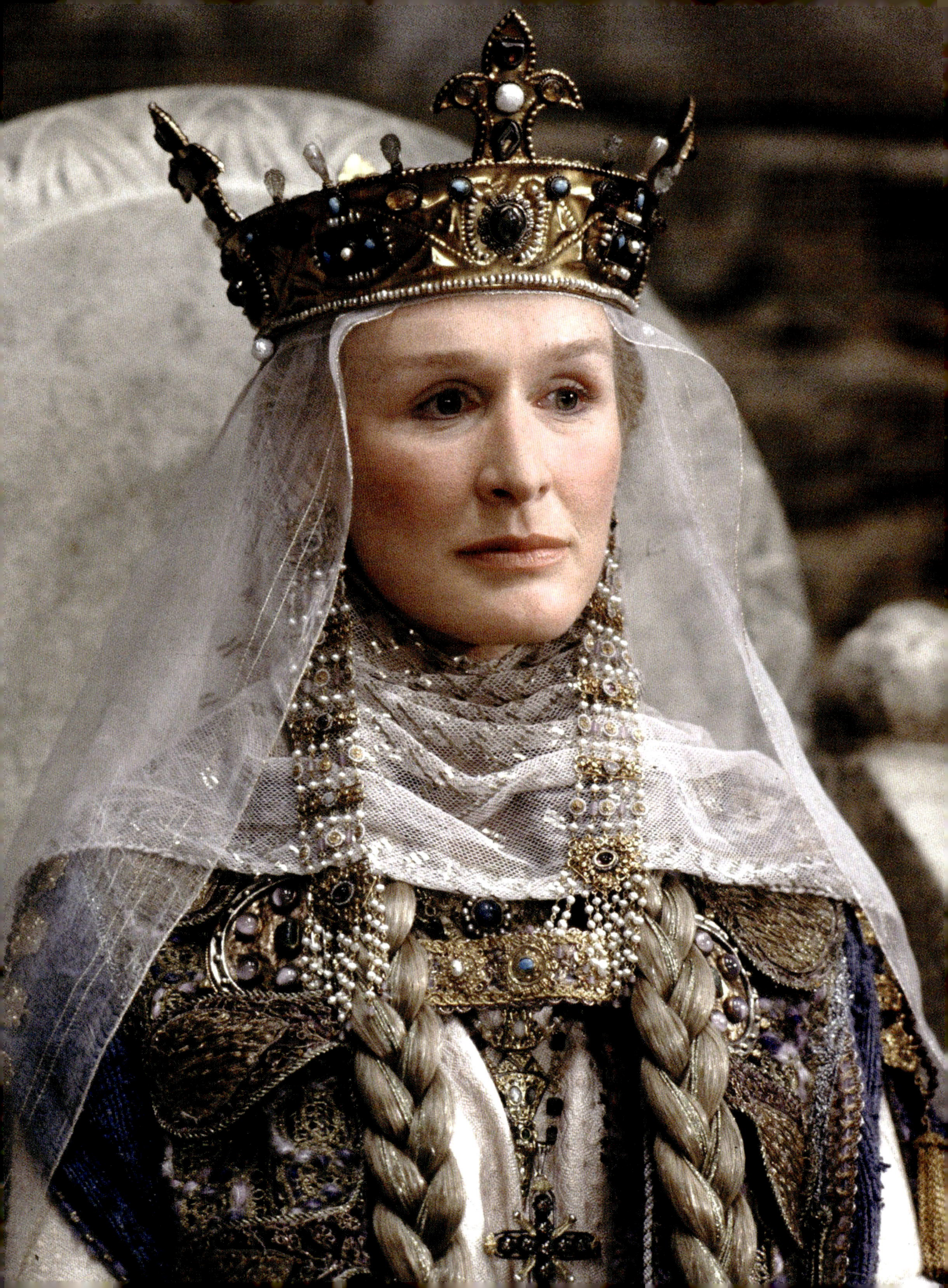

Collaborating Behind the Scenes

Linda Pisano

Clothing is personal. Almost everyone has preferences in the clothing they wear, from color choice to comfort level, to what the garment or combination of garments communicates about themselves. Characters in a film, play, musical, or any other performance have preferences, too, but since they only exist on the page, they require costume designers to navigate these choices. What makes costume design more complex than it might appear at first glance is the extensive knowledge of sociohistorical dress—including the culture, psychology, and economics of silhouettes, textiles, and accoutrements—required of a costume designer.

Costume designers must acquire expertise in dressing any character, in any time period, fantasy or reality, in any possible situation that may manifest itself. From the eighteenth-century grandeur of the Marquise de Merteuil to the science-fiction/fantasy-clad Nova Prime to the infamous Blanche DuBois, a costume designer must understand the nuances and details that will reflect the character outwardly while evoking an emotional response from the audience. Yet this is only a scratch on the surface: the expansive world of the costume designer includes ballet, contemporary dance, installations, film, television, documentaries, commercials, magazines, performance art, photography, and cosplay—and the detail of each piece and the biography of each character must be clear. It is this constant decision-making that requires such a breadth of understanding of the intention and perception of dress.

Navigation of the fundamental elements and principles of design—for example, understanding the powerful aesthetic and physiological responses that color often elicits from viewers—is another crucial component of the costume designer's skill set, as is mastery of collaboration with an artistic team.

The proverb "don't judge a book by its cover" seems axiomatic, yet for most people it is almost instinctive to assess others on their choice of clothing. Through clothing, we can quickly form an opinion—accurate or not—of a person's socioeconomic class, nationality, the climate where they live, a general idea of their occupation, and even their religious and political leanings. Many societies depend on clothing to uphold and enforce the stratification of socioeconomic classes. The costume designer must be finely attuned to a design, as the director, choreographer, and other members of the artistic team depend on the designer's knowledge to navigate these personal choices. Furthermore, the performer who will breathe life into the character will also have questions and perspectives on how the pieces

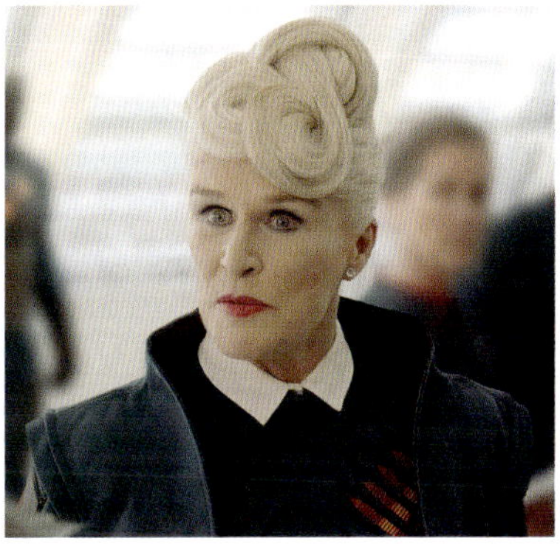

Glenn Close as Nova Prime in *Marvel Studios' Guardians of the Galaxy*, 2014

OPPOSITE
Glenn Close as Queen Gertrude in *Hamlet*, 1990

Glenn Close as the Marquise de Merteuil in *Dangerous Liaisons*, 1988

Glenn Close and Jonathan Pryce in *The Wife*, 2017

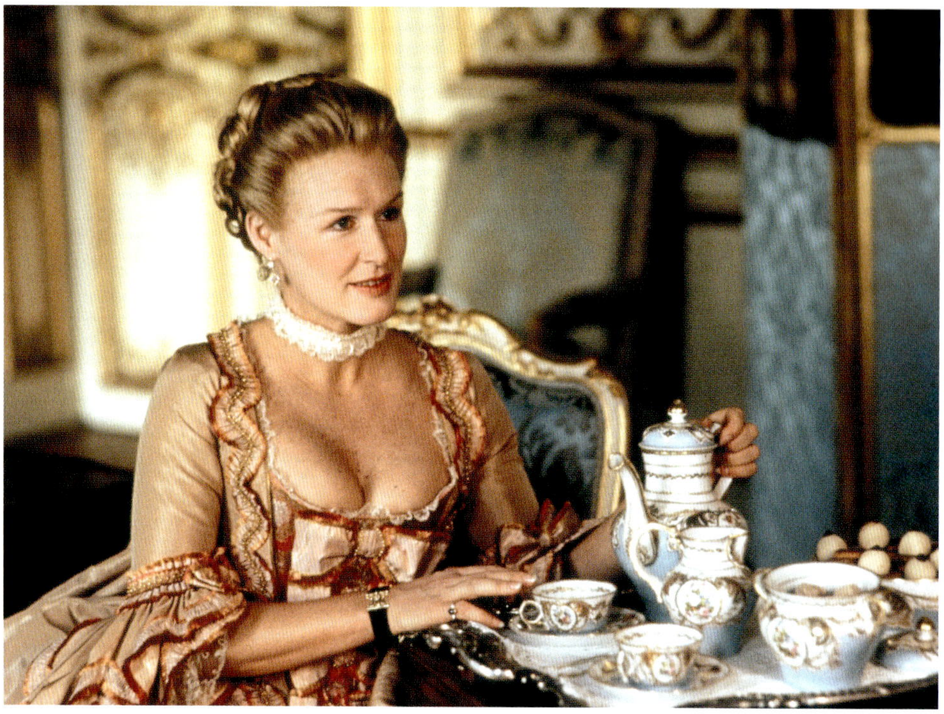

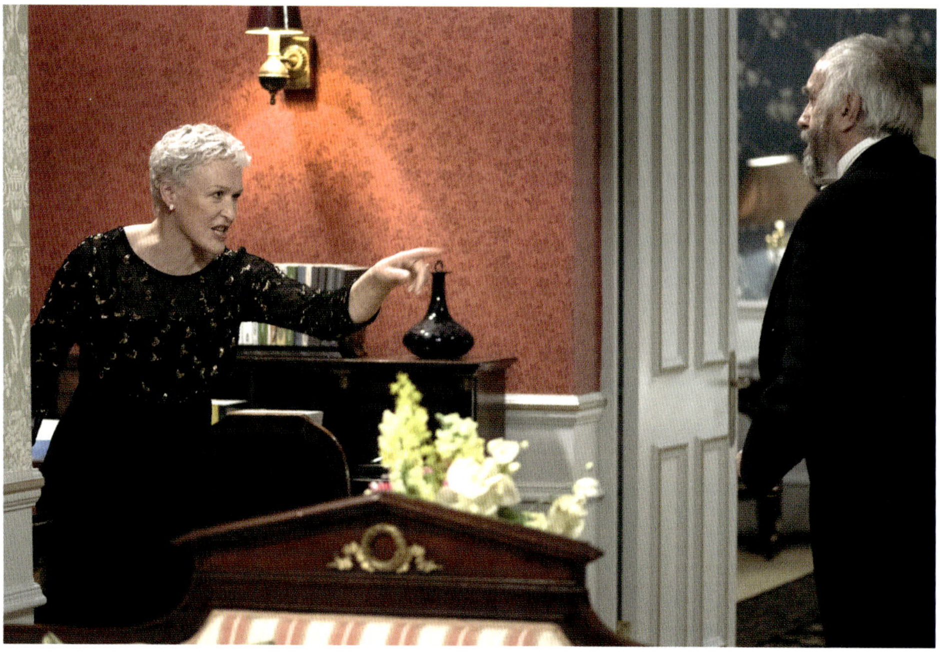

are worn and fit. The more seasoned the performer, the more expertise they will have in understanding how a garment or accessory will impact their performance. It is in this collaboration between designer and performer that a character comes to life.

The Glenn Close Costume Collection is a demonstration of the importance of a performer's contribution to costume design and fabrication, including accessories, hair, and makeup. At its most fundamental, it is a testament to a great performer's reverence for a holistic approach to storytelling and character building: from the designer, through the makers and the performer, and ultimately to the spectator.

According to Glenn Close, "what's so fascinating about people is what they don't show. People are masters at it; usually actors show too much."[1] Understanding the complexity and subtlety of each character is achieved most effectively when the performer and designer have a clear dialogue. Close's dedication to the preservation and archiving of costumes designed for her in a wide range of roles from film, stage, and television reinforces the idea that the costume was an integral part of the physical embodiment of her portrayal of each character. Rather than words living on the page of the script, the character came to life through Close; the costumes are in many ways the skin of the character, both hiding and revealing their biography.

In many ways, Close's comment regarding "what [people] don't show" points to an important part of the actor's job. A professional actor will determine through expert technique of the craft (and sometimes through experiential instinct) those subsurface characteristics that the designer can hide or reveal through clothing. When communication in the spirit of collaboration occurs, the combined creative resources of the performer and costume designer can lay the foundations for truly inspired work.

Glenn Close as Norma Desmond in *Sunset Boulevard*, 2017

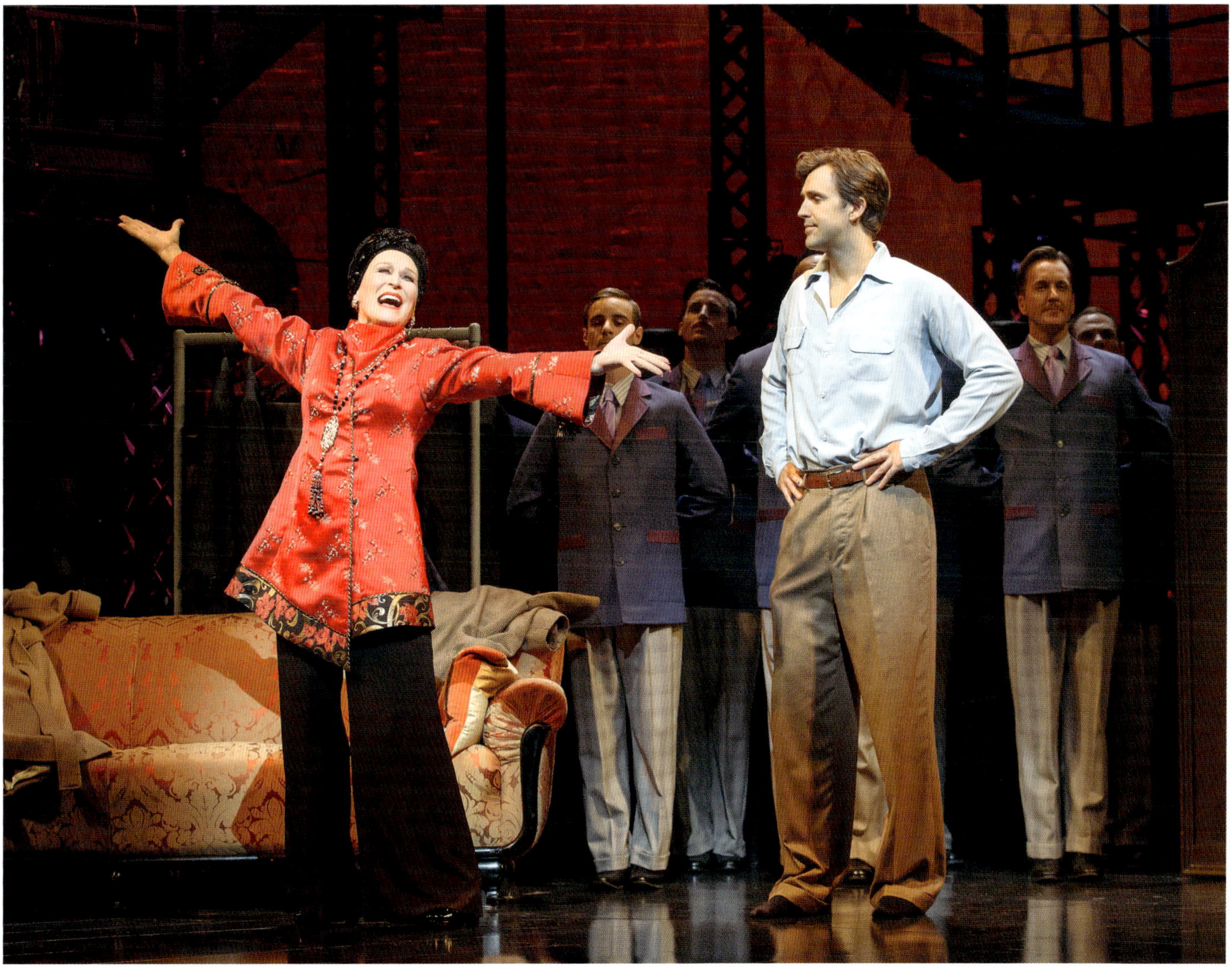

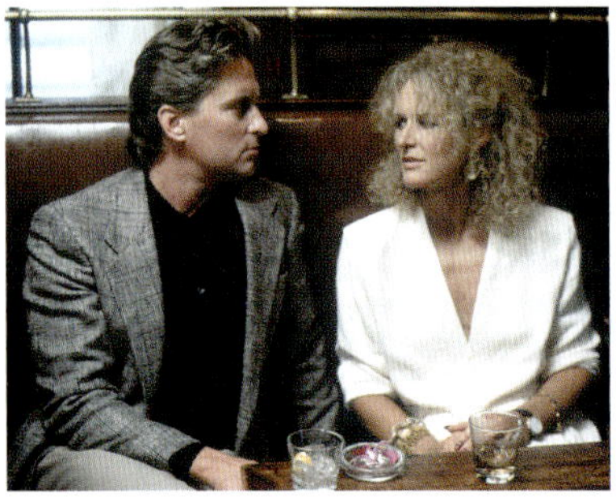

Michael Douglas and Glenn Close in *Fatal Attraction*, 1987

The Glenn Close Costume Collection includes pieces that offer a vivid biography of a character, yet at the same time conceal much. Characters such as Albert Nobbs from the film of the same name (2011), Claire Wellington from *Stepford Wives* (2004), and Alex Forrest in *Fatal Attraction* (1987) each have hidden stories—some in tragedy, some in comedy.

Perhaps of further interest to the viewer is not simply *what* is hidden, but *why* it is hidden. Beyond the writer's original intention, the context of a story's time and culture can impact these hidden histories. For example, *Albert Nobbs* is a relatively contemporary film and today's audience may more fully see the tragedy of Albert's life. A character forced by society, and for her own safety, to hide her gender and identity has a different meaning to a turn of the nineteenth-century community (the film's setting) versus a twenty-first-century one (the film's audience), or even to the 1927 society that existed when the original story was written. The character of Alex Forrest in *Fatal Attraction* wore clothing that was stylish and somewhat affluent—certainly indicative of a successful New York City career woman of the late 1980s. It was so realistic that several of the garments and shoes were off-the-rack rather than fabricated by a costume shop. The quality and style of the clothing communicated social and financial independence, stability, strength, and steadiness, yet by the end of the film Alex appears unstable, hysterical, and frantic. Would this perception be different if told from a post-#MeToo world? And if so, how would the clothing be different? Ultimately, context is important.

Reading a script, screenplay, or any story that is to have realized garments requires looking at the individual distinctions of a character and the overarching development of the ensemble. Balancing the mise-en-scène with a character's individuality is critical to the believability of a story. No matter how fantastic or realistic the plotline, whatever world is built must be believable for the characters who live in it. There are two ways that we approach this: (1) Operationally, the designer ensures that the quality of the costumes' fabrics and construction meets the standards of the production value and genre; and (2) Aesthetically, the designer collaborates with the artistic team to ensure that the conventions of a specific world establish its values and boundaries immediately and are consistent throughout the story.

In the 2004 remake of the 1975 film *The Stepford Wives*, based on Ira Levin's 1972 novel, we can clearly see the conventions set up in the overall production design. The film begins by inviting us into the slick, urban, affluent work life of a high-powered network executive.

Glenn Close as Albert Nobbs in *Albert Nobbs*, 2011

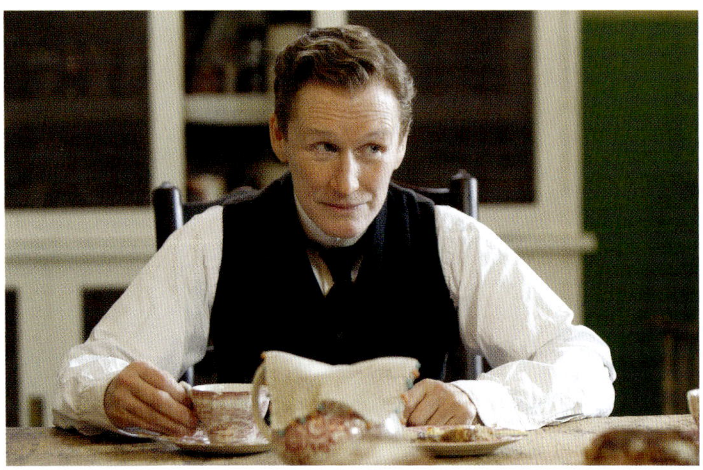

Glenn Close and Mia Wasikowska in *Albert Nobbs*, 2011

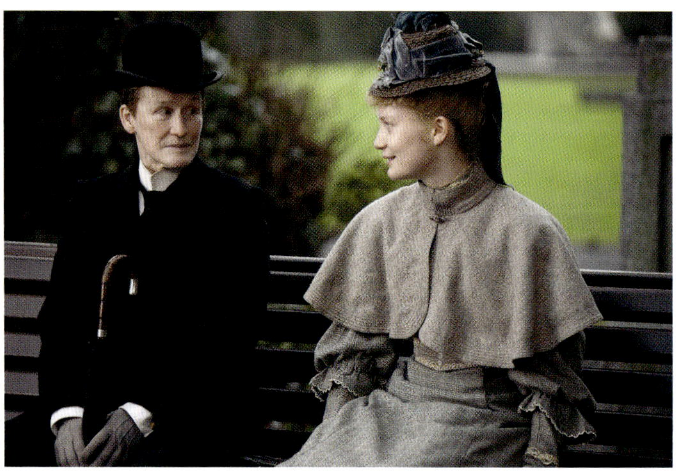

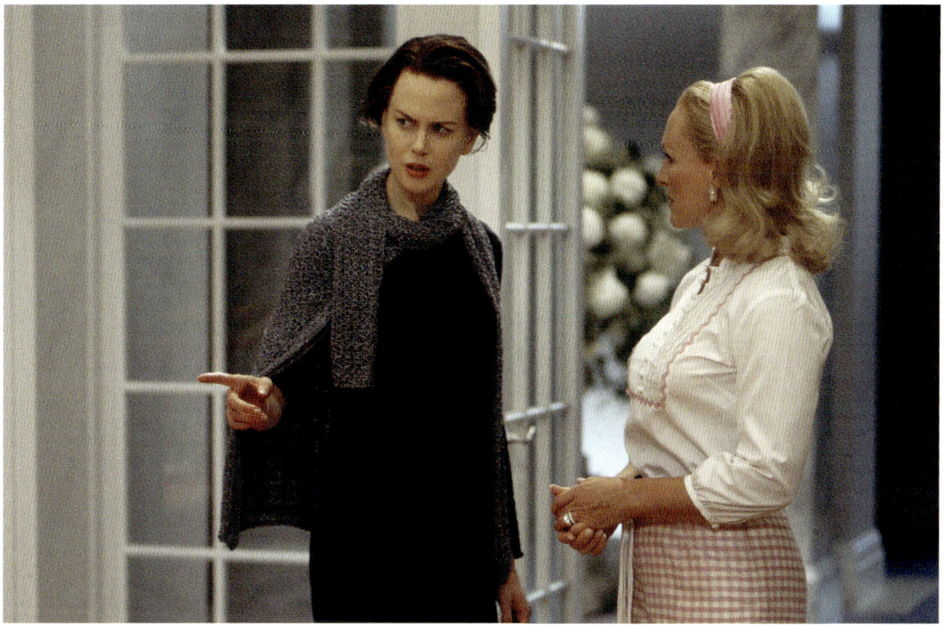

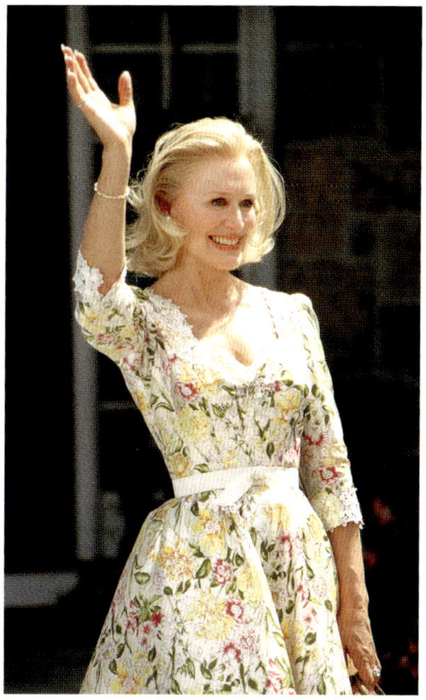

Nicole Kidman and Glenn Close in *The Stepford Wives*, 2004

Glenn Close as Claire Wellington in *The Stepford Wives*, 2004

The character Joanna Eberhart (Nicole Kidman) exudes confidence, intelligence, and independence—thanks in part to her chic, cropped hair and stylishly tailored suit—and her overall appearance is minimalist and sophisticated. The black and gray of her high-end, designer clothing emulates that of the streamlined city buildings and even her car. This facade is important at the top of the story, as it visually creates an armor around the character that we must see collapse in order to drive the narrative forward. After stifling her emotion while being fired, Joanna immediately spirals into a nervous breakdown. The next time we see her, in the hospital, she is disheveled. And although she is still attired in shades of gray and black, the clothing is loose-fitting, knitted casual wear and her auburn hair is unbrushed and frizzy. The mise-en-scène of the world has been established quickly through color and stylistic choices. The hard lines and palette are important to dramatically set up a transformation in this character.

When Joanna and her family move to Stepford, the shift in design is dramatic. The first character they encounter in the security-laden, gated community, with exquisitely manicured landscapes flanking ornamental mansions, is the flawlessly coiffed, brightly clad, and overly cheerful Claire Wellington (Glenn Close). Although her demeanor exudes optimism and happy perfection, dressed in a colorful ensemble reminiscent of a 1950s advertisement for domestic bliss, the facade is as artificial as that which Joanna wore as a broadcast executive in New York City.

In a June 1, 2004, *New York Times* article, costume designer Ann Roth explained, "I wanted the audience to look at the women and think 'where did she get those clothes, that face, those toenails, those feet?' I wanted not smart, not hip, nothing that vaguely said TriBeCa or SoHo or the Lower East Side or Paris. I wanted dopey pretty. Do you know the phrase 'roundheeled woman'? Well, like that."[2] Claire Wellington's ensembles all have nipped waistlines and small heels. Even her exercise ensemble includes heels, a headband, and a decorative belt around a pair of pastel capris. It is in the scene at the spa that she comments on Joanna's clothing choices as an indicator of unhappiness.

Anthony Powell fitting Glenn Close in a *102 Dalmatians* costume at Barbara Matera Ltd. Used by permission from Disney Enterprises, Inc.

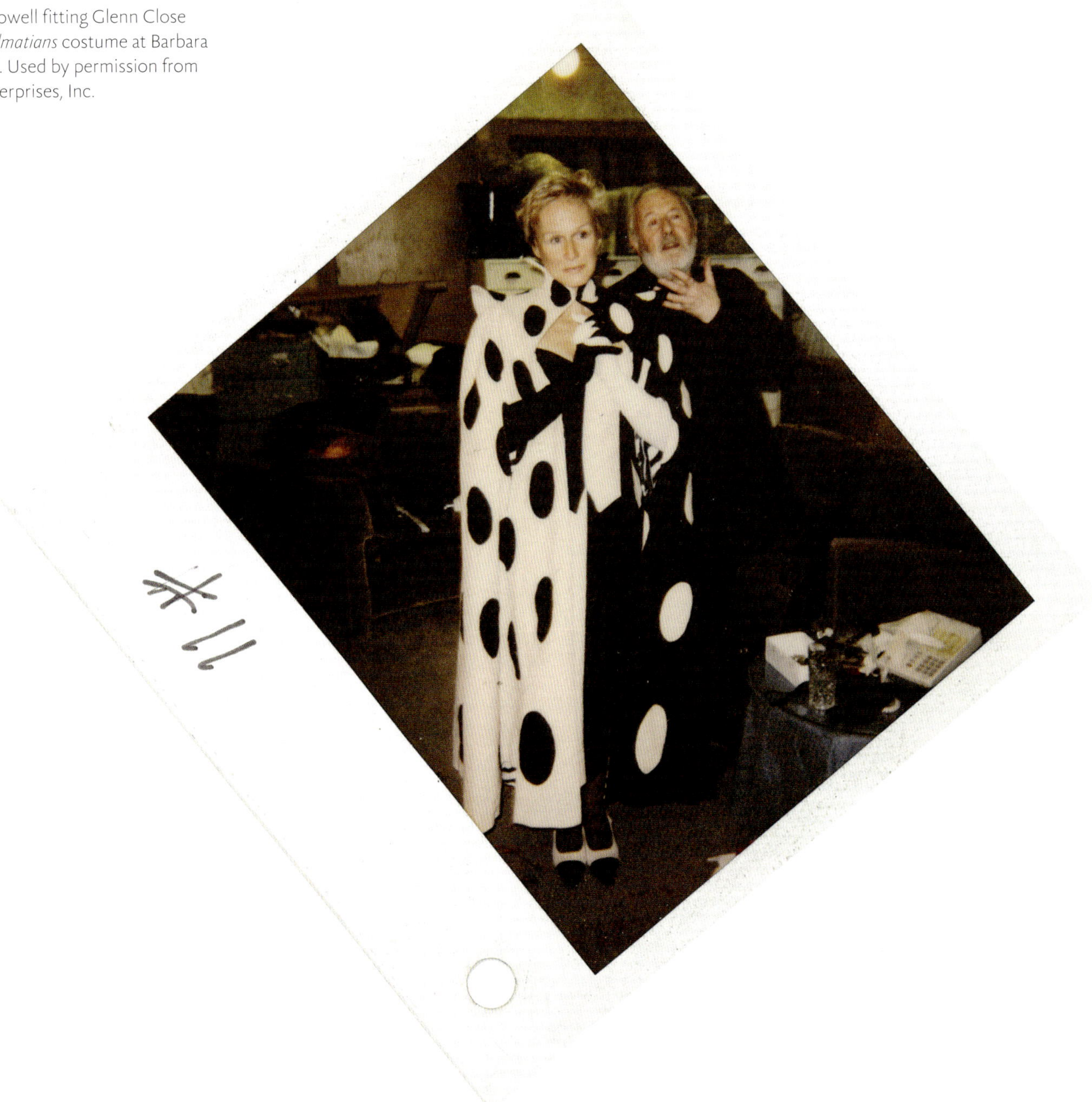

The most successful costume design is a collaboration not only between designer and director, or designer and maker, but between designer and performer. From the exquisite detail and theatricality of Anthony Powell's costumes for Cruella De Vil in Disney's *101 Dalmatians* (1996) to the period style of Consolata Boyle's designs for the 2003 film version of *The Lion in Winter*, to the realism of Trisha Biggar's designs for *The Wife* in 2017, the designer and performer work together to consider the character, of which clothing is such an important part. Furthermore, the makers who construct and build everything, from the shoes to the clothing to the headwear, are an integral part of bringing these ideas to life. The costume collection that Glenn Close has compiled is a testament to the importance of collaboration in storytelling. Concerning the importance of collecting and preserving her costumes, Close has said, "You spend hours in the fitting room and on set living in these works of art by some of the greatest working designers," continuing that donating these to a collection ensures that they "won't be pulled apart, reconstructed or redesigned."[3]

When a performer embodies a character, and a designer and makers work with a performer in bringing to life that story, it remains part of one's experience. Clothing can be difficult to part with even in our real lives as we connect it to special events, important moments, or a time we would like to relive. Close's collection is a tangible memory of these characters and their stories; indeed, in discussing the donation of her collection to Indiana University, Close explained, "I feel quite emotional when I talk about it. . . . To know that it's going out and won't be under my roof anymore."[4]

As in any industry, the opportunity for like-minded artists to collaborate over and over again is important. When a director and/or performer work continually with the same designer or design team, they have often formed a relationship based on shared vision and mutual respect. Costume designer Anthony Powell expressed this well in discussing *102 Dalmatians* (2000): "Glenn is a dream for a costumer. . . . She'll also try anything." He continued, reporting that after Close had asked him if she should do the role of Cruella, "I said, 'When in our entire careers have we been given carte blanche to completely go over the top? Wouldn't that be fun?' Little did we know that we'd be given a chance to do it again."[5]

At the end of the day, working and creating together is such an important part of what we do. Why would we not want to keep the artifacts of our happiest or fondest memories and experiences?

Endnotes

BRINGING FANTASIES TO LIFE

1 E. Shura Pollatsek, *Unbuttoned: The Art and Artists of Theatrical Costume Design* (New York: Routledge, 2017), xi.

2 Triffin Morris and Gregory D. L. Morris, "The History of the Broadway Costume Business," *Theatre Design & Technology* 4, no. 1 (Winter 2011): 13.

3 Morris and Morris, "History of the Broadway Costume Business," 14.

4 Morris and Morris, "History of the Broadway Costume Business," 18.

FASHIONING INTRA-FEMININE FASCINATION

1 Annette Kuhn, quoted in Jane Gaines, *Fabrications: Costume and the Female Body* (London: Routledge, 1990).

2 Charlie Carballo, "Glenn Close Explains Why Cruella De Vil's Heels Made Her So Angry," *Footwear News*, February 20, 2019, https://footwearnews.com/2019/fashion/awards/glenn-close-cdga-2019-red-carpet-1202748255/.

3 Gaines, *Fabrications*, 188.

4 Laura Mulvey, "Visual Pleasure and Narrative Cinema," in *Film Theory and Criticism: Introductory Readings*, ed. Leo Braudy and Marshall Cohen (New York: Oxford University Press, 1999), 833–44. "To-be-looked-at-ness" is a term from Mulvey to indicate the general role of the female body in much of classical Hollywood cinema, that the camera pauses in moments of erotic contemplation whereby the male star's point of view (and hence the camera's point of view) lingers on an ostensibly pleasurable female body in the film.

5 Mulvey, "Visual Pleasure and Narrative Cinema," 833–44.

6 Mulvey, "Visual Pleasure and Narrative Cinema." Of course, critiques of Mulvey's paradigm soon arose, earliest from Black feminism and lesbian feminism, as well as authors such as Linda Williams, who makes the case that the classical "Woman's Film" does not rely on such easily gendered visual pleasures. Psychoanalysis can be viewed as an overly closed system that does not account for the specific material conditions through which a film is watched, and has since begun to be supplanted by more intersectional analyses of race, sexuality, and film outside of the classical Hollywood canon.

7 John Berger, *Ways of Seeing* (London: British Broadcasting Corporation, 1973), 47.

8 Mulvey is careful to note, though, that Hitchcock is invested in pulling the rug out from under Scottie's/our fetishization of Madeleine at the same time as he mobilizes it. As anyone who has seen the film will know, she is neither the person she claims to be nor the person Scottie tries to create her into.

9 The protest included a trash can into which protesters dumped girdles, bras, and a variety of clothing symbolic of this oppression. Contrary to popular belief, no one ever burned a bra, as they were too afraid it might set the wooden Atlantic City pier on fire.

10 Robin Morgan, *Sisterhood Is Powerful: An Anthology of Writing from the Women's Liberation Movement* (New York: Vintage Books, 1970), 522.

11 Simone de Beauvoir, *The Second Sex* (New York: Vintage Books, 1973), 301.

12 Gaines, *Fabrications*, 3.

13 Carballo, "Glenn Close Explains."

14 Ilya Parkins, "Building a Feminist Theory of Fashion: Karen Barad's Agential Realism," *Australian Feminist Studies* 23, no. 58 (2008), 507.

15 Karen Barad, *Meeting the Universe Halfway: Quantum Physics and the Entanglement of Matter and Meaning* (Durham, NC: Duke University Press, 2007), 292.

16 Close has said more than once that she did not play or see Alex as the epitome of backlash feminism out for revenge, but rather as a woman with mental illness. Most readings of the film see it differently though: as director Adrian Lyne's fantasy of revenge on the feminist career woman.

17 Pandora Sykes, "Why Glenn Close in Fatal Attraction Is Our Unexpected Style Icon," *Grazia*, March 20, 2014, https://graziadaily.co.uk/fashion/news/glenn-close-fatal-attraction-unexpected-style-icon/.

18 Gaines, *Fabrications*, 16.

19 Jackie Stacey, "Desperately Seeking Difference," in *Issues in Feminist Film Criticism*, ed. Patricia Erens (Bloomington: Indiana University Press, 1991).

20 Stacey, "Desperately Seeking Difference," 369.

21 Carballo, "Glenn Close Explains."

22 Hilton Als, "Dressing Like a Woman in 'Sunset Boulevard,'" *New Yorker*, February 27, 2017, https://www.newyorker.com/magazine/2017/02/27/dressing-like-a-woman-in-sunset-boulevard.

TELLING HISTORY THROUGH COSTUMES

1 Jimmy Kimmel Live!, "Chris Hemsworth Reveals Where He Keeps His Hammer," *YouTube*, January 11, 2018, https://www.youtube.com/watch?v=Su6KVN33Bew.

2 In 2018, for example, the collection grew with costumes from *Mother of the Maid* (an off-Broadway play) and *The Wife* (a film for which Close received her seventh Academy Award nomination).

3 Heather Akou, "The Elizabeth Sage Historic Costume Collection: A Critical Review of Uses for Teaching and Research," *American Craft Inquiry* 2, no. 2 (2018): 52–60, https://craftcouncil.org/post/elizabeth-sage-historic-collection.

4 Cosplay is a portmanteau of "costume" and "play," referring to people who wear costumes to create and embody fictional characters such as Sailor Moon, Harry Potter, or even Nova Prime from Marvel's 2014 film *Marvel Studios' Guardians of the Galaxy* (a character played by Close).

5 Joanne Eicher, "Dress," in *Routledge International Encyclopedia of Women: Global Women's Issues and Knowledge*, ed. Cheris Kramarae and Dale Spender (New York: Routledge, 2004), 422–23.

6 In a nutshell, the study of aesthetics is about how human beings sense objects (by sight, smell, touch, etc.) and attach social meanings to them. I might think a costume is beautiful, but why?

7 Unusually, Close has retained the right to borrow and wear her costumes again. In the 2017 revival of *Sunset Boulevard*, she reused some of the costumes from her first appearance as Norma Desmond in 1994.

8 Taylor Healy, "Creating Custom Storage Forms for Charles James Masterpieces," *Now at The Met* (blog), Metropolitan Museum of Art, October 20, 2016, https://www.metmuseum.org/blogs/now-at-the-met/2016/custom-storage-forms-charles-james.

9 Common brands for nursing uniforms in the 1940s–60s included Barco, White Swan, and Paul Jones.

10 Ginia Bellafante, "Dressing the Post-Feminist Stepford Wife," *New York Times*, June 1, 2004, B7, https://www.nytimes.com/2004/06/01/nyregion/dressing-the-post-feminist-stepford-wife.html.

11 In numerous cultures, snakes symbolize transformation and the extremes of good and evil.

12 Heather Akou, "Prison Uniforms on the Outside: Intersections with US Popular Culture," *Fashion, Style & Popular Culture* 7, no. 4 (2020), 473–99.

13 Not to be confused with the former host of *The Price is Right*, Bob Barker is a North Carolina–based supplier of uniforms and other products used in prison systems throughout the United States.

COLLABORATING BEHIND THE SCENES

1 "Glenn Close Quotes," *IMDb*, https://m.imdb.com/name/nm0000335/quotes.

2 Ginia Bellafante, "Dressing the Post-Feminist Stepford Wife," *New York Times*, June 1, 2004, B7, https://www.nytimes.com/2004/06/01/nyregion/dressing-the-post-feminist-stepford-wife.html.

3 John Wogan, "Glenn Close's Theatrical Costumes, Illustrated," *T: The New York Times Style Magazine*, February 14, 2018, https://www.nytimes.com/2018/02/14/t-magazine/entertainment/glenn-close-costumes.html.

4 Yohana Desta, "The Gorgeous Cruella De Vil Costumes That Made Glenn Close Nearly Faint," *Vanity Fair*, November 8, 2017, https://www.vanityfair.com/hollywood/2017/11/glenn-close-cruella-de-vil-costumes.

5 Michael Quintanilla, "It's a Case of Evil Is as Evil Dresses," *Los Angeles Times*, November 12, 2000, https://www.latimes.com/archives/la-xpm-2000-nov-12-ca-50531-story.html

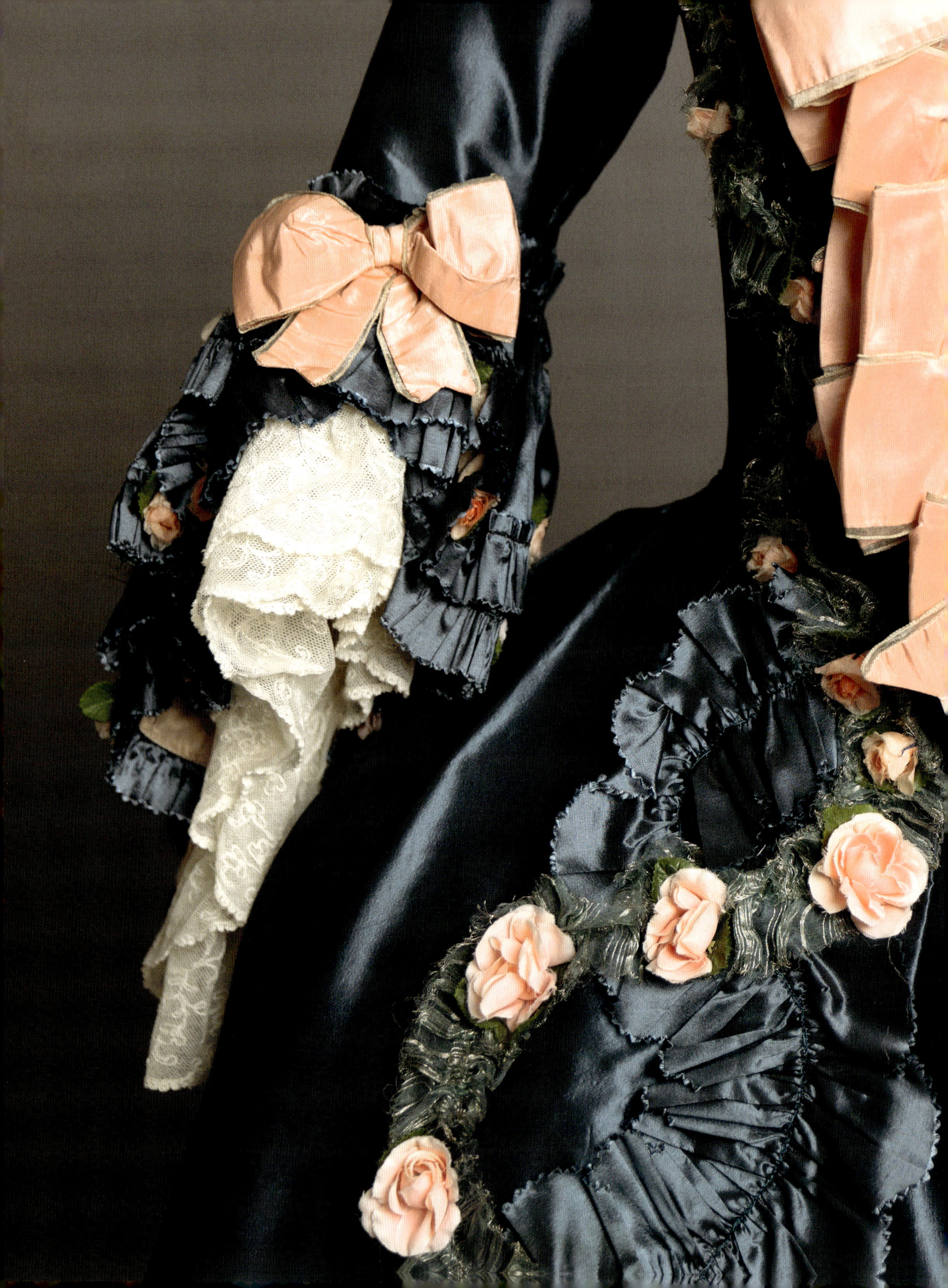

Catalogue

Kelly Gallett Richardson
and Galina Olmsted

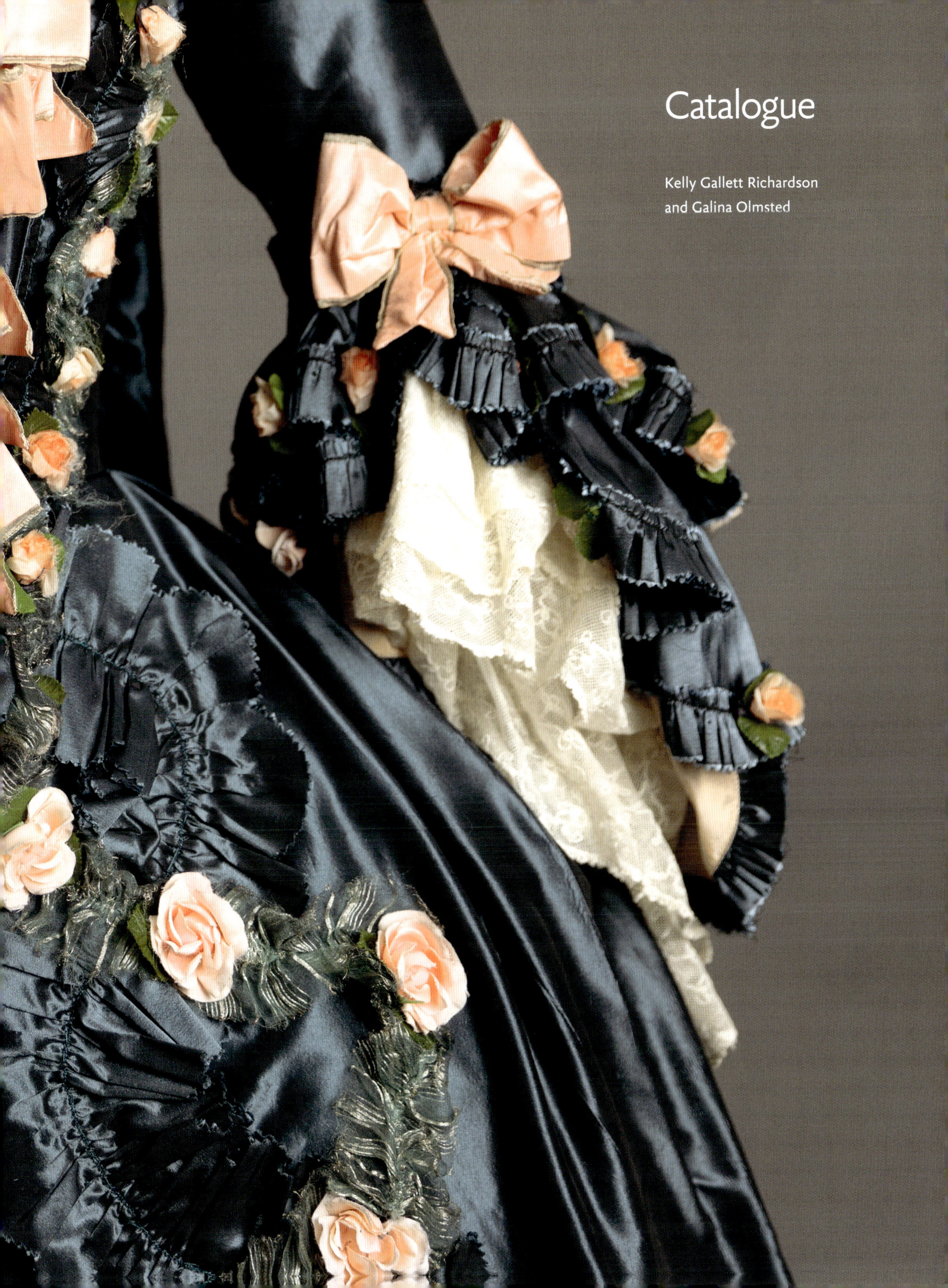

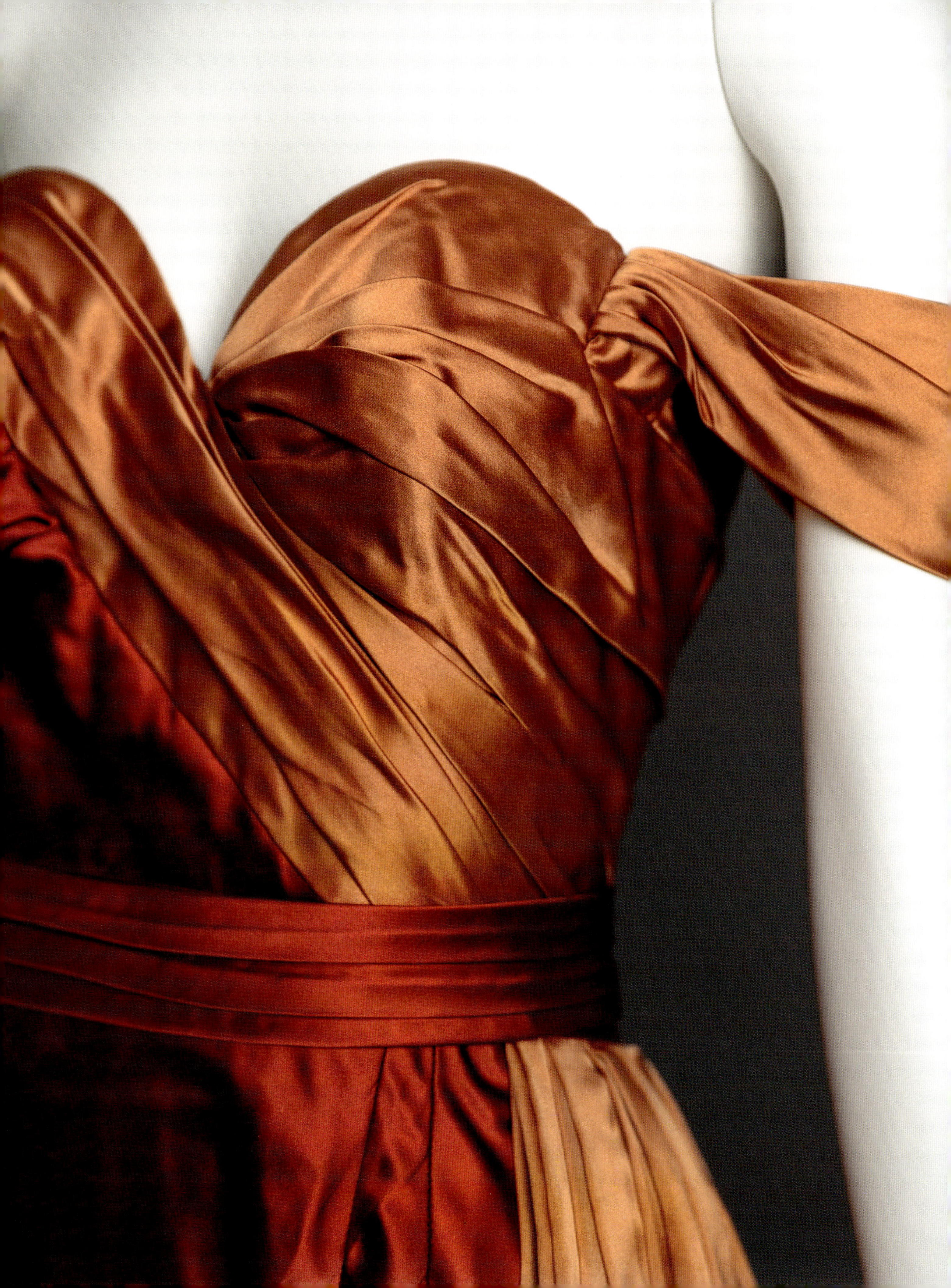

Costuming the Contemporary

Contemporary costuming is perhaps the most misunderstood genre of costume design. A costume designer must be able to conceptualize a character's wardrobe in the midst of an overwhelming barrage of present-day images. While the lens of history allows designers to filter out only the most relevant silhouettes and while clothing bodies for an imagined place grants enormous freedom, a designer working on a contemporary project must create within the constraints of his or her own era to develop a sartorial vocabulary for characters that will endure. Ellen Mirojnick (*Fatal Attraction*) acknowledged the difficulty of the genre in 2010: "As a designer of contemporary work, you are creating history. Remember, in 20 years the designer's work in a contemporary film will be history and reference of that time and place. We are all creating stories with characters that live on."[1]

The best contemporary costuming disappears when the character and what they are wearing become a believable unit that furthers the narrative and the director's vision. In the years ahead, it becomes a part of our collective memory of that era. Some costume elements may be purchased off-the-rack and altered if necessary; however, a costume designer often needs to create custom garments to achieve the desired fit, color, and mood needed to fully realize a character.

Before the widespread popularity of film, theater actors were the celebrities of their day and were featured in magazines like *Vogue*, which also published illustrations of gowns worn on stage. During the Golden Age of Hollywood in the 1930s and 1940s, costumers such as Adrian, Travis Banton, and Edith Head helped craft the glamorous personas of performers whose on-screen fashions were coveted by moviegoers. The costumes worn in these films influenced trends that reappeared in magazines and department stores. Today, costume designers might not set out to influence fashion or cultivate glamour, but their work to bring a character and their story to life can have a lasting impact beyond the screen.

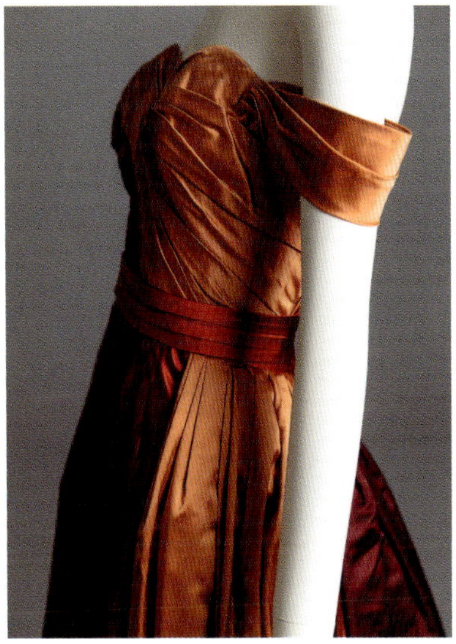

Judianna Makovsky (American)
Sunny von Bülow
Reversal of Fortune, 1990
Silk
GC 2017.149.1

CHARACTER
Sunny von Bülow

Reversal of Fortune, 1990

IN THE 1990 FILM *REVERSAL OF FORTUNE*, Close plays Sunny von Bülow, an American socialite who spent the final decades of her life hospitalized in a persistent vegetative state. Based on Alan Dershowitz's book by the same name, *Reversal of Fortune* recounts the events leading up to von Bülow's unexplained coma, her husband's arrest and trial, and his eventual acquittal. Told through the perspective of Dershowitz's work on the appeal, the film weaves together von Bülow's voiceover with flashbacks to the years leading up to her coma.

In her work on the film, Judianna Makovsky creates an identity for Sunny von Bülow that spans several important moments in her life. She is a dazzling dinner party guest in an off-the-shoulder evening gown, surreptitiously reaching for Klaus von Bülow's hand for the first time. She is a fearless young socialite in a pink organza dress, inviting a pet tiger to drink from the table at a garden party. As she settles into her life with Klaus, she begins to turn more often to alcohol and pills, still impeccably dressed in silk nightgowns with matching bed jackets and robes. In Dershowitz's telling, Sunny von Bülow was a woman obsessed with appearances—"Brain dead, body better than ever," as she says in the film's opening sequence—and through Makovsky's careful costuming, Close is able to embody and give voice to the real-life character despite her literal absence from the main narrative of the film.

DESIGNER
Judianna Makovsky

Judianna Makovsky began her career as a member of the children's chorus and ballet school of New York City's Metropolitan Opera at Lincoln Center. She earned a BFA from the School of the Art Institute of Chicago and attended both the Goodman School of Drama and the MFA program at the Yale University School of Drama. Her first credit as a costume designer was as an assistant to Milena Canonero on Francis Ford Coppola's *The Cotton Club* (1984). She worked with Coppola again in 1987, as the costume designer for *Gardens of Stone*. Over the course of her career in film, Makovsky has earned Academy Award nominations in the category of Best Costume Design for *Pleasantville* (1998), *Harry Potter and the Sorcerer's Stone* (2001), and *Seabiscuit* (2003). Makovsky first worked with Close in 1990 on Barbet Schroeder's *Reversal of Fortune*.

In recent years, Makovsky has become best-known for her intricate, fantastical costumes, designing for *The Last Airbender* (2010), *The Hunger Games* (2012), and for various films in the Marvel Cinematic Universe, including *Captain America: The Winter Soldier* (2014), *Captain America: Civil War* (2016), *Marvel Studios' Guardians of the Galaxy 2* (2017), *The Avengers: Infinity War* (2018) and *The Avengers: Endgame* (2019). In addition to her Academy Award nominations, Makovsky's designs have been recognized by a BAFTA nomination for *Harry Potter and the Sorcerer's Stone* and four Costume Designers Guild Awards, including the Career Achievement in Film Award in 2013. In addition to her extensive work on films, Makovsky has designed for television, theater, and opera.

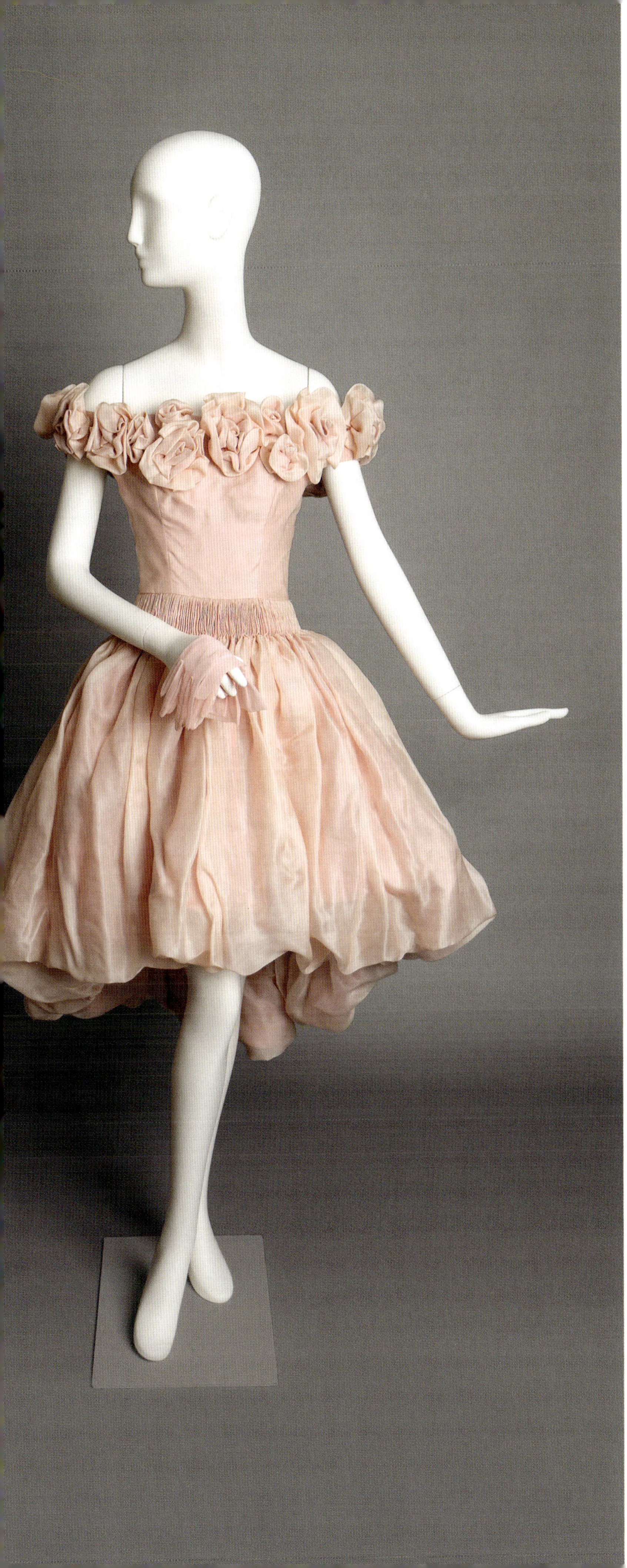

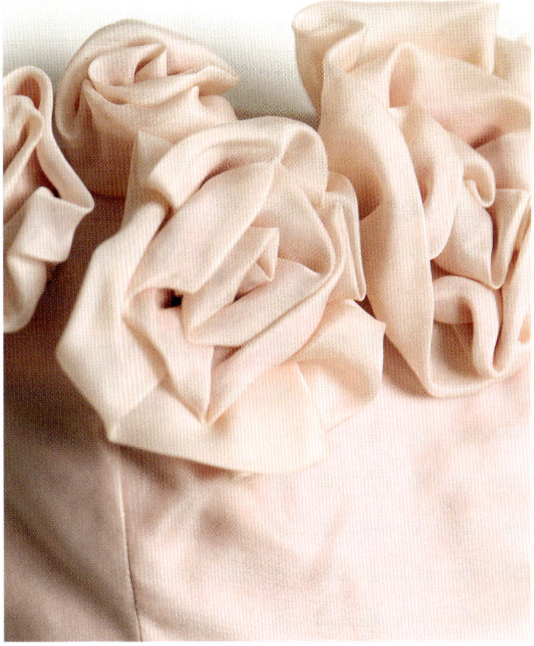

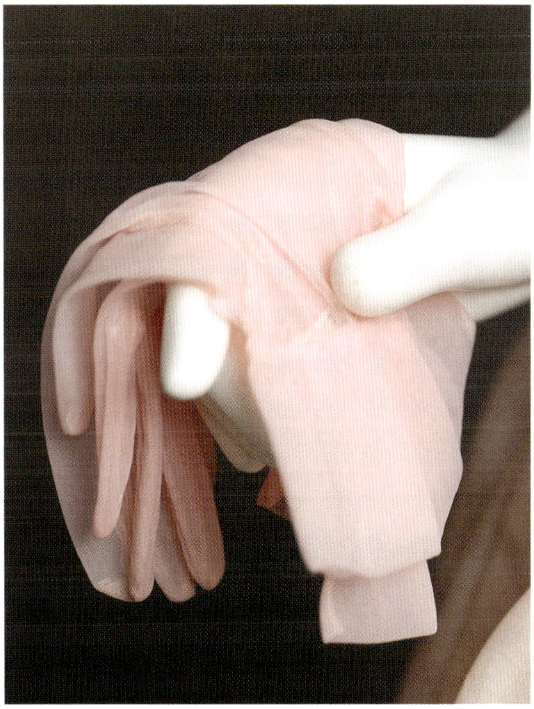

Judianna Makovsky (American)
Sunny von Bülow
Reversal of Fortune, 1990
Silk, nylon
GC 2017.148.1–.2 AB

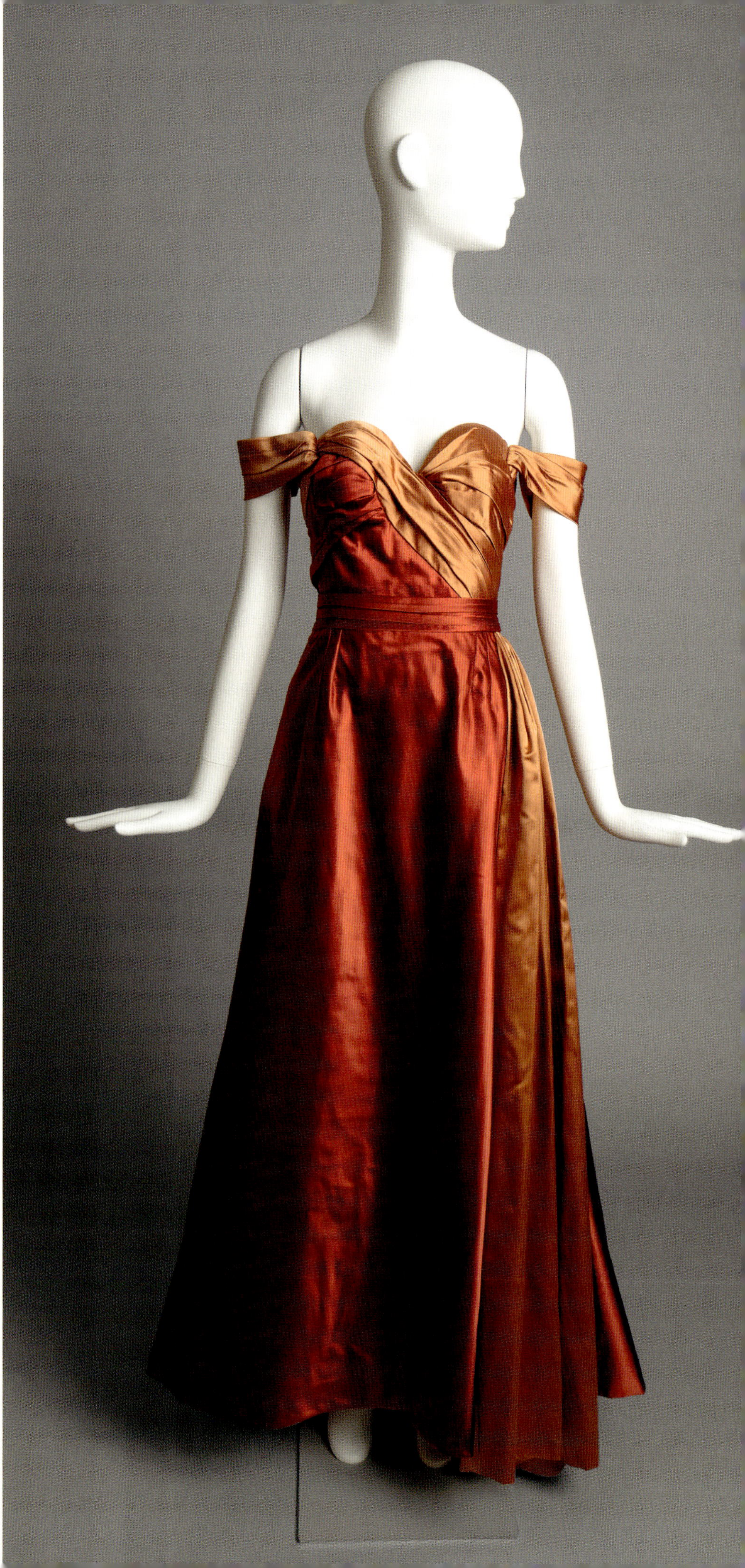

Judianna Makovsky (American)
Sunny von Bülow
Reversal of Fortune, 1990
Silk
GC 2017.149.1

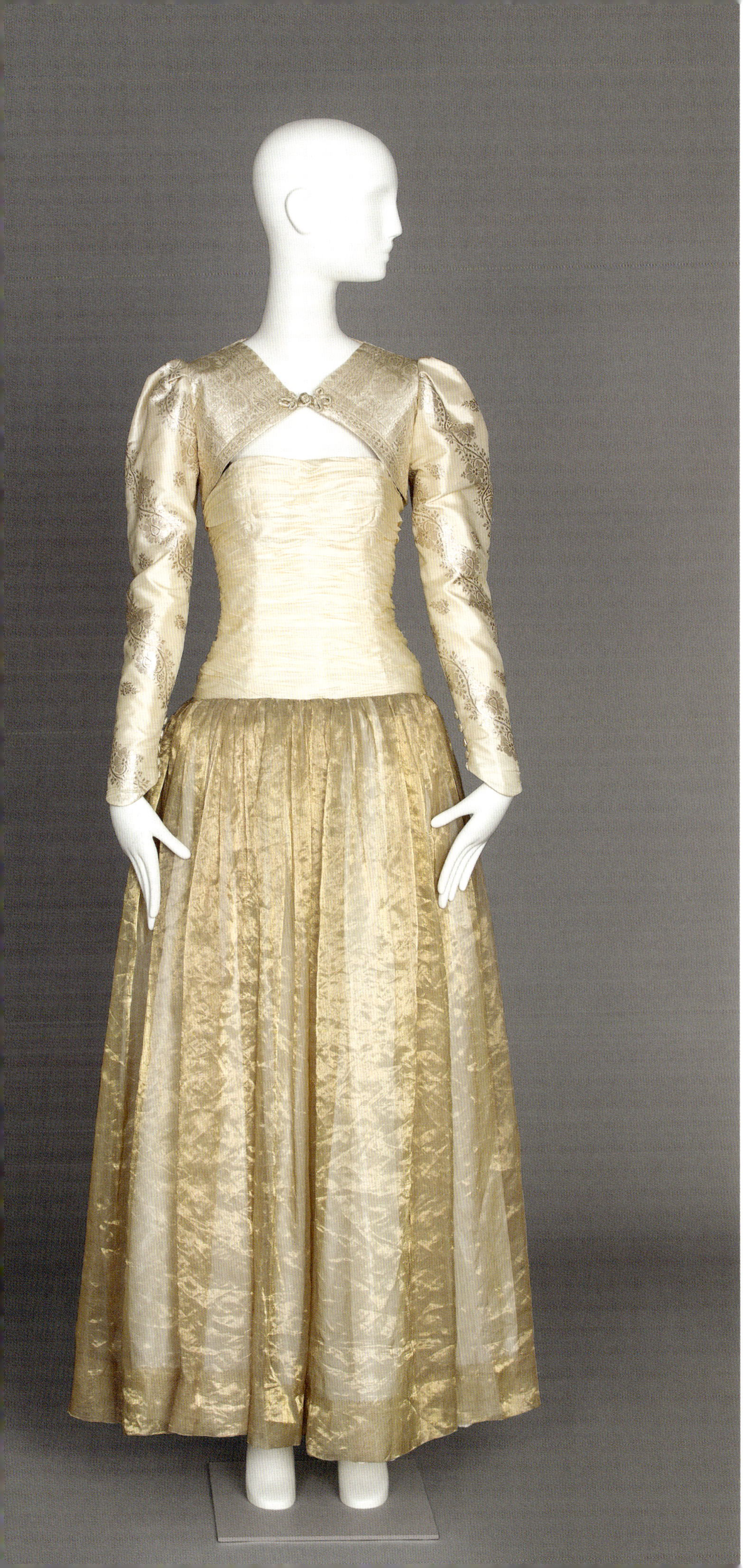

Judianna Makovsky (American)
Sunny von Bülow
Reversal of Fortune, 1990
Silk
GC 2017.150.1

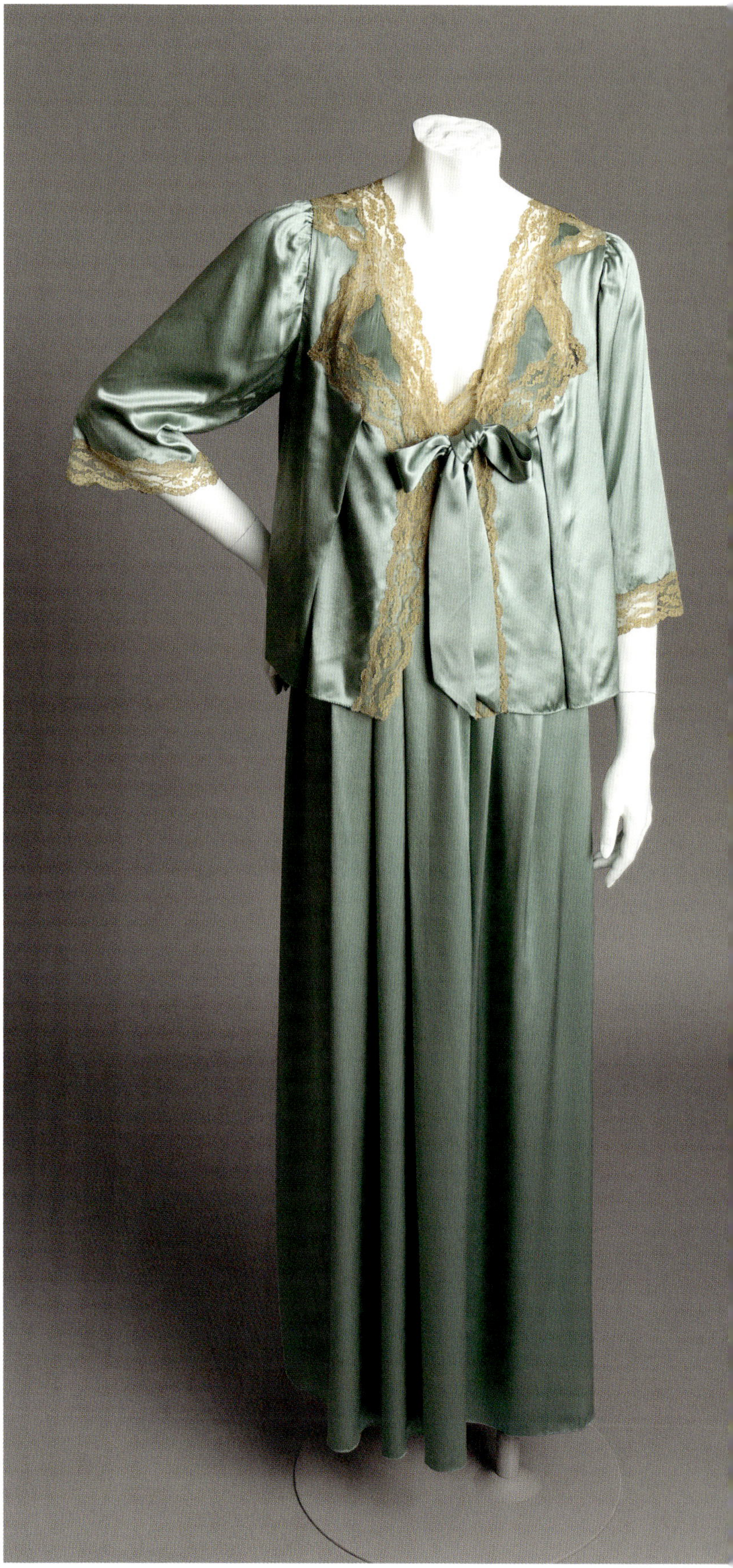

Judianna Makovsky (American)
Sunny von Bülow
Reversal of Fortune, 1990
Silk
GC 2017.142.1 AB

OPPOSITE
Judianna Makovsky (American)
Sunny von Bülow
Reversal of Fortune, 1990
Silk
GC 2017.144.1–.2

Judianna Makovsky (American)
Sunny von Bülow
Reversal of Fortune, 1990
Silk
GC 2017.141.1

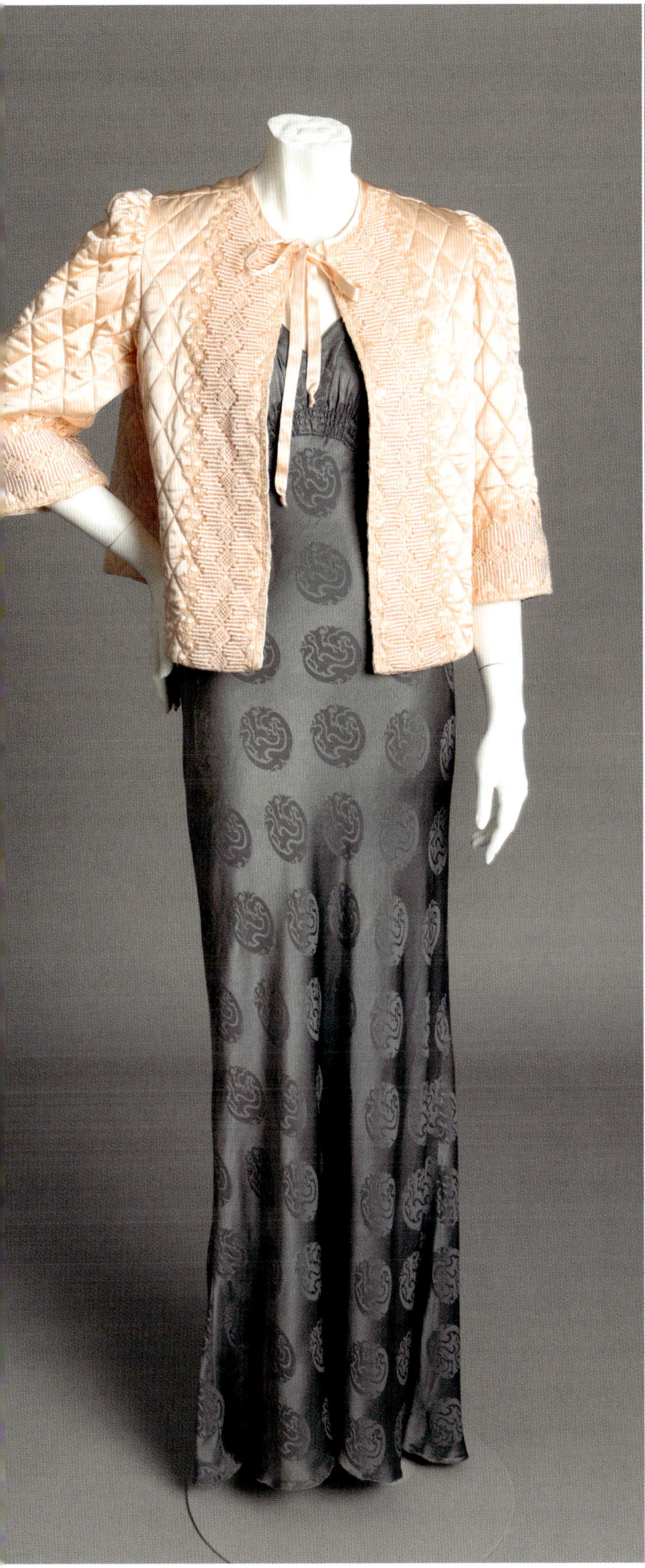

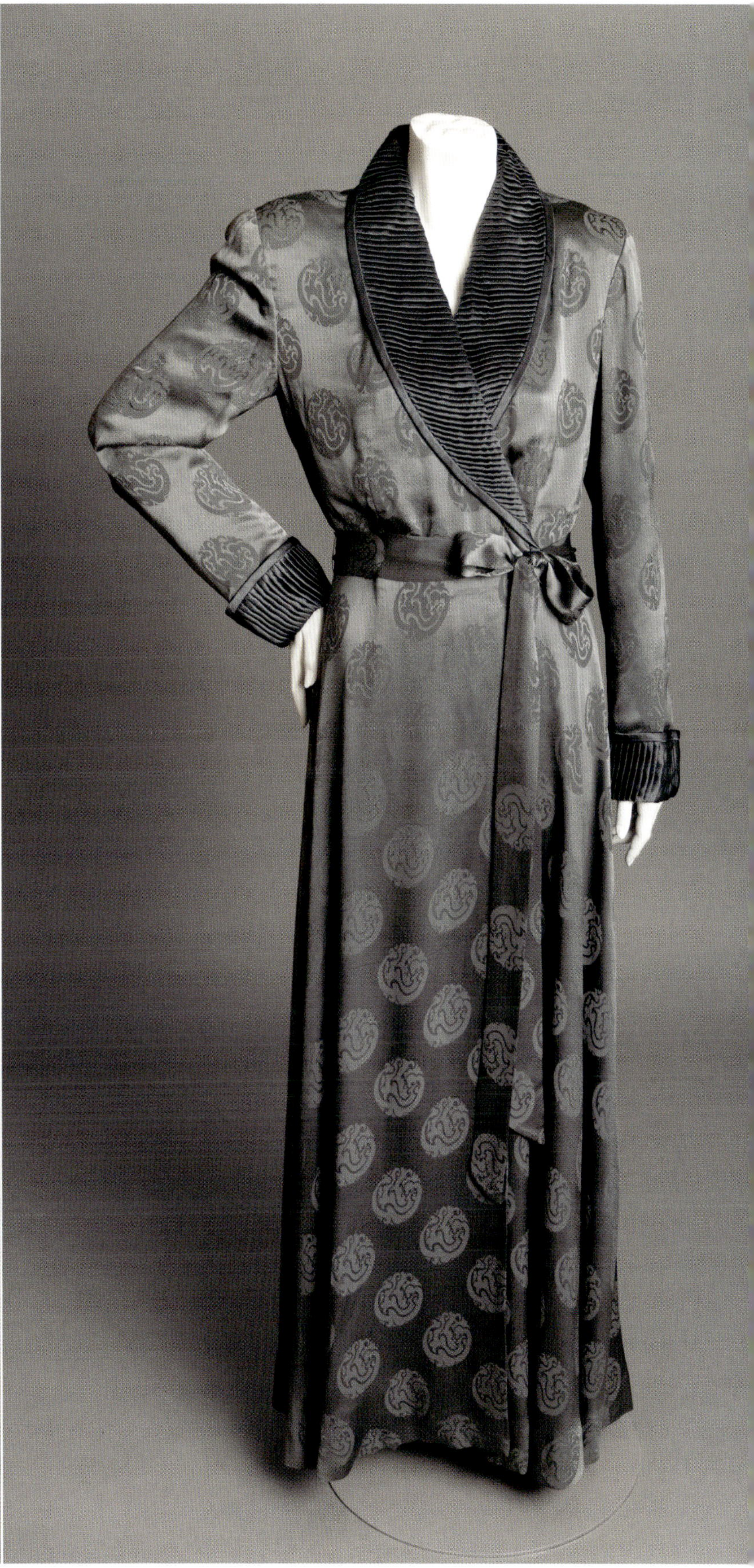

CHARACTER

Alex Forrest

Fatal Attraction, 1987

GLENN CLOSE'S PORTRAYAL OF ALEX FORREST became a cultural phenomenon when *Fatal Attraction* was released in 1987. After a brief affair with Dan Gallagher (Michael Douglas), Forrest's interest in him turns into obsession, spiraling into violence and wreaking havoc on his wife and daughter. In its own time, the film was viewed as a cautionary tale for married men tempted by infidelity and the derogatory term "bunny boiler" entered the popular lexicon as shorthand for women whose passions were deemed excessive. In the decades ahead, Close's own organization, Bring Change to Mind, has helped encourage an empathetic and nuanced understanding of mental illness. This cultural shift has allowed for a more complex understanding of Forrest as a character suffering from an unnamed personality disorder and as a probable victim of childhood sexual abuse.

In the film, Ellen Mirojnick repeats light and dark contrasts in Forrest's wardrobe to lend visual emphasis to the character's erratic temperament. In an off-the-rack, black leather coat with fashionably oversize 1980s shoulders, Forrest commands authority and attention in a material that conveys both individuality and rebellion. By contrast, the simple cotton shift she wears at home and the white knit dress worn in the film's denouement evoke a near-angelic vulnerability. Mirojnick's thoughtful costuming highlights the contrast between Forrest's wardrobe of lights and darks and the earthy, maternal ensembles worn by Gallagher's wife, Beth (Anne Archer).

DESIGNER

Ellen Mirojnick

A native New Yorker, Ellen Mirojnick is a graduate of both the School of Visual Arts and Parsons School of Design. She first worked with Glenn Close on *Fatal Attraction* (1987), designing the iconic white dress that Close's character Alex Forrest wears in her final confrontation with Dan Gallagher, played by Michael Douglas. Mirojnick went on to collaborate extensively with Douglas through the 2010s, designing costumes for *Wall Street* (1987), *Basic Instinct* (1992), *A Perfect Murder* (1998), and *Behind the Candelabra* (2013), a biopic about the relationship between Liberace, played by Douglas, and Scott Thorson, played by Matt Damon. The wardrobe that Mirojnick created for Douglas's character Gordon Gekko in *Wall Street* inspired a number of men's fashion trends in the late 1980s and early 1990s, including boldly patterned ties, contrast collar shirts, and brightly colored suspenders. In 1988 she was honored with the Cutty Sark Menswear Award for her sartorial statement in *Wall Street*.

Having built her career on contemporary film projects in the 1980s and 1990s, Mirojnick turned to period films such as *Behind the Candelabra*, set in the late 1970s and early 1980s, and *The Knick* (2014–15), a television series set in the early part of the twentieth century. An innovator at the crossroads of fashion, art, and film, Mirojnick collaborated with the actor James Franco to create images for *Visionaire 59: Fairytale* (2011) and, in 2011, her video collaboration with artist Richard Phillips was exhibited at the Venice Biennale. Her costume designs have been recognized with numerous awards, including an Emmy for Outstanding Costumes for *Behind the Candelabra* and four Costume Designers Guild Awards, including the Career Achievement Award for Film and Television in 2016.

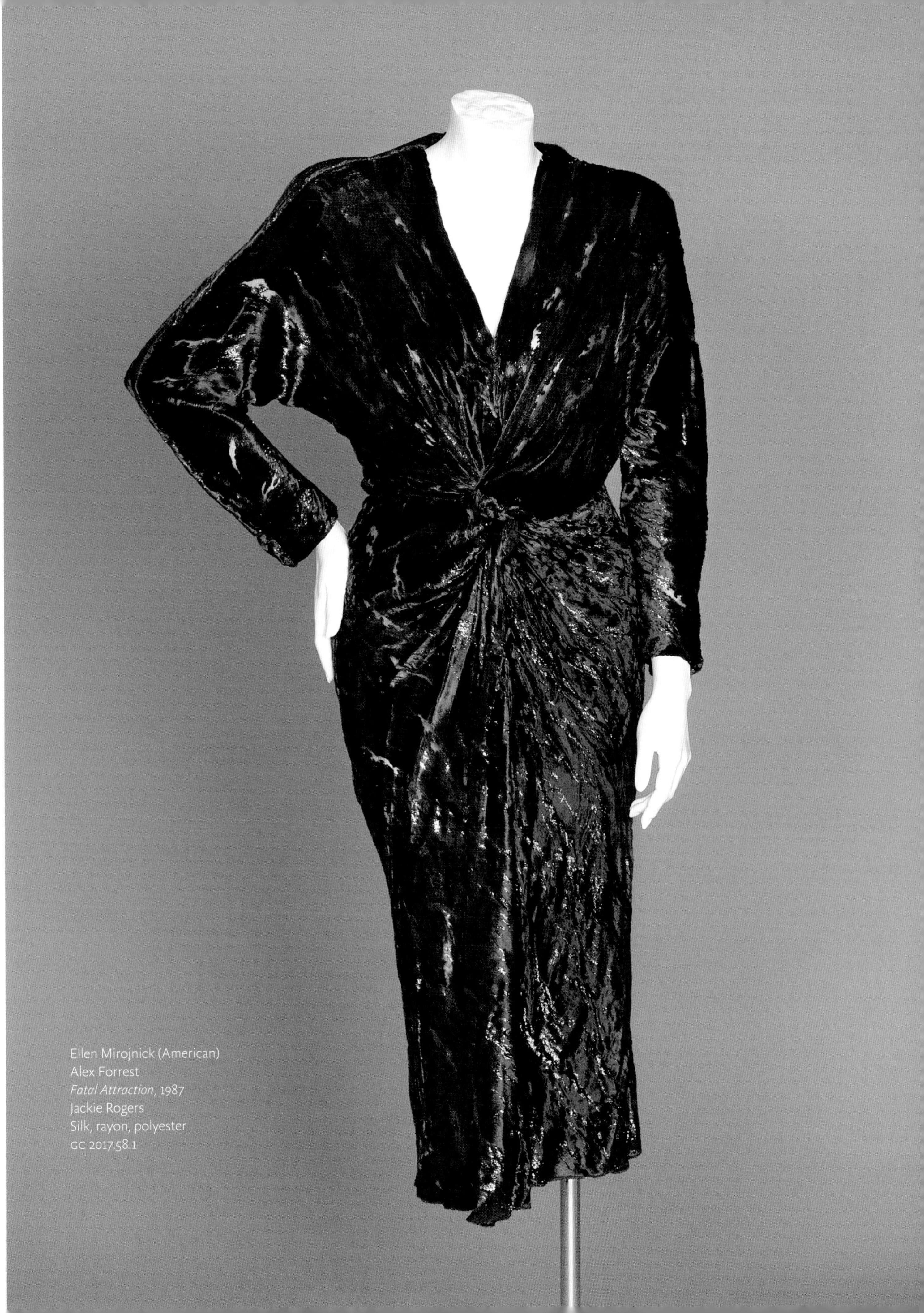

Ellen Mirojnick (American)
Alex Forrest
Fatal Attraction, 1987
Jackie Rogers
Silk, rayon, polyester
GC 2017.58.1

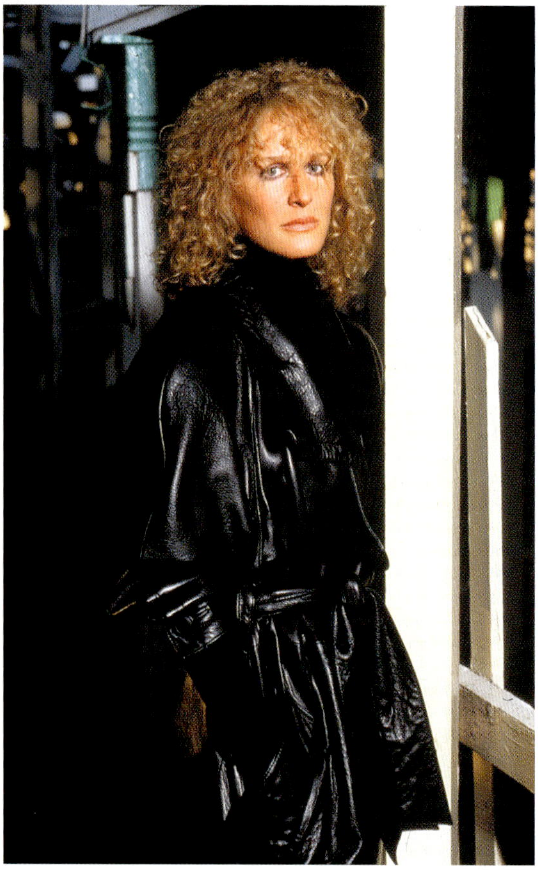

ABOVE
Publicity still of Glenn Close as Alex Forrest in *Fatal Attraction*, 1987

RIGHT
Ellen Mirojnick (American)
Alex Forrest
Fatal Attraction, 1987
Maxima
Leather
GC 2017.66.1 AB

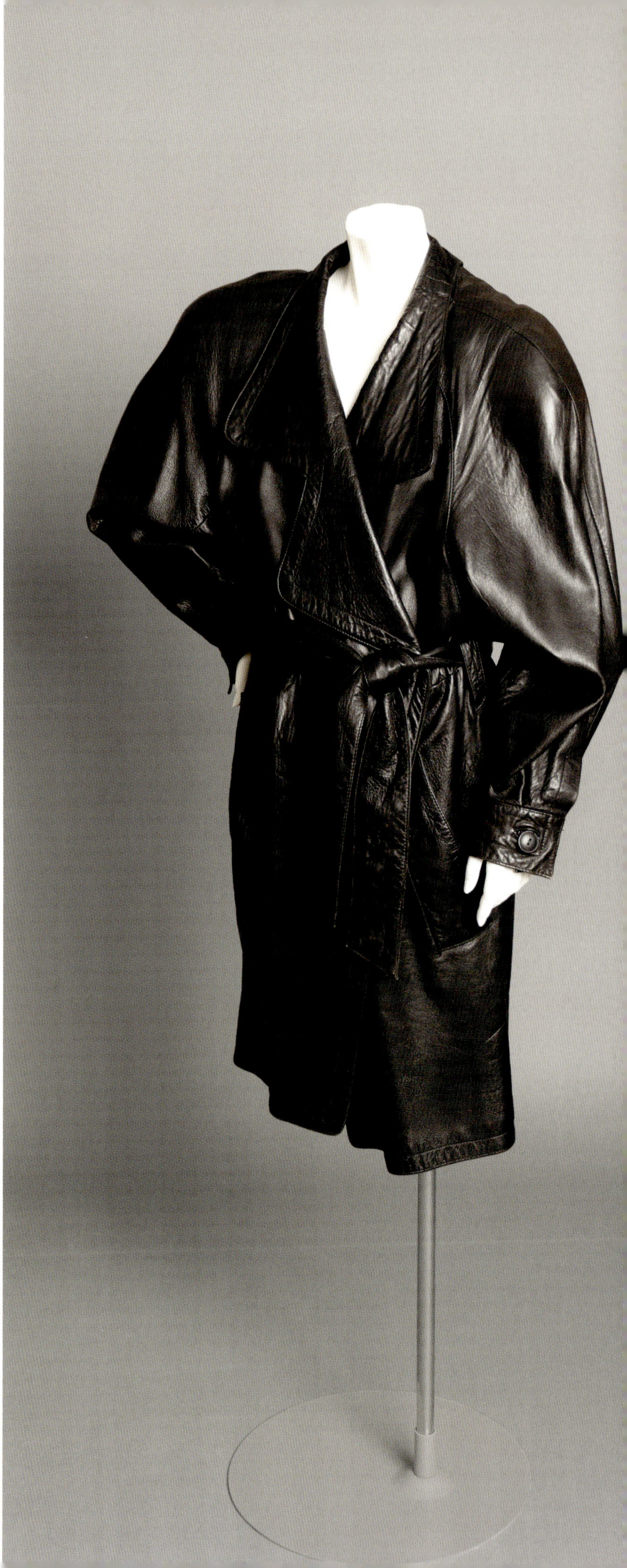

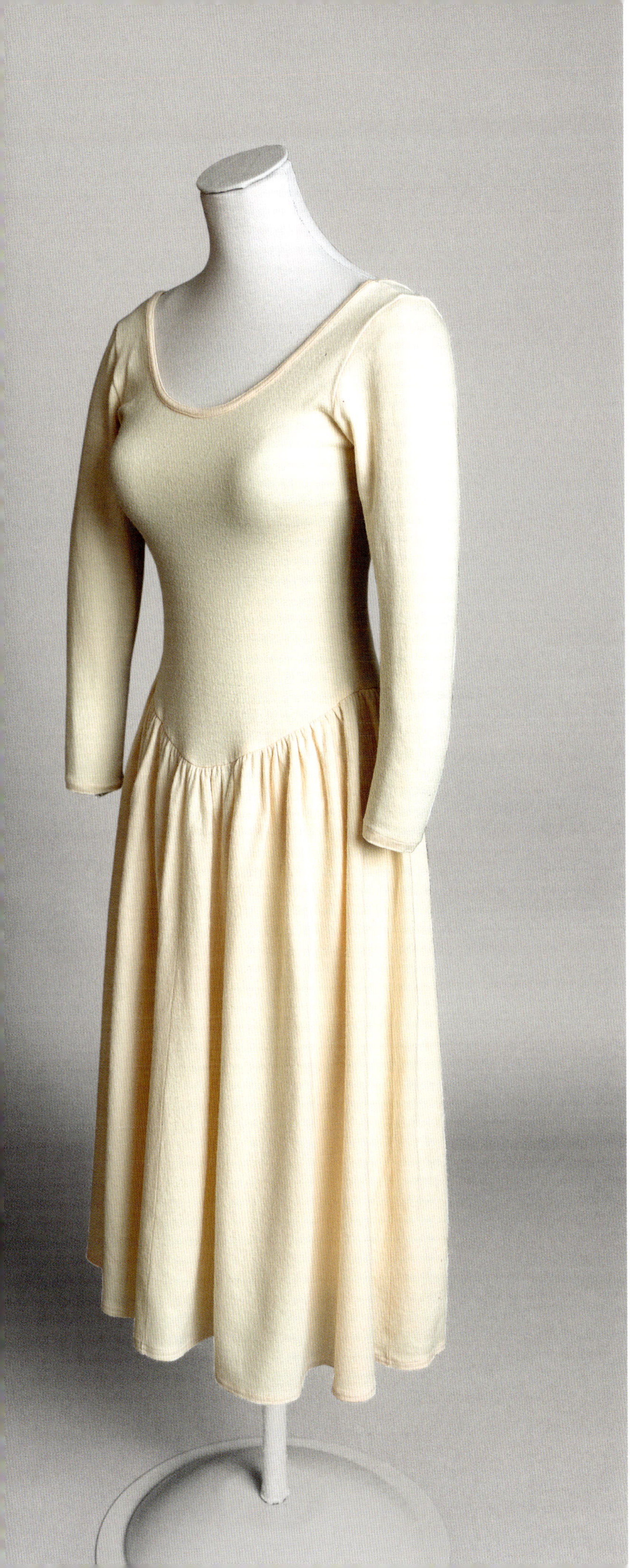

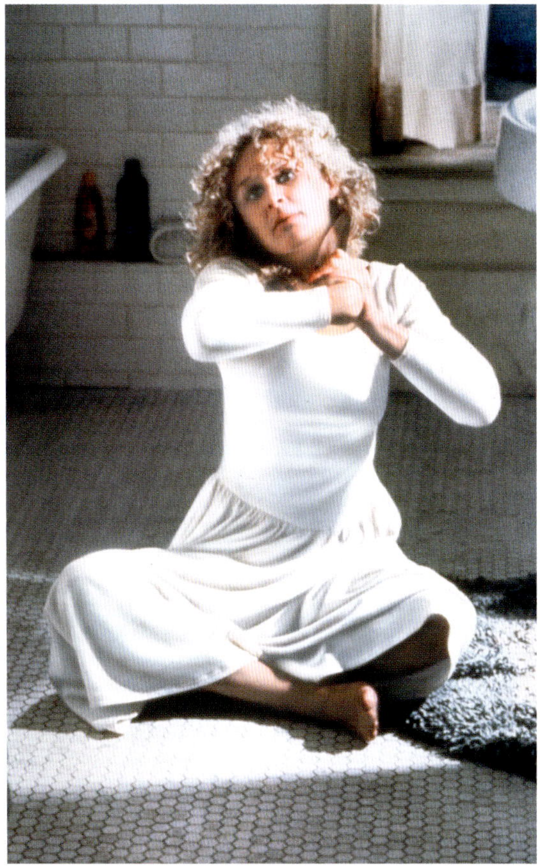

ABOVE
Glenn Close as Alex Forrest in *Fatal Attraction*, 1987

LEFT
Ellen Mirojnick (American)
Alex Forrest
Fatal Attraction, 1987
Wool
GC 2017.57.1

CHARACTER

Teddy Barnes

Jagged Edge, 1985

GLENN CLOSE'S TIMELY TURN AS LAWYER TEDDY BARNES was the first in a batch of late 1980s and early 1990s Hollywood courtroom dramas featuring women attorneys, a trend that reflected real-life demographics as the number of women graduating with professional degrees was on the rise since the 1970s. These films brought to light the ongoing challenges of professional women, including gender bias in the workplace, sexual harassment, and work-life balance. In *Jagged Edge*, Barnes is lured into a personal relationship with her client, the handsome and wealthy accused murderer Jack Forrester, played by Jeff Bridges.

In the courtroom, Barnes holds her own among the men who surround her. At home, she shares custody of her two children and maintains an amicable relationship with her ex-husband. In her work on the film, Ann Roth designed a number of influential costumes for Barnes, ensembles that have come to be part of our collective visual memory of professional women at the time. When *Jagged Edge* was released, workplace attire for women was evolving beyond conservative, skirted versions of men's business suits. As the number of women in the workplace rose, so did their desire to feminize and individualize their wardrobes while still projecting an air of authority. The "power suits" that emerged in the 1980s and early 1990s were characterized by strong shoulders, delineated waists, and narrow skirts. At home, Barnes wore soft oversize sweaters and casual pants or jeans, emphasizing the contrast between her personal and work lives.

DESIGNER

Ann Roth

Born in Hanover, Pennsylvania, Ann Roth earned a BFA at Carnegie Mellon University before beginning her career as a scenery painter for the Pittsburgh Opera. Roth first became interested in costume design when she met Irene Sharaff, who invited her to Los Angeles to assist with the costumes for *Brigadoon* (1954). Sharaff earned an Academy Award nomination for Best Costume Design for the film and Roth's work on the project launched a career that has spanned seven decades and that includes over two hundred film and theater credits. Best known for her work on *The English Patient* (1996), *The Birdcage* (1996), and *The Talented Mr Ripley* (1999), Roth has won accolades for her work designing costumes for both film and stage productions.

Roth has earned nine Tony Award nominations for Best Costume Design, with a win for *The Nance* (2013), as well as four Academy Award nominations for Best Costume Design, winning in 1997 for her work on *The English Patient*. Her other honors and awards include three Emmy Award nominations for Outstanding Costumes; three BAFTA Award nominations for Best Costume Design, with a win in 1976 for *The Day of the Locust*; and five Costume Designers Guild Award nominations, in addition to the Career Achievement Award for Film, which she won in 2003. Roth first worked with Glenn Close on *The World According to Garp* (1982), designing the nurse's uniform and long coat that Close wore in the role of Jenny Fields. They have worked together on a number of subsequent projects, including *Jagged Edge* (1985), *Maxie* (1985), *Death and the Maiden* (1992), and *The Stepford Wives* (2004).

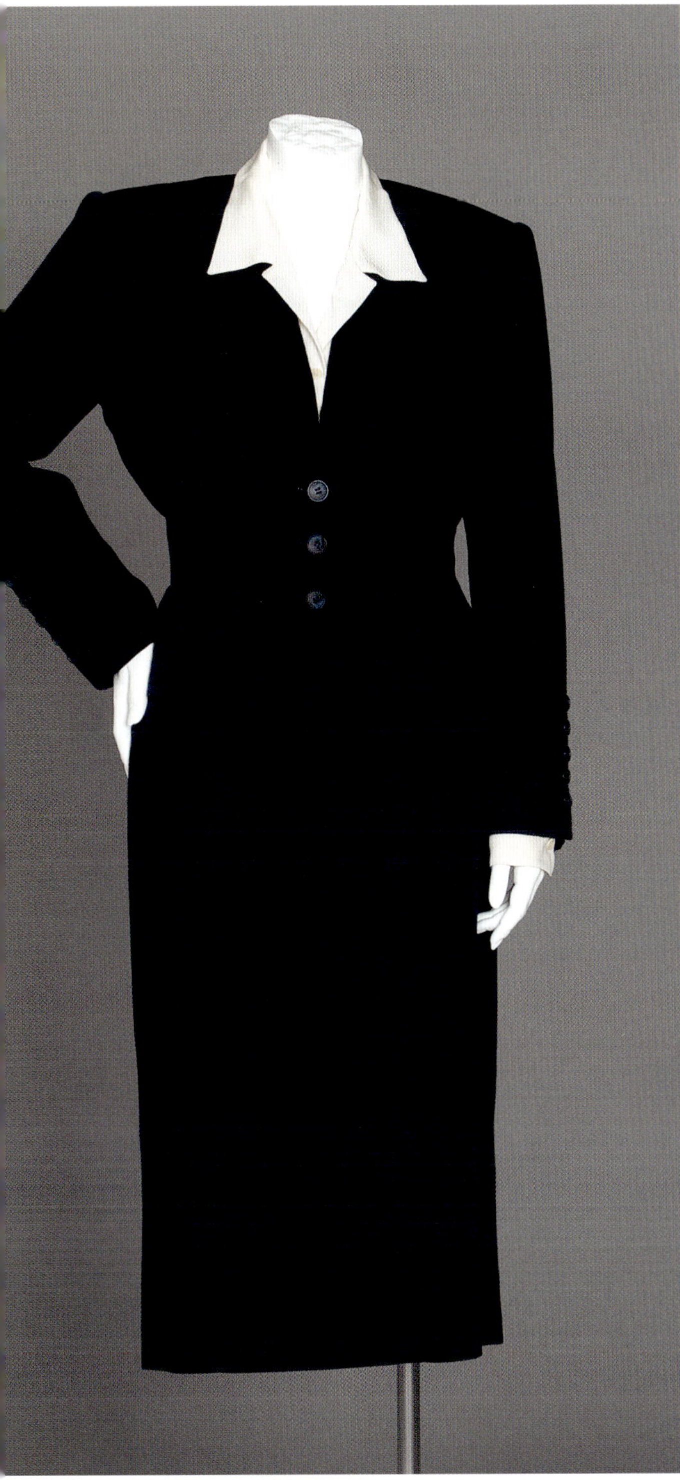

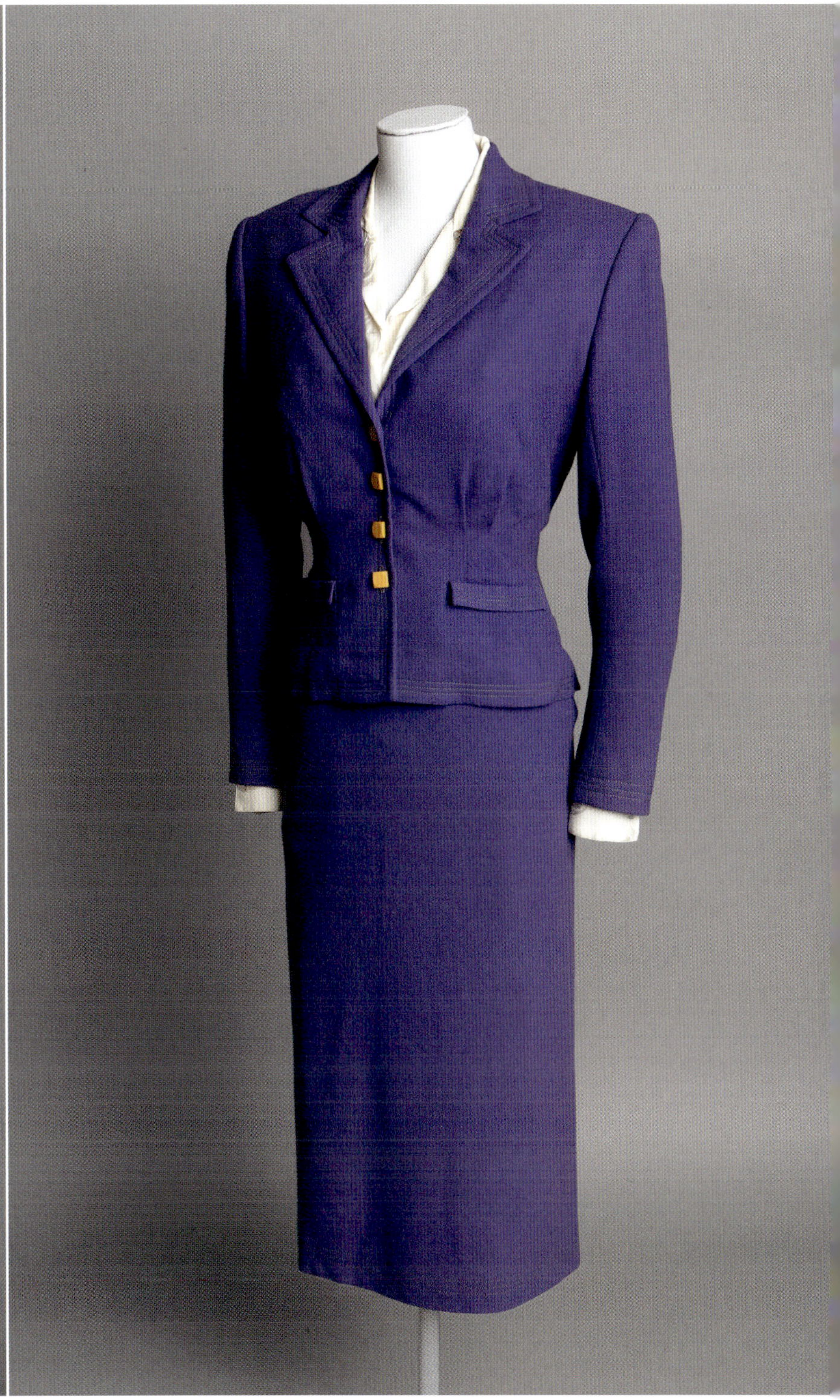

Ann Roth (American)
Barbara Matera Ltd.
Teddy Barnes
Jagged Edge, 1985
Wool, silk
GC 2017.76.1–.2

Ann Roth (American)
Barbara Matera Ltd.
Teddy Barnes
Jagged Edge, 1985
Wool, silk
GC 2017.78.1–.2

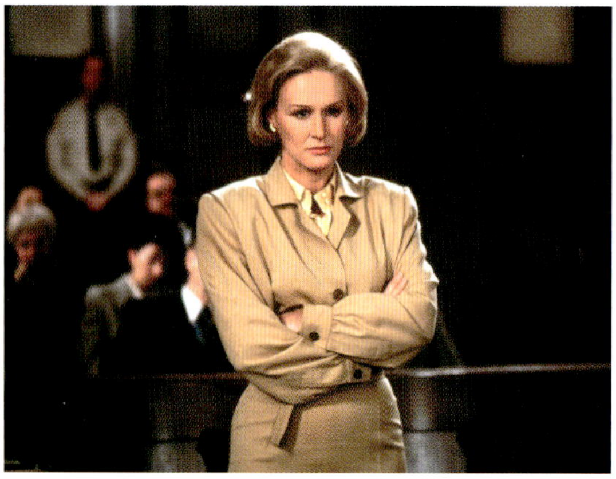

ABOVE
Glenn Close as Teddy Barnes in *Jagged Edge*, 1985

RIGHT
Ann Roth (American)
Barbara Matera Ltd.
Teddy Barnes
Jagged Edge, 1985
Wool, leather
GC 2017.79.1 AB

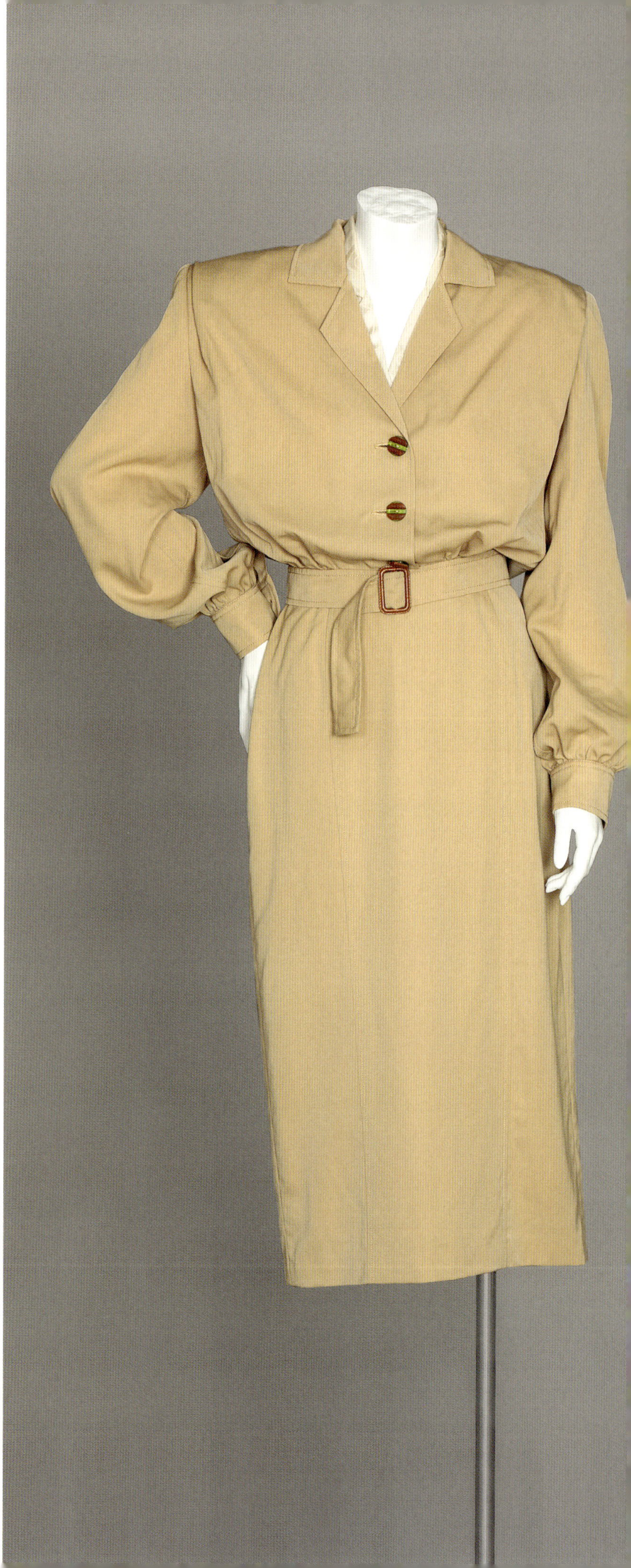

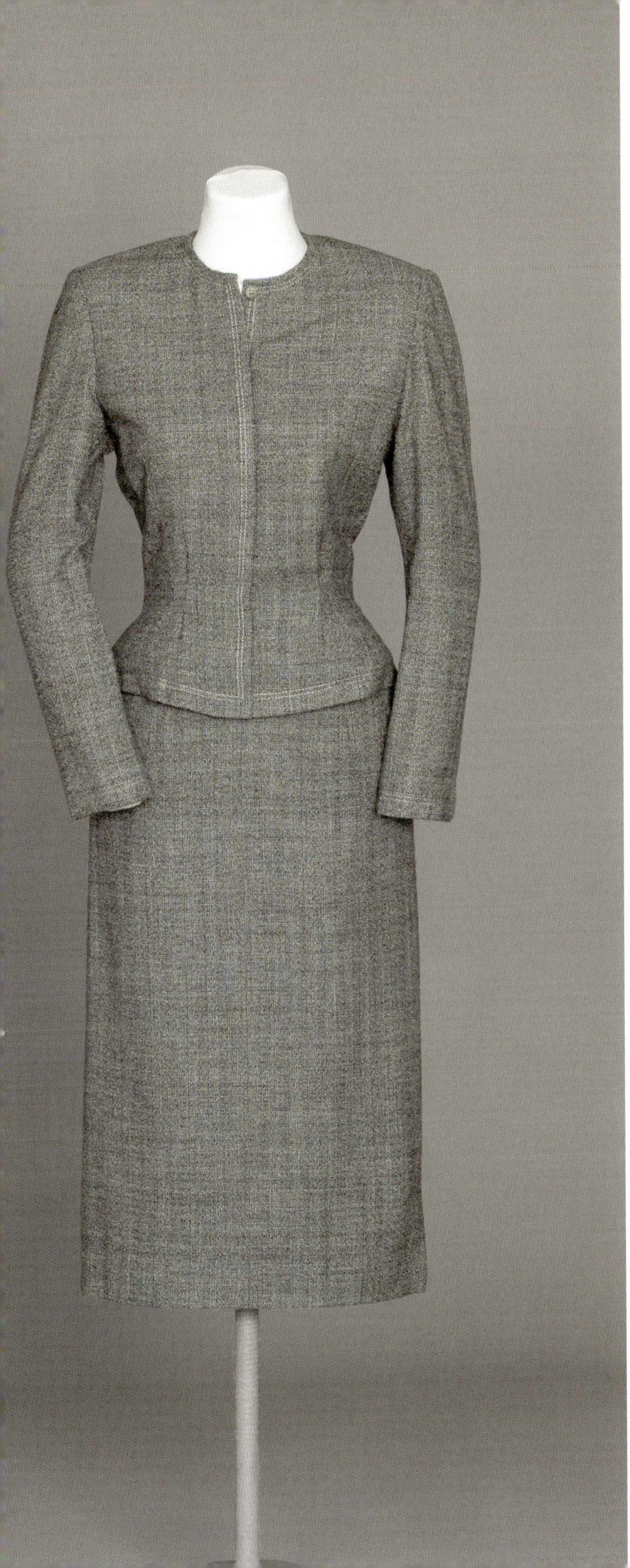

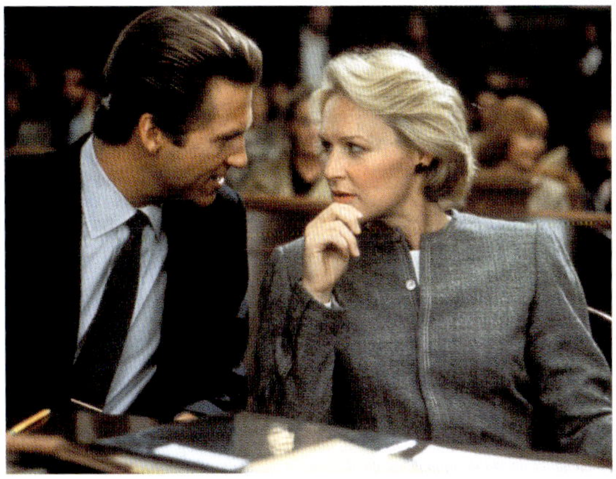

ABOVE
Glenn Close as Teddy Barnes in *Jagged Edge*, 1985

LEFT
Ann Roth (American)
Barbara Matera Ltd.
Teddy Barnes
Jagged Edge, 1985
Wool, silk
GC 2017.77.1–.2

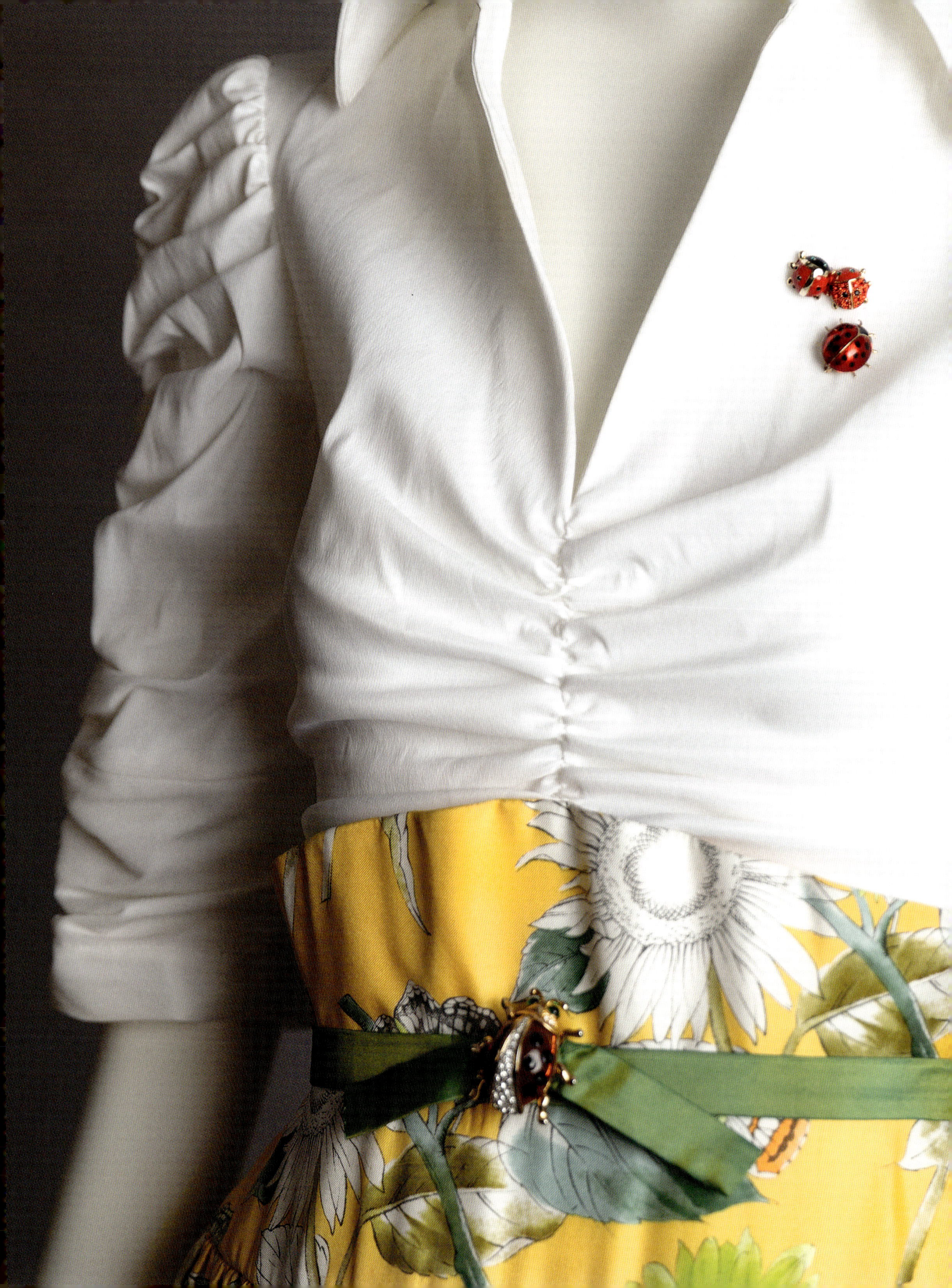

Crafting Identity

When first conceptualizing a character's look, a costume designer takes into account visual clues that signal characteristics such as age, socioeconomic status, gender, and cultural and religious values. Designers take these factors into consideration when building a character's wardrobe and can silently convey aspects of their personality through the skillful selection of fabric color, pattern, and weight, as well as expert manipulation of fit and silhouette. A character's motivations may be clearly communicated through their outward appearance or their wardrobe may serve as a disguise, concealing or distracting from their true self.

Costumes tasked with reflecting hidden or complex aspects of a character's identity require especially close collaboration among directors, designers, makers, and actors. Carefully fitted garments can alter an actor's manner of walking, speaking, and presenting themselves on film or on stage. By working closely with hairstylists and prosthetic makeup artists, costume designers help actors fully immerse themselves into a role, becoming unrecognizable to audiences as anyone but the character at hand.

Throughout her long career, the art of costuming has enabled Glenn Close to play a range of characters, including doting mother, unhappy wife, troubled socialite, groundbreaking military general, and manipulative queen. In *The Stepford Wives* (2004), Close plays Claire Wellington, a villainous former brain surgeon who weaponizes her overt femininity through a wardrobe that costume designer Ann Roth compared to simplistic, larger-than-life paper dolls.[2] In *The World According to Garp* (1982), the feminist heroine Jenny Fields wears her nurse's uniform in a conscious crafting of her public identity. In a demonstration of powerful transformative costuming, Close disappeared into the role of the titular Irish servant in *Albert Nobbs* (2011), a film which earned Close her sixth of seven Academy Award nominations. Whether the designer seeks to highlight or obfuscate aspects of a character's identity, costuming is often used to help shape the audience's understanding of the character over the course of the production.

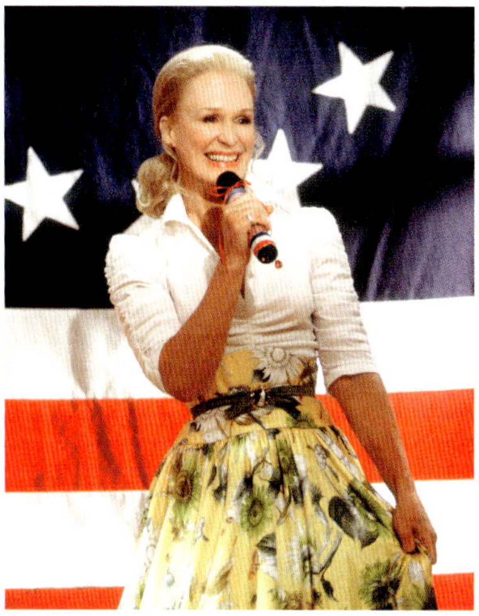

Ann Roth (American)
Eric Winterling Inc.
Claire Wellington
The Stepford Wives, 2004
Silk, cotton, spandex, metal, enamel, rhinestones
GC 2017.300.1–.2 AB

CHARACTER

Claire Wellington

The Stepford Wives, 2004

AFTER A PROFESSIONAL CRISIS SENDS JOANNA EBERHART (Nicole Kidman) into a spiral, she and her husband Walter Kresby (Matthew Broderick) move their family from Manhattan to the quiet, fictional suburb of Stepford, Connecticut. They are welcomed to town by the local real estate agent, Claire Wellington, played by Glenn Close. A remake of the 1975 film of the same name, *The Stepford Wives* is a piece of distinctly twentieth-century feminist satire that veers closer to comedy than the original. In Stepford, the women are impeccably dressed at every occasion, including an aerobics exercise class where Claire—dressed in pink and white gingham capri pants with matching blouse, headband, and heels—leads the housewives in a routine based on domestic chores, calling out "Let's all be washing machines!"

In a 2004 interview, the designer Ann Roth describes the 1950s-inspired costuming as essential to the film's plot: "There should be nothing hip, nothing edgy. The women should—in their own dopey way—look like paper dolls. They should look simplistic. . . . They should be larger than life, meaning that they're perfect in a not real way."[3] The costumes in *The Stepford Wives* aligned with a resurgence of gingham capris and retro sundresses in the mid-2000s, led by designers such as Lilly Pulitzer and Kate Spade. In the film's final scenes, Claire wears a yellow silk plaid evening gown with a matching lace bolero that epitomizes her role as the town's reigning housewife and, in the end, its wicked mastermind.

DESIGNER

Ann Roth

See p. 88 for biography and Afterword on p. 177.

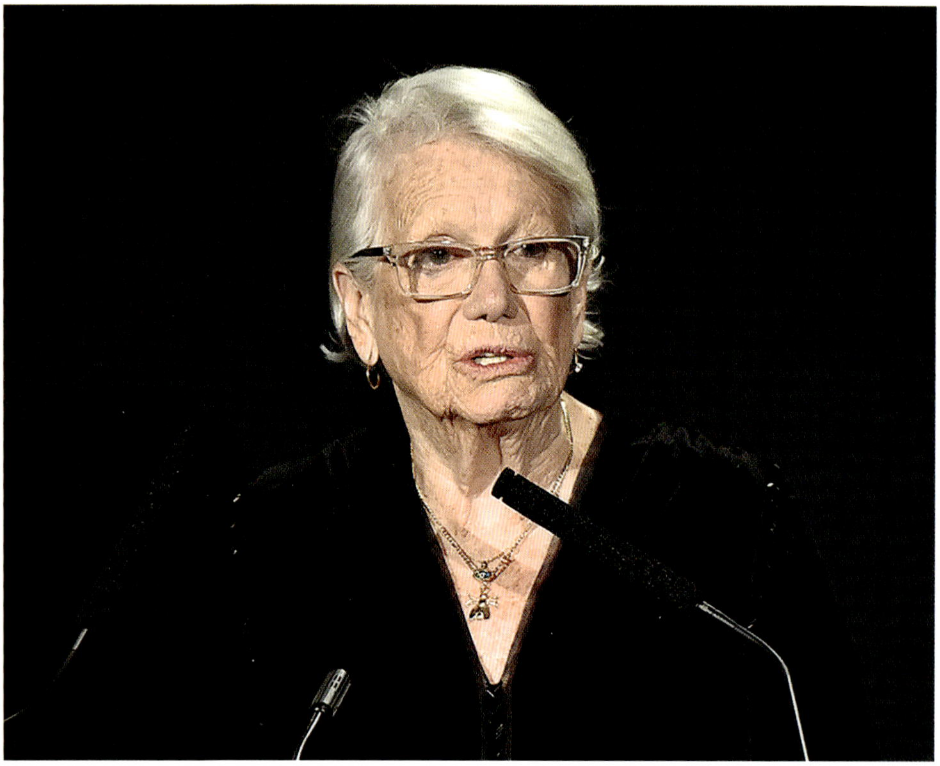

Ann Roth speaks onstage during the 2018 DGA Honors Show at DGA Theatre on October 18, 2018 in New York City

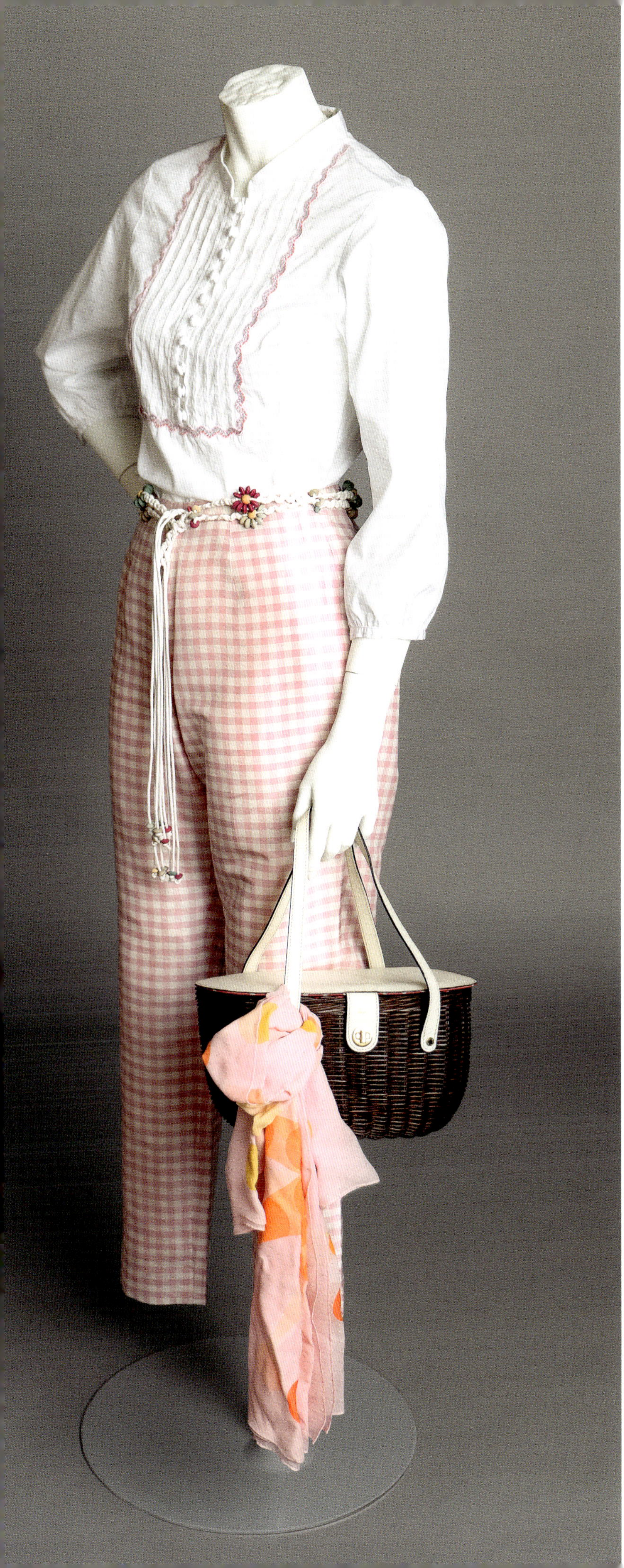

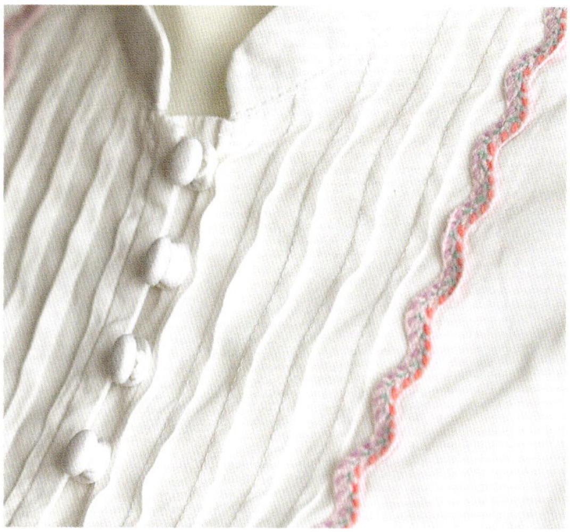

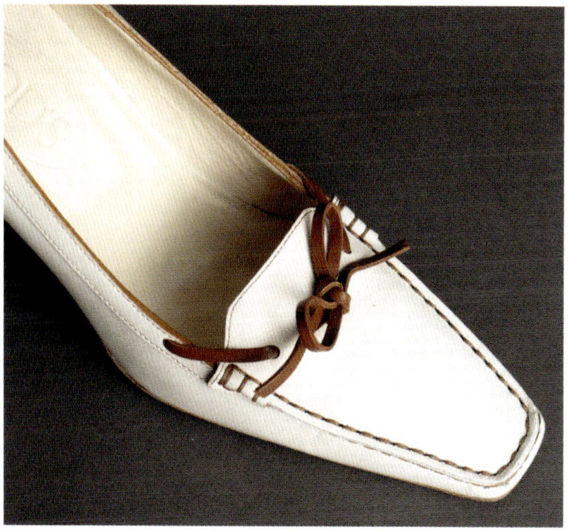

ABOVE
Ann Roth (American)
Claire Wellington
The Stepford Wives, 2004
Tod's
Leather
GC 2017.294.4 AB

LEFT
Ann Roth (American)
Claire Wellington
The Stepford Wives, 2004
Pink, Ralph Lauren, Kate Spade
Cotton, spandex, silk, wooden beads
GC 2017.294.1-.3, .5

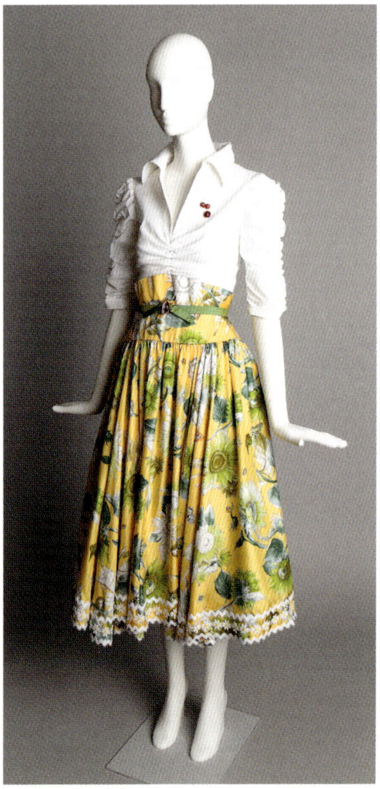

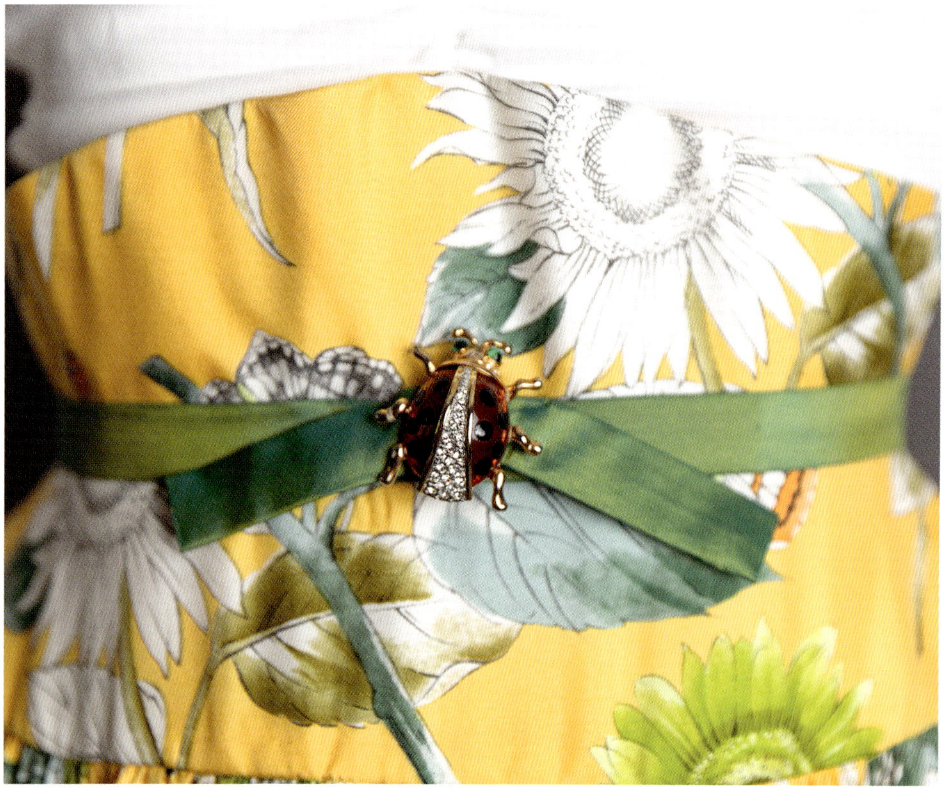

Ann Roth (American)
Eric Winterling Inc.
Claire Wellington
The Stepford Wives, 2004
Silk, cotton, spandex, metal, enamel, rhinestones
GC 2017.300.1–.2 AB

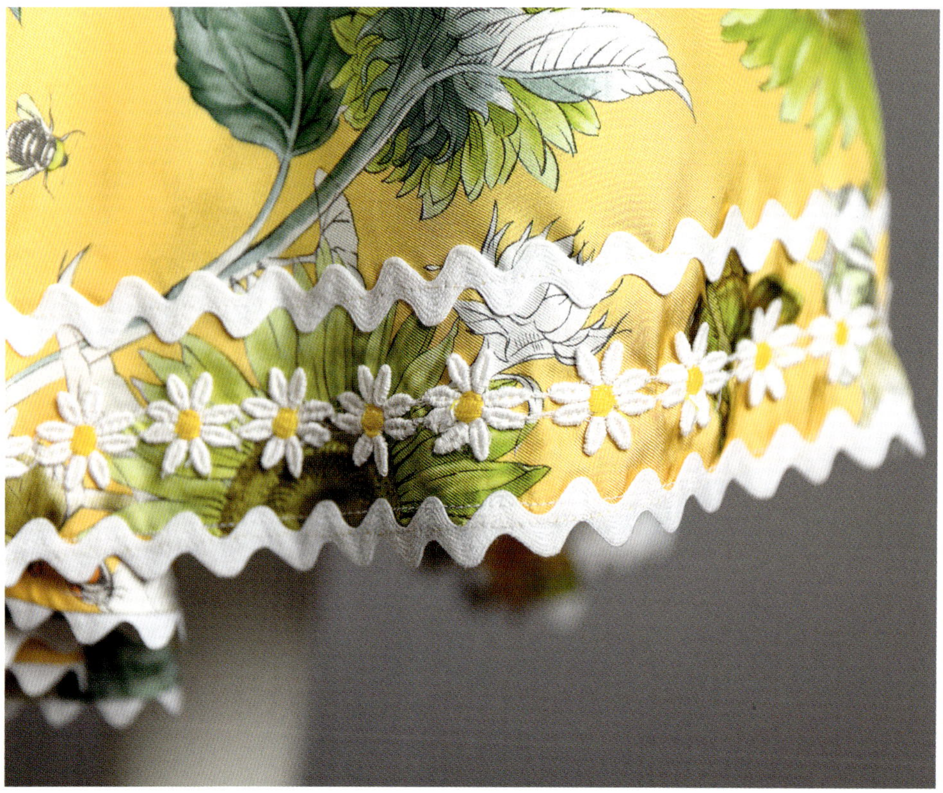

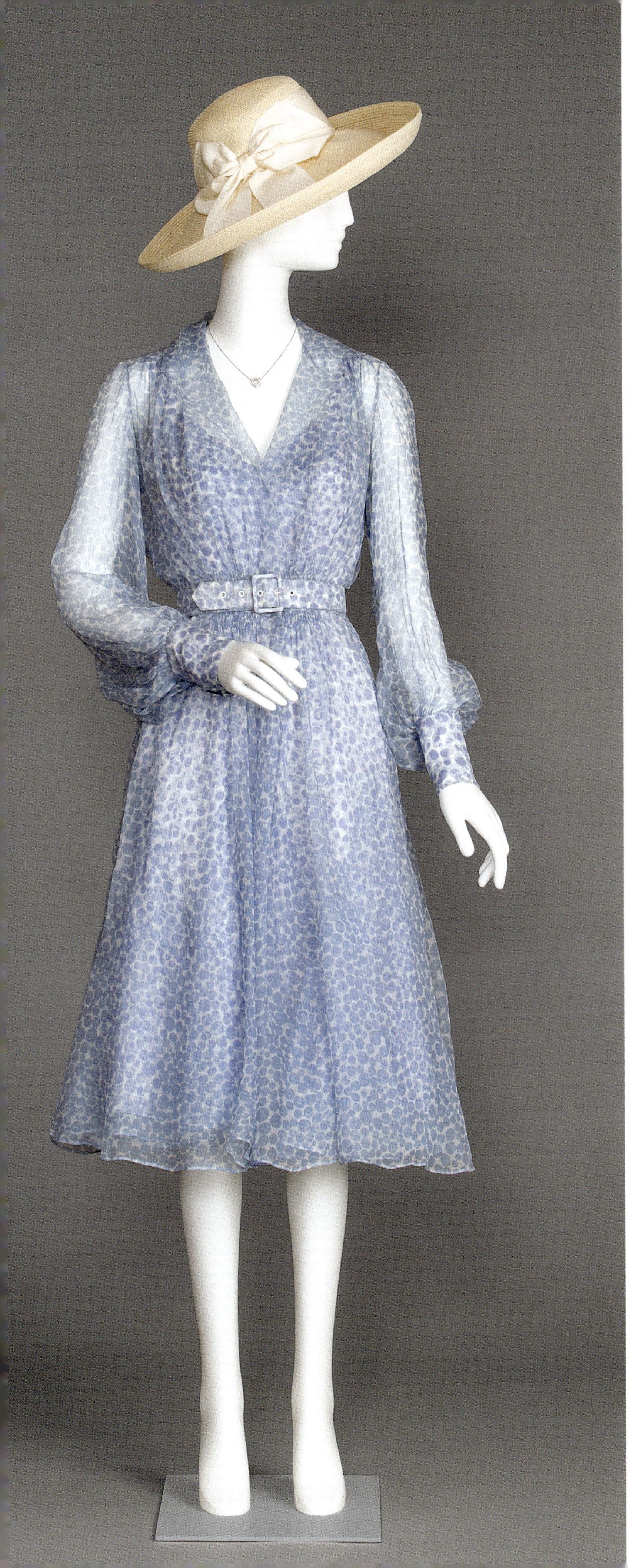

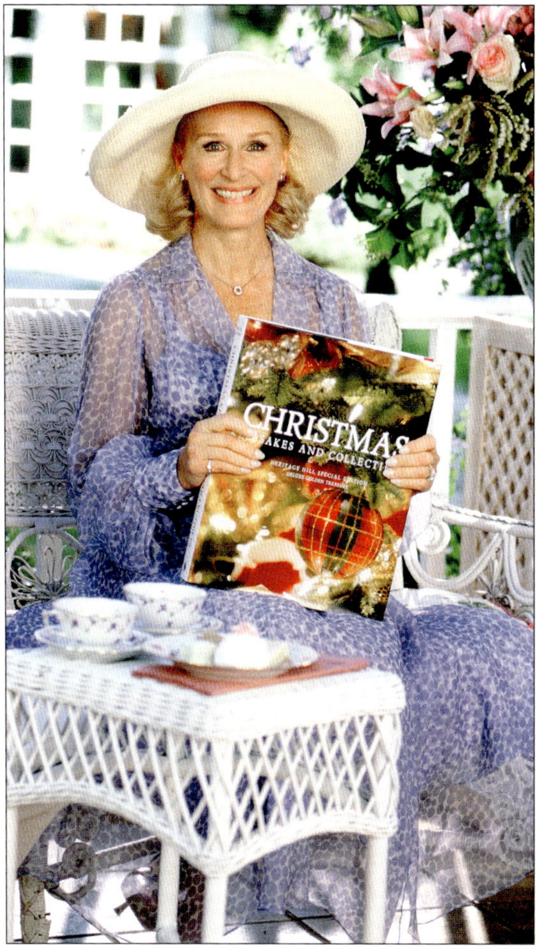

Ann Roth (American)
Eric Winterling Inc.
Claire Wellington
The Stepford Wives, 2004
Silk
GC 2017.296.1-.3, .5

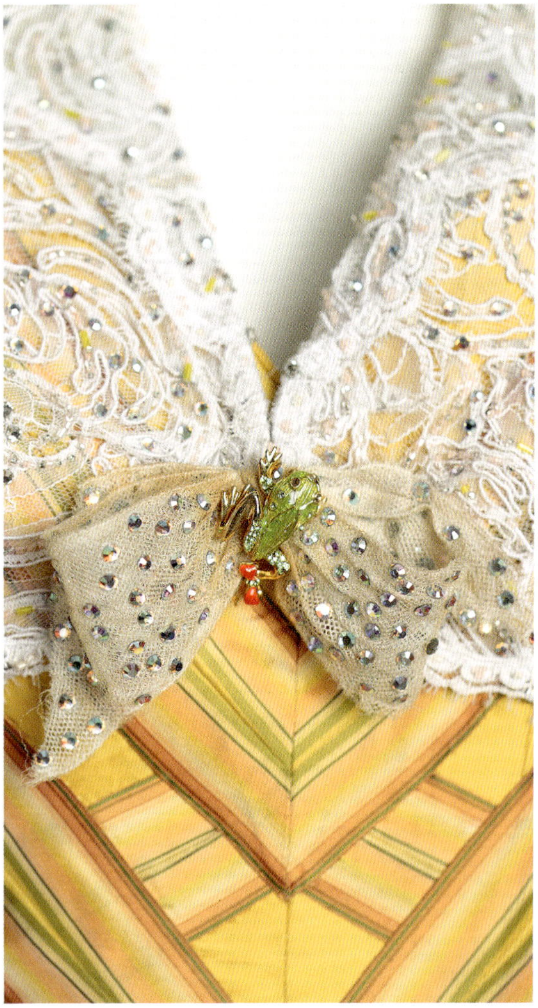

Ann Roth (American)
Eric Winterling Inc.
Claire Wellington
The Stepford Wives, 2004
Silk, cotton, rhinestones, metal, enamel
GC 2017.301.1–.2, .10

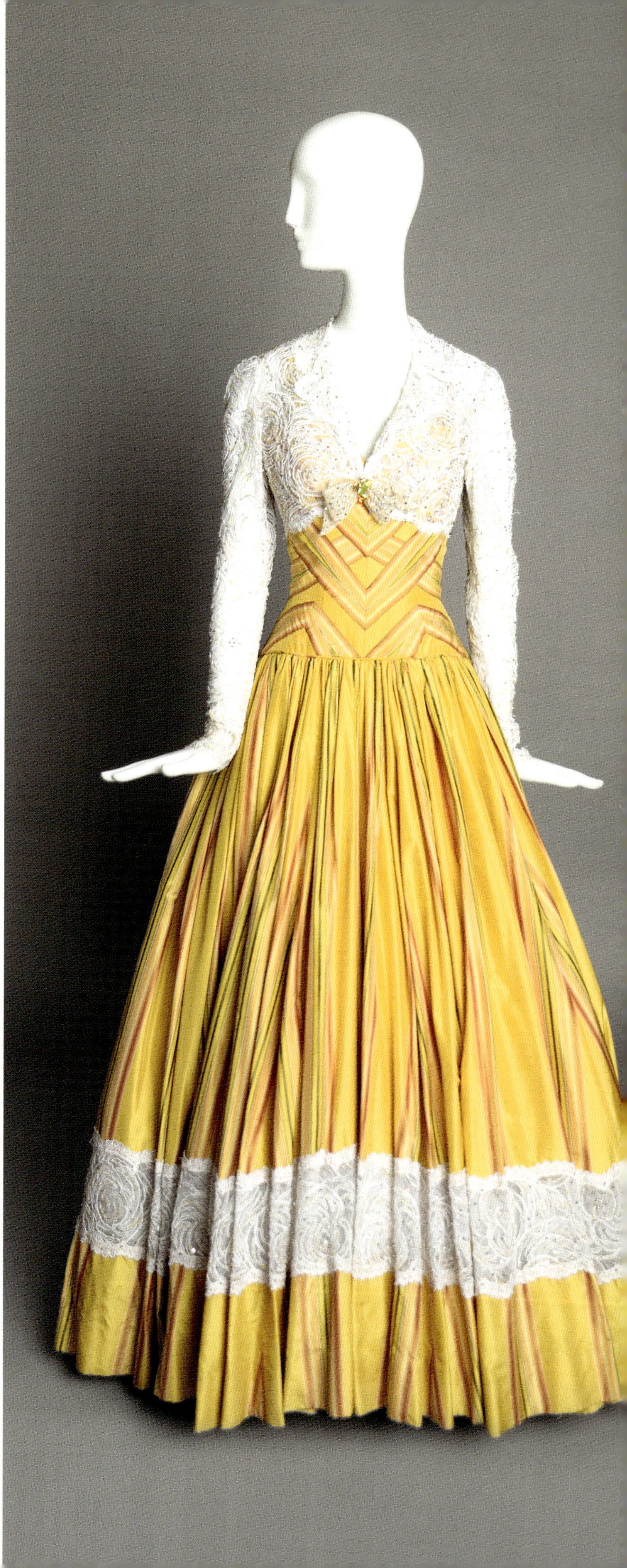

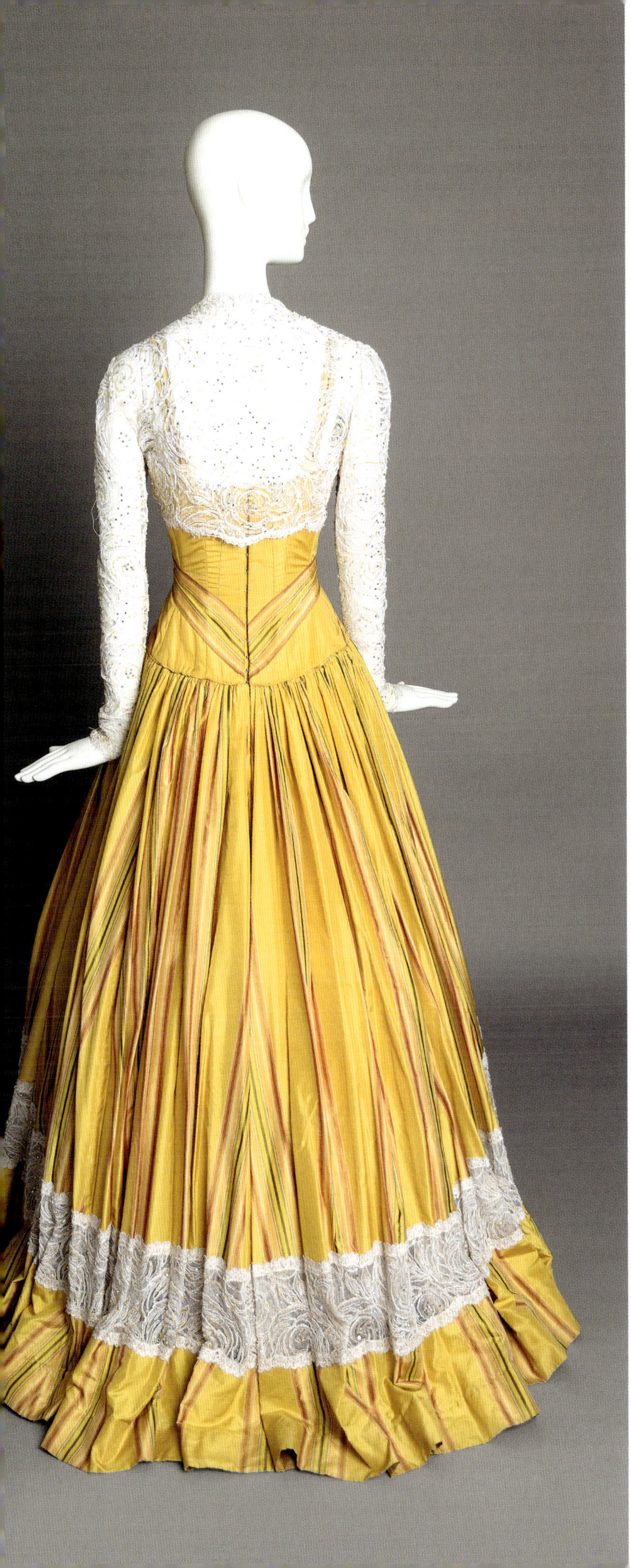

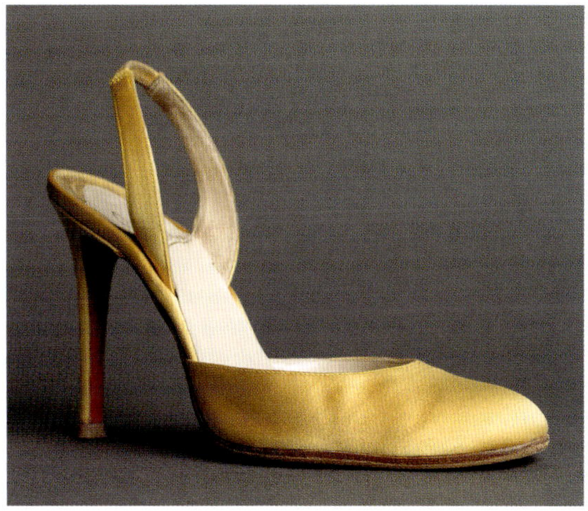

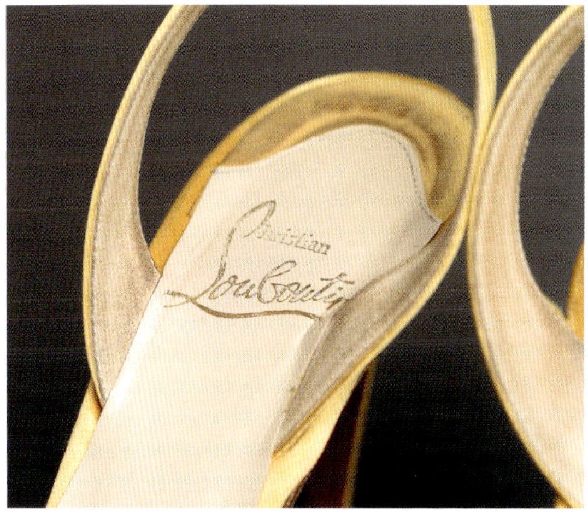

Ann Roth (American)
Claire Wellington
The Stepford Wives, 2004
Christian Louboutin
Silk, leather
GC 2017.301.7 AB

CHARACTER
Jenny Fields

The World According to Garp, 1982

THE DESIGNER ANN ROTH'S LONG WORKING RELATIONSHIP with Glenn Close began with the film adaptation of John Irving's 1978 novel, *The World According to Garp*. Close plays Jenny Fields, a strong-willed nurse who conceives a child via an unconscious soldier under her care during World War II. A single mother, she raises a successful novelist son and, inspired by his writing, she pens her own book, *A Sexual Suspect*, which transforms her into a feminist hero and icon. Using the proceeds from her book, Fields founds a home for abused and traumatized women and uses her influence to advocate for political candidates who share her views.

Fields is a straightforward, caring woman who is utterly committed to her beliefs. Roth's wardrobe for Close is practical and utilitarian, eschewing unnecessary details or accessories. The simple 1940s nursing uniform would have been originally manufactured in a factory or home-sewn. The costume version was designed by Roth and carefully constructed by the skilled hands at Barbara Matera Ltd. Once Fields becomes an activist in the public eye, she wears her nurse's uniform almost exclusively, deliberately telegraphing both her professional authority and her compassion for those in need. While the nurse's uniform once served a functional purpose as she cared for wounded soldiers, by the end of the film it has become an emblem of Fields's commitment to a set of political and social beliefs that drive her every move. The meticulous care taken to design and build the seemingly everyday garment inspired Close to begin collecting the costumes worn by her characters in film, television, and on stage.

DESIGNER
Ann Roth

See p. 88 for biography and Afterword on p. 177.

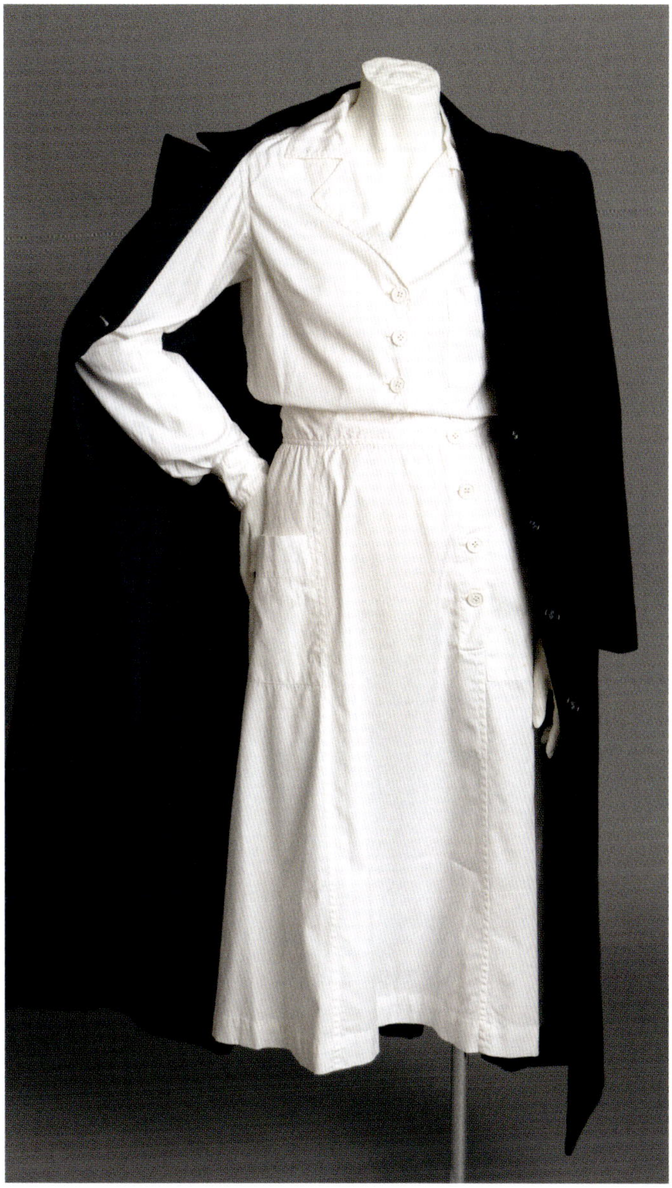

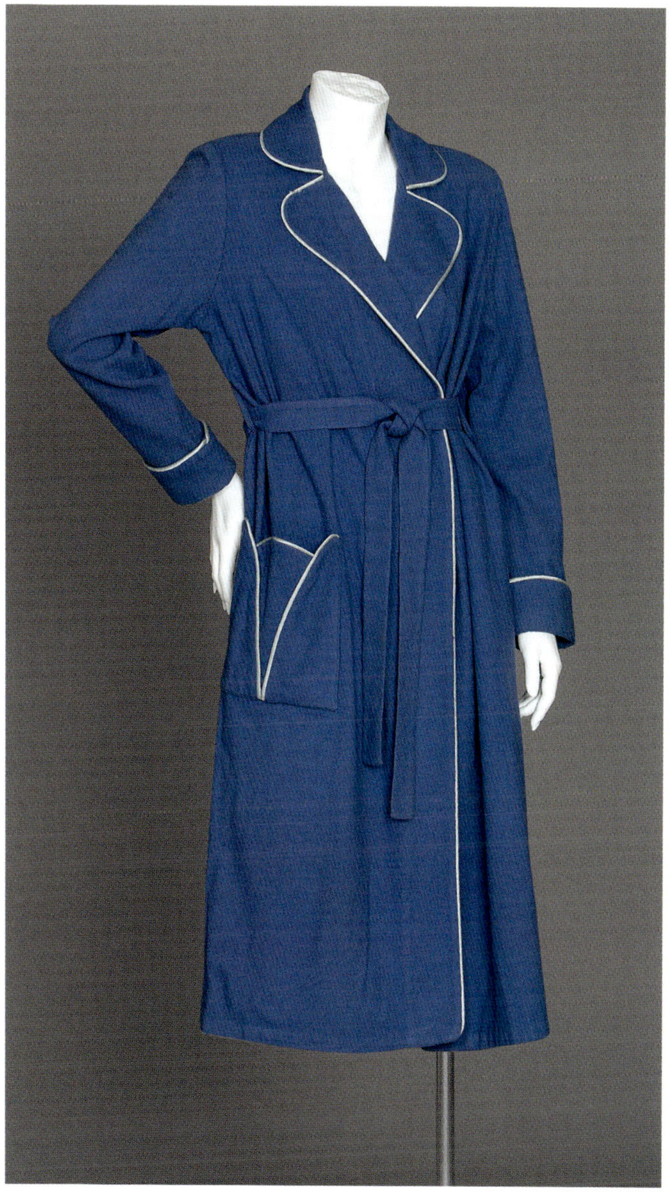

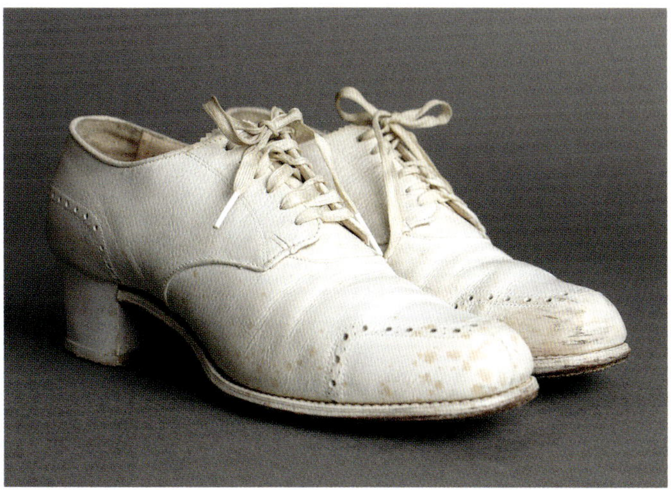

ABOVE LEFT
Ann Roth (American)
Barbara Matera Ltd.
Jenny Fields
The World According to Garp, 1982
Cotton, wool
GC 2017.309.1 B, .310

LEFT
Ann Roth (American)
Jenny Fields
The World According to Garp, 1982
Leather
GC 2017.309.2 AB

ABOVE RIGHT
Ann Roth (American)
Jenny Fields
The World According to Garp, 1982
Wool, silk
GC 2017.307.1 AB

CHARACTER

Albert Nobbs

Albert Nobbs, 2011

BASED ON THE 1927 NOVELLA BY GEORGE MOORE, the film adaptation of *Albert Nobbs* was cowritten and coproduced by Glenn Close. The 2011 film was not her first turn playing the titular character; in 1982, Close starred in an off-Broadway adaptation of the story and her performance was recognized with an Obie Award. Her film portrayal earned an Academy Award nomination for Best Actress in 2012.

A woman born into difficult circumstances, Albert Nobbs begins to live as a man at the age of fourteen after a violent rape and the death of her adoptive mother. This masquerade ensures her economic survival through her employment as a hotel butler and servant in Dublin, where she encounters another man living with the same secret. This new friend, Hubert, inspires Nobbs to seek a wife who could help her realize her dream of opening a tobacco shop with her saved wages. The film is set in nineteenth-century Dublin and Pierre-Yves Gayraud's costumes reflect both Nobbs's socioeconomic status as a butler who could not afford a custom, tailored suit, and her secret, which kept her from being properly fitted for her clothes. Weighted, oversize boots add to the awkwardness of Nobbs's appearance and contribute to the heaviness of the character's gait. In a pivotal scene, Hubert and Nobbs trade their trousers for dresses during a seaside outing. Liberated by the opportunity to wear a skirt after so many years in men's clothing, the usually cautious and guarded Nobbs breaks into a run while Hubert's unease is made visible through her clumsily laced corset and ill-fitting gown.

DESIGNER

Pierre-Yves Gayraud

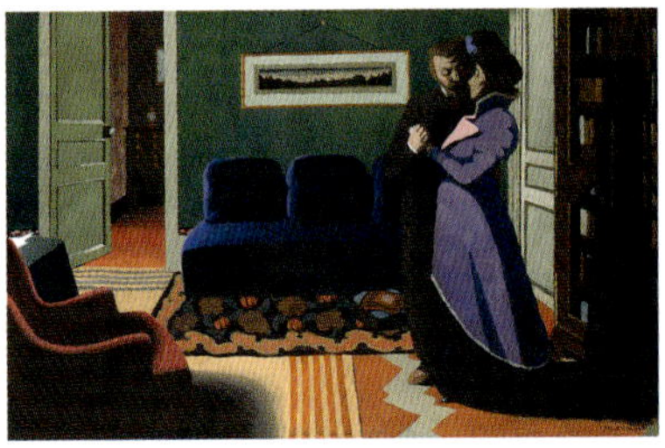

Felix Vallotton (Swiss, 1865–1925), *The Visit*, 1899, Gouache on cardboard, $21\frac{7}{8} \times 34\frac{1}{4}$ in., Kunsthaus Zurich, 1909

Born in Lille, France, the designer Pierre-Yves Gayraud had his first major success with Régis Wargnier's *Indochine* (1992), which won the Academy Award for Best Foreign Language Film in 1993. Set during the 1930s to 1950s, Gayraud created costumes that transported viewers to Vietnam during a particularly tumultuous moment in French colonial history. Together with Gabriella Pescucci, Gayraud received a César Award nomination for his work on the film. In the years following, Gayraud worked on other period films, including *Total Eclipse* (1995) and *Est-Ouest* (1999). Gayraud had his breakthrough into big-budget American films with *The Bourne Identity* (2002), directed by Doug Liman and starring Matt Damon in the titular role of Jason Bourne.

Gayraud first worked with Glenn Close on the costumes for *Albert Nobbs*, directed by Rodrigo García. In his research for the film, Gayraud found inspiration in early twentieth-century films made by the Mitchell & Kenyon film company. Sagar Mitchell and James Kenyon filmed street scenes, crowds, and parades in England, Ireland, and Scotland at the turn of the century, providing rich, active source material for the designer. In a 2012 interview, Gayraud cited French and Irish paintings from the late nineteenth and early twentieth centuries as another source of inspiration: "I particularly love Félix Valloton, who had such an incredible sense to sketch the silhouettes with strong colors, which was unusual for this time."[4] In recent years, Gayraud has worked on both French and American films, including *Cloud Atlas* (2012) and *L'Empereur de Paris* (2018). He is a three-time César Award nominee, two-time Costume Designers Guild Award nominee, and in 2018, his work on the television series *Babylon Berlin* (2017 to present) earned him the Deutschen Fernsehpreis for Best Costume Design.

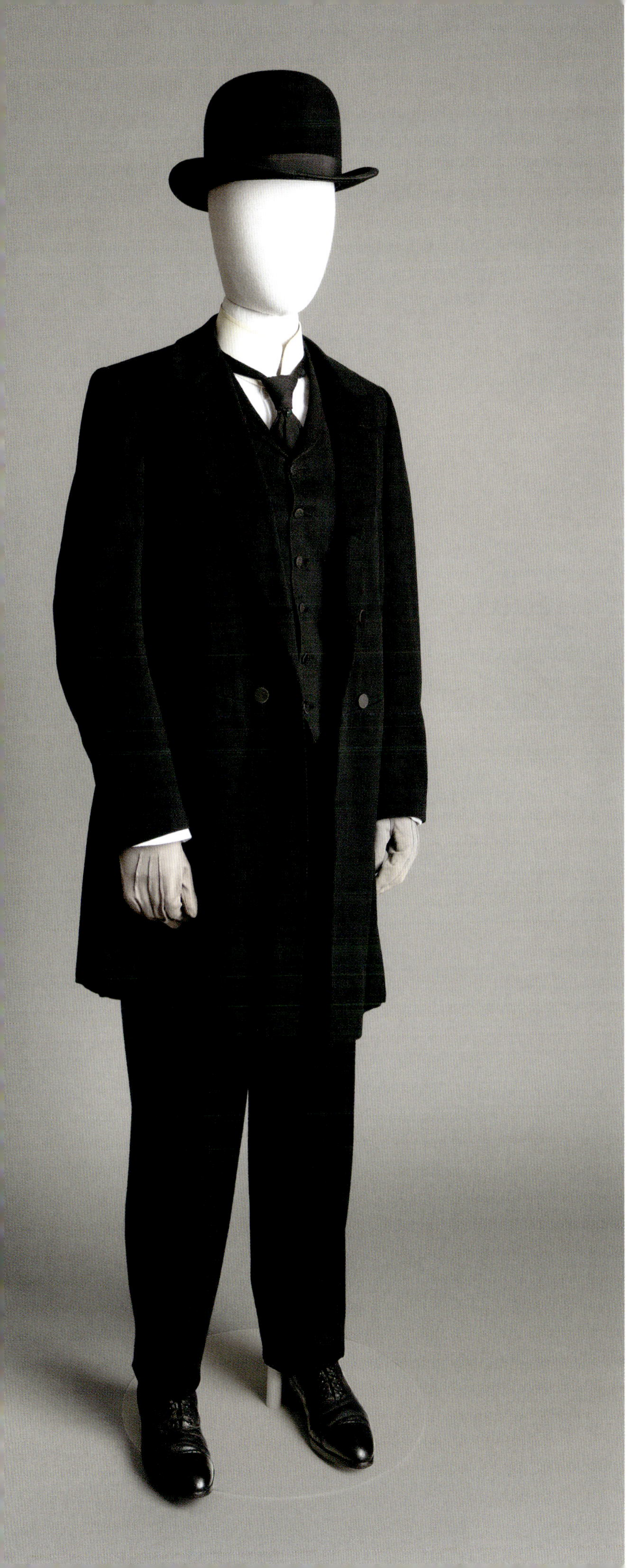

Pierre-Yves Gayraud (French)
Angels Costumes
Albert Nobbs
Albert Nobbs, 2011
Wool, cotton, silk, leather
GC 2017.31.1,.3–.8, .10

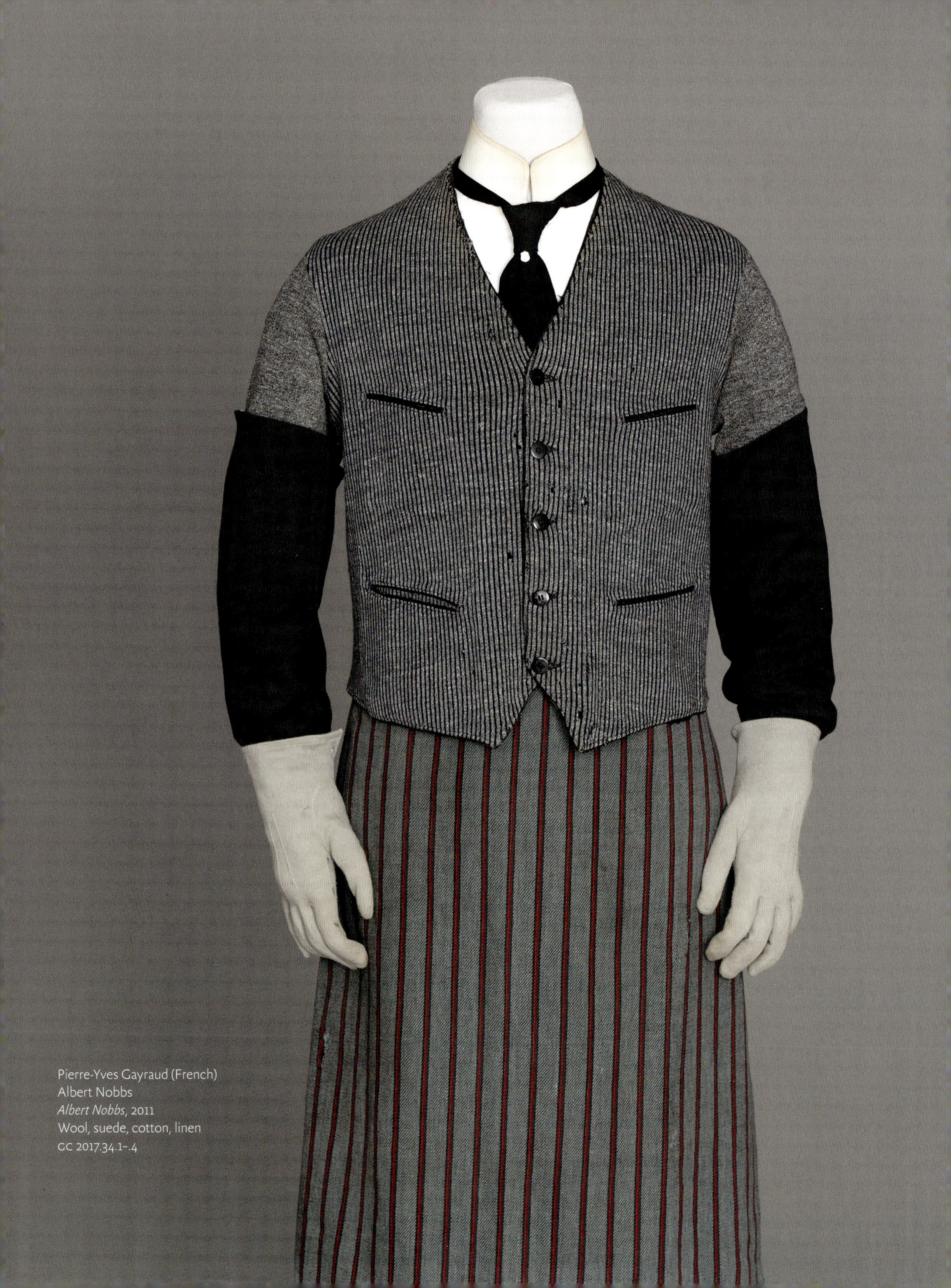

Pierre-Yves Gayraud (French)
Albert Nobbs
Albert Nobbs, 2011
Wool, suede, cotton, linen
GC 2017.34.1–.4

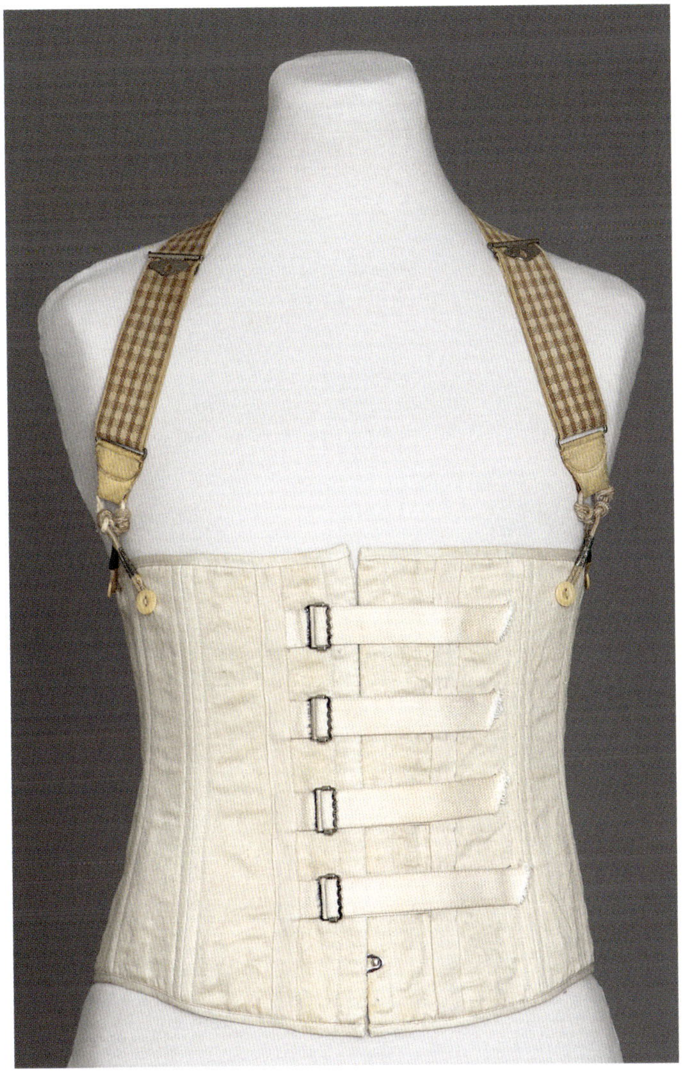

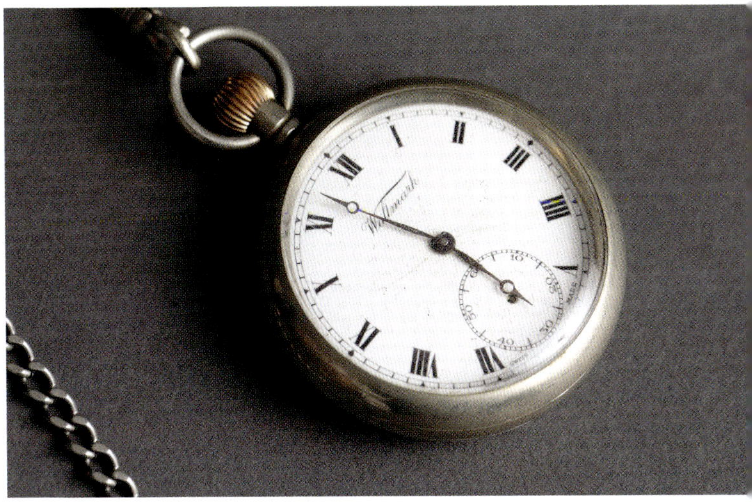

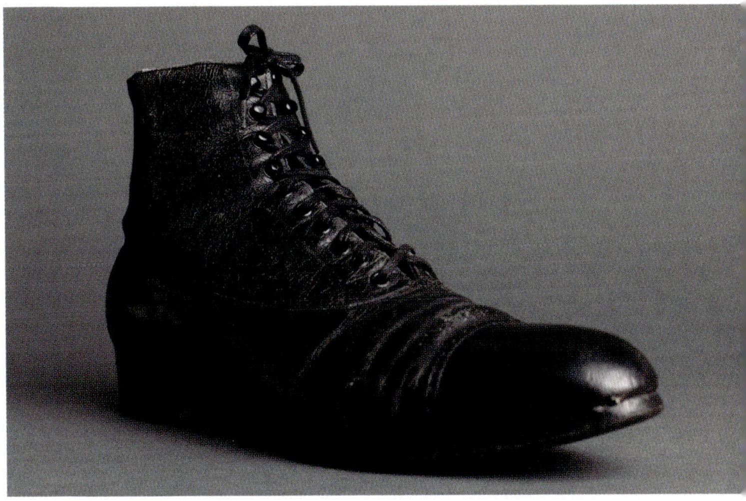

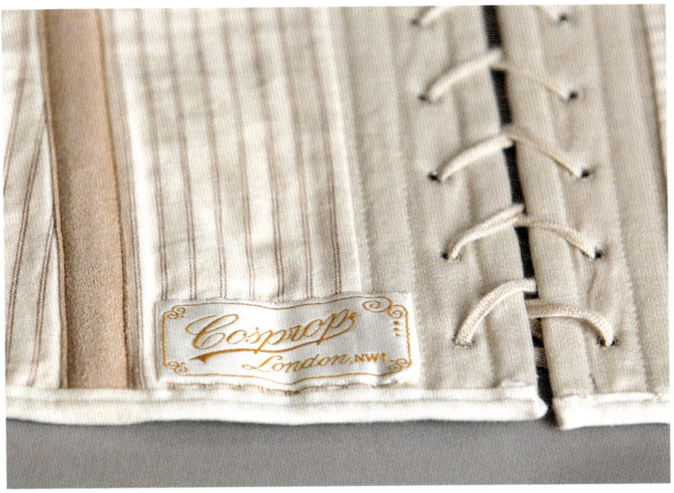

LEFT
Pierre-Yves Gayraud (French)
Cosprop
Albert Nobbs
Albert Nobbs, 2011
Cotton, metal, leather
GC 2017.32.1

TOP
Pierre-Yves Gayraud (French)
Albert Nobbs
Albert Nobbs, 2011
Waltmark
Metal, crystal
GC 2017.31.9

ABOVE
Pierre-Yves Gayraud (French)
Albert Nobbs
Albert Nobbs, 2011
Saxone
Leather, metal, cotton
GC 2017.31.10 AB

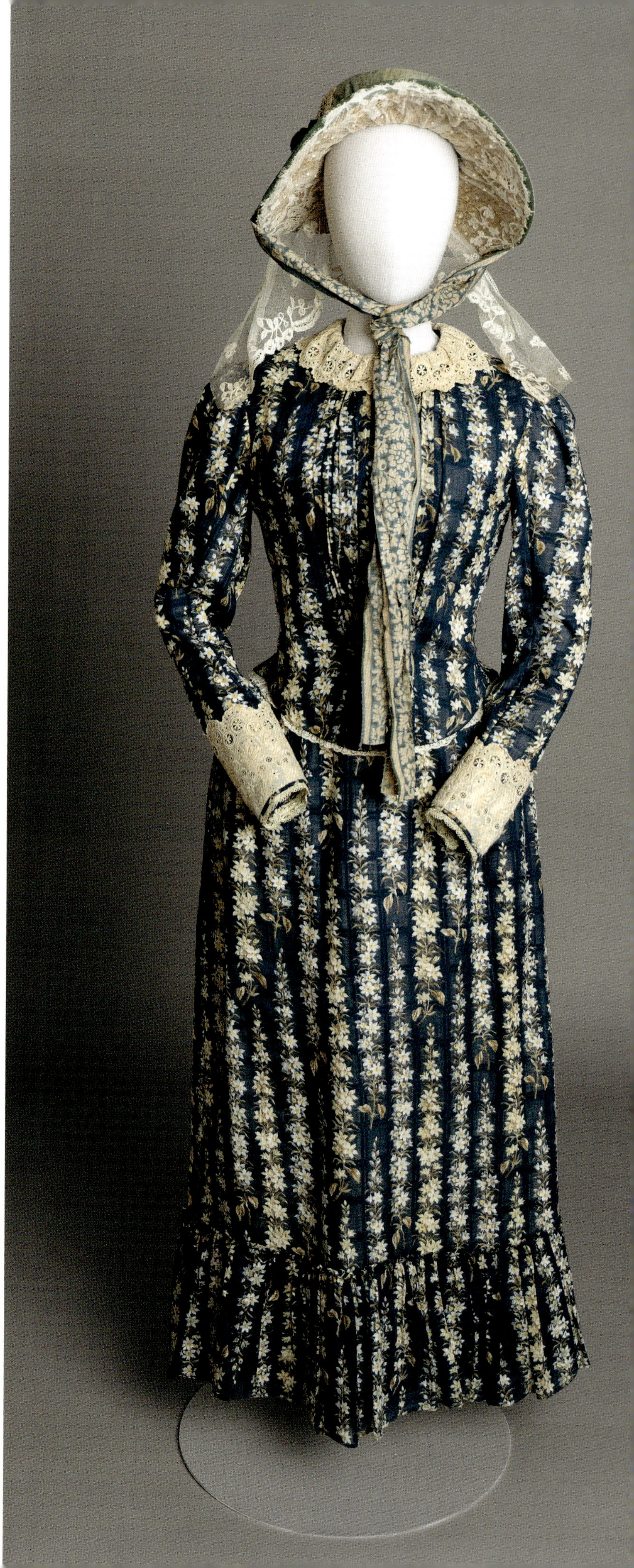

Pierre-Yves Gayraud (French)
Albert Nobbs
Albert Nobbs, 2011
Cotton, linen
GC 2017.36.1–.2

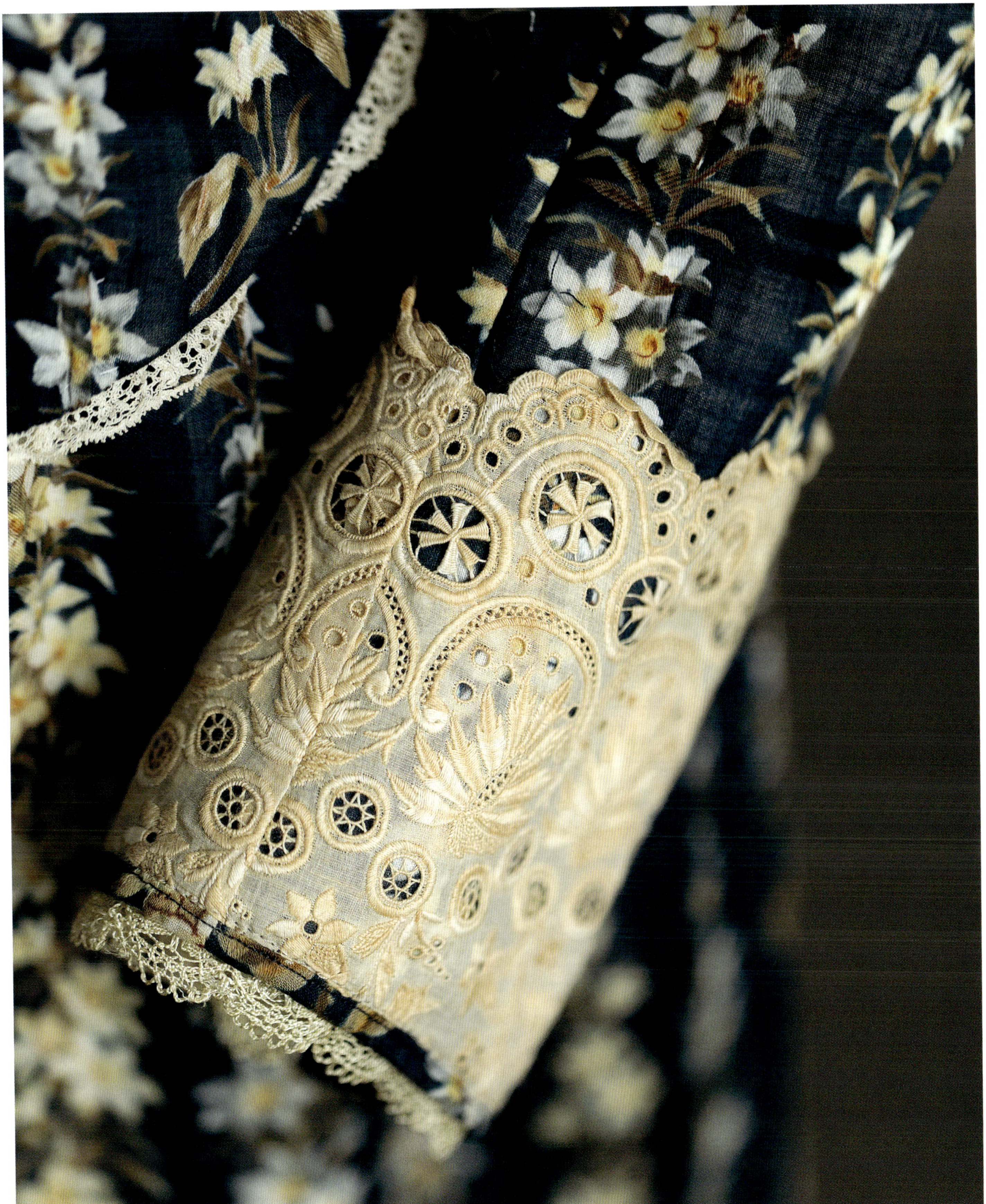

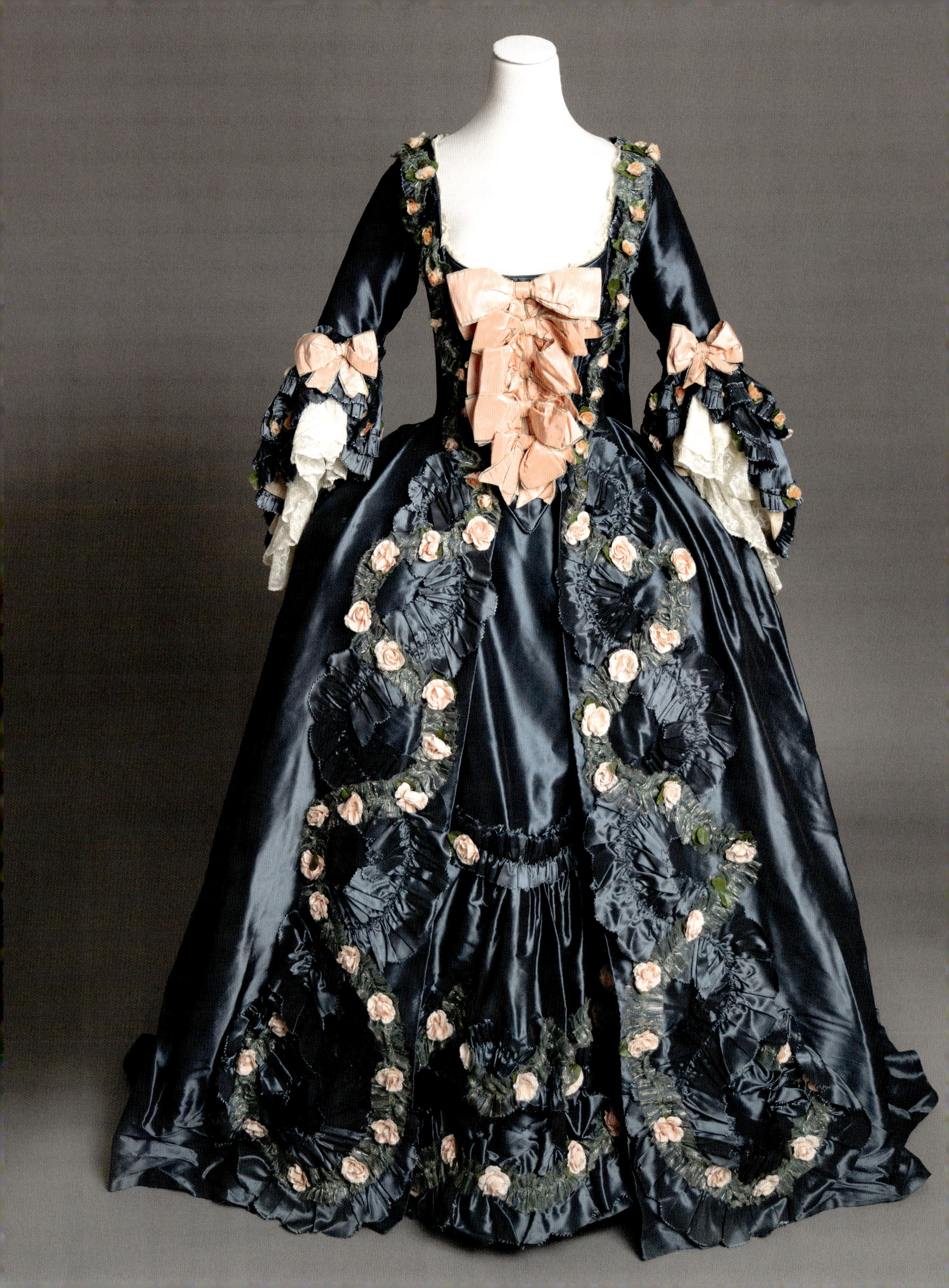

Bringing History to Life

There is no category in film that is more evocative of visual splendor than that of costume drama. The term is used to describe a production set in an era perceived to be more glamorous or beautiful than one's own, wherein the characters' period clothing is a feast for the eyes. These compelling films are eagerly awaited by audiences, who revel in the sumptuous silhouettes, colors, and textures. Costume designers are tasked with making a historical character's appearance visually pleasing, but not distracting, and historically appropriate, but still relatable to contemporary audiences.

For costume designers, certain attributes of dress such as the length and width of the hem, waist placement, and sleeve shape are crucial for historical correctness, as well as the support of proper undergarments and fabrics of the appropriate weight.[5] These efforts by costume designers become part of our modern, collective understanding of history. Costume designers often collect extant historical pieces to use as research and references for their work. One of the most important collections of fashion and dress in the world, the Costume Institute at the Metropolitan Museum of Art, has its origins in a group of historic fashion pieces gathered for theatrical costuming purposes in the early 1900s.

Due to the cost and labor involved in producing period costumes, these garments are often sold for reuse or returned to the costume shop or studio, where they are dismantled, altered, and remodeled for future productions. It is evidence of Glenn Close's passion for the art of costuming that her collection found a home in the Sage Collection at Indiana University.

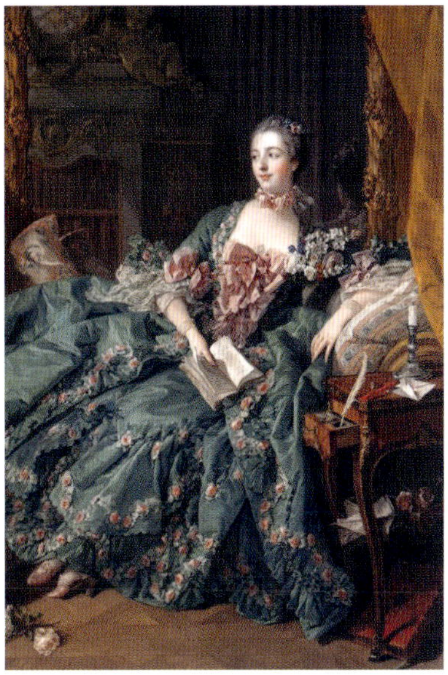

François Boucher (French, 1703–1770)
Madame de Pompadour, 1756
Oil on canvas, 201 × 157 cm
Alte Pinakothek, Munich
permanent loan from HypoVereinsbank, Member of UniCredit—acquired in 1971 by the Bayerische Hypotheken- und Wechsel-Bank

OPPOSITE
James Acheson (English)
Annie Hadley
Marquise de Merteuil
Dangerous Liaisons, 1988
Silk, metallic thread, cotton
GC 2017.50.1, .3

CHARACTER

Marquise de Merteuil

Dangerous Liaisons, 1988

BASED ON THE EIGHTEENTH-CENTURY EPISTOLARY NOVEL by Pierre Choderlos de Laclos and adapted first for the stage and later for film by Christopher Hampton, *Dangerous Liaisons* is a story of sex, power, and deception set in the final decade of the French ancien régime. Two former lovers—the Marquise de Merteuil, played by Glenn Close, and Vicomte de Valmont, played by John Malkovich—conspire to have Valmont seduce the fiancée of a fellow aristocrat who has left the Marquise. Their mutual devotion to manipulation and seduction as a means of wielding power binds the Marquise and Valmont, even as their plot unravels and their betrayals multiply.

Filmed on location in Île-de-France and in eighteenth-century buildings across Val-de-Marne, Essonne, and Versailles, the authenticity of the film's setting is matched by James Acheson's attention to historically correct silhouettes, fabrics, and decorations that represented the height of French court fashion in the second half of the century. Each ensemble was accompanied by period shoes, hats, makeup, hair, and jewelry, and fitted over panniers and undergarments that were appropriate for the historical moment. Acheson's use of eighteenth-century French paintings as source material for the film's costumes is evident in the Marquise's blue court dress with pink roses, a design reminiscent of the dress worn by Madame de Pompadour in François Boucher's 1756 portrait.

DESIGNER

James Acheson

Born in Leicester, England, James Acheson trained at the Wimbledon School of Art before launching his career as a costume and set designer for television, theater, opera, ballet, and film. He got his start with BBC Television, designing the costumes for thirty-six episodes of *Doctor Who* from 1972 to 1976. He established the costume for the fourth incarnation of the Doctor, including the character's signature long scarf. Acheson also played a crucial role in developing the monsters that appeared on the show during that time, using materials such as latex rubber, molded plastic, and fiberglass to craft the creatures.

Acheson's film credits are varied and include ambitious period films, such as *Wuthering Heights* (1992) and *The Man in the Iron Mask* (1998), as well as superhero films, such as *Spider-Man* (2002) and its sequels *Spider-Man 2* (2004) and *Spider-Man 3* (2007). He first collaborated with Glenn Close on *Dangerous Liaisons* (1988), crafting the intricate eighteenth-century French court costumes worn by the actress, who was nominated for an Academy Award for her portrayal of the Marquise de Merteuil. Acheson's work has been recognized with three Academy Awards for Best Costume Design for *The Last Emperor* (1987), *Dangerous Liaisons*, and *Restoration* (1995), as well as a BAFTA Award for Best Costume Design for *The Last Emperor* and the 2004 Costume Designers Guild Award for Career Achievement in Film. Throughout his career, he has designed costumes for the stage, including Jonathan Kent's production of *Hamlet* in London (1994) and on Broadway (1995), and Sir Jonathan Miller's *The Marriage of Figaro* at the Metropolitan Opera (1998). He now lives in Wellington, New Zealand, and in 2017, he designed both the sets and the costumes for *Romeo and Juliet*, choreographed by Francesco Ventriglia, at the Royal New Zealand Ballet.

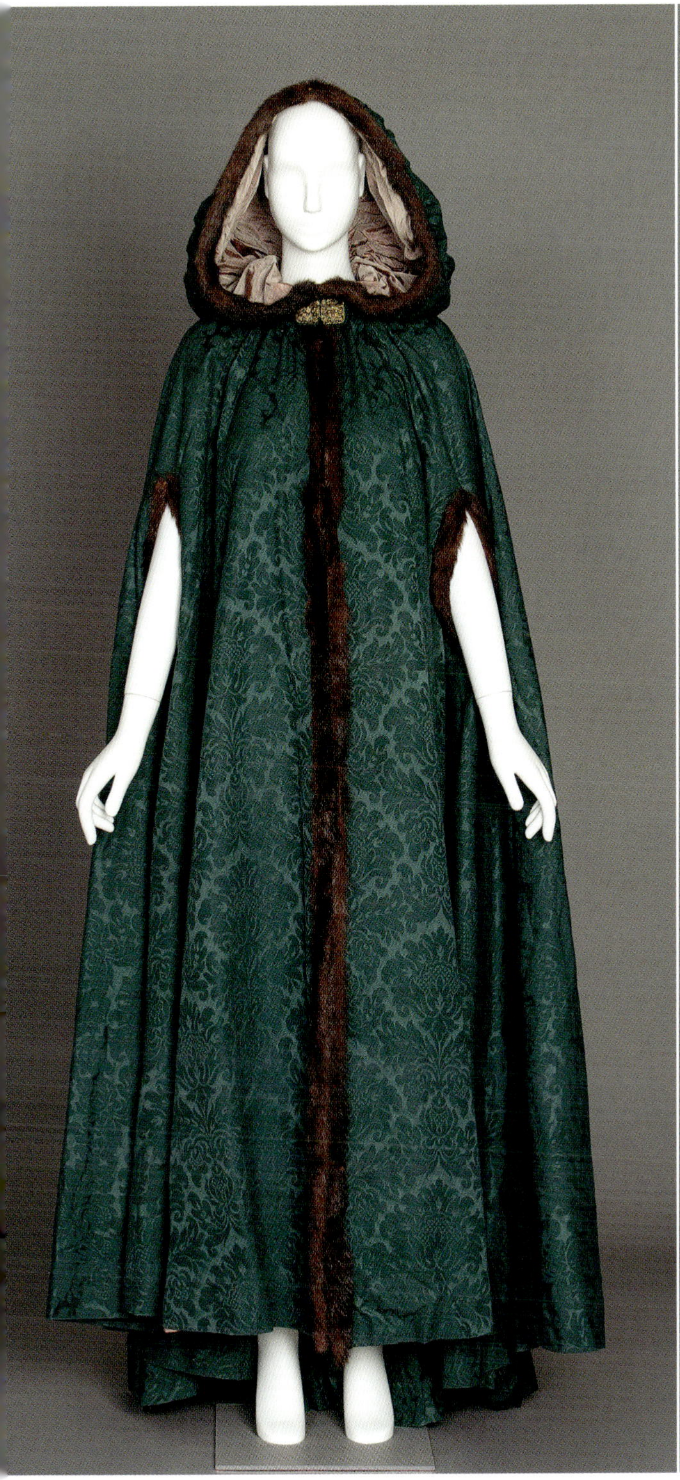

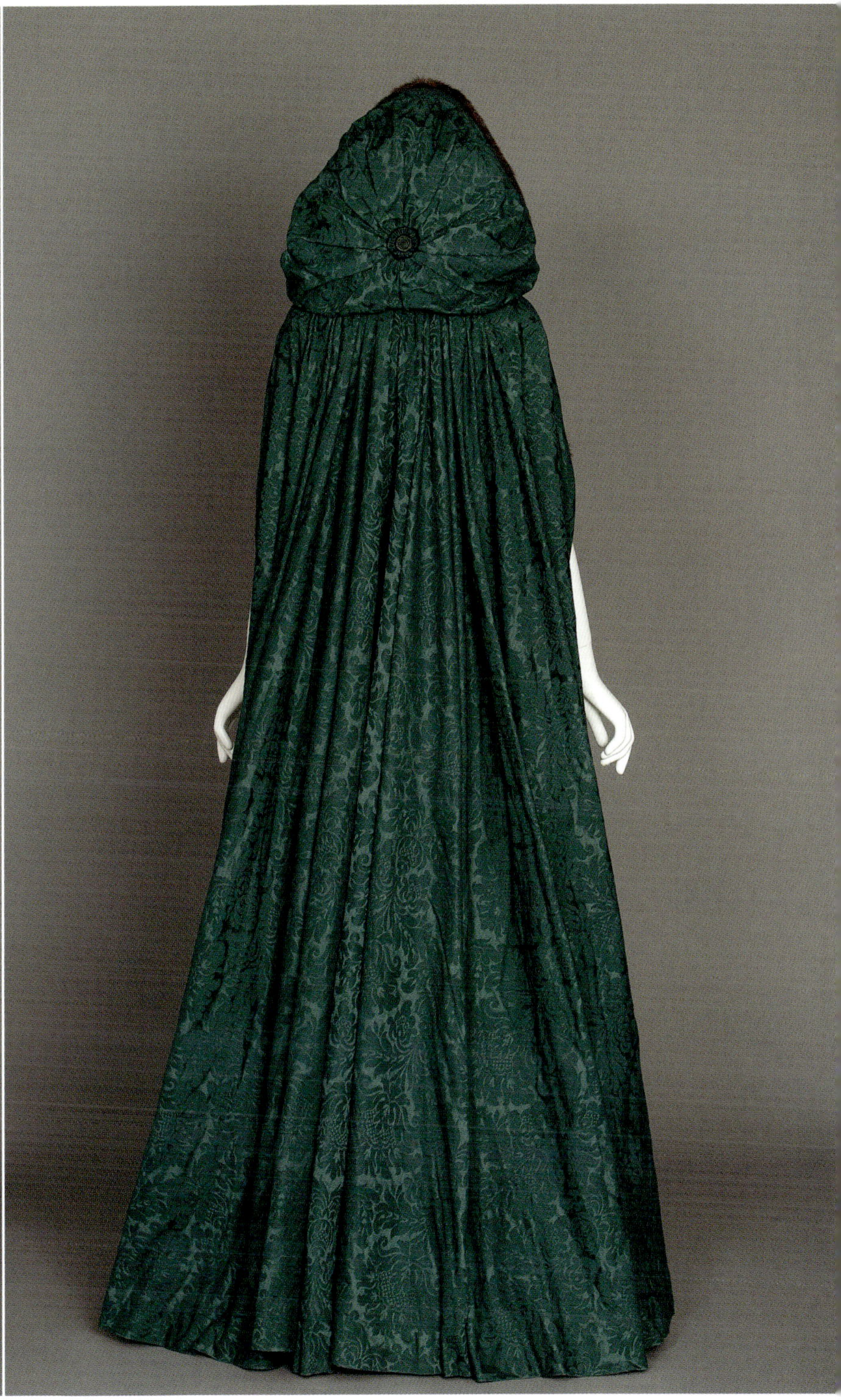

James Acheson (English)
Annie Hadley
Marquise de Merteuil
Dangerous Liaisons, 1988
Silk, mink fur
GC 2017.53.1
(Note: This cape was not seen in the film.)

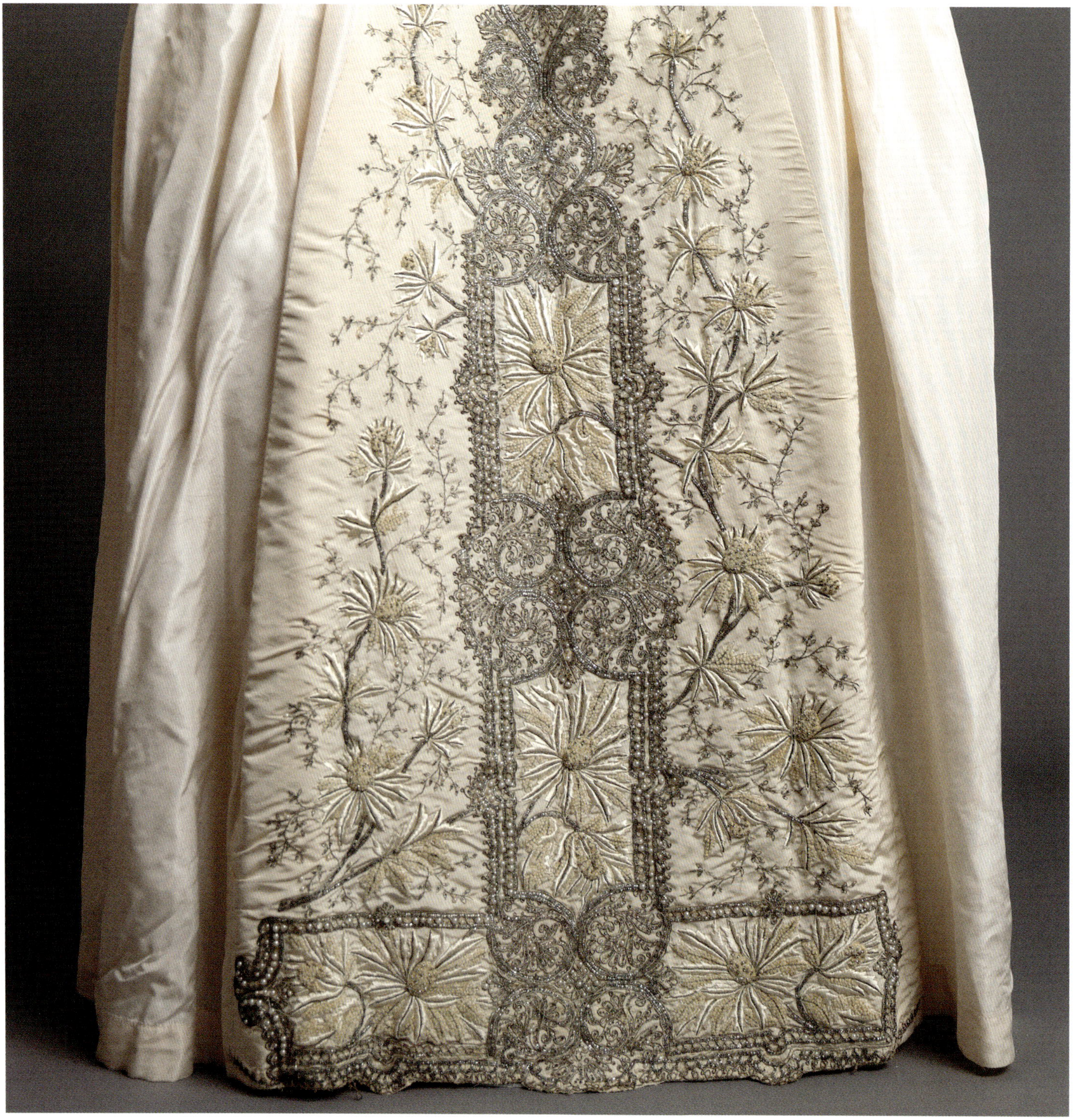

James Acheson (English)
Annie Hadley
Marquise de Merteuil
Dangerous Liaisons, 1988
Silk, metallic thread, glass beads,
faux pearls
GC 2017.51.1 AB

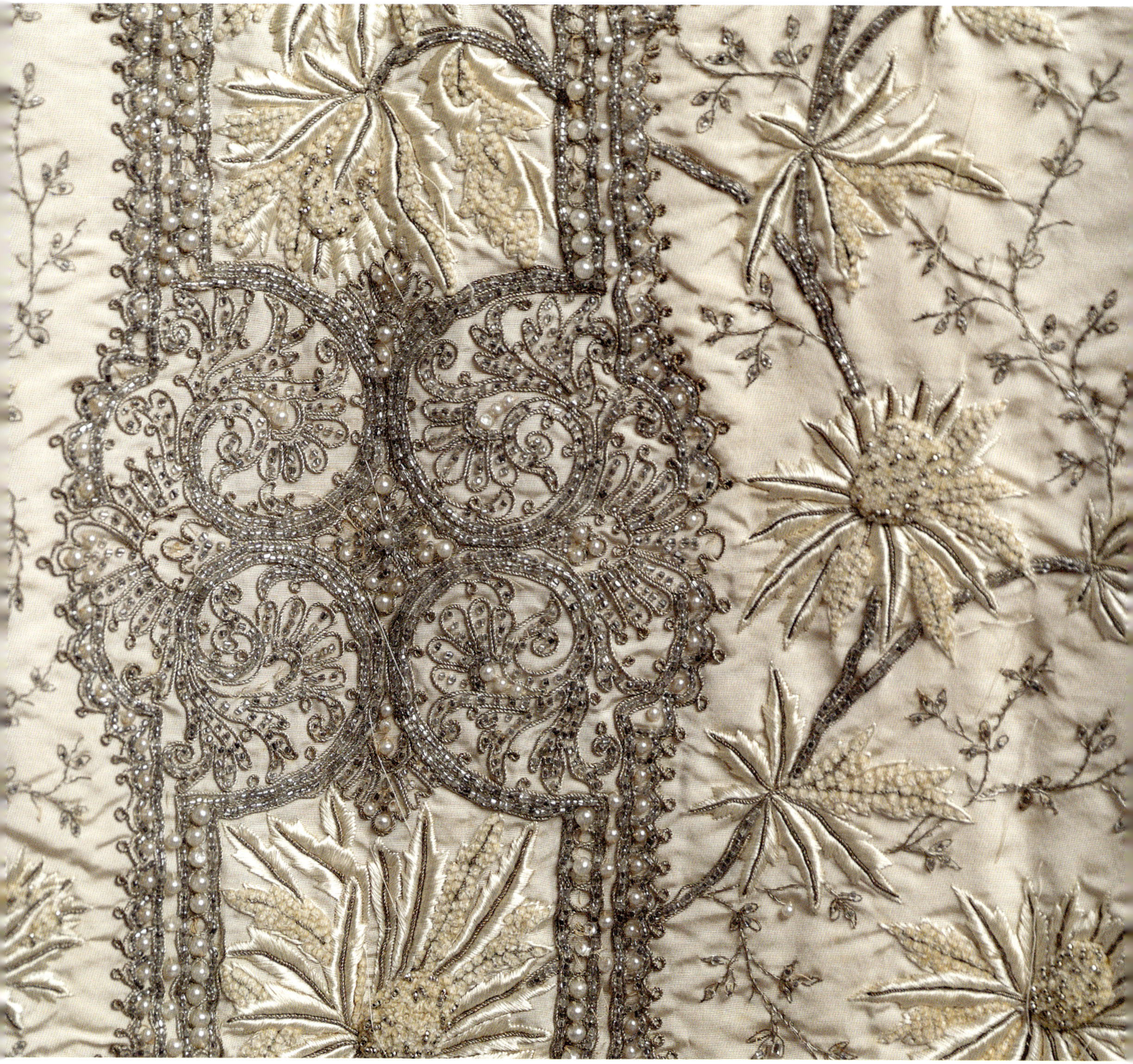

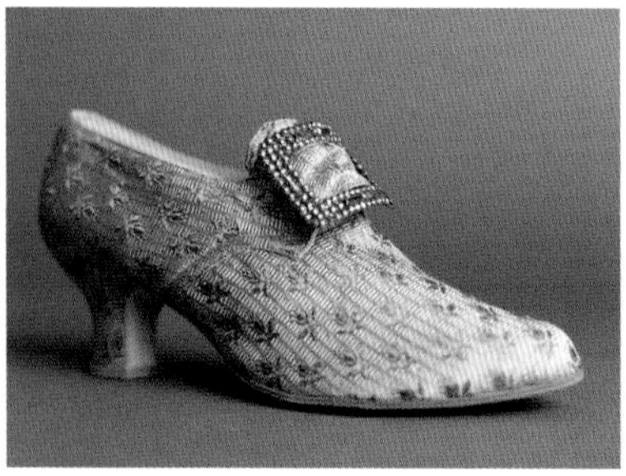

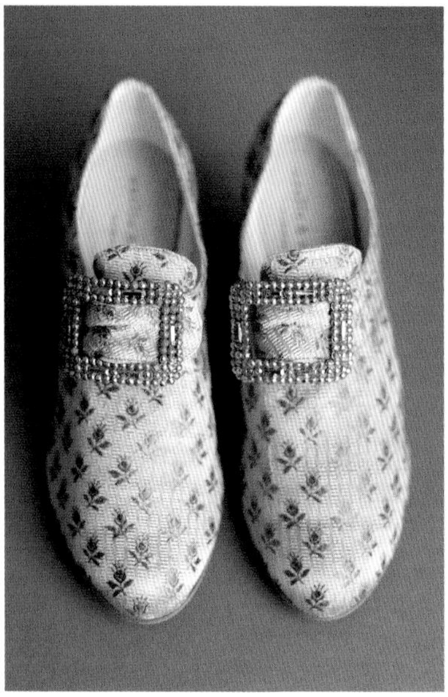

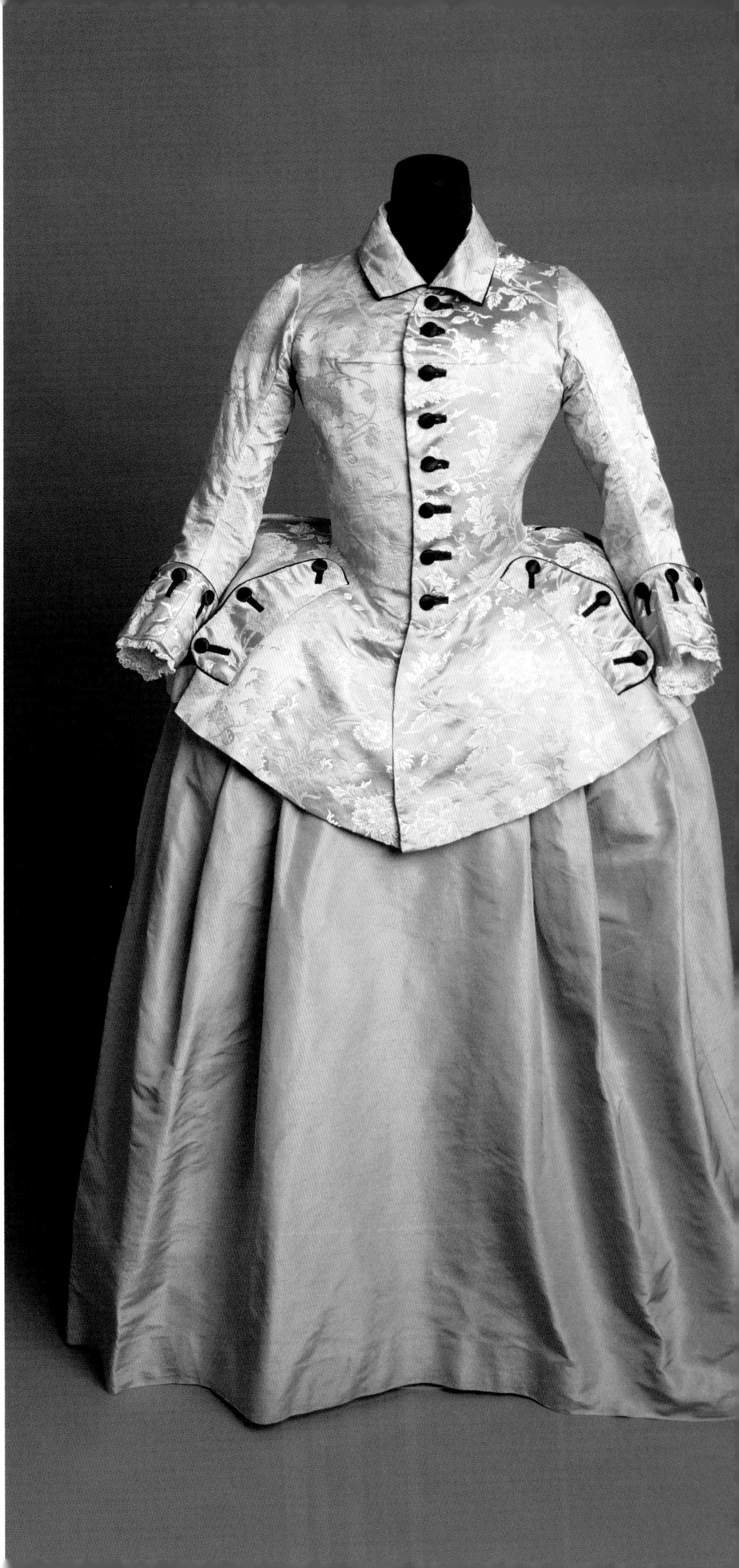

ABOVE
James Acheson (English)
Anello and Davide
Marquise de Merteuil
Dangerous Liaisons, 1988
Leather, silk, metal,
cut steel beads
GC 2017.52.5 AB

RIGHT
James Acheson (English)
Annie Hadley
Marquise de Merteuil
Dangerous Liaisons, 1988
Silk, cotton
GC 2017.52.1 AB

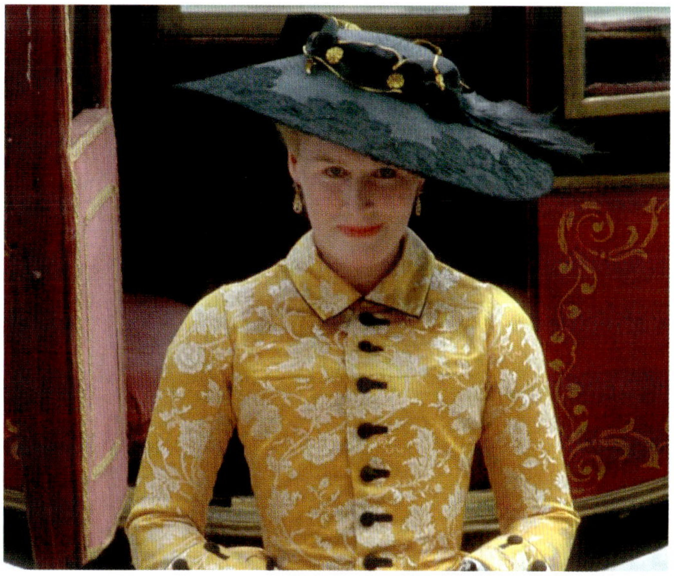

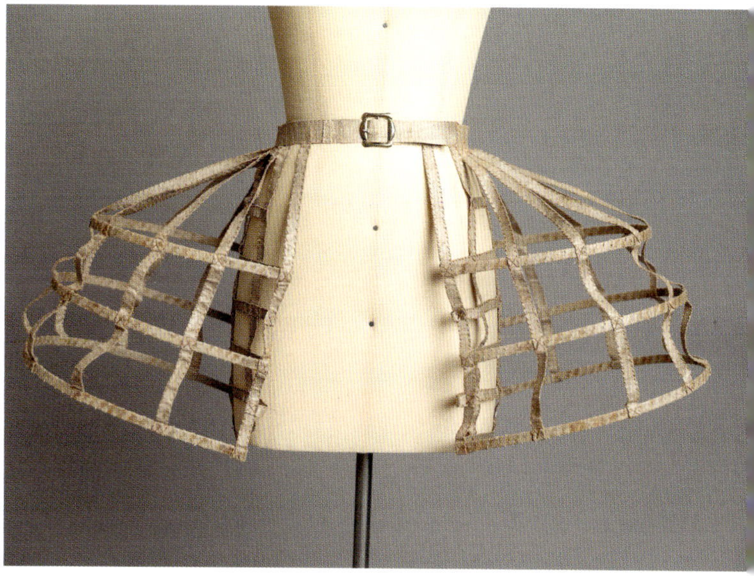

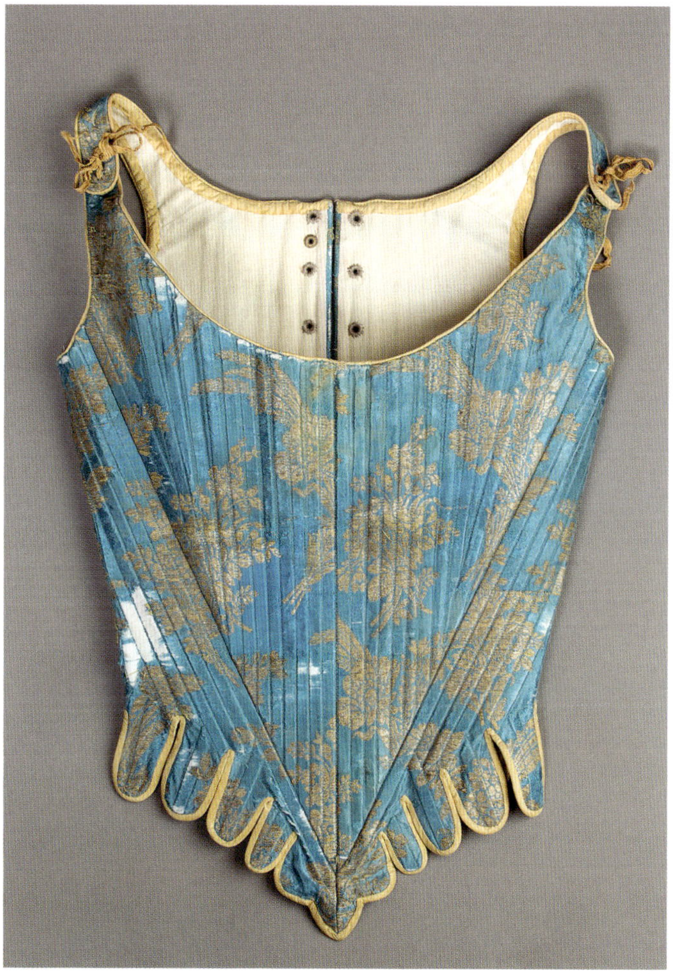

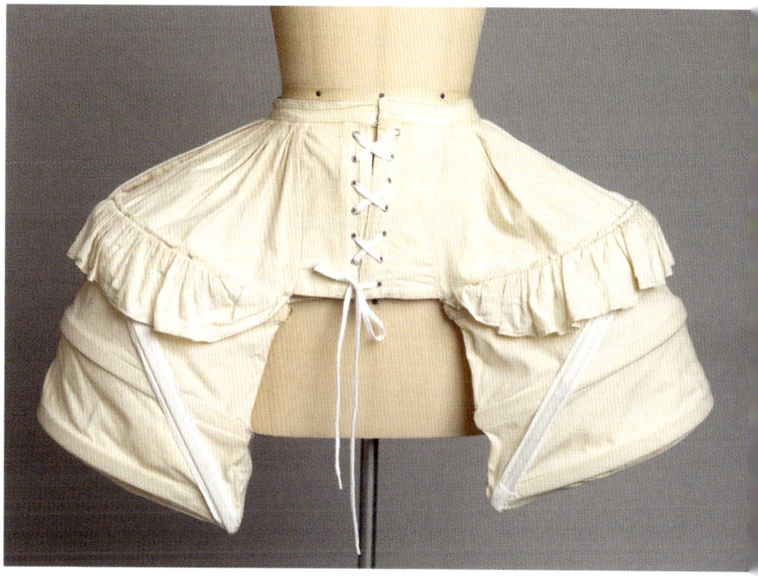

TOP LEFT
Glenn Close in *Dangerous Liaisons*, 1988

LEFT
James Acheson (English)
Annie Hadley
Marquise de Merteuil
Dangerous Liaisons, 1988
Silk, metallic thread
GC 2017.53.2

TOP RIGHT
James Acheson (English)
Annie Hadley
Marquise de Merteuil
Dangerous Liaisons, 1988
Linen, steel
GC 2017.52.3

ABOVE
James Acheson (English)
Annie Hadley
Marquise de Merteuil
Dangerous Liaisons, 1988
Linen, polyester, cotton
GC 2017.52.2

CHARACTER

Eleanor of Aquitaine

The Lion in Winter, 2003

IN THE 2003 MADE-FOR-TELEVISION MOVIE *THE LION IN WINTER*, Glenn Close and Patrick Stewart take on the roles played by Katharine Hepburn and Peter O'Toole in the 1968 film adaptation of a 1966 Broadway play of the same name. Set in 1183 at Chinon, the castle of Henry II of England in present-day France, the film follows the gamesmanship among Henry II (Stewart); Eleanor of Aquitaine (Close); their three surviving sons, Richard, Geoffrey, and John; and Phillip II, King of France. Eleanor has been imprisoned since 1173 for supporting a revolt against Henry II, but she is brought to Chinon following the death of Henry, their eldest son. Henry II must choose a new heir to the throne and while he favors their youngest son, John, Eleanor instead favors Richard, now their eldest.

In the film's opening scene, Eleanor appears in armor and on horseback, having just failed to overthrow her husband. Cutting a magnificent figure, with the horsehair tassel at the peak of her helmet flying defiantly in the wind, the strong-willed noblewoman accepts defeat and consoles her two eldest sons, with whom she had formed an alliance. This prologue—which was not part of the original film—offers the viewer a glimpse of the formidable spirit of this legendary queen before her lengthy imprisonment. Close's portrayal of Eleanor earned her a Golden Globe Award for Best Performance by an Actress in a Miniseries or Motion Picture for Television and Consolata Boyle's work on the project was recognized with an Emmy Award for Outstanding Costumes.

DESIGNER

Consolata Boyle

Consolata Boyle was born in Dublin, graduating from University College Dublin with degrees in archaeology and history before training in costume design at the Abbey, Ireland's national theater. She also completed a postgraduate degree in textiles at the West Surrey College of Art and Design, now part of the University for the Creative Arts. Her early theater credits include costume and set design for the world premiere of Brian Friel's *Translations* (1980) and costume design for Joe Dowling's acclaimed production of *Juno and the Paycock* (1986), which transferred to Broadway.

Boyle began her career in film with *The Outcasts* (1982) and is well-known for her collaborations with the director Stephen Frears, receiving Academy Award nominations for Best Costume Design for her work on *The Queen* (2006), *Florence Foster Jenkins* (2016), and *Victoria & Abdul* (2017). She has been nominated for numerous other awards throughout her career, including two BAFTA nominations for Best Costume Design. Her work has been recognized by seven Irish Film and Television Awards since 2000. A four-time Costume Designers Guild Award nominee, Boyle won in 2007 for her work on *The Queen*. Boyle and Glenn Close first worked together on Frears's film *Mary Reilly* (1996).

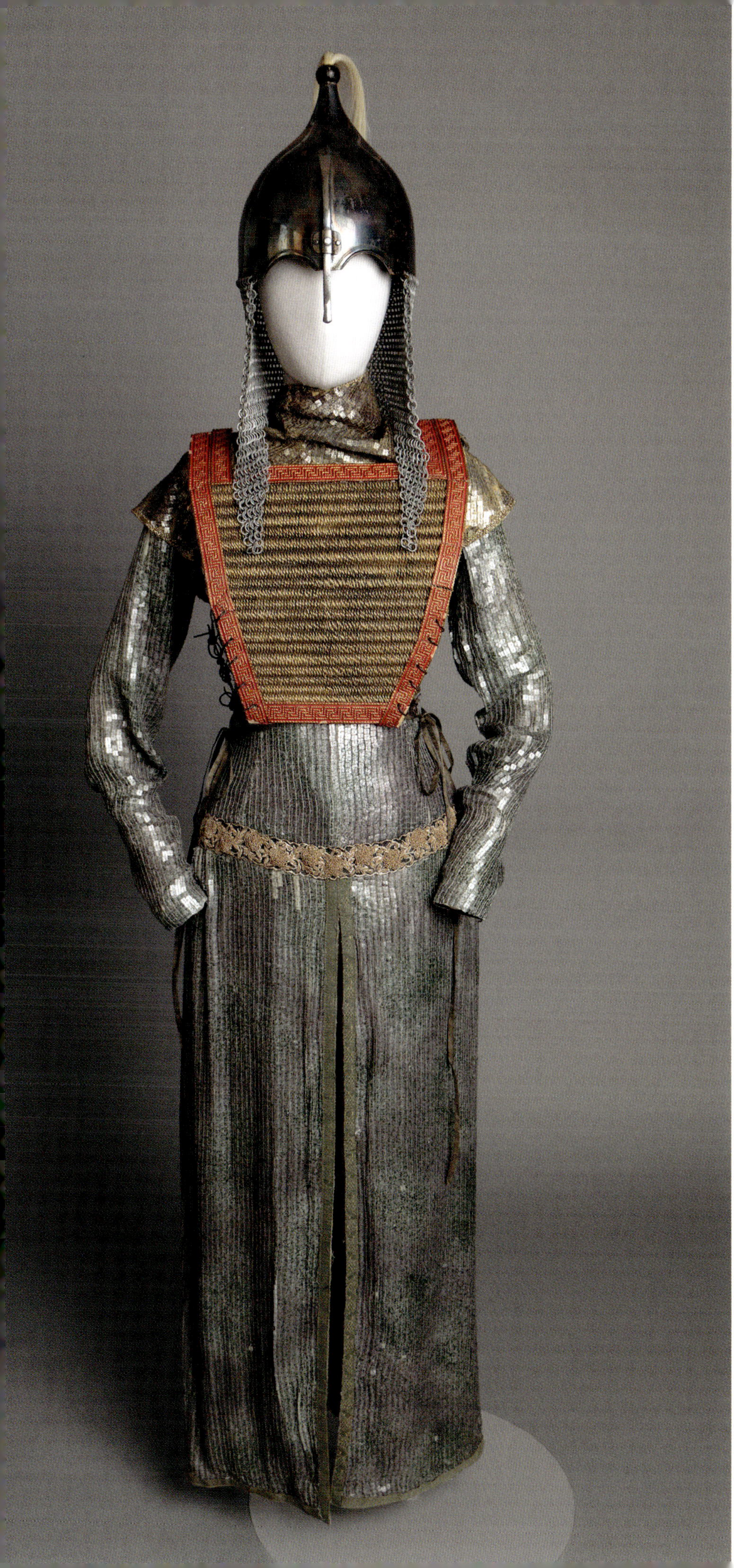

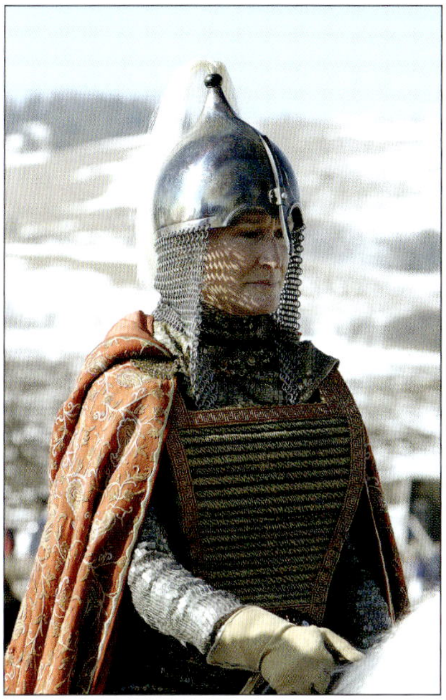

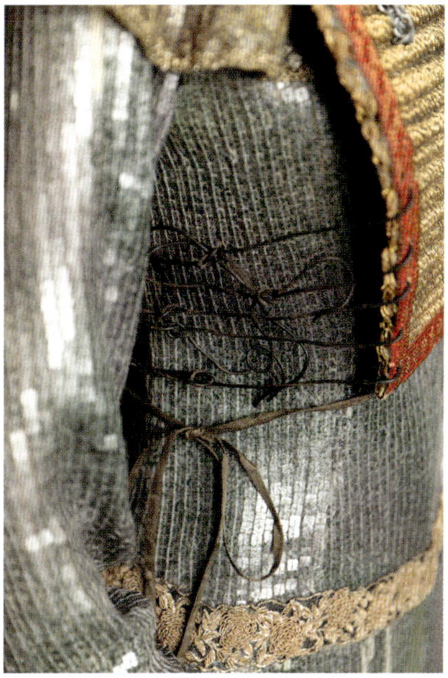

TOP
Glenn Close as Eleanor of Aquitaine in
The Lion in Winter, 2003

LEFT
Consolata Boyle (Irish)
Angels Costumes
Eleanor of Aquitaine
The Lion in Winter, 2003
Silk, plastic sequins, bamboo,
metallic yarn, leather, cotton,
metal, steel, horsehair
GC 2017.287.1–.5

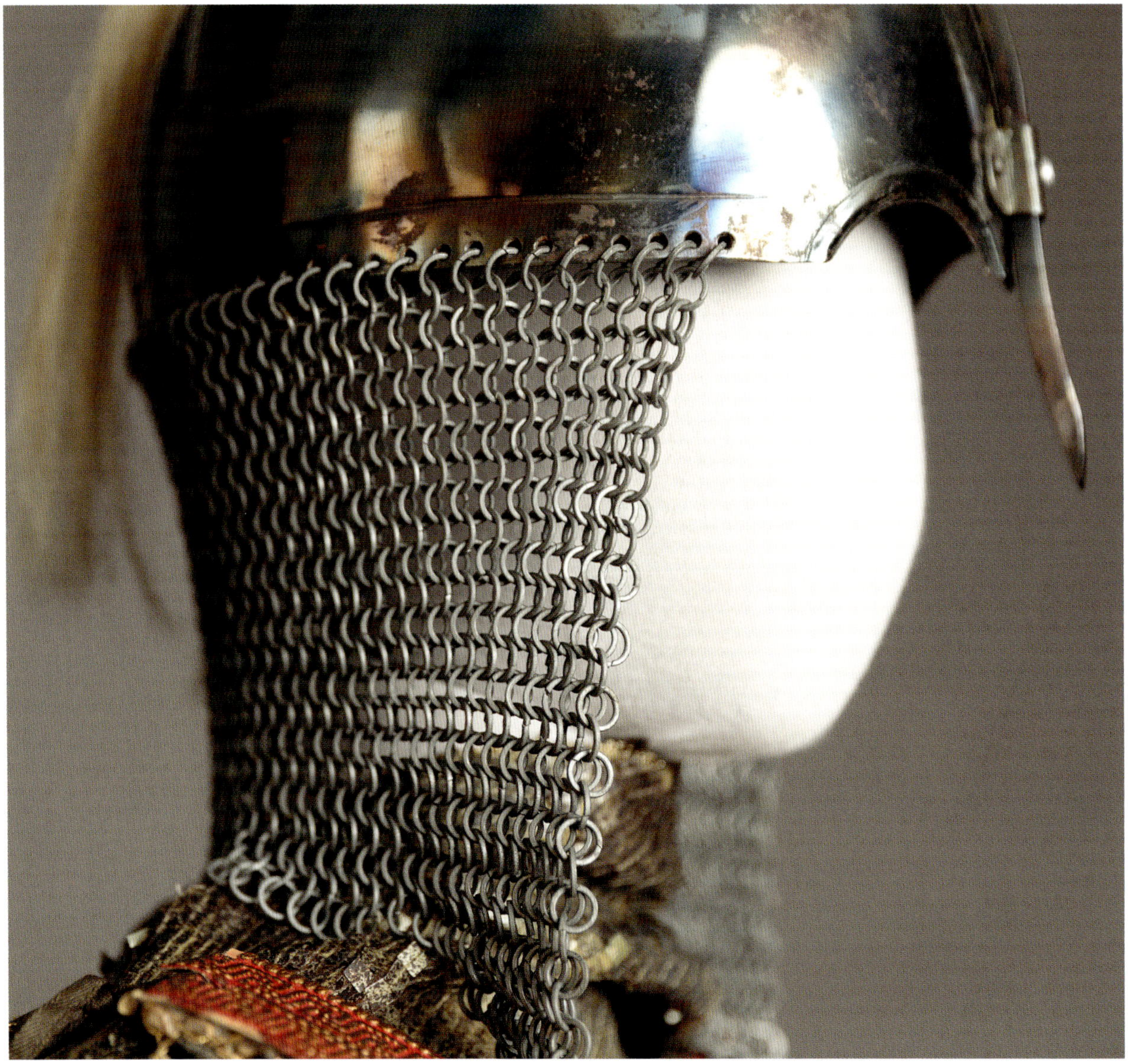

Consolata Boyle (Irish)
Angels Costumes
Eleanor of Aquitaine
The Lion in Winter, 2003
Silk, plastic sequins, bamboo, metallic yarn, leather, cotton, metal, steel, horsehair
GC 2017.287.1-.5

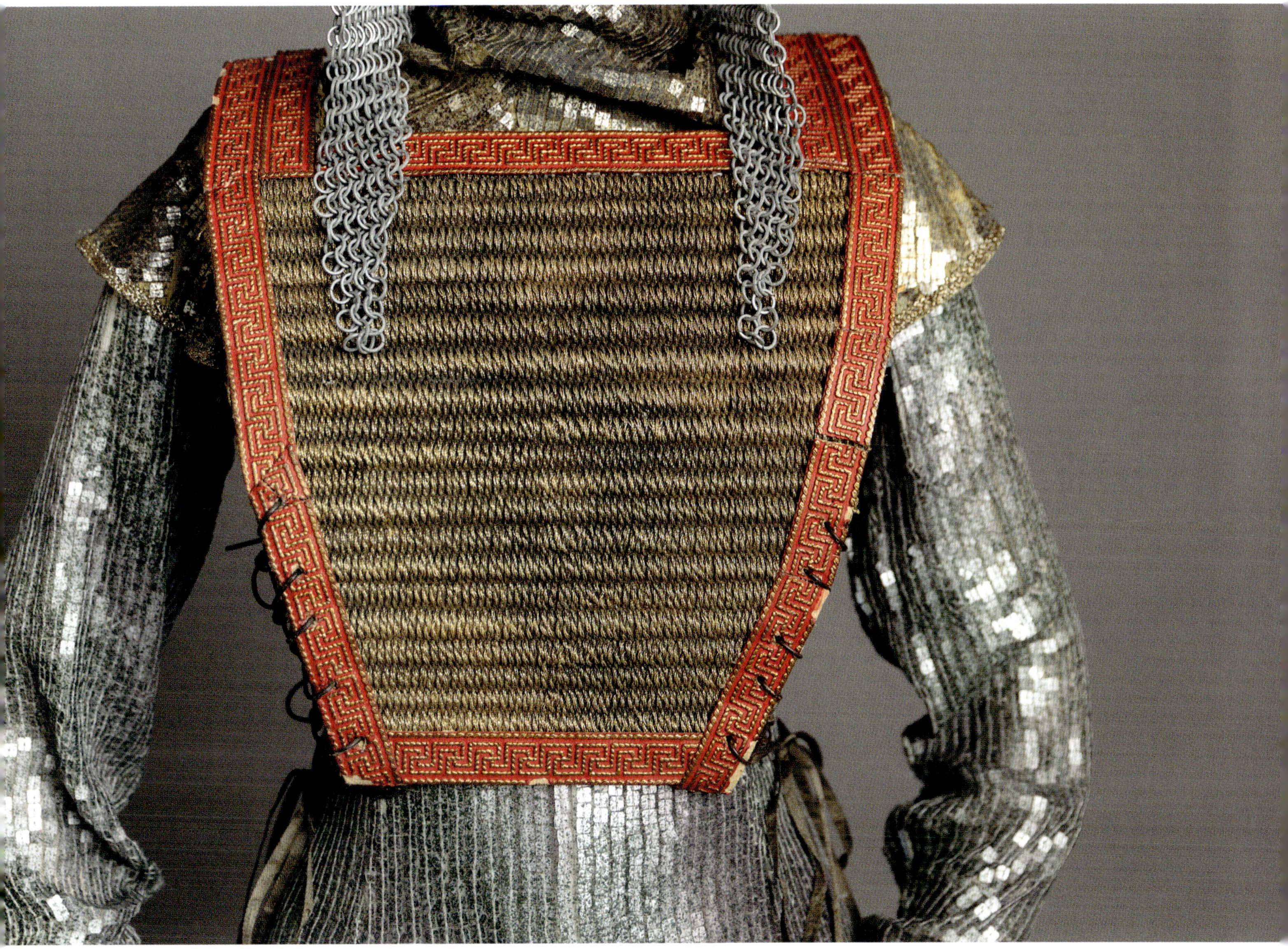

CHARACTER

Sarah Wheaton Witting

Sarah, Plain and Tall, 1991
Skylark, 1993
Sarah, Plain and Tall: Winter's End, 1999

AUTHOR PATRICIA MACLACHLAN TURNED DOWN SEVERAL OFFERS to adapt her award-winning children's books before she heard Glenn Close read the audiobook of *Sarah, Plain and Tall*. Close starred in and executive produced all three of the *Sarah, Plain and Tall* television films, which center on themes of family, home, and belonging. In the namesake novel, Sarah Wheaton travels to the Kansas prairie from her beloved Maine in the early 1900s in response to an advertisement placed by widower Jacob Witting for a farmwife and mother to his children. The Wittings fear that a homesick Sarah will leave, but she instead chooses to stay and build a life with them in Kansas. Over the course of three films, the family experiences Jacob and Sarah's marriage and the birth of their child, drought, separation, fire, the Spanish flu, and the return of Jacob's absent father.

Costume designer Van Broughton Ramsey was selected for the *Sarah, Plain and Tall* films after earning an Emmy Award for Outstanding Costume Design for a Miniseries or a Special for his work on *Lonesome Dove* (1989). Ramsey's historical costuming is characterized by his extensive research process and his attention to detail, including visible wear and mending in his costumes. His designs for *Sarah, Plain and Tall* were informed by period sources such as magazines, catalogues, and historic photographs of early twentieth-century Kansas. Using fine cottons, linens, and wools, the staff at Barbara Matera's atelier brought an authenticity to the wardrobe of the hardworking and "not mild-mannered" Sarah. Visual sleight of hand costuming elements like vertical stripes and shortened sleeves helped Close embody the self-described tall character.

DESIGNER

Van Broughton Ramsey

Born in the small town of Wharton, Texas, Van Broughton Ramsey earned a BA in botany and chemistry from Baylor University and an MA in restoration architecture from the University of Texas before moving to New York City in 1978 to pursue a career in costume design. Ramsey worked as an architect by day and took theater costume design classes by night until the director Gene Frankel gave him his first break designing for an off-Broadway production of *The Marriage/War Play* (1980). In 1983 Ramsey designed the costumes for the play *1918* by fellow Wharton native Horton Foote.

Ramsey's first foray into designing for television came with the 1989 miniseries *Lonesome Dove*, a cultural phenomenon credited with reviving both television westerns and the miniseries format. The series was wildly popular with both viewers and critics, earning nineteen Emmy nominations and seven wins, including Ramsey's award for Outstanding Costume Design for a Miniseries or a Special. Over the course of his career in television, Ramsey has been nominated for six Emmys, winning a second time in 1994 for his costume designs for *Oldest Living Confederate Widow Tells All*. In 1991 Ramsey worked with Glenn Close on the costume designs for *Sarah, Plain and Tall*, the first of three installments of a made-for-television film adaptation of Patricia MacLachlan's novel of the same name. Ramsey received an Emmy nomination for his work on the project and a Costume Designers Guild Award nomination for the third installment, *Sarah, Plain and Tall: Winter's End* (1999). Ramsey continues to work as a costume designer for both theater and television, having served as a Governor for the Academy of Television Arts and Sciences and as a ten-year member of the Executive Board of the Costume Designers Guild.

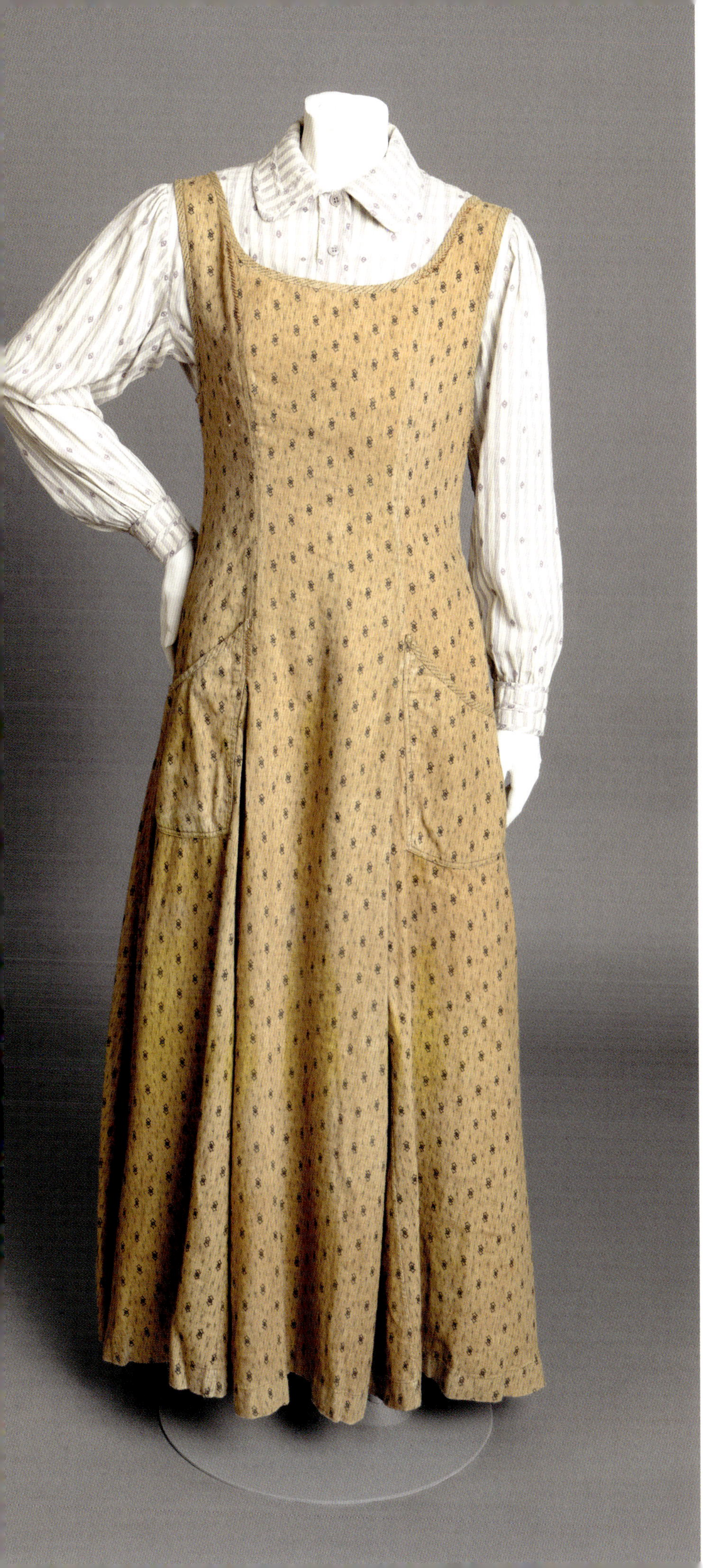

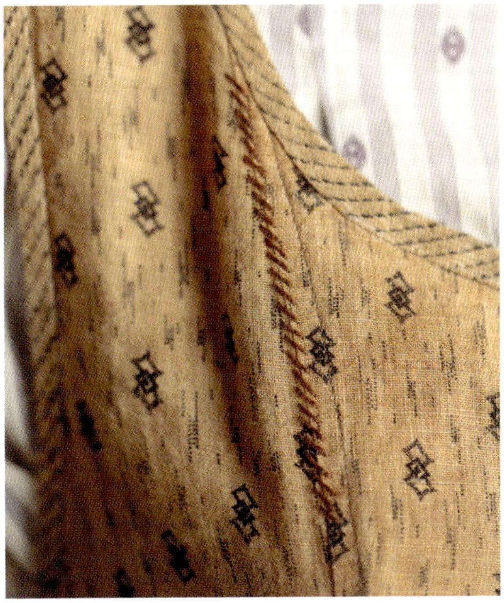

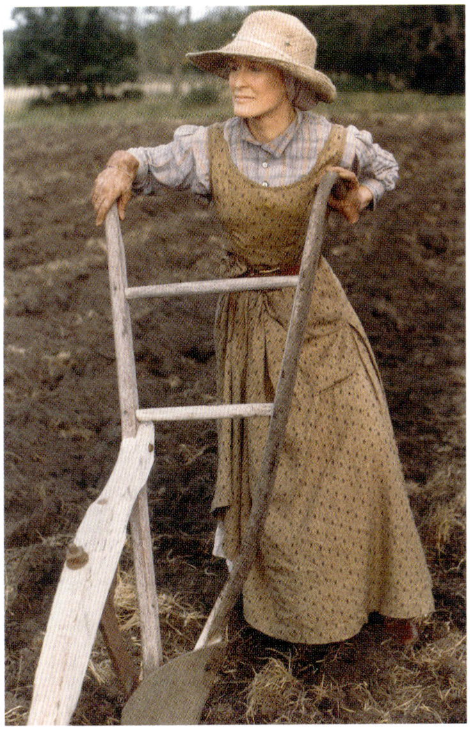

ABOVE
Glenn Close as Sarah Wheaton Witting,
Sarah, Plain and Tall (1993)

LEFT
Van Broughton Ramsey (American)
Barbara Matera Ltd.
Sarah Wheaton Witting,
Sarah, Plain and Tall, 1991
Linen, cotton
GC 2017.161.1, .162.1

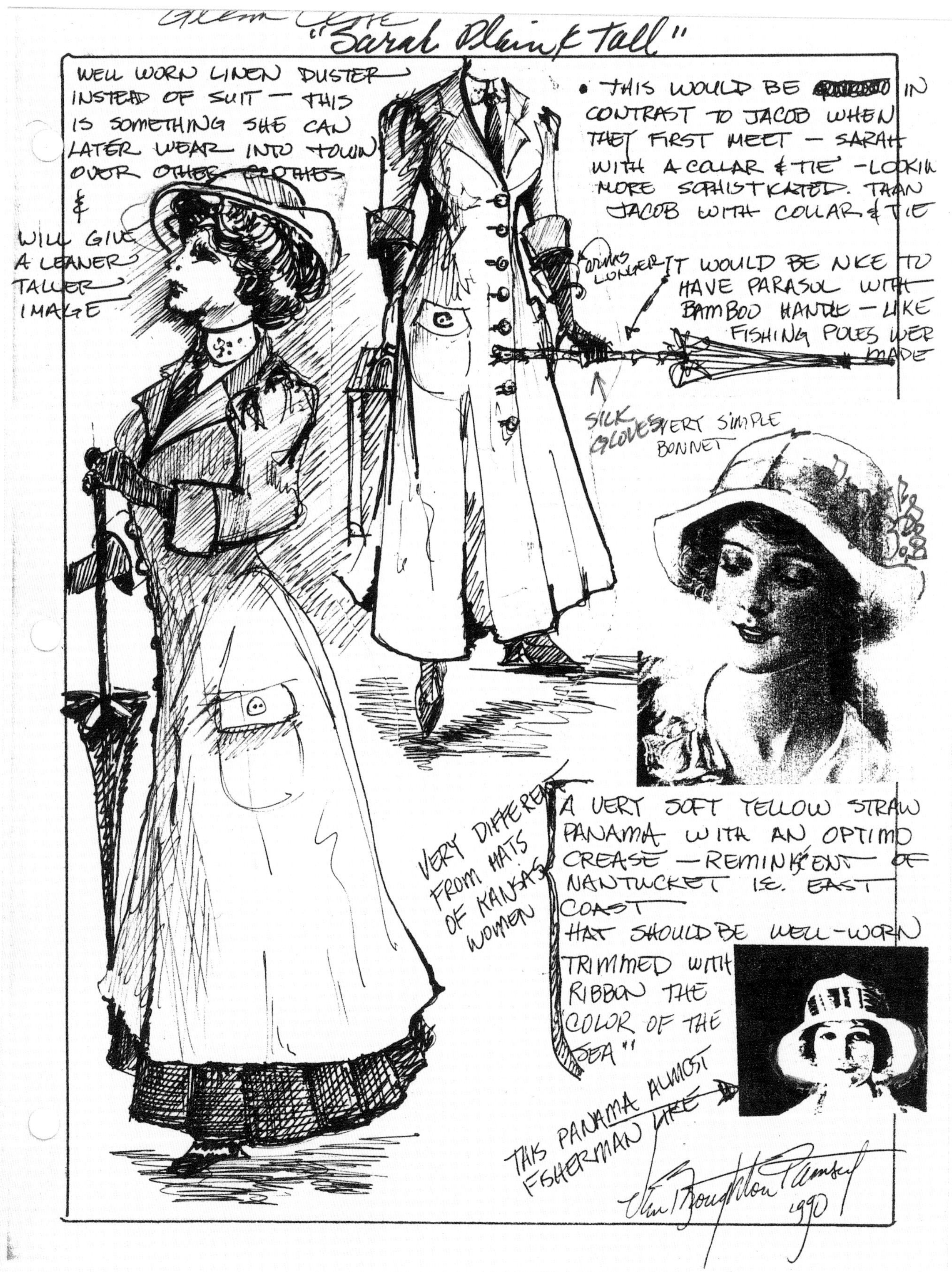
"Sarah Plain & Tall"
WELL WORN LINEN DUSTER INSTEAD OF SUIT — THIS IS SOMETHING SHE CAN LATER WEAR INTO TOWN OVER OTHER CLOTHES
& WILL GIVE A LEANER TALLER IMAGE
• THIS WOULD BE IN CONTRAST TO JACOB WHEN THEY FIRST MEET — SARAH WITH A COLLAR & TIE — LOOKING MORE SOPHISTICATED THAN JACOB WITH COLLAR & TIE
IT WOULD BE NICE TO HAVE PARASOL WITH BAMBOO HANDLE — LIKE FISHING POLES WERE MADE
SILK GLOVES
VERY SIMPLE BONNET
VERY DIFFERENT FROM HATS OF KANSAS WOMEN
A VERY SOFT YELLOW STRAW PANAMA WITH AN OPTIMO CREASE — REMINISCENT OF NANTUCKET I.E. EAST COAST
HAT SHOULD BE WELL-WORN TRIMMED WITH RIBBON THE "COLOR OF THE SEA"
THIS PANAMA ALMOST FISHERMAN LIKE
1990

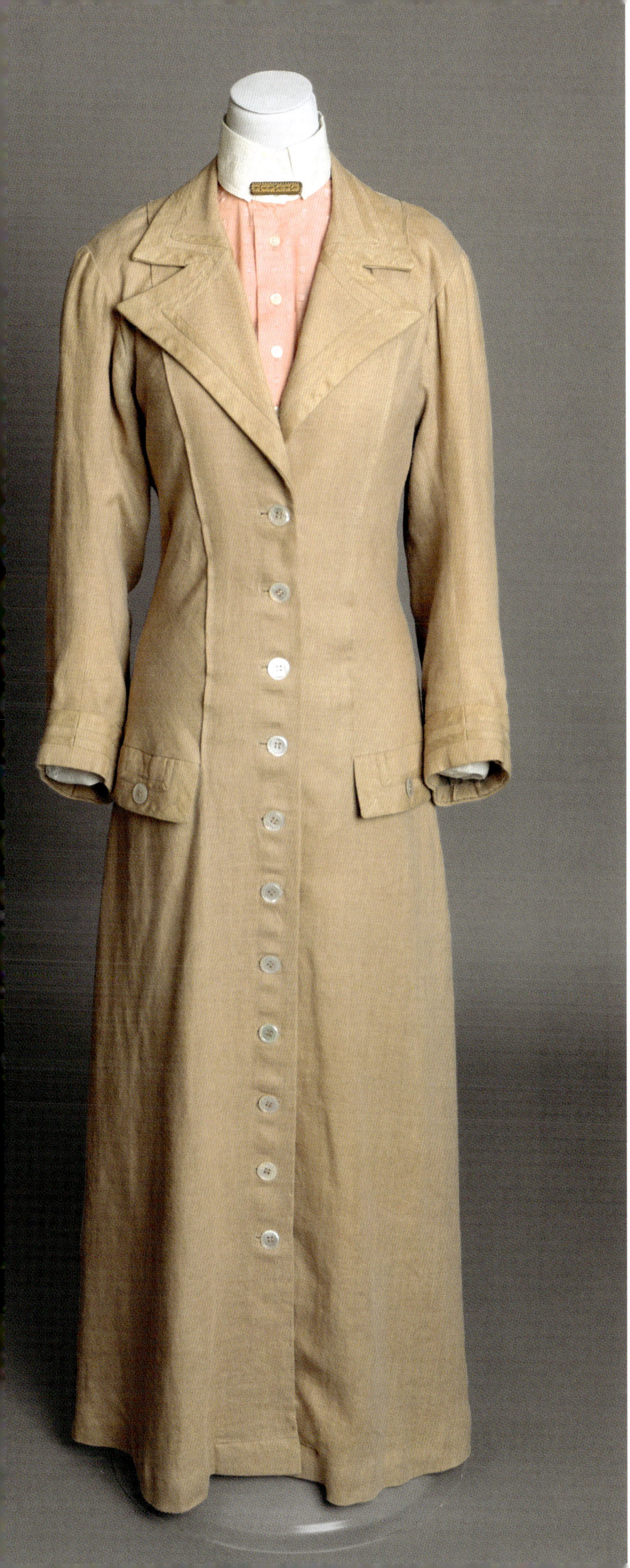

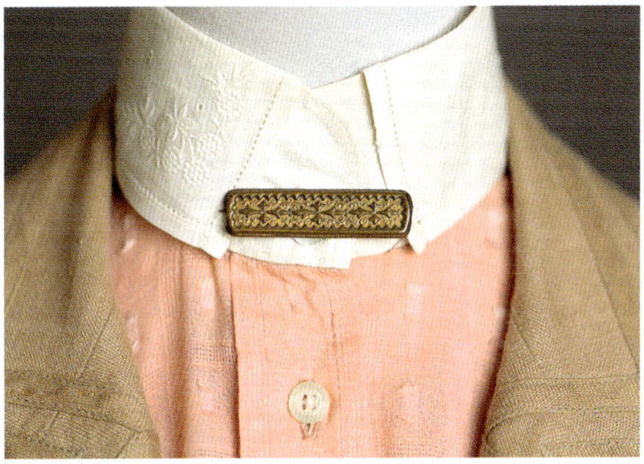

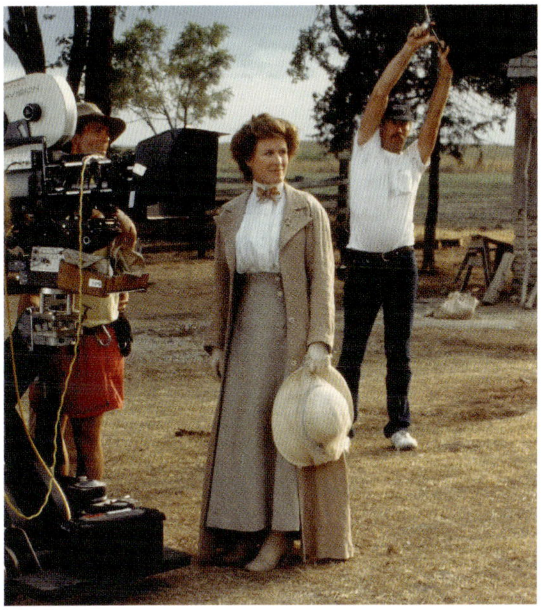

ABOVE
Glenn Close as Sarah Wheaton Witting
on the set of *Skylark*, 1993

LEFT
Van Broughton Ramsey (American)
Barbara Matera Ltd.
Sarah Wheaton Witting
Sarah, Plain and Tall, 1991
Skylark, 1993
Linen, cotton, silk
GC 2017.171.1, .175.1

OPPOSITE
Van Broughton Ramsey
Annotated sketch for Duster
Sarah, Plain and Tall, 1990

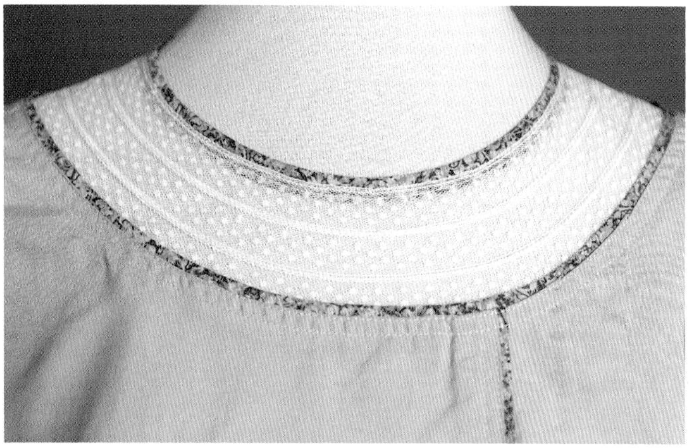

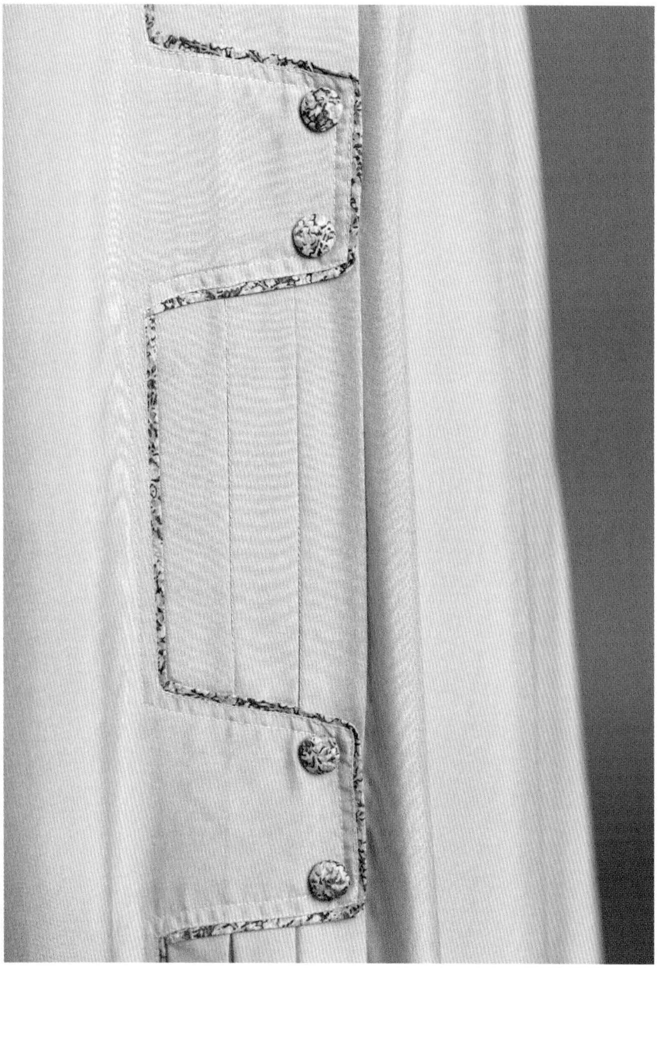

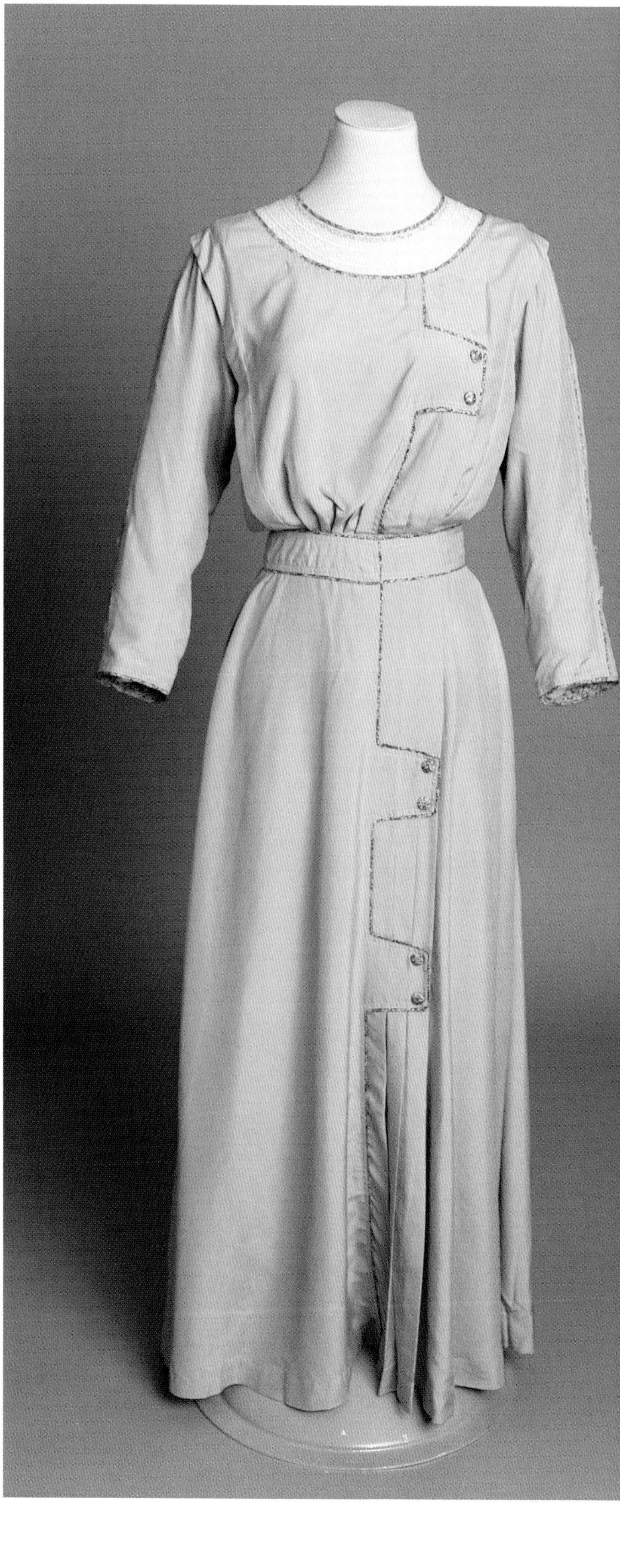

Van Broughton Ramsey (American)
Barbara Matera Ltd.
Sarah Wheaton Witting
Sarah, Plain and Tall, 1991
Rayon, cotton
GC 2017.152.1

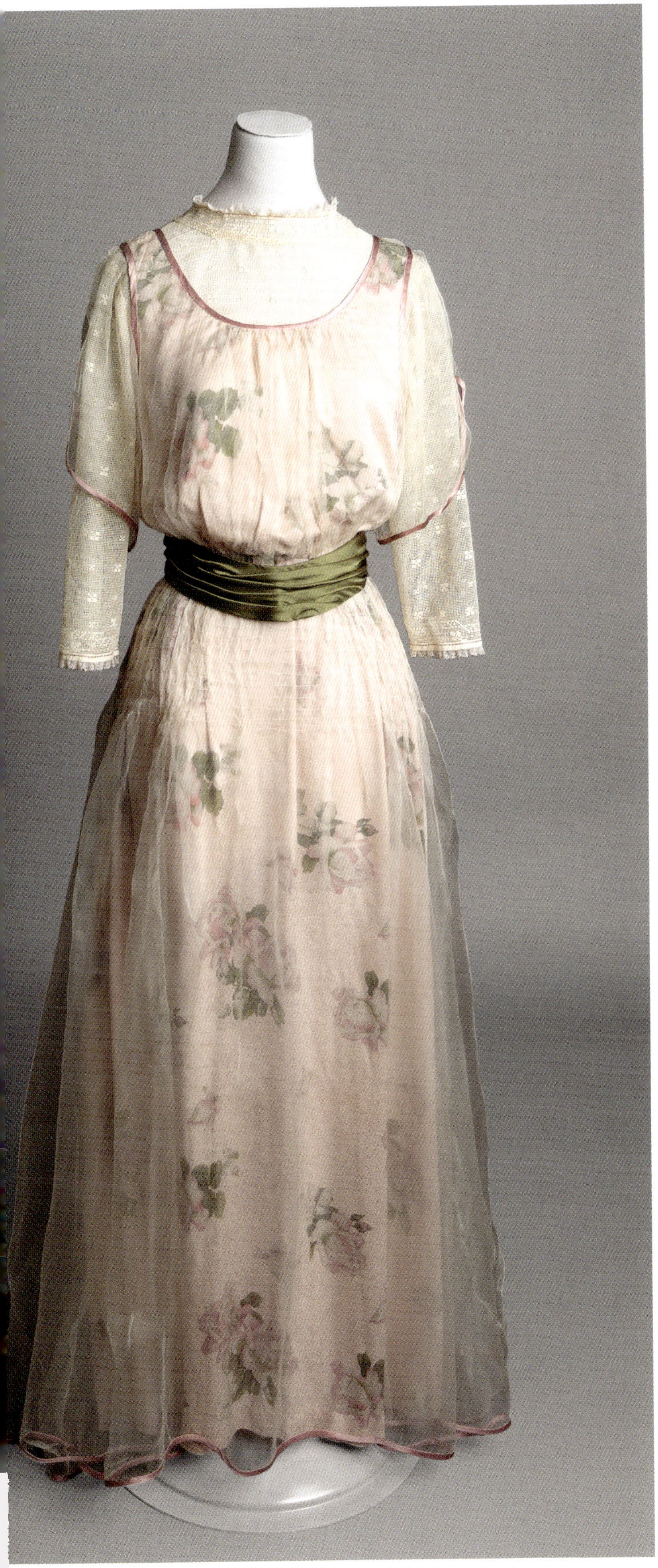

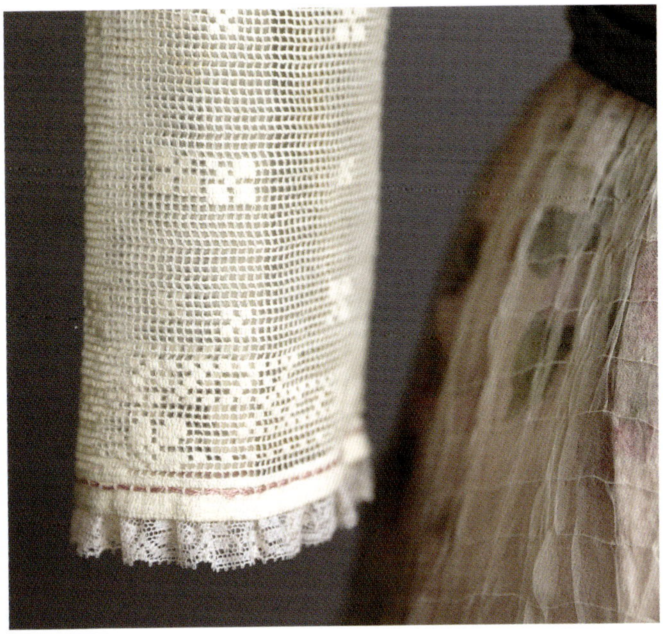

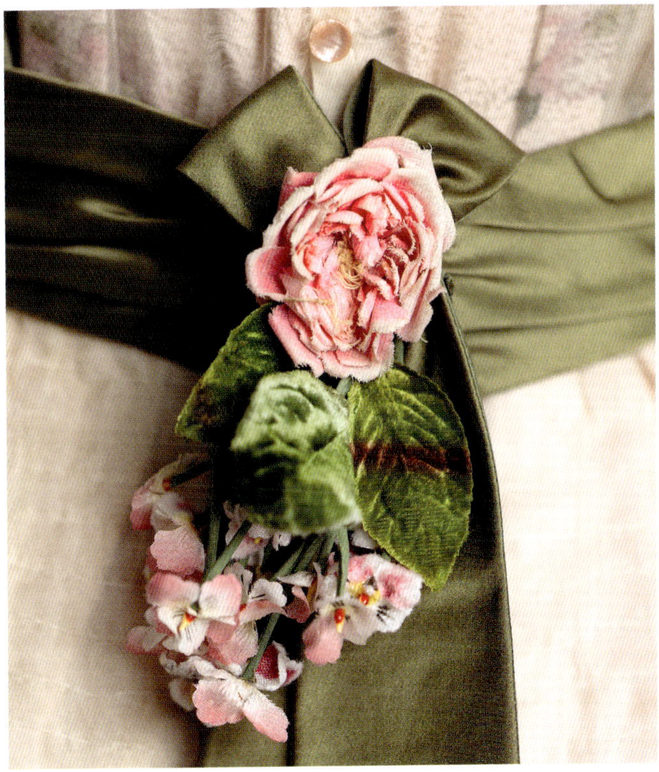

Van Broughton Ramsey (American)
Barbara Matera Ltd.
Sarah Wheaton Witting
Skylark, 1993
Silk, cotton
GC 2017.167.1 AB

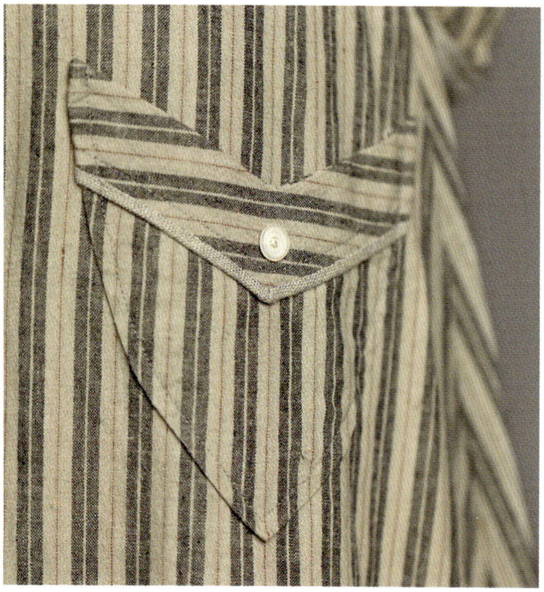

Van Broughton Ramsey (American)
Barbara Matera Ltd.
Sarah Wheaton Witting
Sarah, Plain and Tall: Winter's End, 1999
Linen
GC 2017.191.1

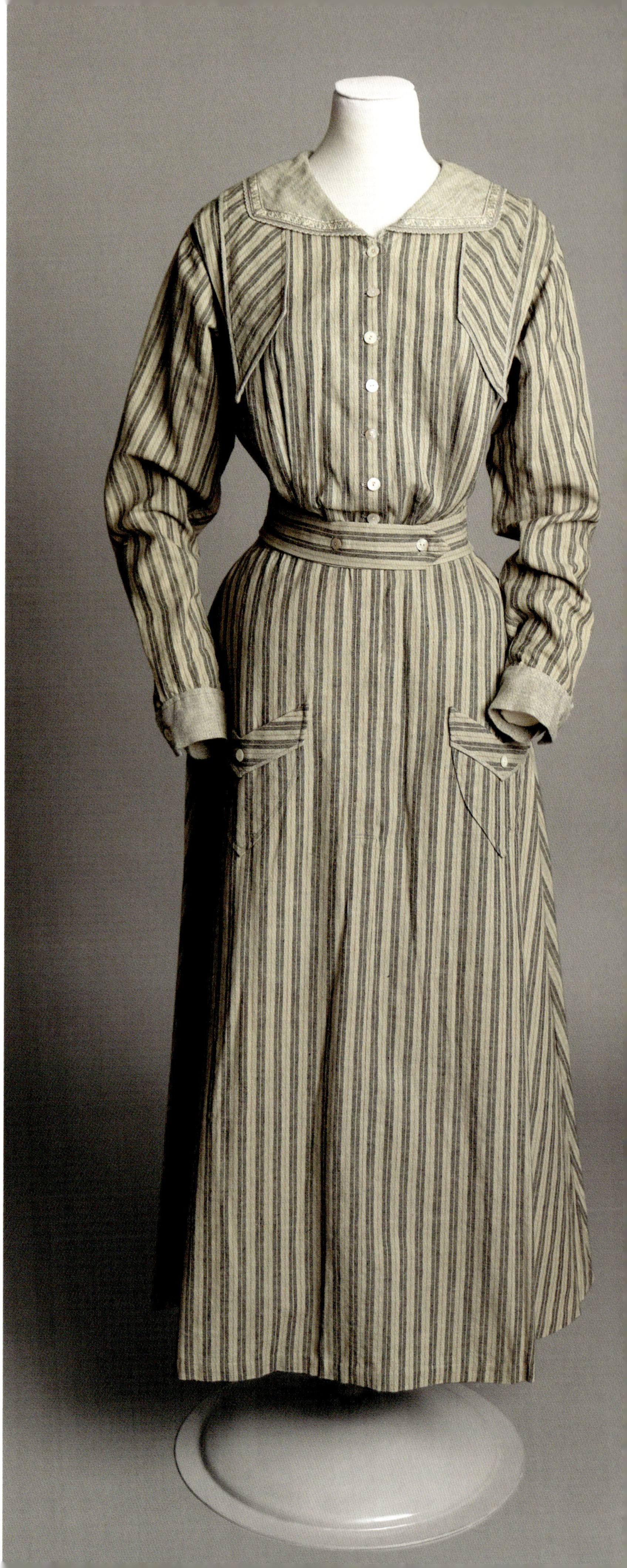

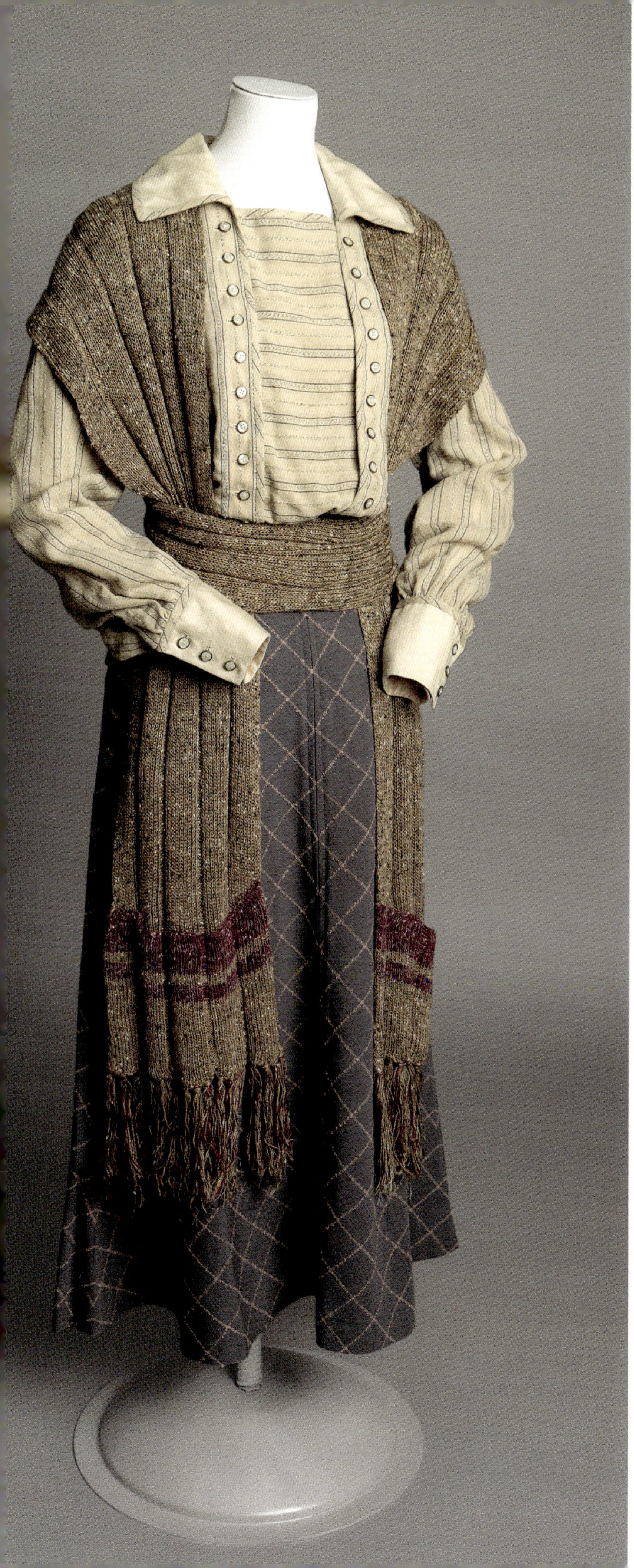

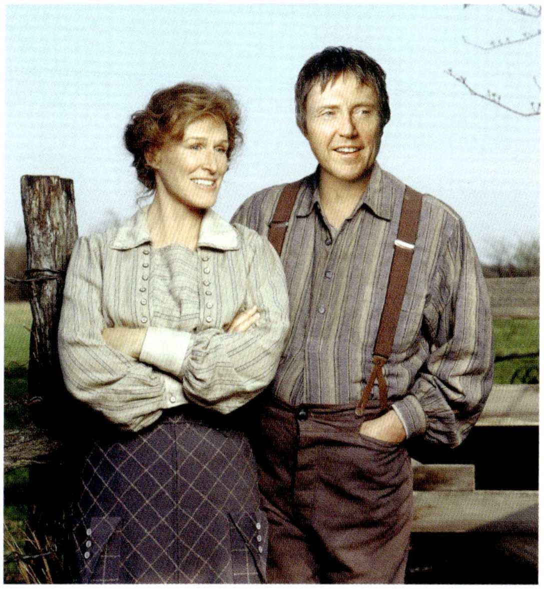

ABOVE

Glenn Close and Christopher Walken in *Sarah, Plain and Tall: Winter's End*

LEFT

Van Broughton Ramsey (American)
Barbara Matera Inc.
Topaz Handloomed Knits
Sarah Wheaton Witting
Sarah, Plain and Tall: Winter's End, 1999
Linen, wool
GC 2017.196.1-.3

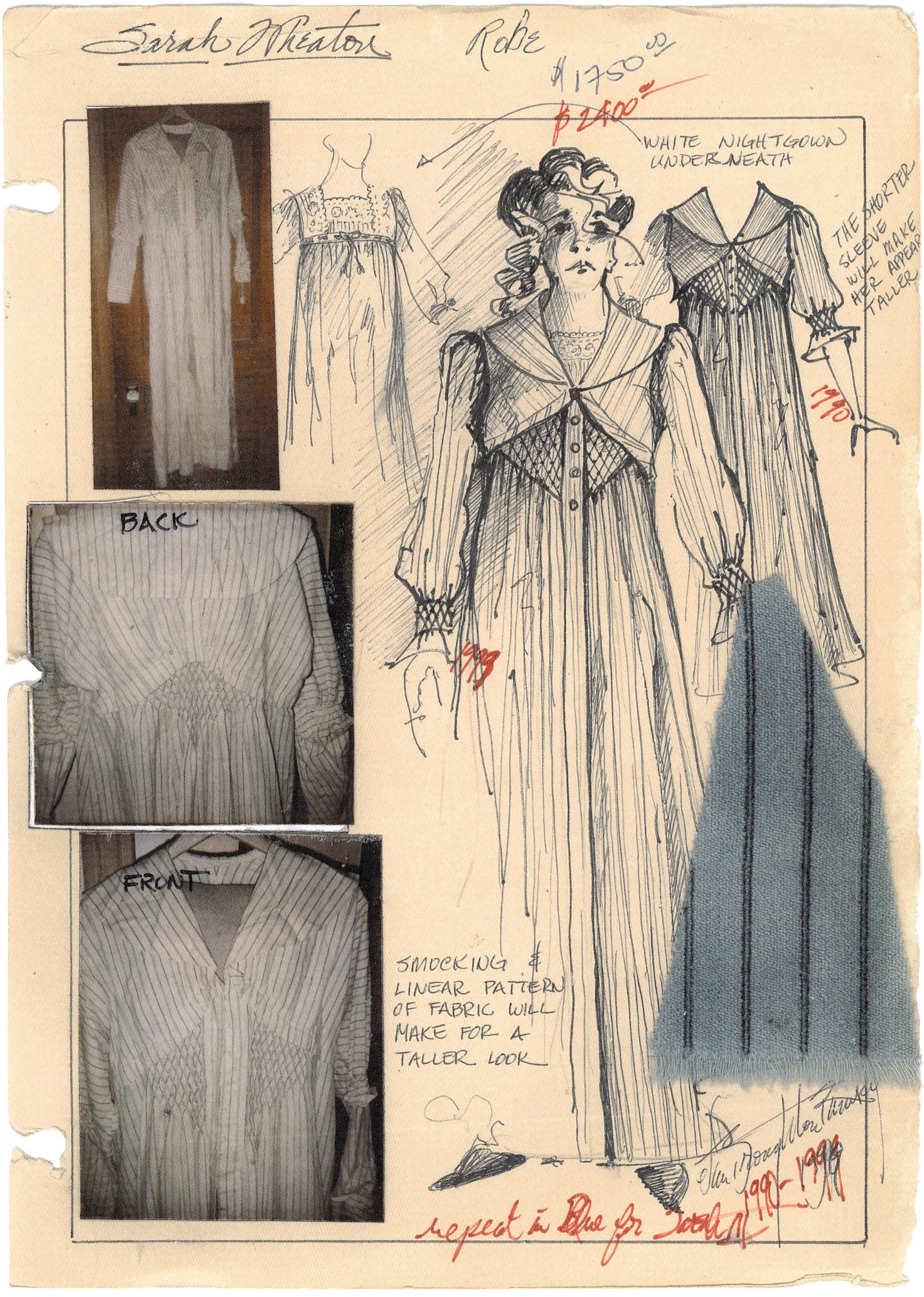
Sarah Wheaton
Robe
$1750.00
$2400.00
WHITE NIGHTGOWN UNDERNEATH
THE SHORTER SLEEVE WILL MAKE HER APPEAR TALLER
BACK
FRONT
SMOCKING & LINEAR PATTERN OF FABRIC WILL MAKE FOR A TALLER LOOK
repeat in Blue for Sarah II
1990-1998

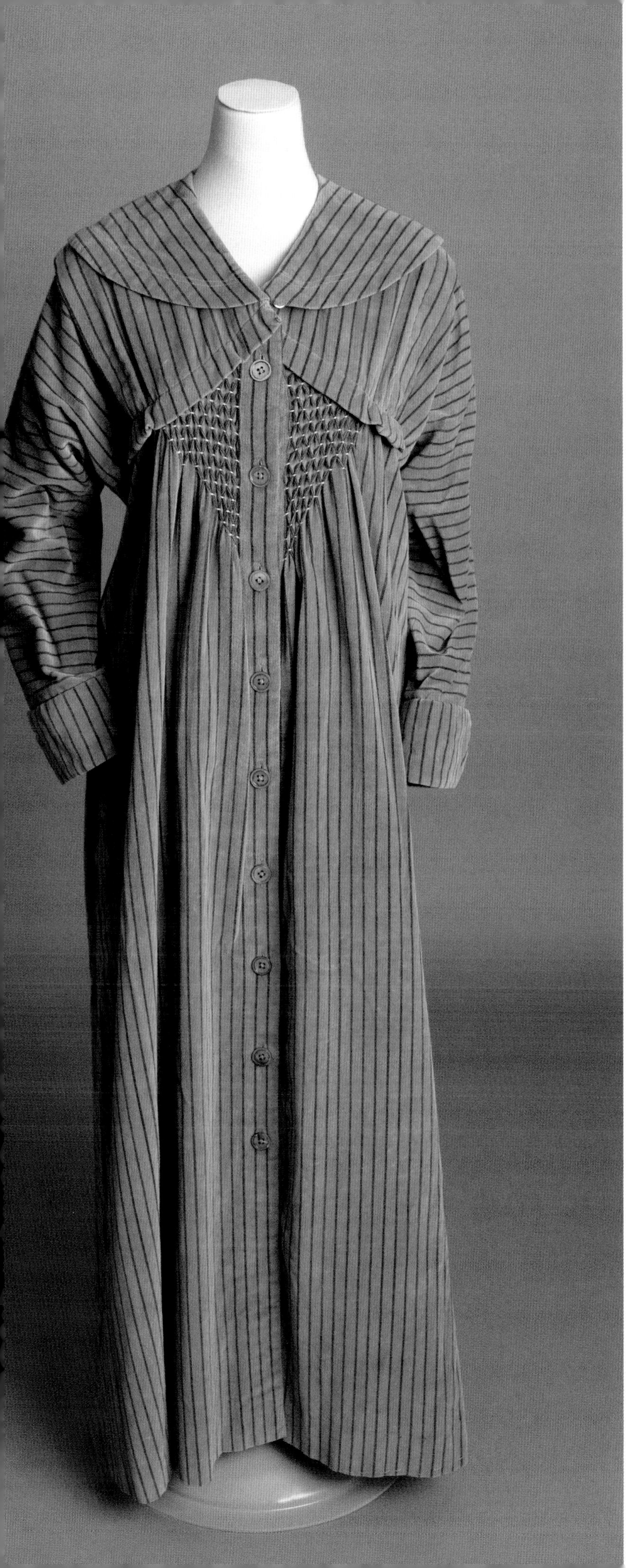

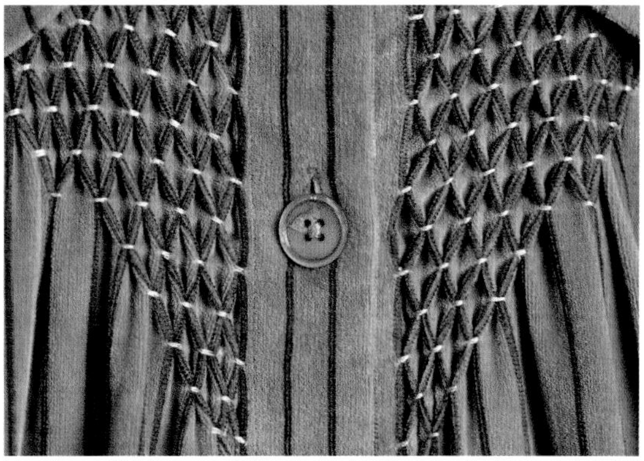

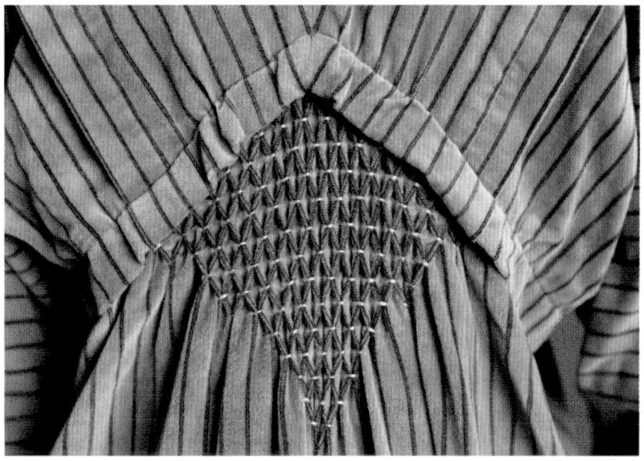

ABOVE
Van Broughton Ramsey (American)
Barbara Matera Ltd.
Sarah Wheaton Witting
Sarah, Plain and Tall: Winter's End, 1999
Cotton
GC 2017.197.1

OPPOSITE
Van Broughton Ramsey
Annotated sketch for Robe
Sarah, Plain and Tall: Winter's End, 1990–99
Courtesy the Witliff Collections
Texas State University

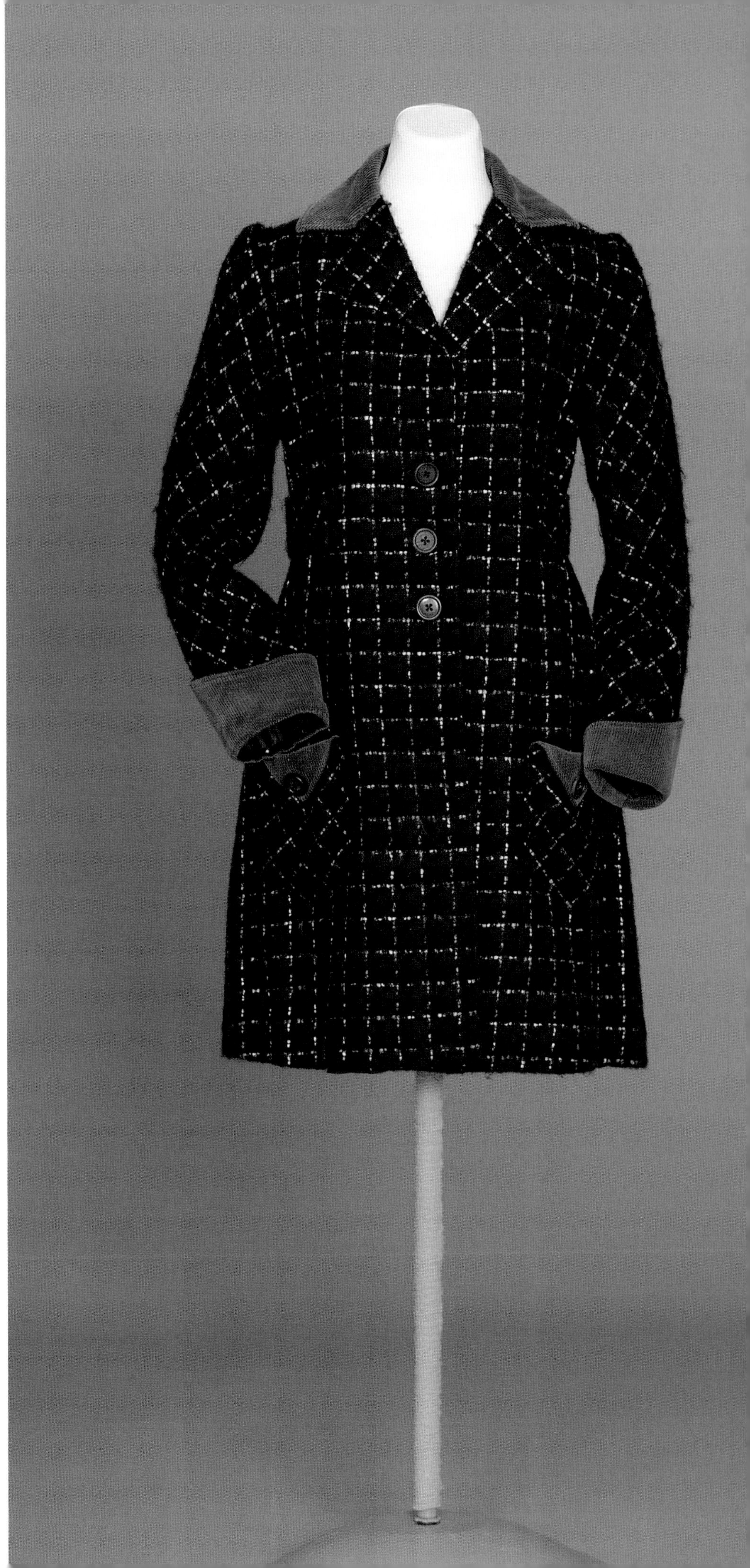

Van Broughton Ramsey (American)
Barbara Matera Ltd.
Sarah Wheaton Witting
Sarah, Plain and Tall: Winter's End, 1999
Wool, silk, cotton
GC 2017.198.1

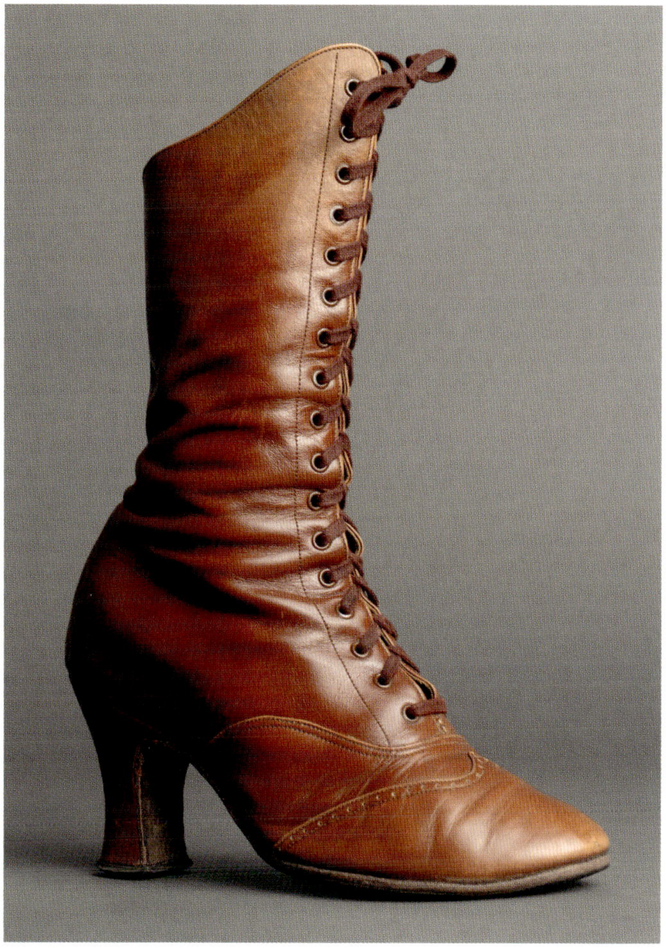

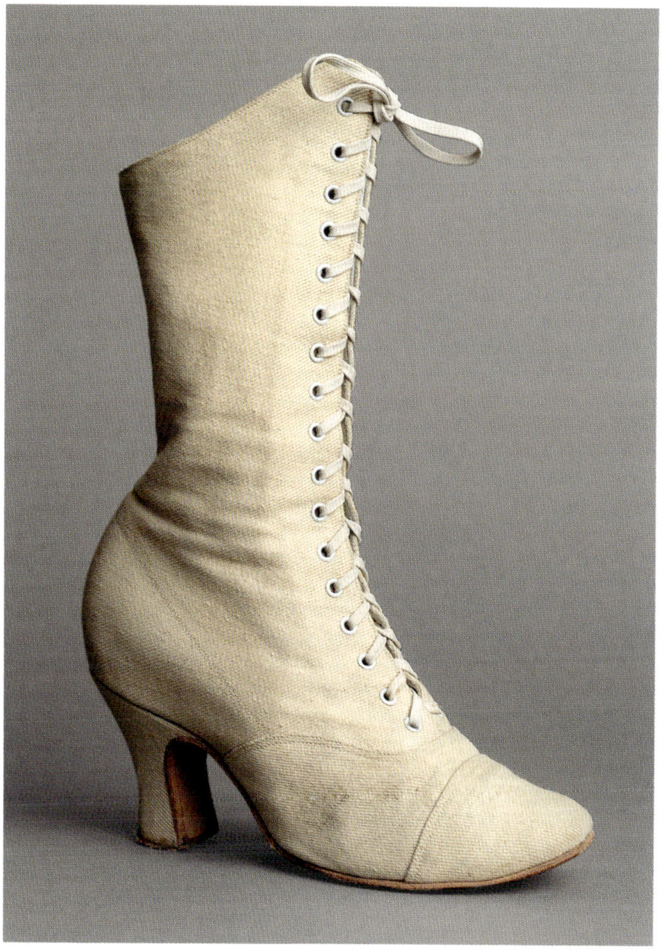

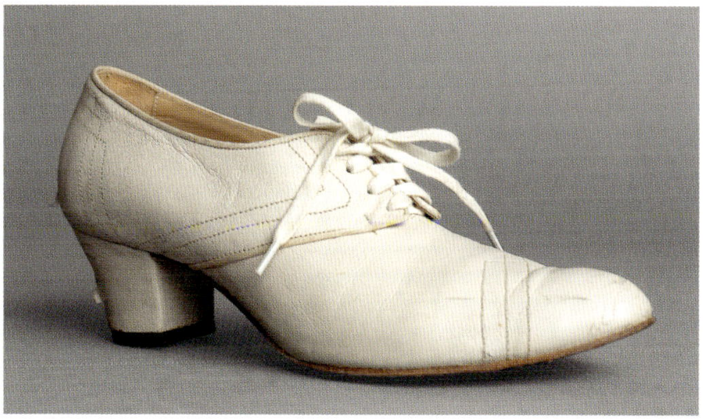

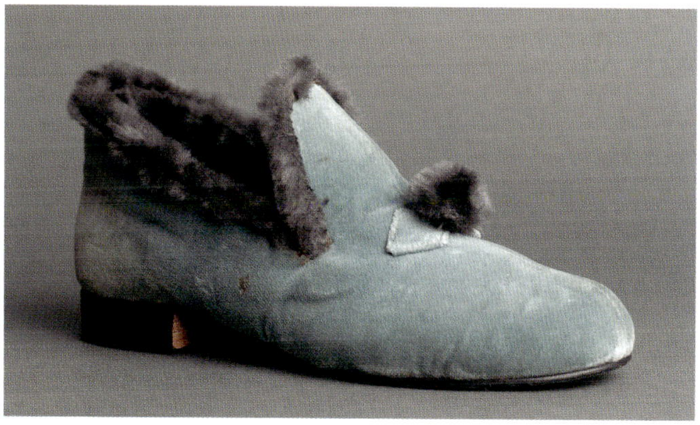

TOP
Van Broughton Ramsey (American)
Sarah Wheaton Witting
Sarah, Plain and Tall series, 1991–99
Leather
GC 2017.235.1 AB

ABOVE LEFT
Van Broughton Ramsey (American)
Sarah Wheaton Witting
Skylark, 1993
Leather
GC 2017.189.1 AB

TOP RIGHT
Van Broughton Ramsey (American)
Sarah Wheaton Witting
Sarah, Plain and Tall series, 1991–99
Canvas, leather
GC 2017.159.1 AB

ABOVE RIGHT
Van Broughton Ramsey (American)
Sarah Wheaton Witting
Sarah, Plain and Tall: Winter's End, 1999
Cotton, acrylic, leather
GC 2017.236.1 AB

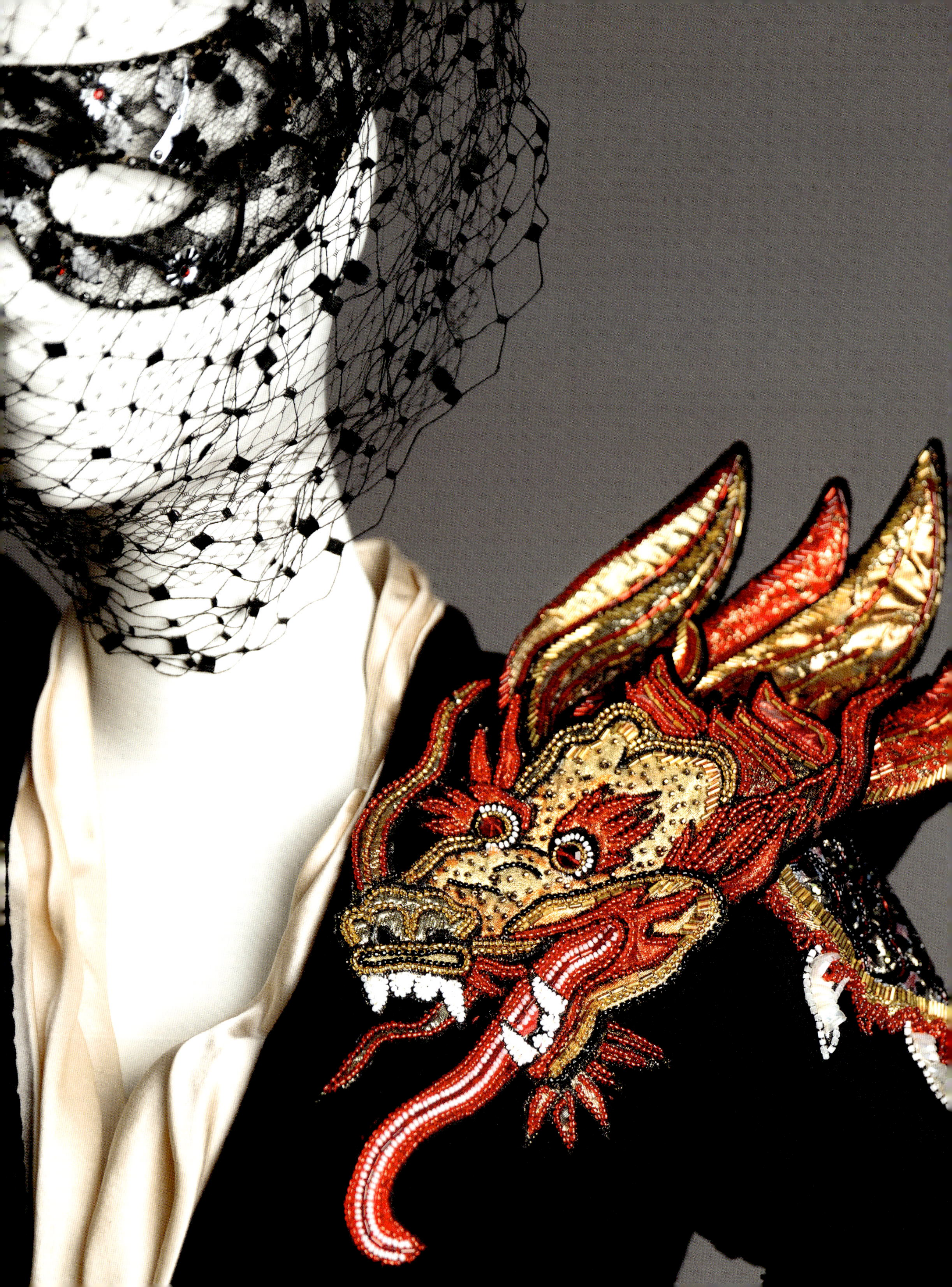

Making Fantasy Real

While some productions are rooted in familiar times and places, it is through conjuring unknown worlds that a costume designer can bring the imagined and fantastic to life. Advancing silhouettes, materials, and textures to new limits, costume designers work closely with directors and production designers to conceptualize wardrobes for characters living in the future; for inhabitants of imagined lands; and for unbelievable bodies and creatures. At the same time, the costume designer must still convey aspects of each character's unique personality, suggesting their temperament, status, and personal narrative.

Embodying fantasy can also entail pushing familiar archetypes to unprecedented heights, as in the ensembles worn by the spectacularly evil Cruella De Vil. Her hyperbolic wardrobe is filled with garments and accessories that reflect her passion for excess and cruelty. For characters with origins in other media, such as the intergalactic commander Nova Prime from *Marvel Studios' Guardians of the Galaxy*, costume designers must fulfill expectations for beloved characters in ways that adhere to the existing story's narrative. Fantastic characters often carry out physically daring feats on-screen and designers must work closely with actors and costume technicians to ensure that their garments allow for free and creative movement.

In a 2000 interview with *The Guardian*, three-time Academy Award-winner Anthony Powell described his responsibility as a costume designer as making it easier for actors to embody their characters—whether the character in question is outrageously overdone or understated and restrained.[6] The costumes Powell designed for Glenn Close's turn as Cruella De Vil in the live-action remake of the animated Disney classic *101 Dalmatians* (1996) and its sequel *102 Dalmatians* (2000) are some of the most stunning and elaborate ensembles in the Glenn Close Costume Collection.

OPPOSITE
Anthony Powell (English)
Barbara Matera Ltd.
Martin Adams
Woody Shelp
Cruella De Vil/Ella
102 Dalmatians, 2000
Wool, silk, polyester, metallic thread, glass beads, glass stones, plastic sequins, metal, feathers
GC 2017.13.1-.3, .7-.8

CHARACTER
Cruella De Vil

101 Dalmatians, 1996

CRUELLA DE VIL MADE HER DEBUT in the 1956 children's book *The Hundred and One Dalmatians*, which Disney first brought to the big screen in 1961 with a successful animated film. Rail-thin, with a fashion model's hips-forward slouch and skeletal face with razor-sharp cheekbones, Cruella was Disney's first contemporary villain. To the dismay and delight of dog lovers and viewers thirty-five years later, Glenn Close's flesh-and-blood Cruella emerged as an enthralling and memorable screen presence with the help of Academy Award–winning designer Anthony Powell. The framing of the character as head of her own fashion atelier, the House of De Vil, provided Powell and Close a foundation for creating one of the most visually compelling and heartless screen villains in history, one who shrieks, "I live for fur, I worship fur! After all, is there a woman in all this wretched world who doesn't?"

As the ultimate coldhearted fashion innovator, Close is most often outfitted in a palette of black, white, and red, with spotted, striped, feathered, and scaled materials and motifs. Powell's designs for Close cleave to no specific time or place—whether she's in a full-skirted, wasp-waisted coat; a high-collared, sweeping cape and bustier; a black-and-white negligee with hanging feather-lined sleeves; or a superlative power suit, the audacious costumes in *101 Dalmatians*, built by the talented makers at Barbara Matera Ltd., inspire awe and delight. Cruella embodies her passion in ensemble after ensemble, her obsession bringing about her downfall as she meets her end in a vat of molasses, clad in one of her beloved fur coats.

DESIGNER
Anthony Powell

Recognized as one of the most important costume designers of his generation, Anthony Powell has worked on film and stage productions in New York, Paris, London, and Los Angeles for over fifty years. Born near Manchester, England, he graduated from London's Central School of Art and Design before launching his career with the costumes for Sir John Gielgud's production of *The School of Scandal* in 1963. He earned both a Tony Award for Best Costume Design and a nomination for Best Scenic Design for that production. Powell began his career in film with *The Royal Hunt of the Sun* (1969) and is a six-time nominee for the Academy Award for Best Costume Design, winning for *Travels with My Aunt* (1972), *Death on the Nile* (1978), and *Tess* (1979). His other film credits include *Indiana Jones and the Temple of Doom* (1984), *Indiana Jones and the Last Crusade* (1989), and *Hook* (1991).

In 1993 Powell designed the lavish costumes for Andrew Lloyd Webber's West End musical *Sunset Boulevard*. The production opened on Broadway in 1994 with Glenn Close in the role of Norma Desmond. Powell worked with Close again for the live-action remake of *101 Dalmatians* (1996) and its sequel *102 Dalmatians* (2000), the latter of which earned an Academy Award nomination for Best Costume Design. In addition to his Tony and Academy Award nominations and wins, Powell won the BAFTA Award for Best Costume Design in 1979 for his work on *Death on the Nile* and the César Award for Best Costume Design in 1987 for *Pirates*. In 2000 the Costume Designers Guild honored Powell's work in film with a Career Achievement Award. He continues to design costumes for the stage, notably for Richard Strauss's *Capriccio* for the Paris Opera in 2004 and the 2015 revival of *Singin' in the Rain* at the Théâtre du Châtelet in Paris.

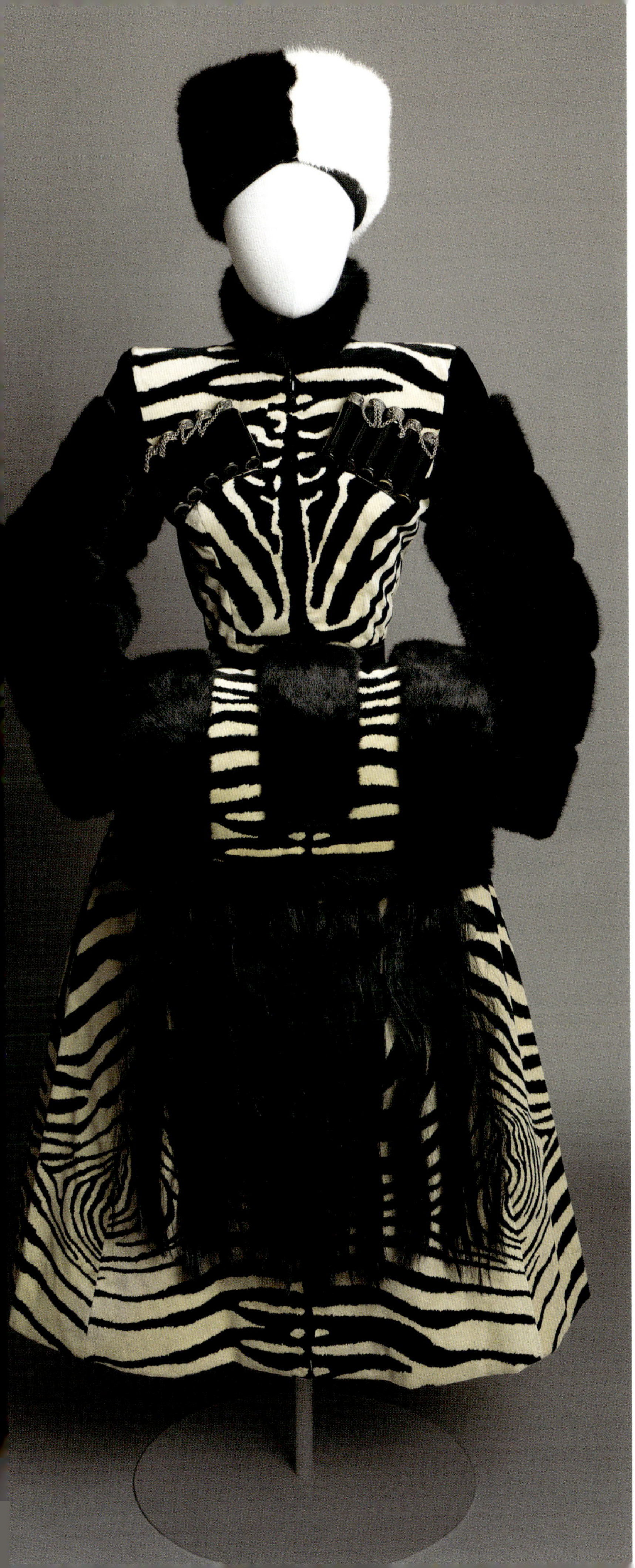

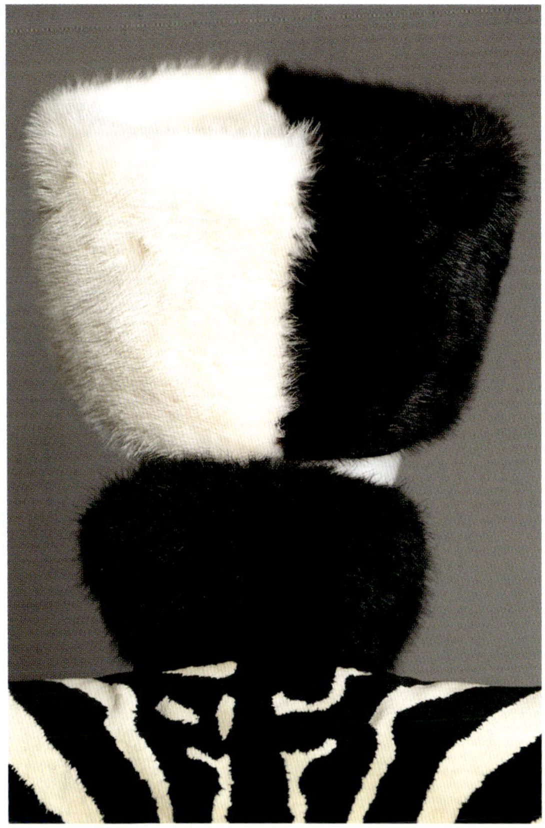

Anthony Powell (English)
Barbara Matera Ltd.
Martin Adams
Woody Shelp
Cruella De Vil
101 Dalmatians, 1996
Acrylic/synthetic fur, mink fur, leather, polyvinyl chloride, metal, horsehair
GC 2017.6.1–.3, .5

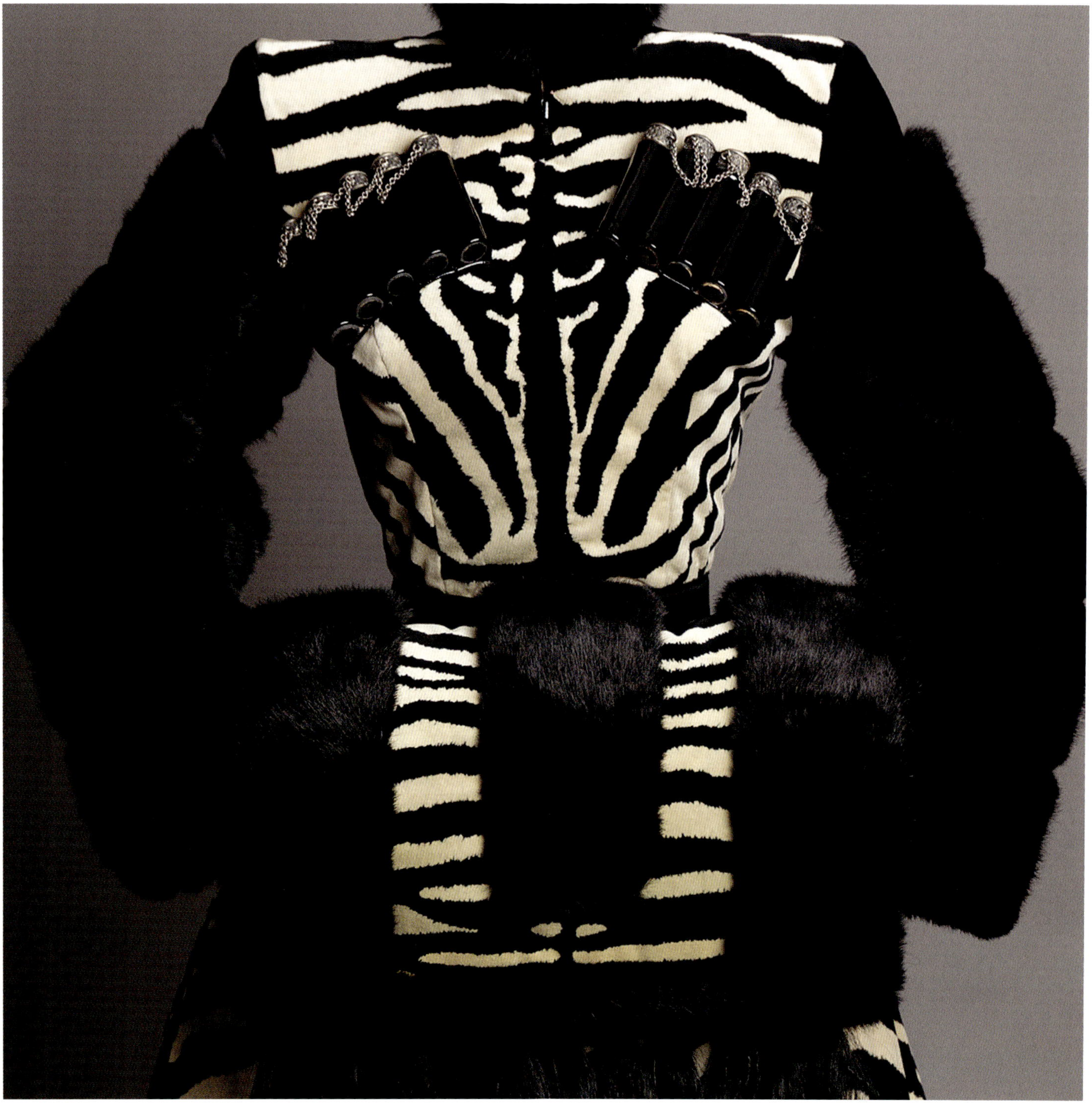

Anthony Powell (English)
Barbara Matera Ltd.
Martin Adams
Woody Shelp
Cruella De Vil
101 Dalmatians, 1996
Acrylic/synthetic fur, mink fur, leather,
polyvinyl chloride, metal, horsehair
GC 2017.6.1–.3, .5

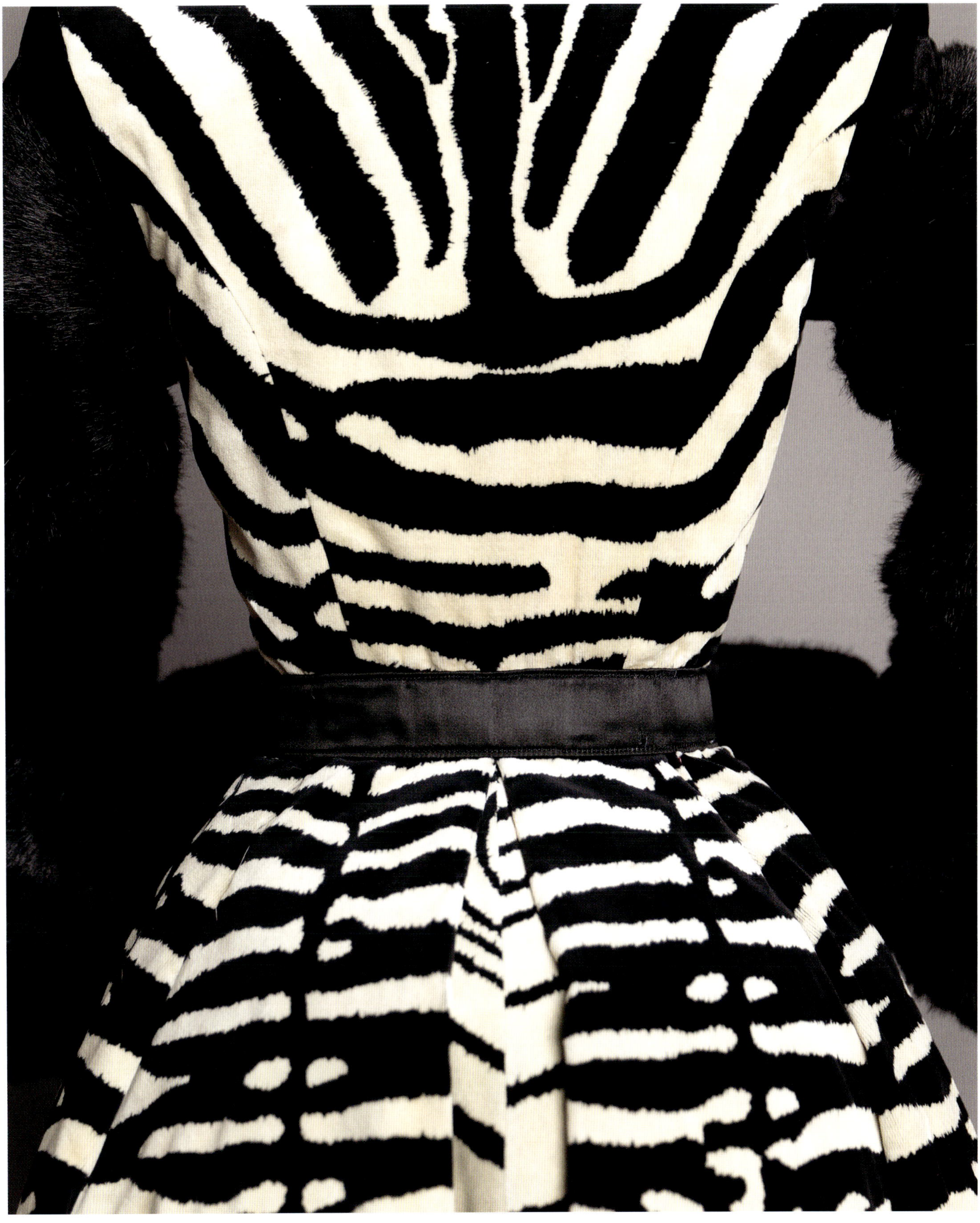

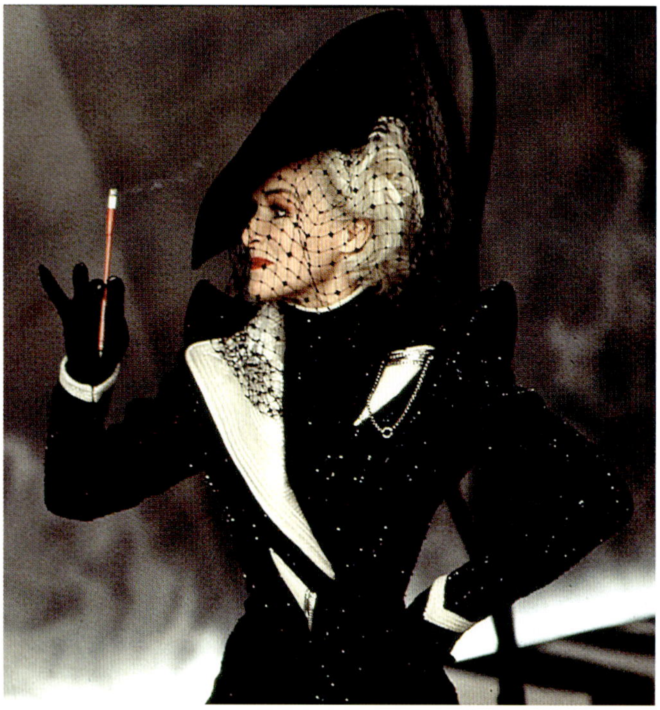

ABOVE
Glenn Close as Cruella De Vil
in *101 Dalmatians*, 1996. © Disney

RIGHT
Anthony Powell (English)
Cruella De Vil
101 Dalmatians, 1996
Manolo Blahnik
Leather, metal
GC 2017.2.2 AB

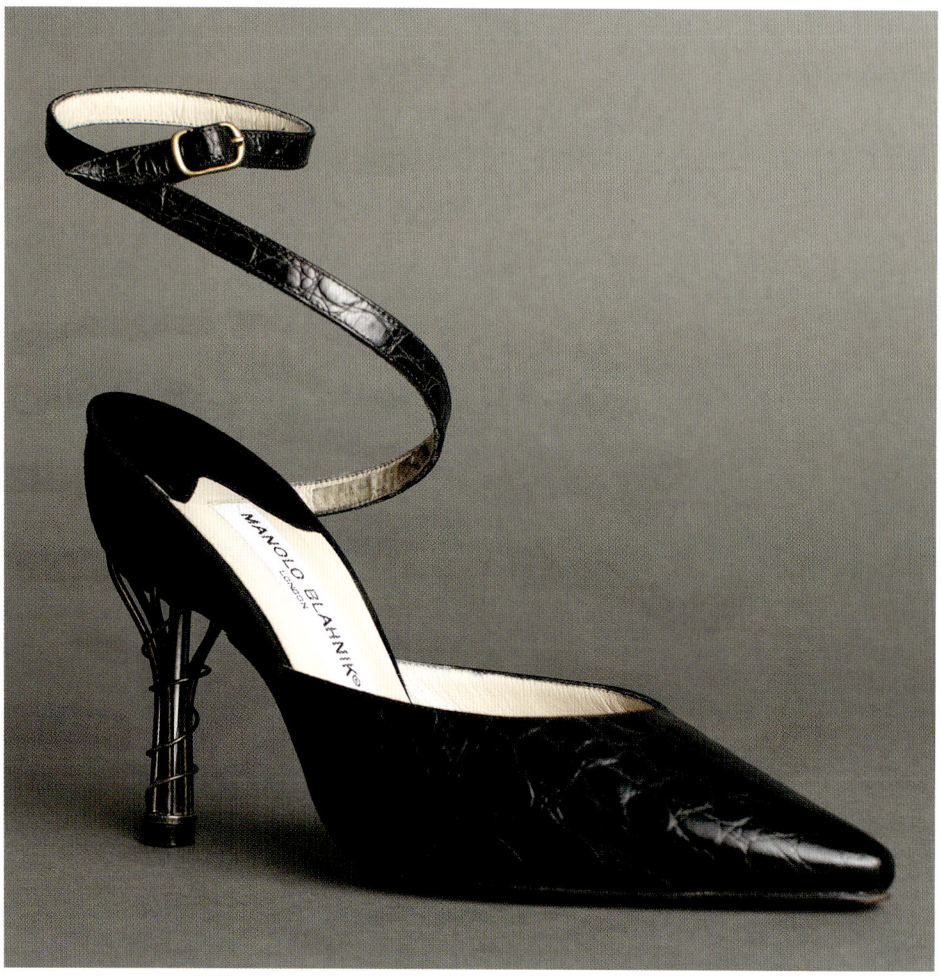

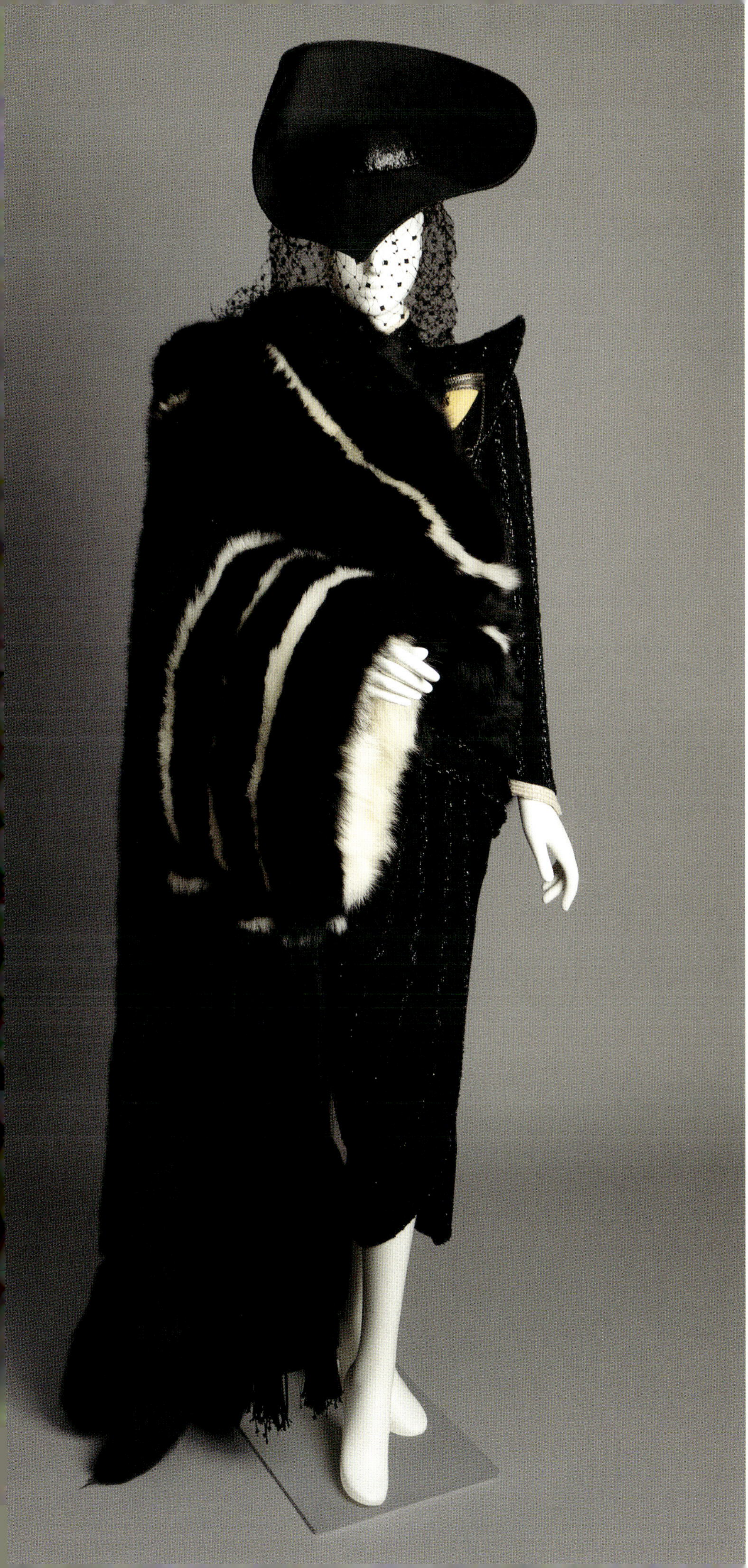

Anthony Powell (English)
Barbara Matera Ltd.
Martin Adams
Woody Shelp
Cruella De Vil
101 Dalmatians, 1996
Wool, glass beads, fox fur, horsehair, plastic, metal, straw, rayon, cotton, silk
GC 2017.2.1, .5–.7

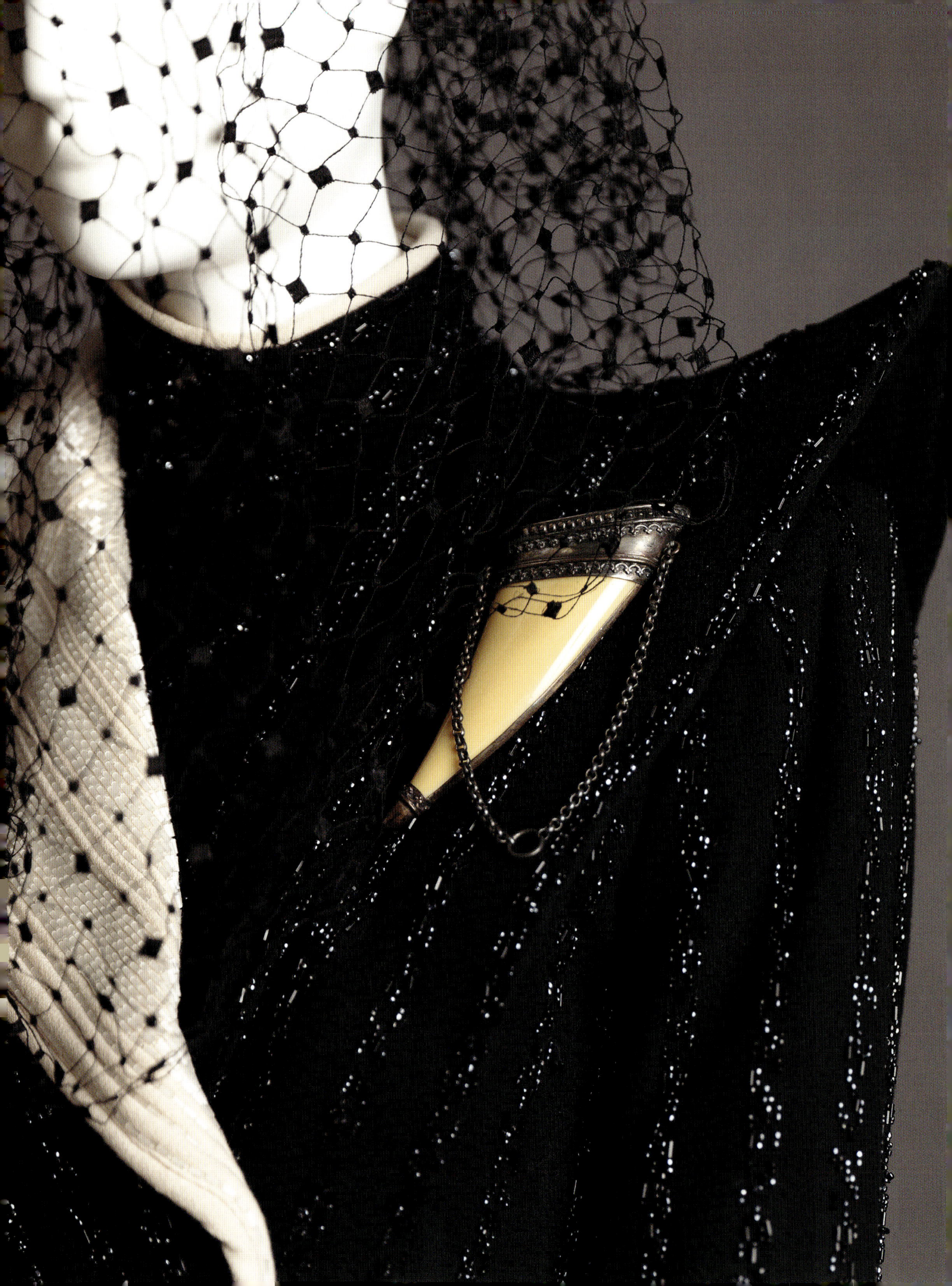

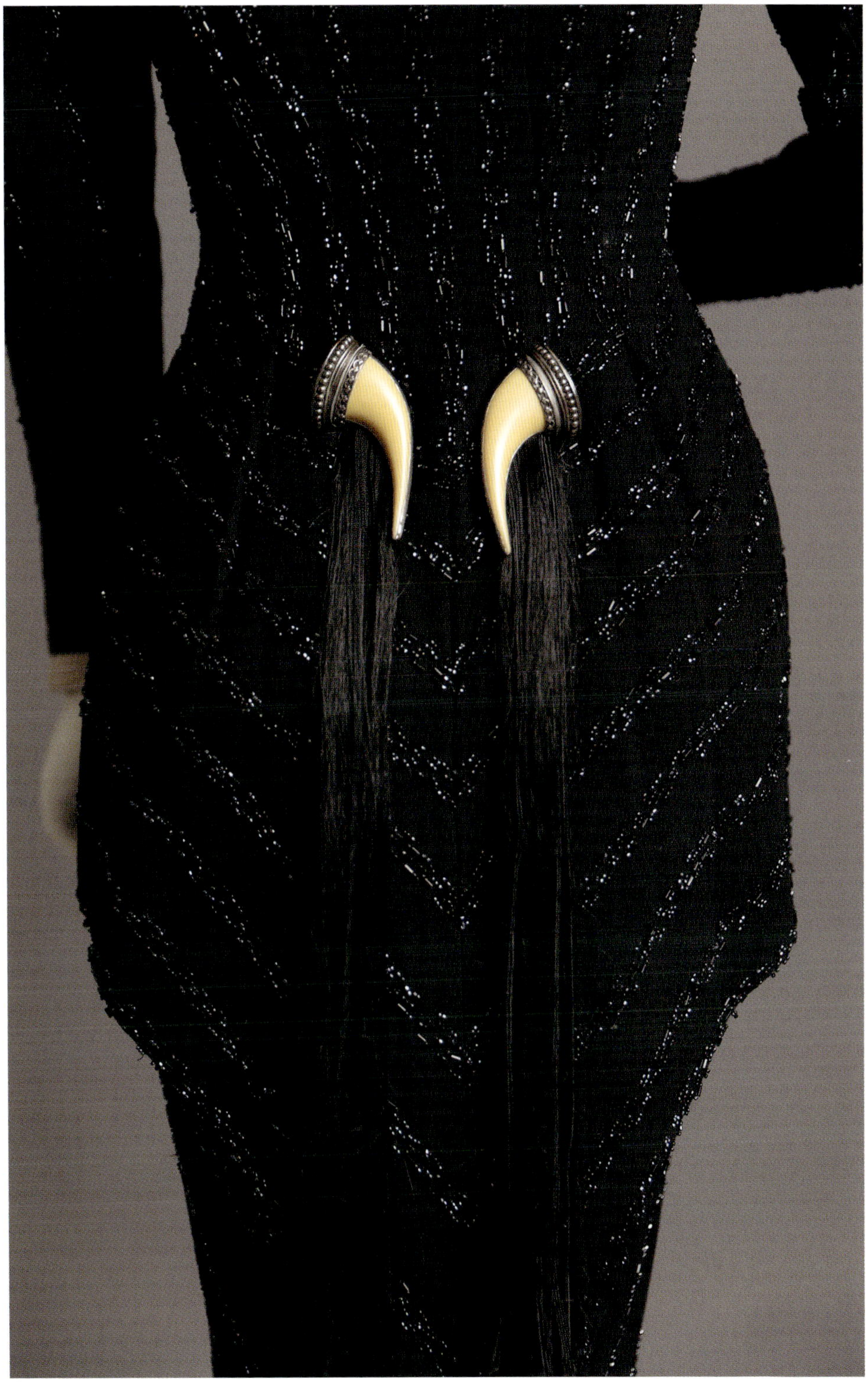

Anthony Powell (English)
Barbara Matera Ltd.
Martin Adams
Woody Shelp
Cruella De Vil
101 Dalmatians, 1996
Wool, glass beads, fox fur, horsehair, plastic, metal, straw, rayon, cotton, silk
GC 2017.2.1, .5–.7

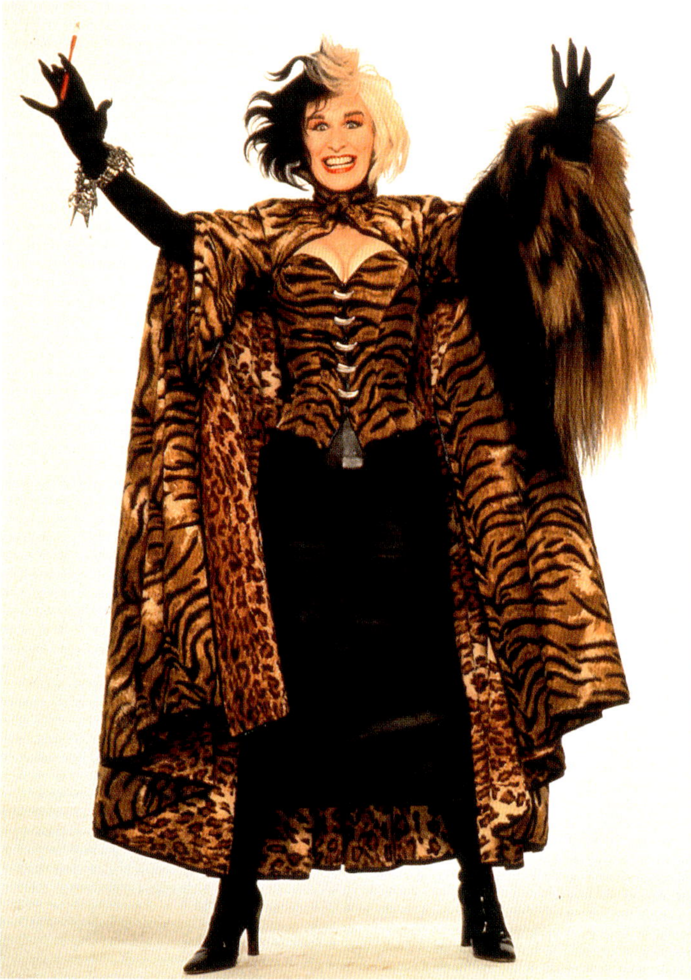

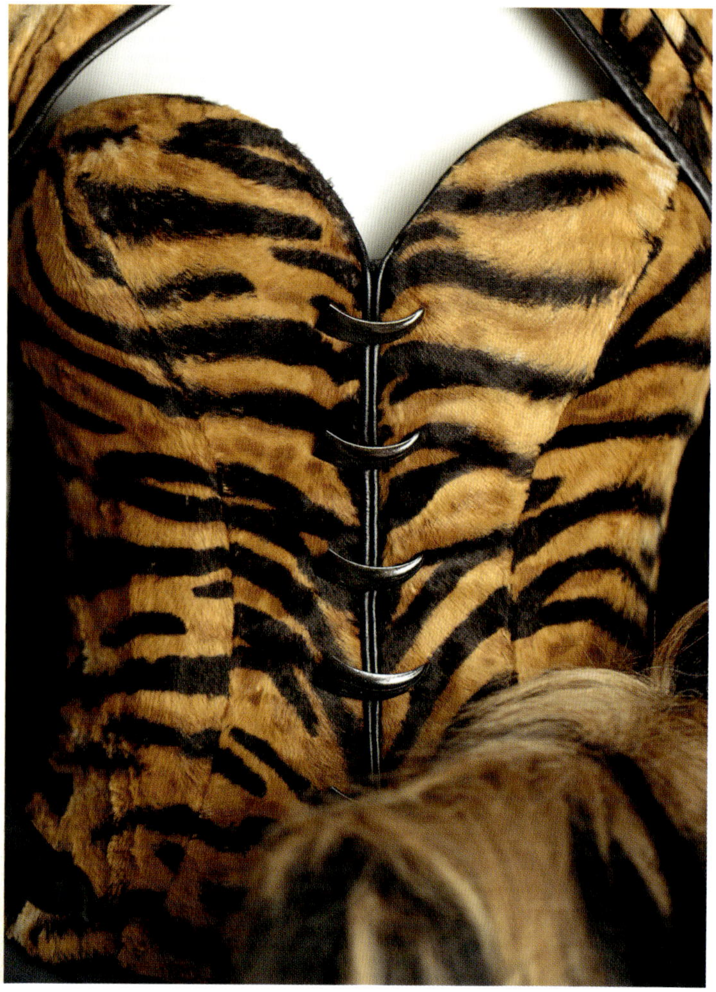

Anthony Powell (English)
Barbara Matera Ltd.
Martin Adams
Cruella De Vil
101 Dalmatians, 1996.
© Disney
Acrylic/faux fur, leather, metal, spandex, plastic
GC 2017.3.1–.4, .6 AB

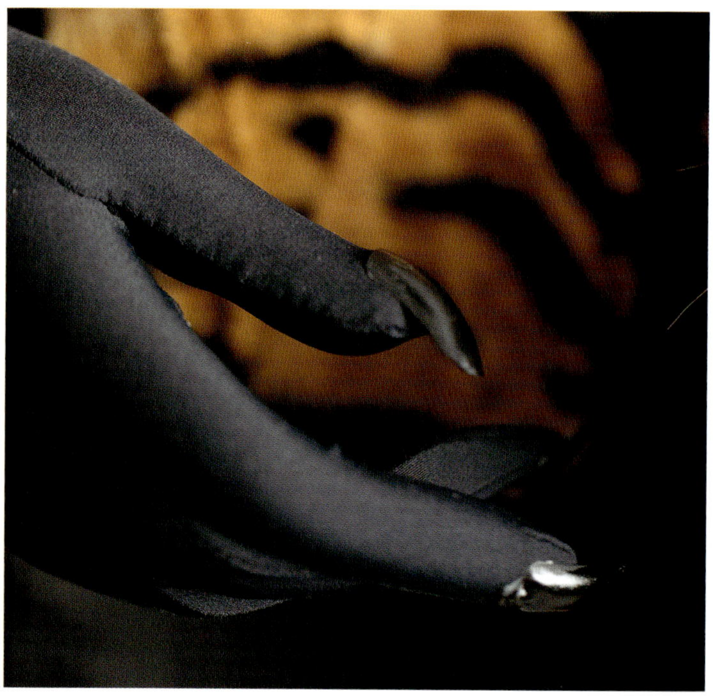

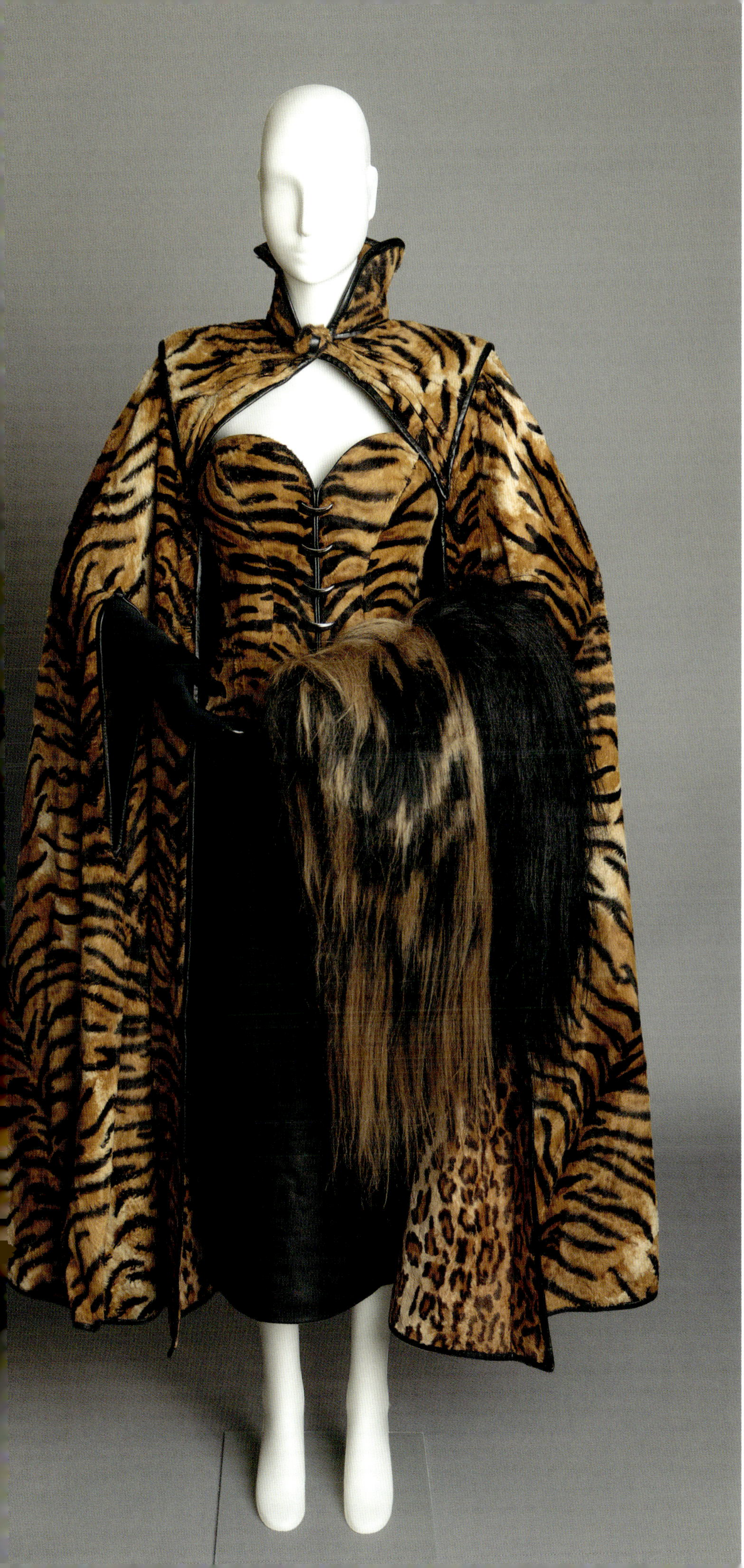

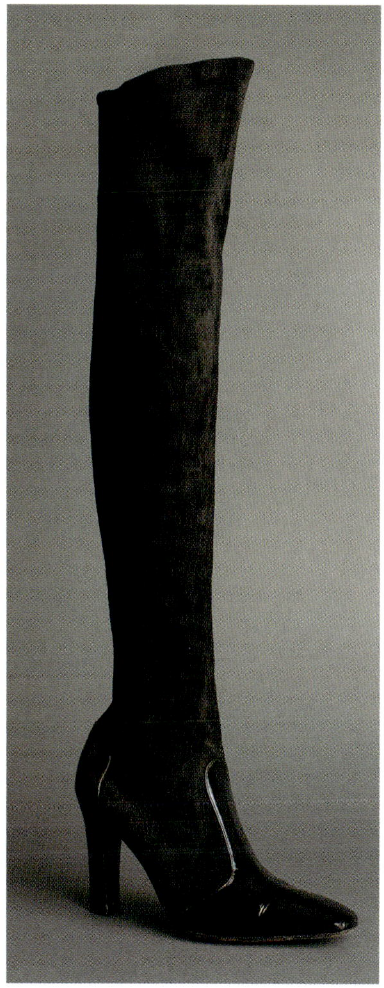

ABOVE
Anthony Powell (English)
Cruella De Vil
101 Dalmatians, 1996
Leather, suede
GC 2017.3.5 AB

LEFT
Anthony Powell (English)
Barbara Matera Ltd.
Martin Adams
Cruella De Vil
101 Dalmatians, 1996
Acrylic/faux fur, leather, metal, spandex, plastic
GC 2017.3.1–.4, .6 AB

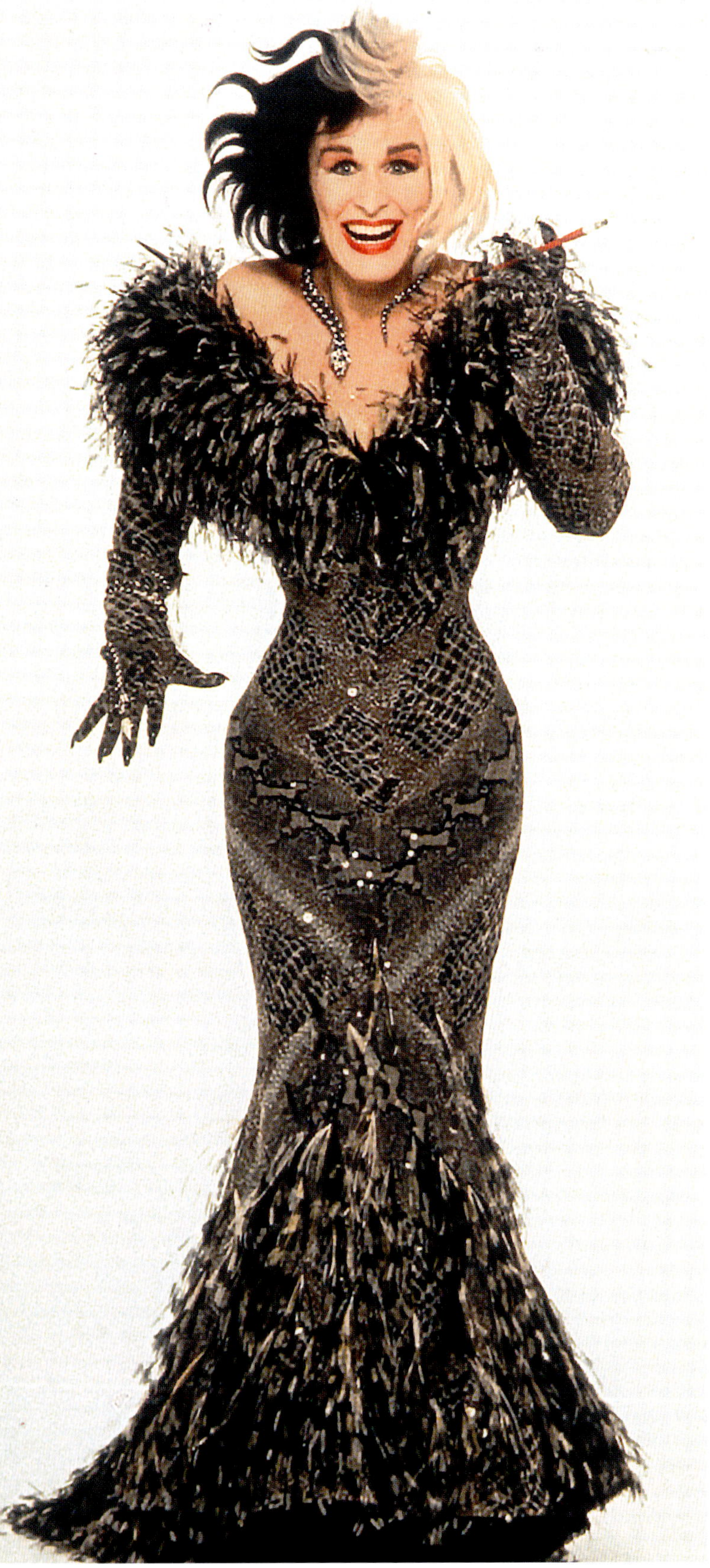

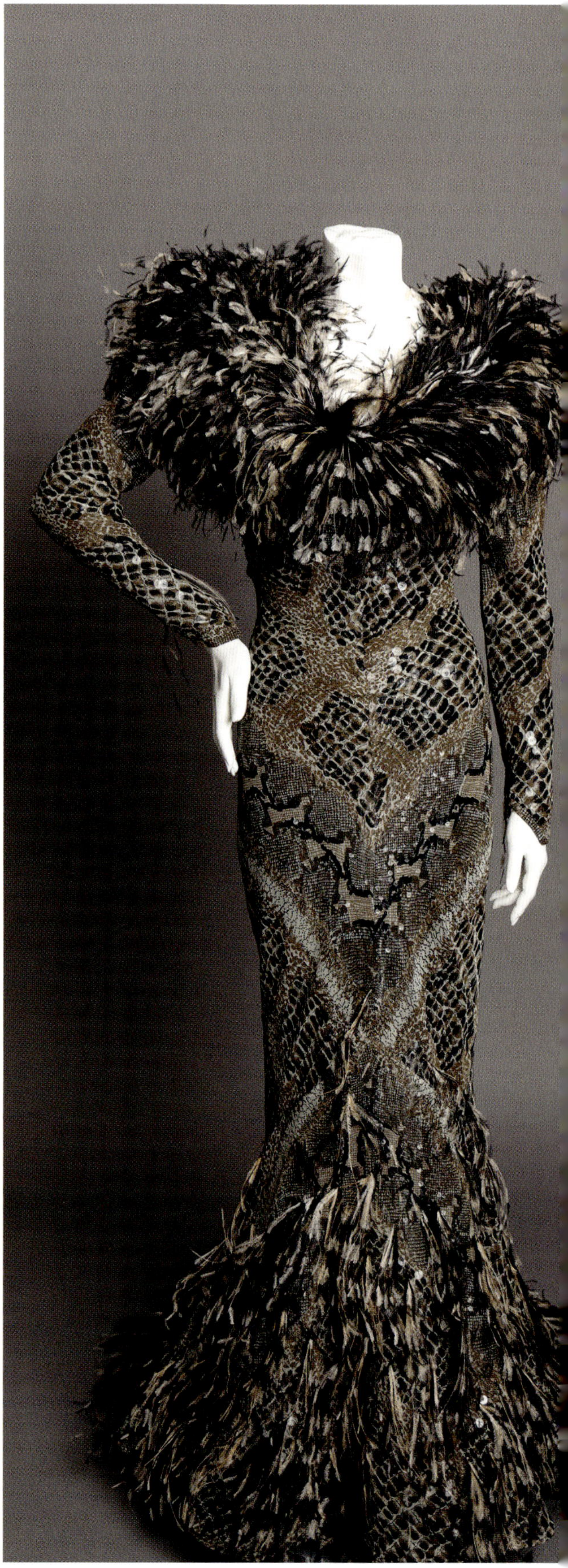

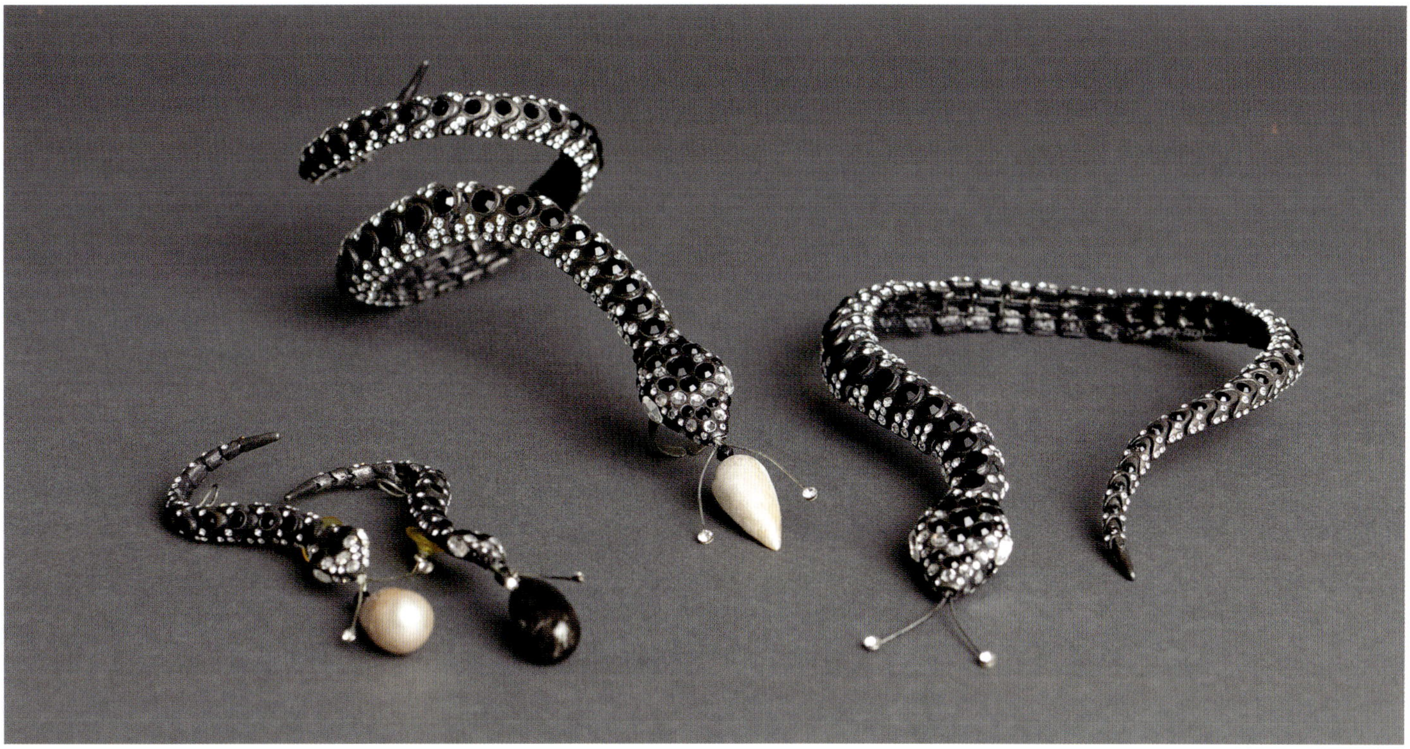

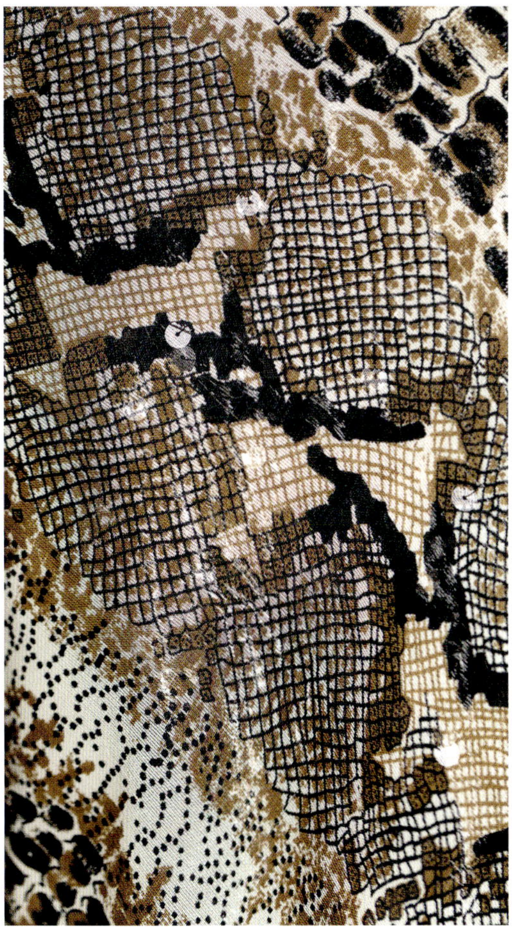

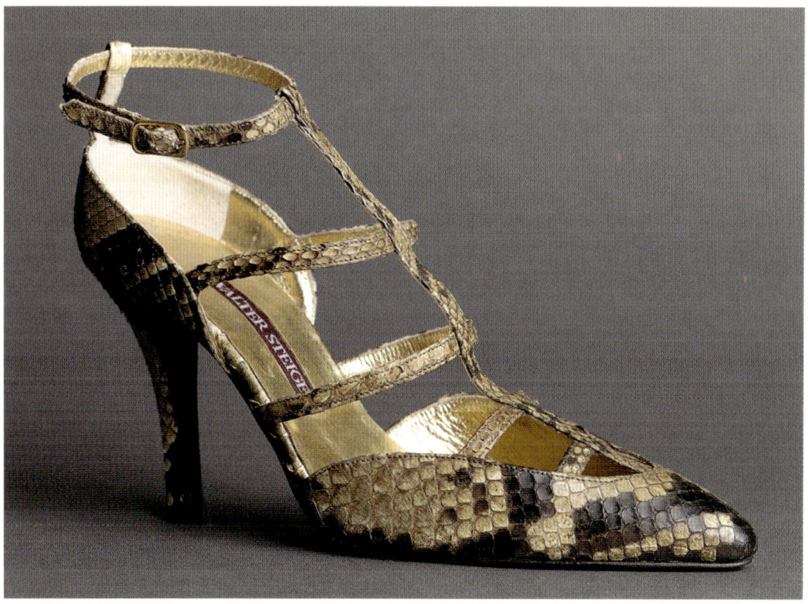

OPPOSITE
Anthony Powell (English)
Barbara Matera Ltd.
Cruella De Vil
101 Dalmatians, 1996
© Disney
Silk, ostrich feathers,
plastic sequins
GC 2017.7.1

TOP
Anthony Powell (English)
Martin Adams
Cruella De Vil
101 Dalmatians, 1996
Metal, crystals,
glass stones, faux pearls
GC 2017.7.4 A–D

ABOVE RIGHT
Anthony Powell (English)
Cruella De Vil
101 Dalmatians, 1996
Walter Steiger
Snakeskin, leather
GC 2017.7.2 AB

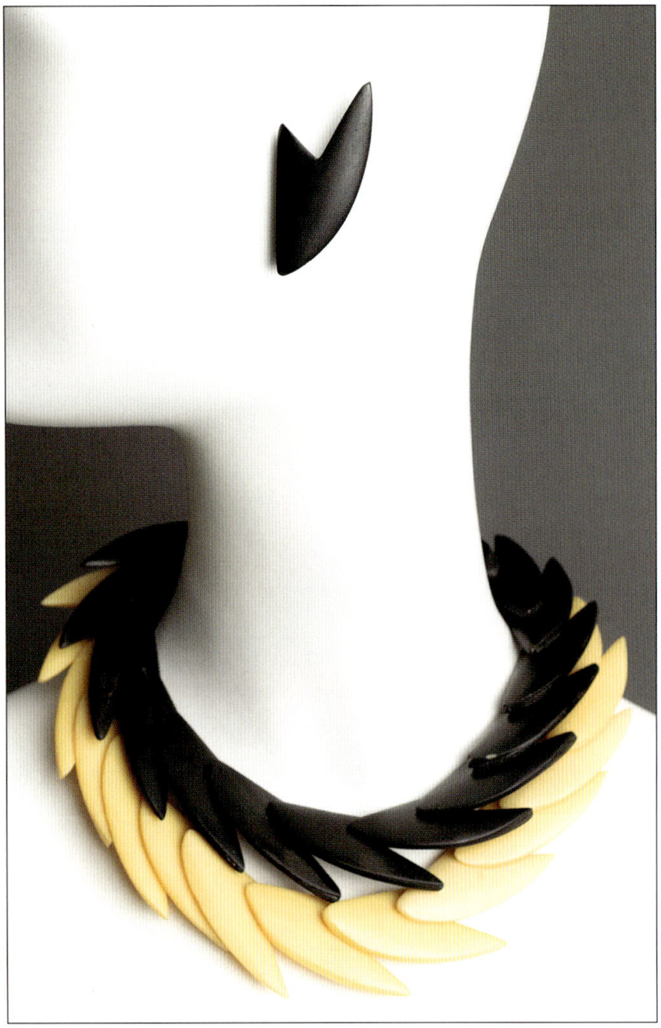

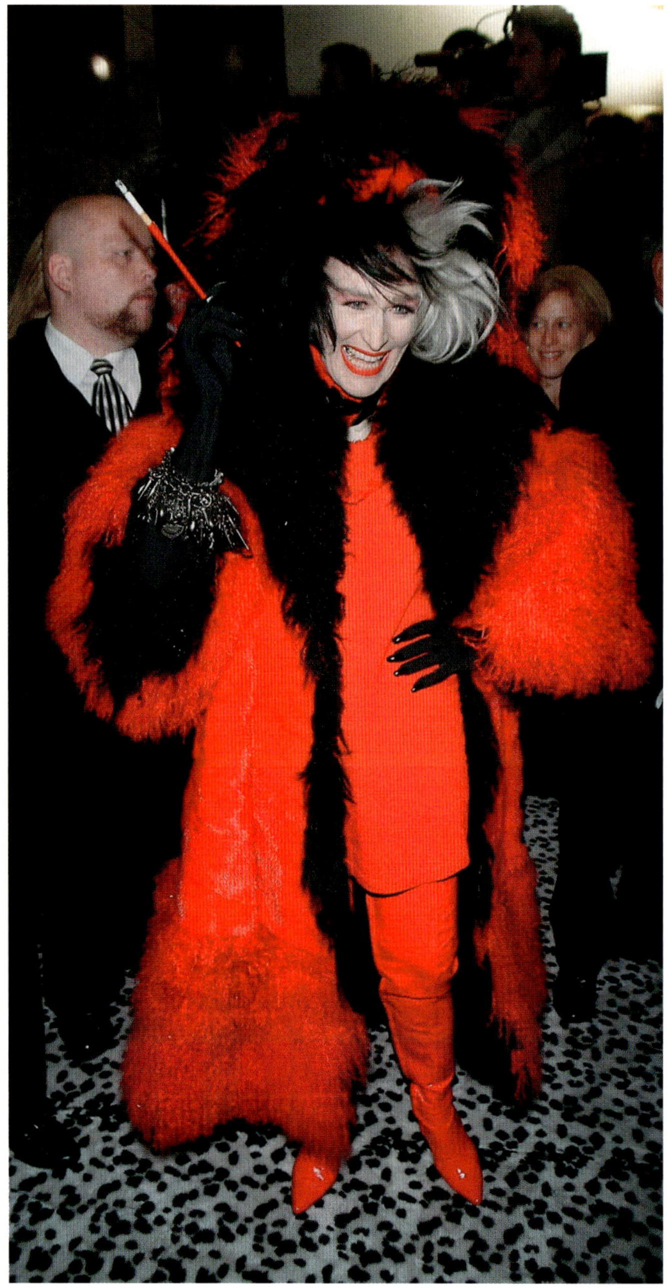

ABOVE
Anthony Powell (English)
Martin Adams
Cruella De Vil
101 Dalmatians, 1996
Plastic, metal
GC 2017.1.7, .12 AB

RIGHT
Glenn Close in Cruella De Vil costume at the New York premiere of *101 Dalmatians*, 1996
Used by permission from Disney Enterprises, Inc.

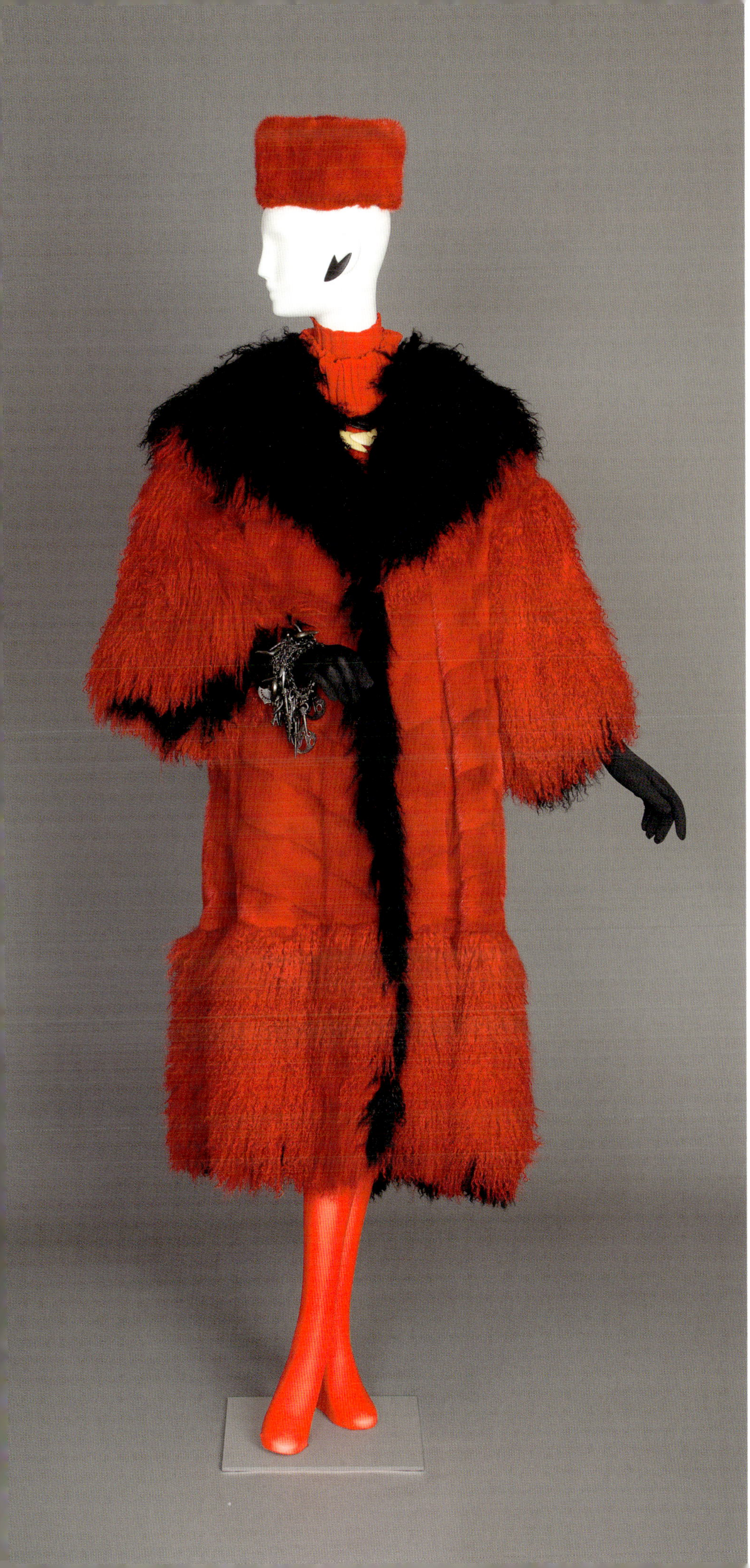

Anthony Powell (English)
Barbara Matera Ltd.
Martin Adams
Woody Shelp
Cruella De Vil
101 Dalmatians, 1996
Mink fur, Mongolian lamb, wool, plastic, metal, rhinestones
GC 2017.1.2, .4–8

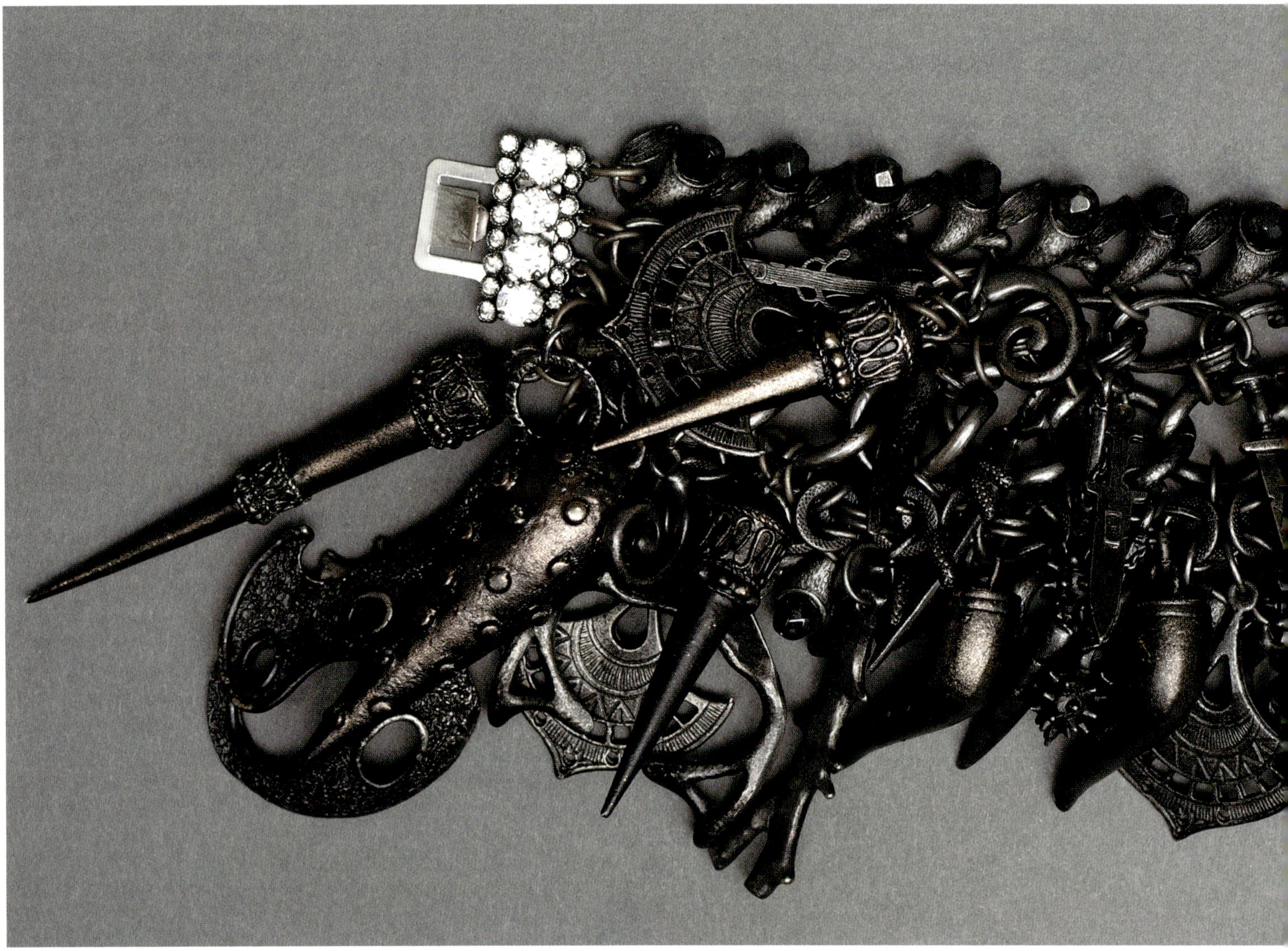

Anthony Powell (English)
Martin Adams
Cruella De Vil
101 Dalmatians, 1996
Metal, rhinestones
GC 2017.1.8

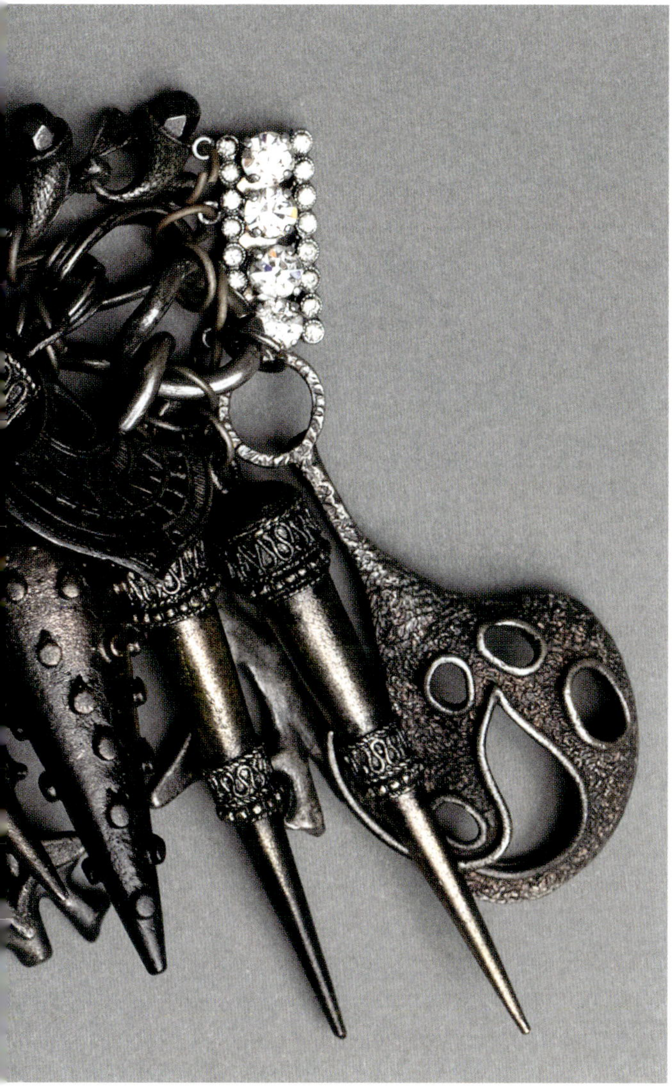

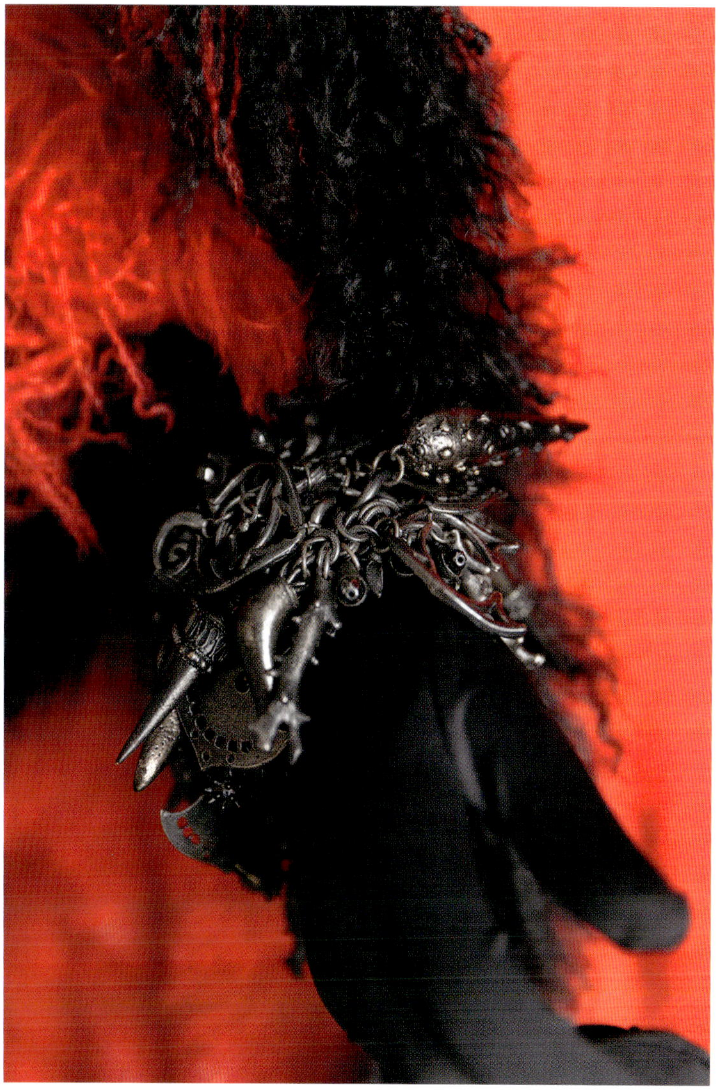

CHARACTER

Cruella De Vil

102 Dalmatians, 2000

CRUELLA DE VIL, THE FUR-CRAZED FASHION VILLAIN, returned to the screen in 2000 in the popular sequel *102 Dalmatians*. In the film's opening, Cruella has undergone aversion therapy by Dr. Pavlov during her three-year prison sentence, emerging as the dog-loving, fur-loathing Ella. She bails out a faltering dog shelter on the brink of eviction, but her conditioning is quickly undone by the bell chimes of Big Ben. The terms of her probation require her to donate her fortune if she commits more crimes against animals, and so she is forced to hide her relapse. She meets her end when she is baked into a giant layer cake by dalmatian puppies, still clad in an enormous black and red fur coat and thigh-high boots.

Glenn Close's character arc and the personalities she played—the reformed Ella; Cruella pretending to be the sweet Ella; and the wicked Cruella—were ideal vehicles for Anthony Powell's creativity. The film's director, Kevin Lima, emphasized the significance of costuming to the narrative, saying in an interview that the wardrobe for each character shift "is among the most important attributes in telling Cruella's story."[7] In addition to the good-to-evil transformation scene, spectacular settings like a fashion show and a dog dinner party inspired over-the-top fabulous fire- and dragon-inspired costumes painstakingly handcrafted at Barbara Matera Ltd. The reformed Ella's fear of fur created opportunities to display her new ethos via ingenious garments constructed out of silk flowers and plastic bubble wrap.

DESIGNER

Anthony Powell

See p. 134 for biography.

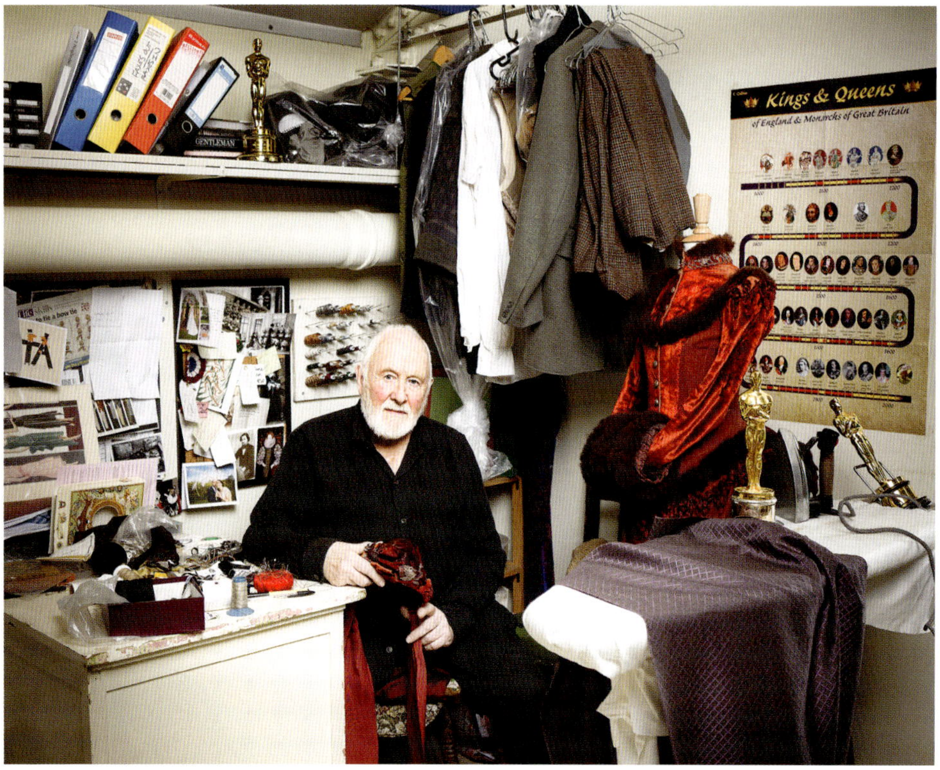

Costume designer Anthony Powell is photographed for the *Guardian* on December 9, 2015 in London, England.

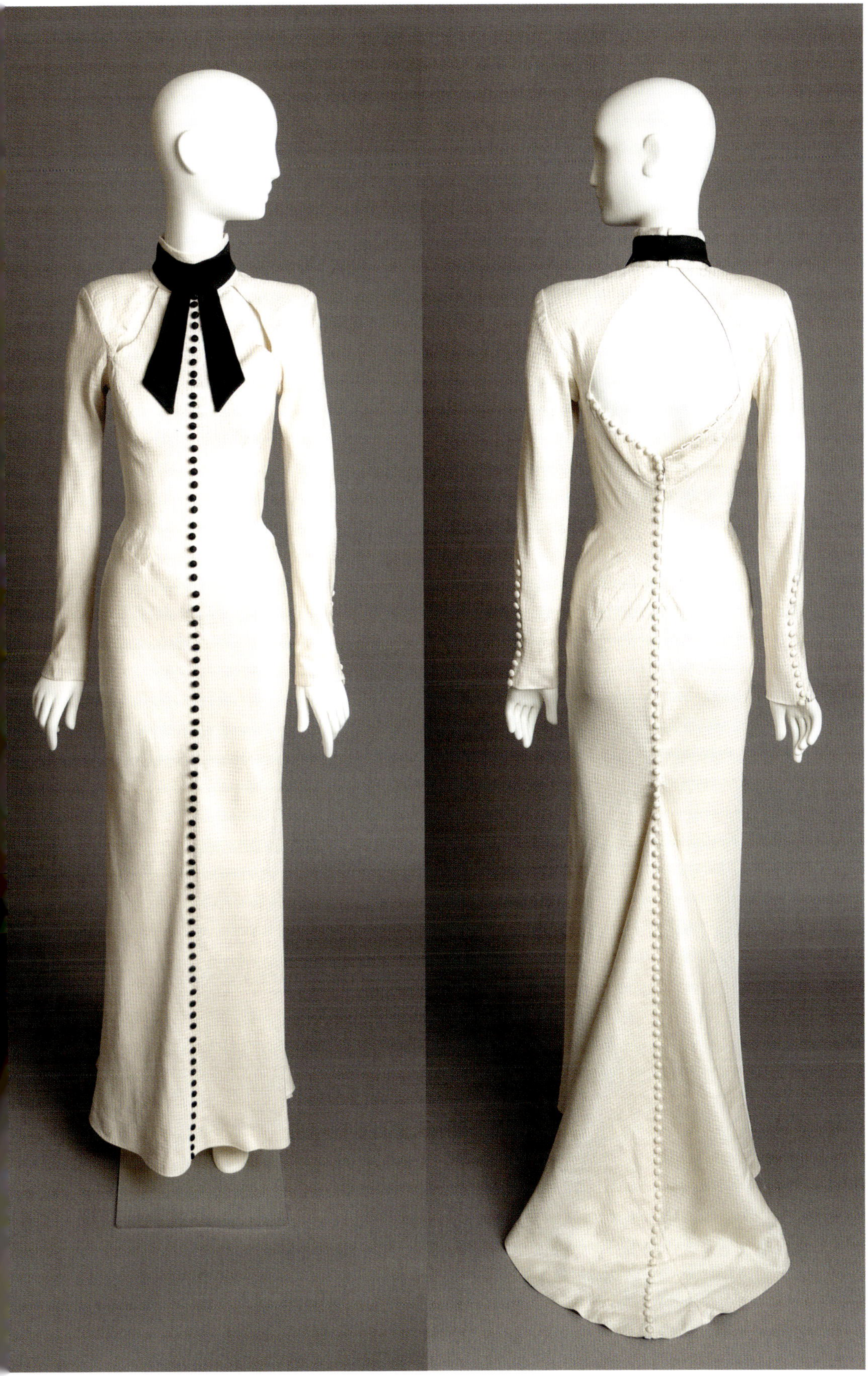

Anthony Powell (English)
Barbara Matera Ltd.
Cruella De Vil/Ella
102 Dalmatians, 2000
Silk
GC 2017.11.1

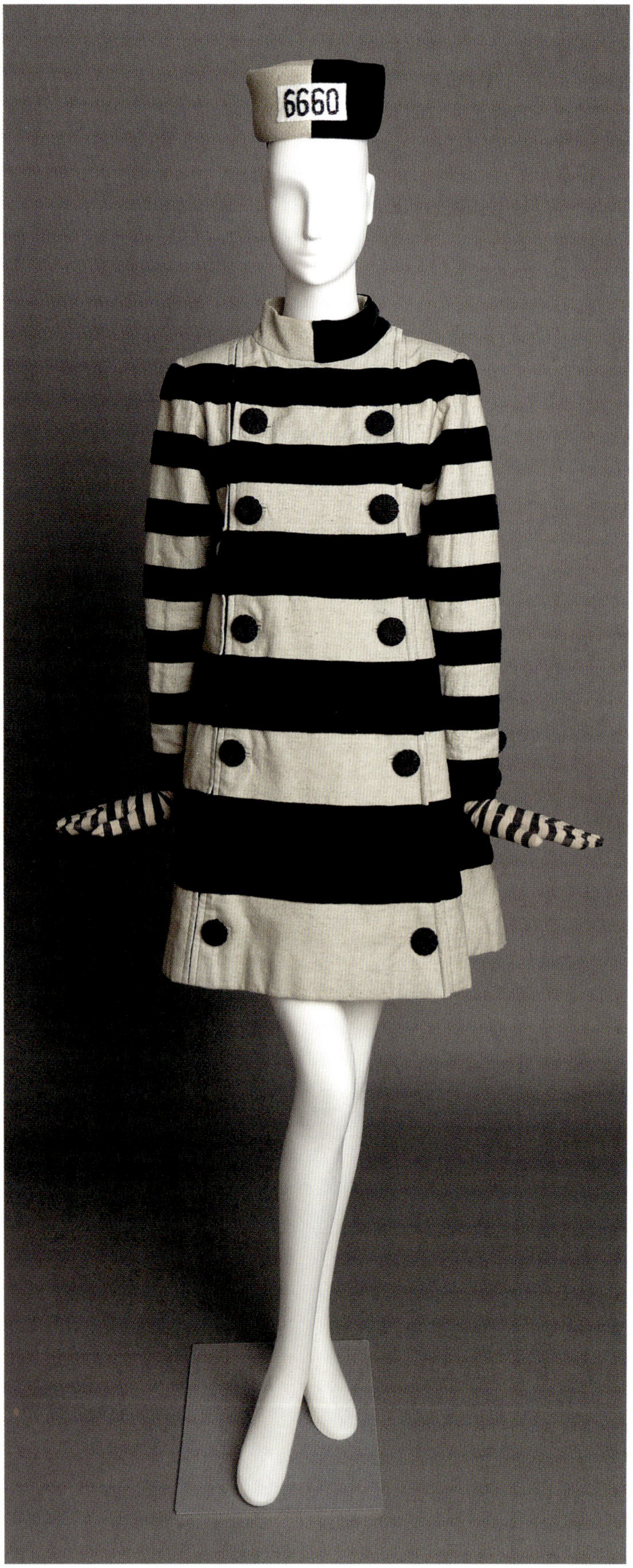

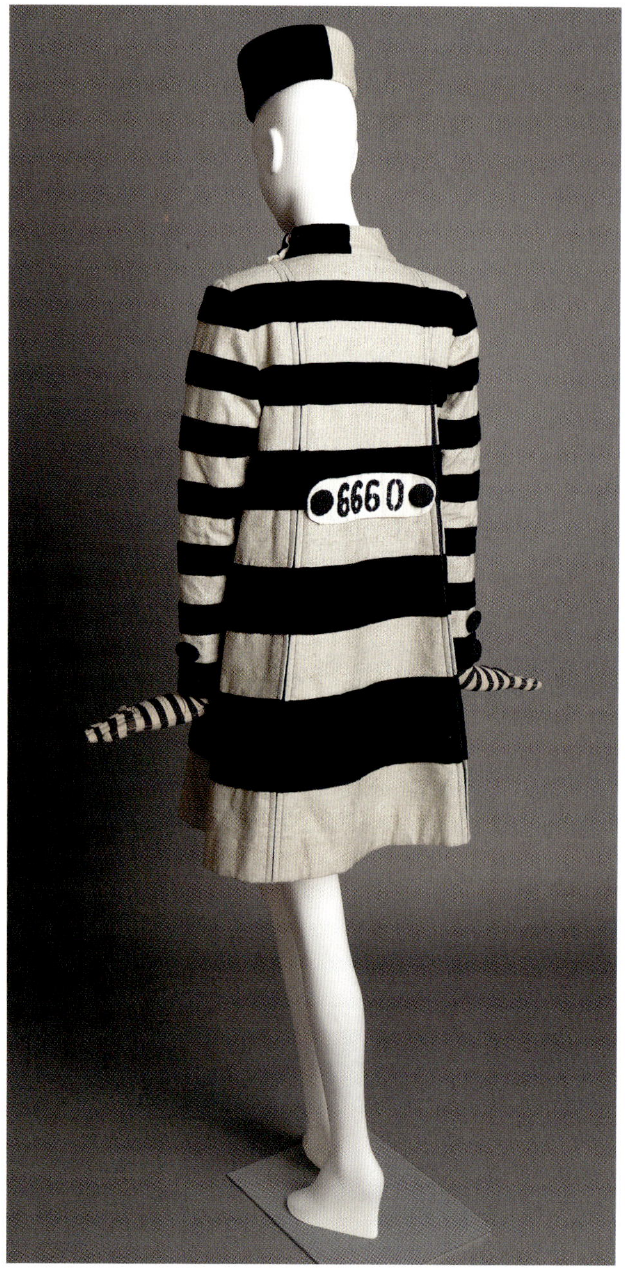

THIS PAGE AND OPPOSITE
Anthony Powell (English)
Barbara Matera Ltd.
Woody Shelp
Cruella De Vil/Ella
102 Dalmatians, 2000
© Disney
Linen, silk, cotton, glass beads
GC 2017.10.1–.2, .4

OPPOSITE BOTTOM LEFT
Anthony Powell (English)
Cruella De Vil/Ella
102 Dalmatians, 2000
Linen, leather
GC 2017.10.3 AB

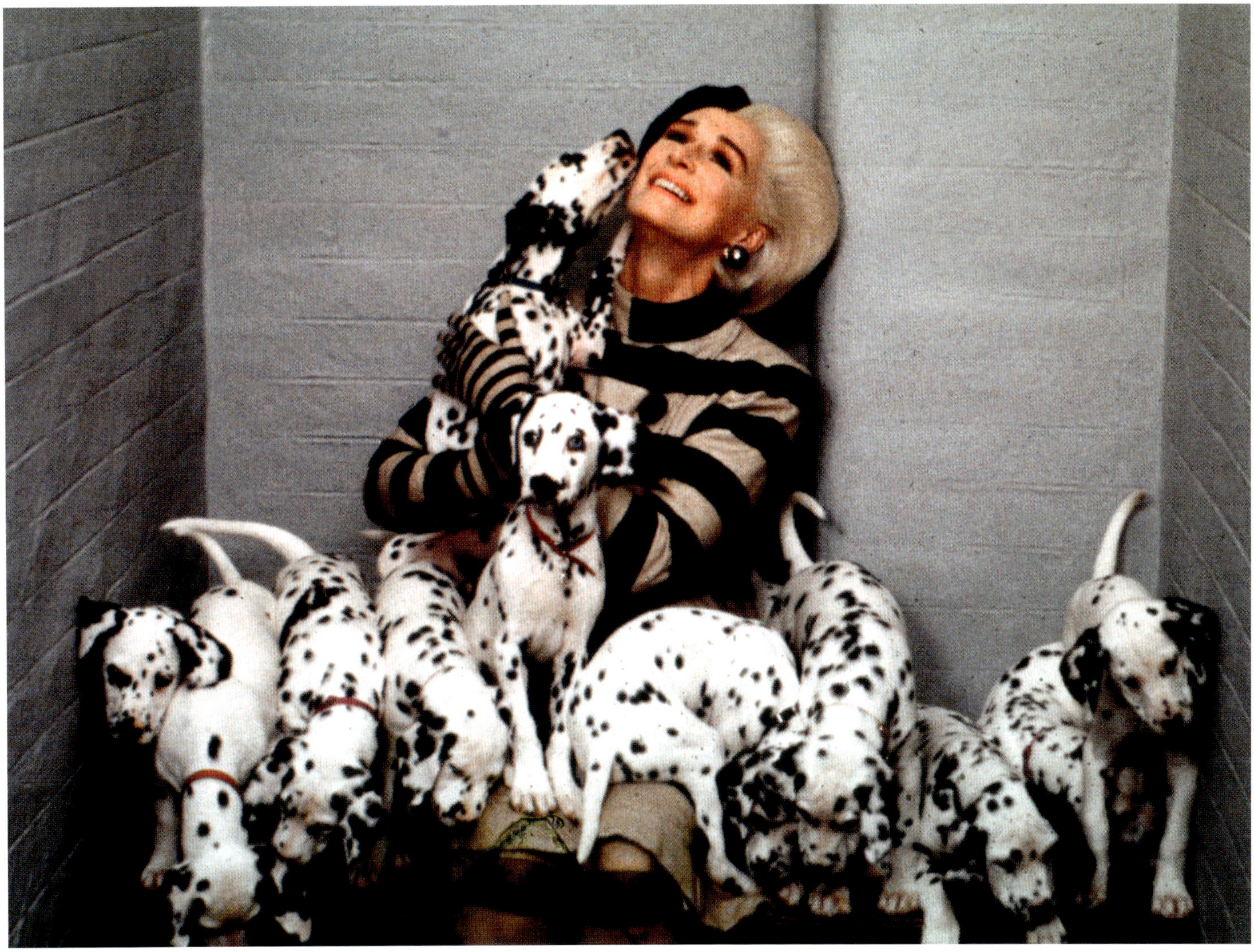

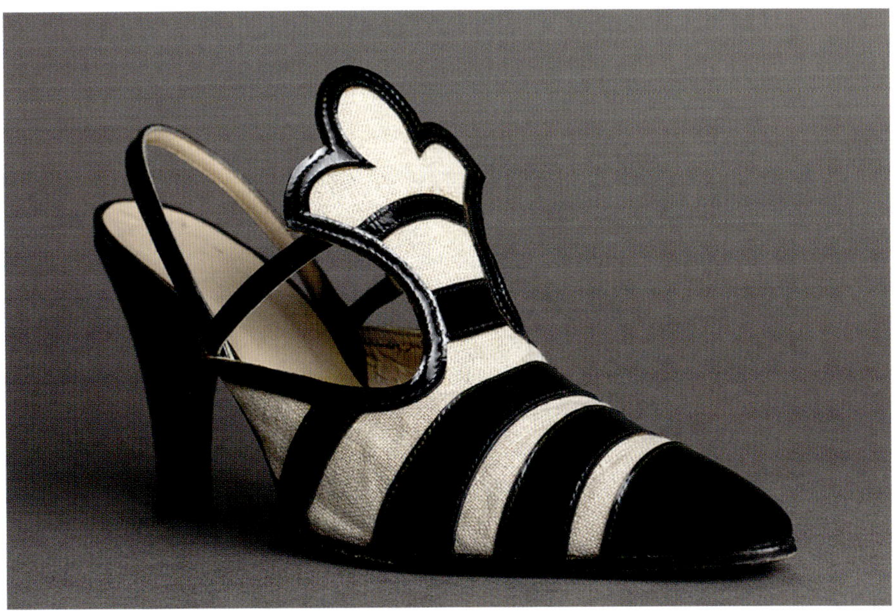

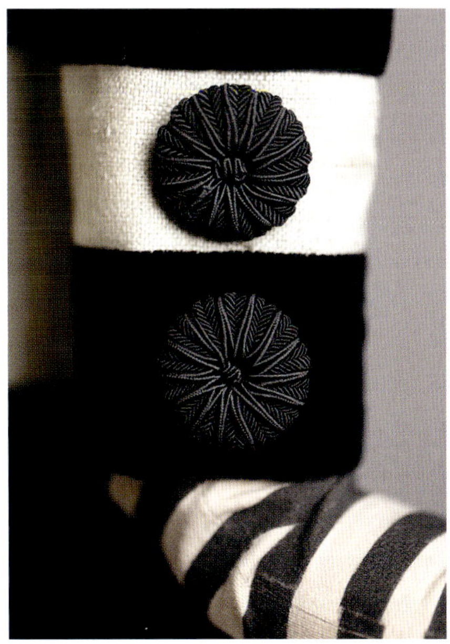

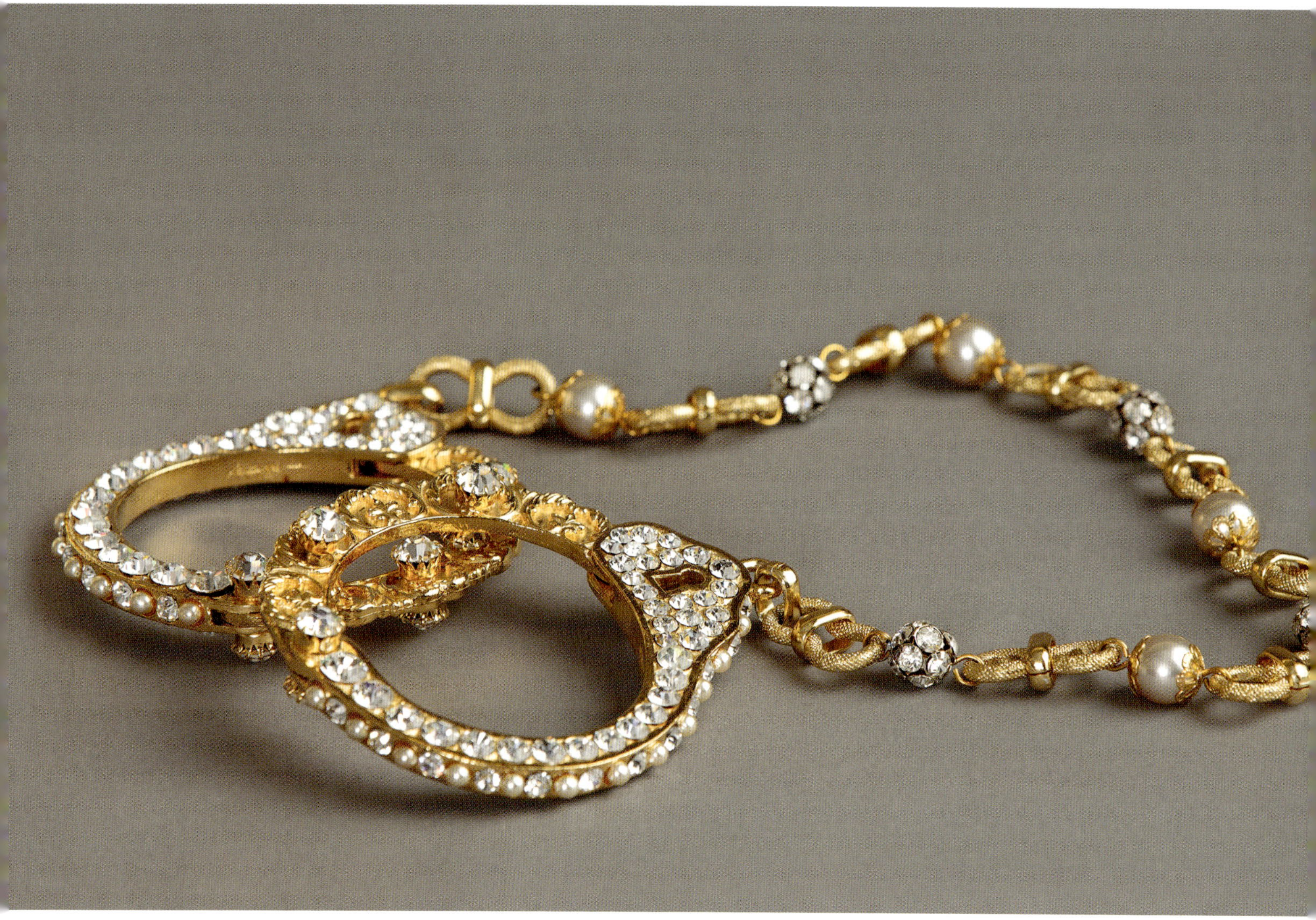

Anthony Powell (English)
Martin Adams
Cruella De Vil/Ella
102 Dalmatians, 2000
Metal, rhinestones, faux pearls, glass
GC 2017.10.7, .8

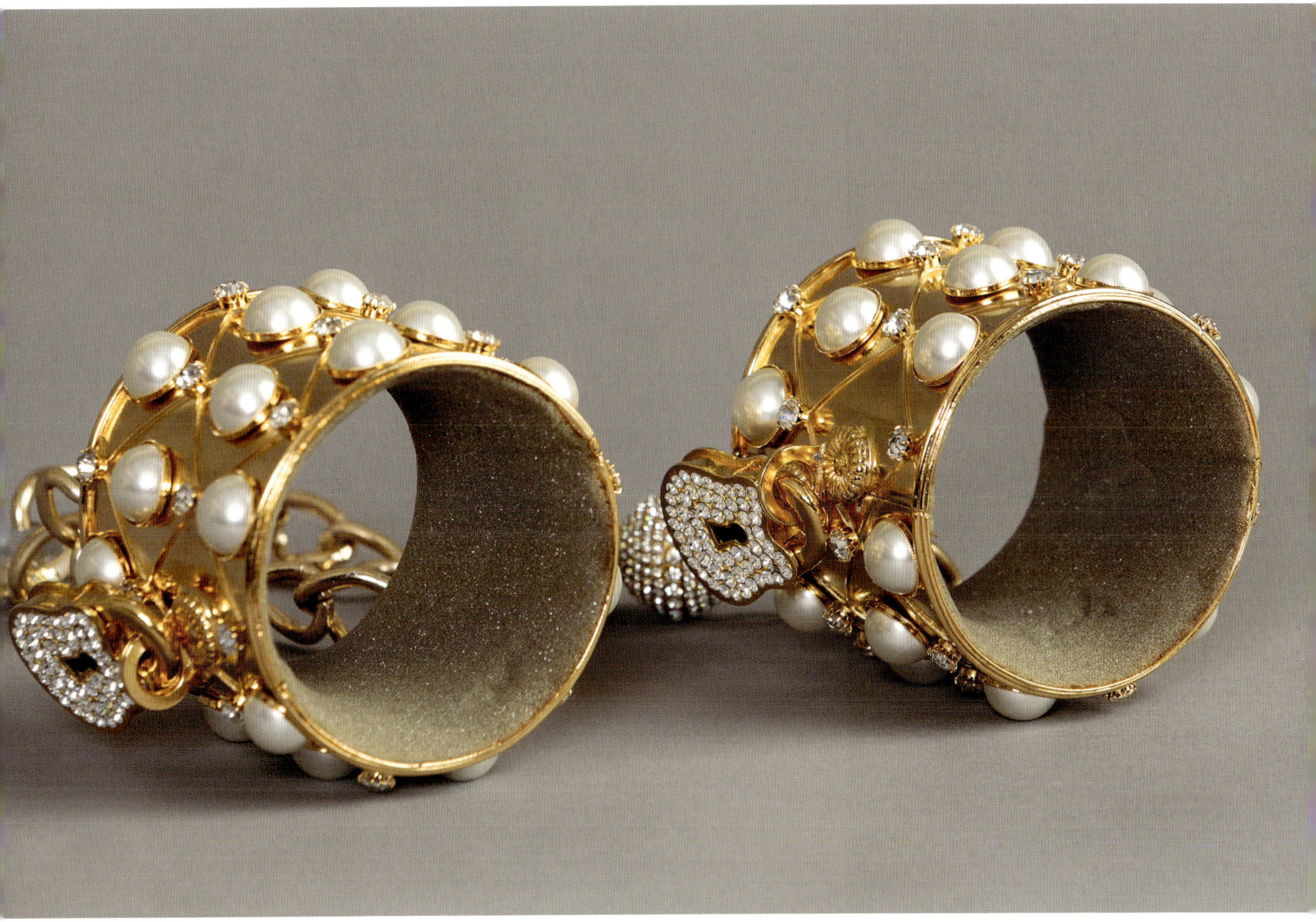

Anthony Powell (English)
Barbara Matera Ltd.
Cruella De Vil/Ella
102 Dalmatians, 2000
Silk
GC 2017.24.1

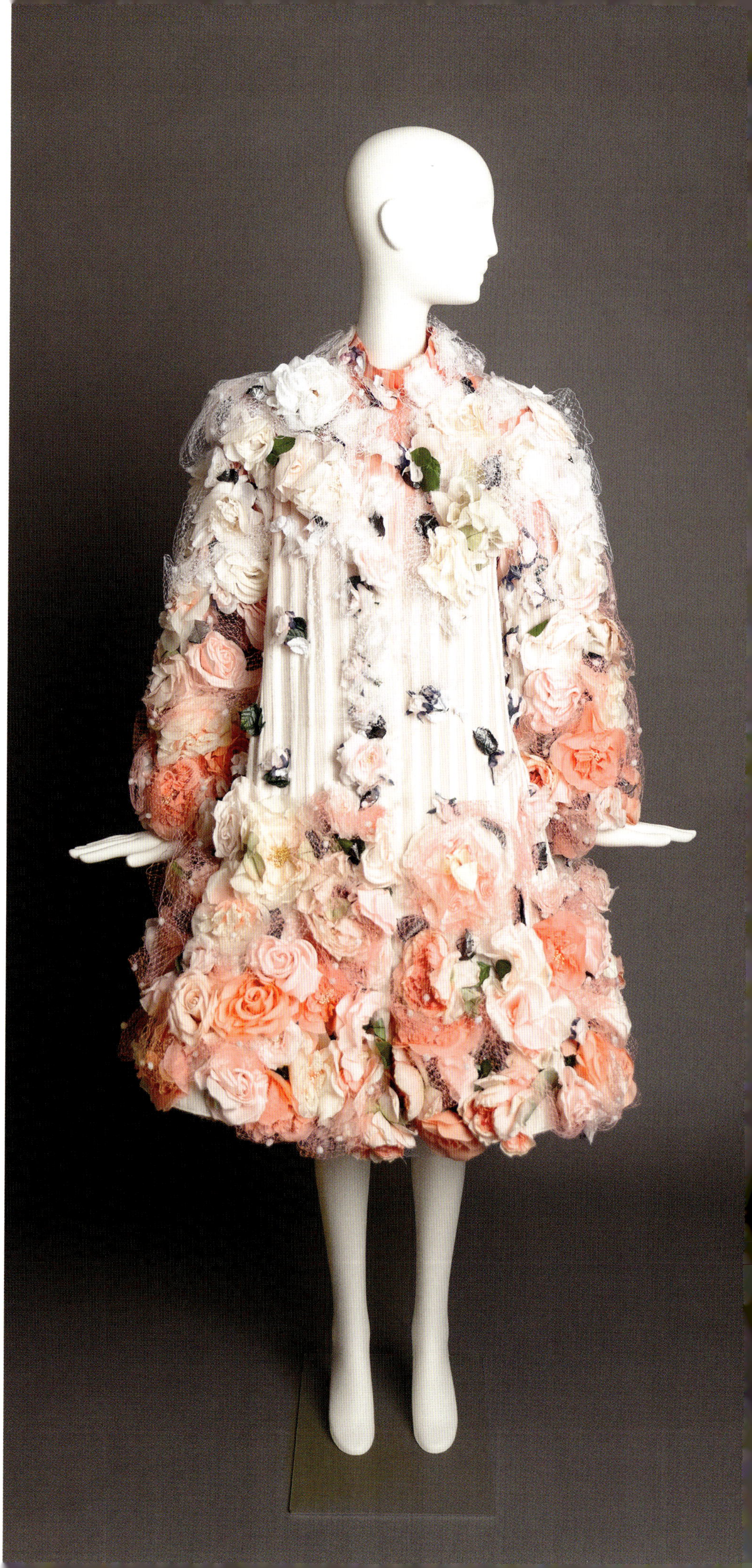

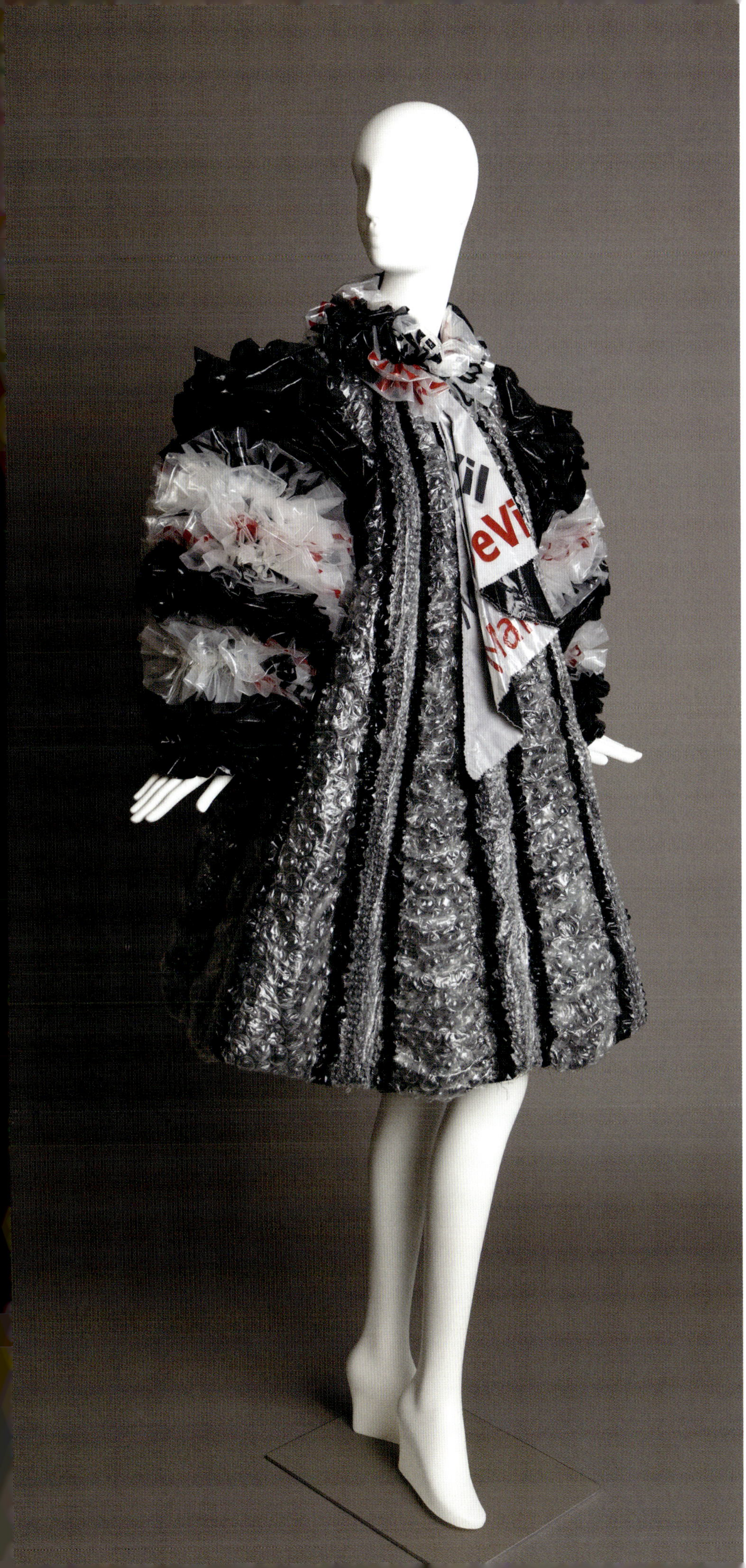

Anthony Powell (English)
Barbara Matera Ltd.
Cruella De Vil/Ella
102 Dalmatians, 2000
Plastic, Lurex, silk, polyester
GC 2017.23.1

Anthony Powell (English)
Barbara Matera Ltd.
Martin Adams
Cruella De Vil/Ella
102 Dalmatians, 2000
Cotton, metal, polyvinyl chloride, rhinestones
GC 2017.12.1, .3–.4

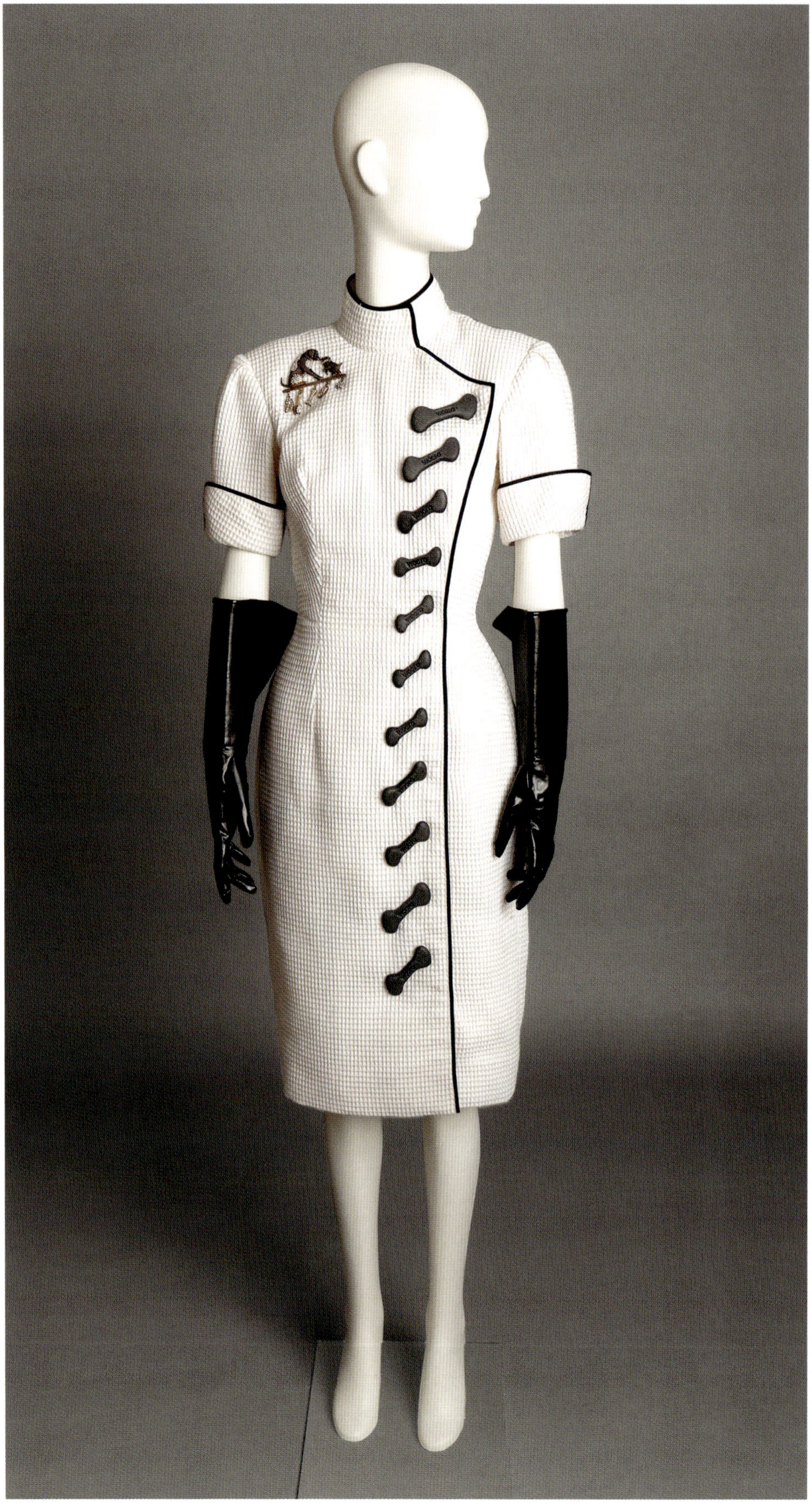

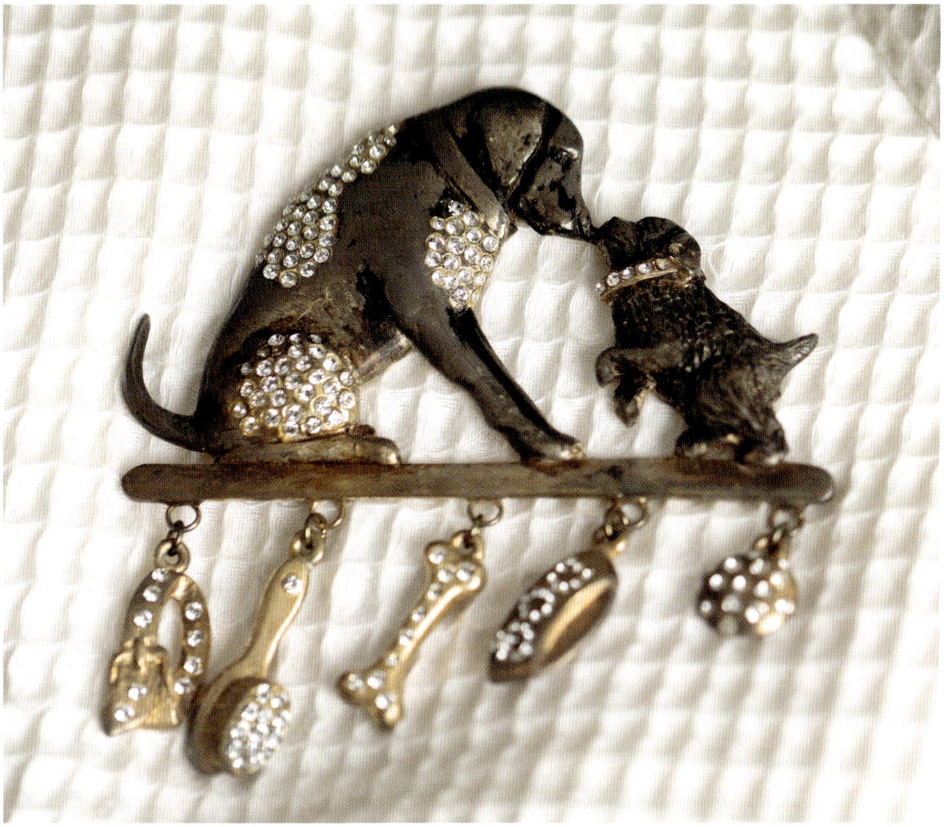

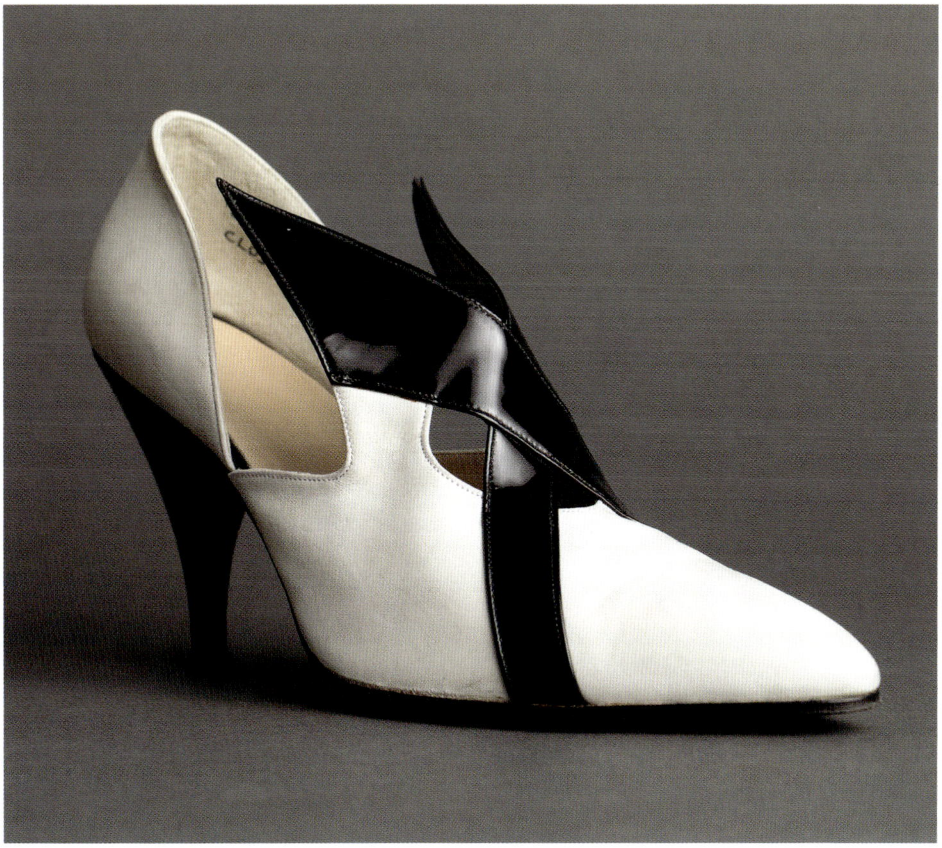

LEFT
Anthony Powell (English)
Barbara Matera Ltd.
Martin Adams
Cruella De Vil/Ella
102 Dalmatians, 2000
Metal and rhinestones
GC 2017.12.1, .4

BOTTOM LEFT
Anthony Powell (English)
Cruella De Vil/Ella
102 Dalmatians, 2000
Buckskin, leather
GC 2017.12.2 AB

RIGHT
Glenn Close as Cruella De Vil/Ella in *102 Dalmatians*, 2000. © Disney

BOTTOM RIGHT
Anthony Powell (English)
Martin Adams
Cruella De Vil/Ella
102 Dalmatians, 2000
Metal, crystals, faux pearls
GC 2017.15.6

OPPOSITE
Anthony Powell (English)
Barbara Matera Ltd.
Martin Adams
Cruella De Vil/Ella
102 Dalmatians, 2000
Wool, silk, metal, plastic sequins, glass beads, crystals, faux pearls
GC 2017.15.1–.2, .5–.6/16.1–.2, .4–5/17.1–.2, .6

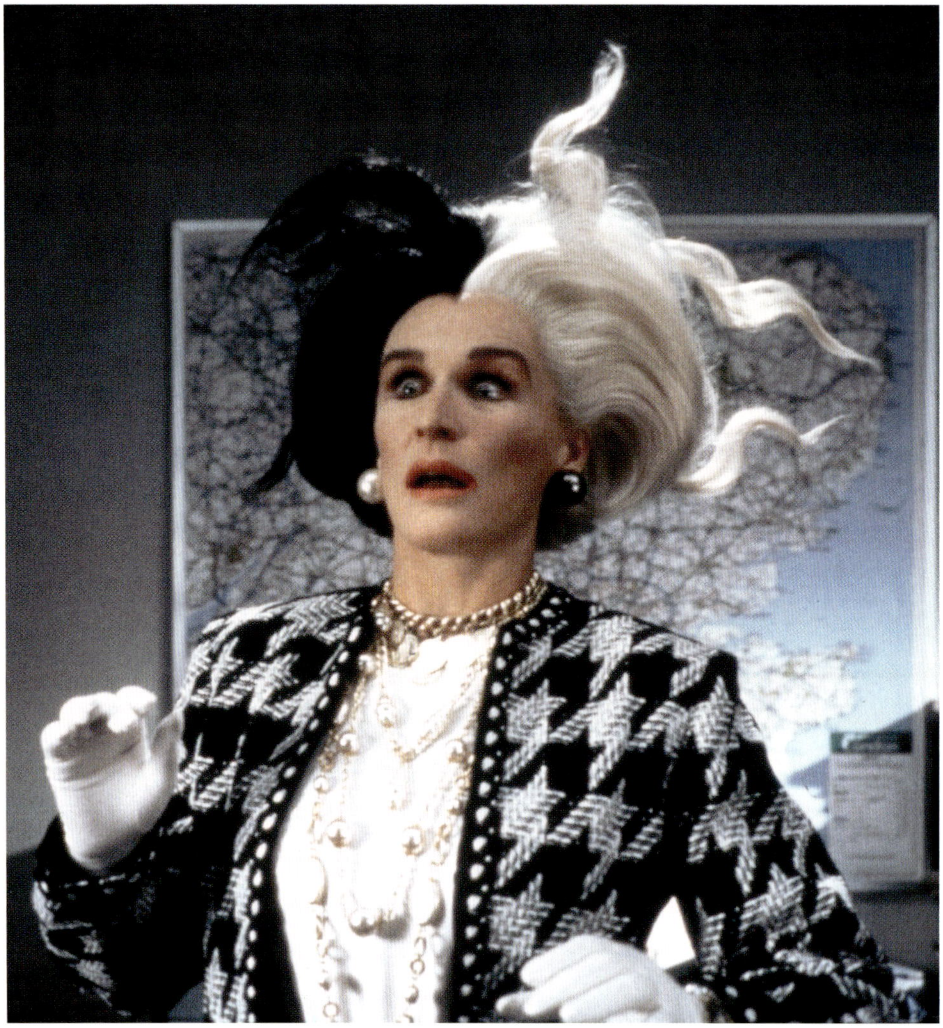

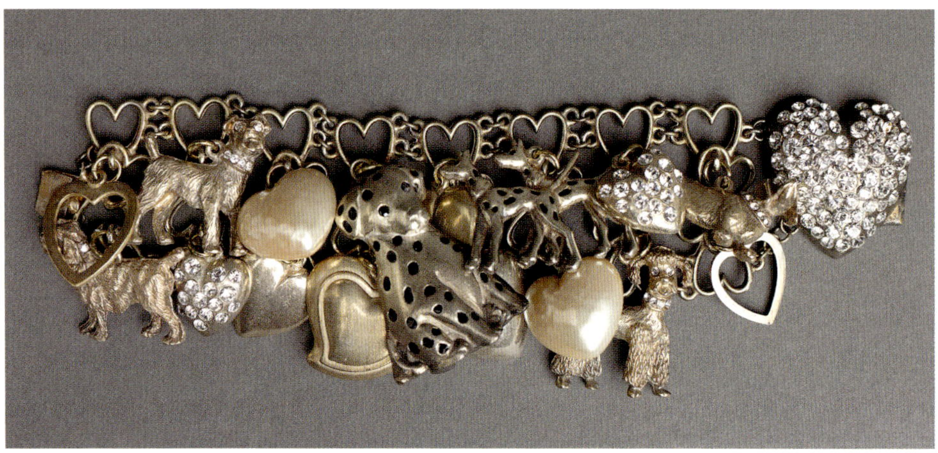

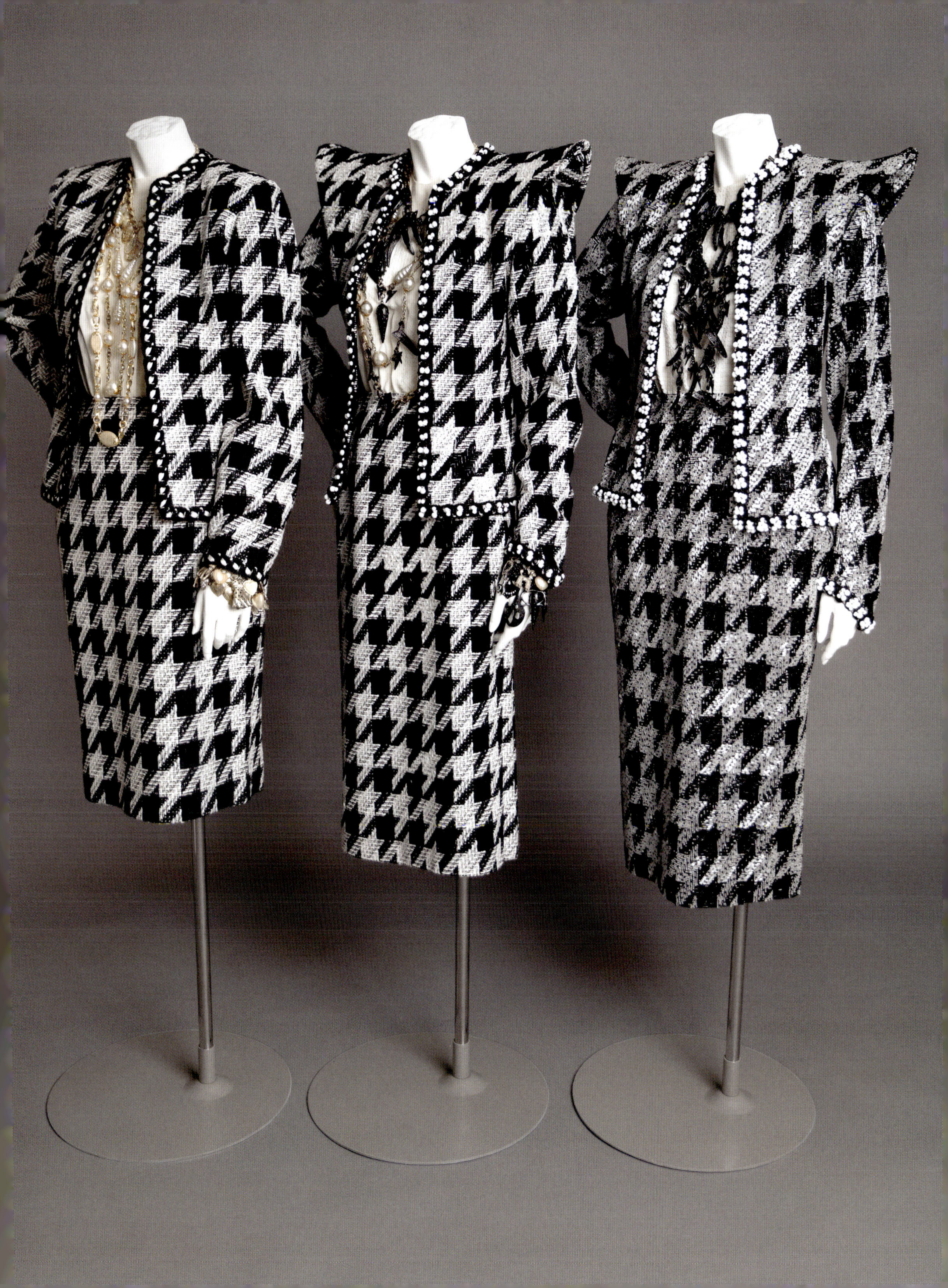

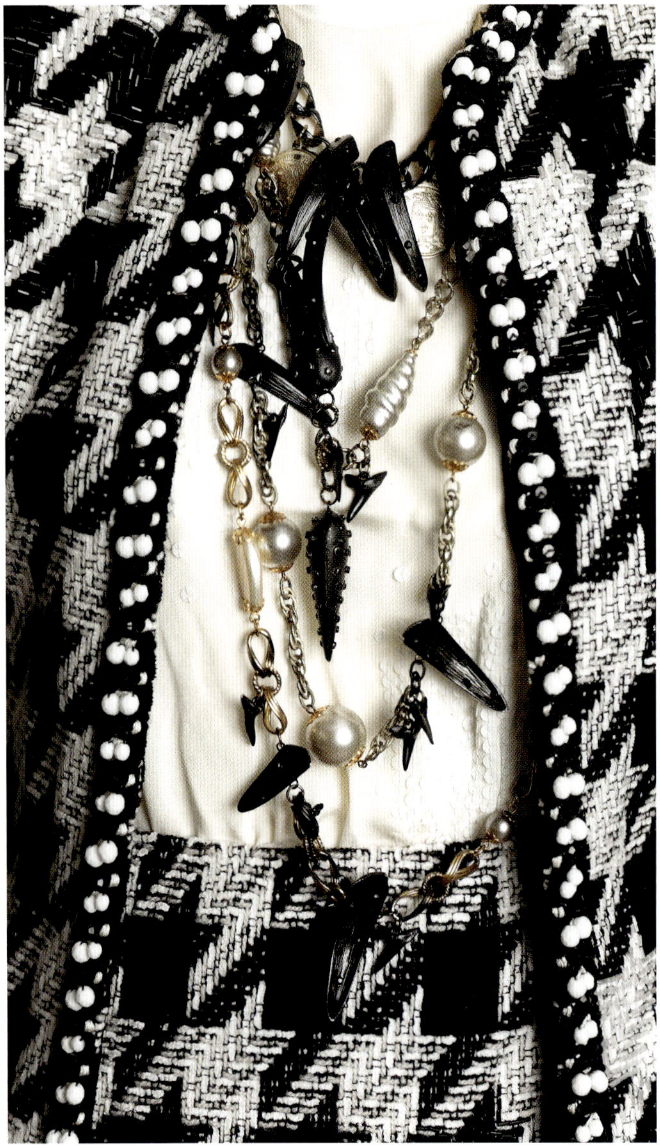

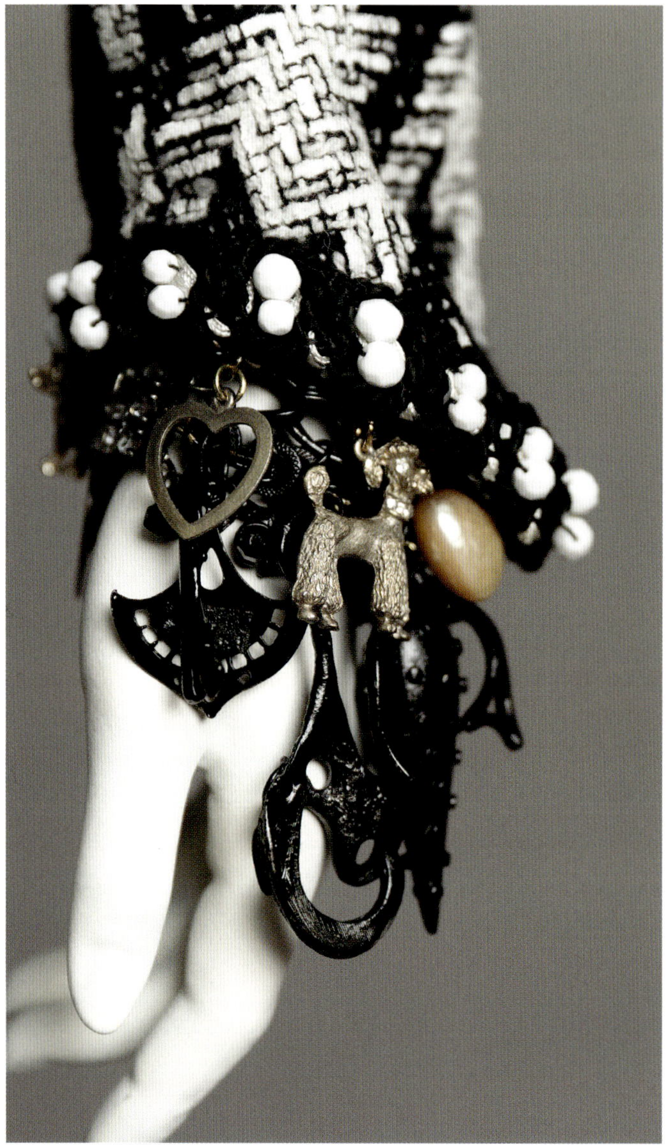

ABOVE
Anthony Powell (English)
Barbara Matera Ltd.
Martin Adams
Cruella De Vil/Ella
102 Dalmatians, 2000
Wool, silk, metal, plastic sequins, glass beads, crystals, faux pearls
GC 2017.16.1-.2, .4-.5

OPPOSITE
Anthony Powell (English)
Barbara Matera Ltd.
Martin Adams
Woody Shelp
Cruella De Vil/Ella
102 Dalmatians, 2000
Silk, spandex, plastic, rhinestones, metal, polyester, feathers, porcupine quills

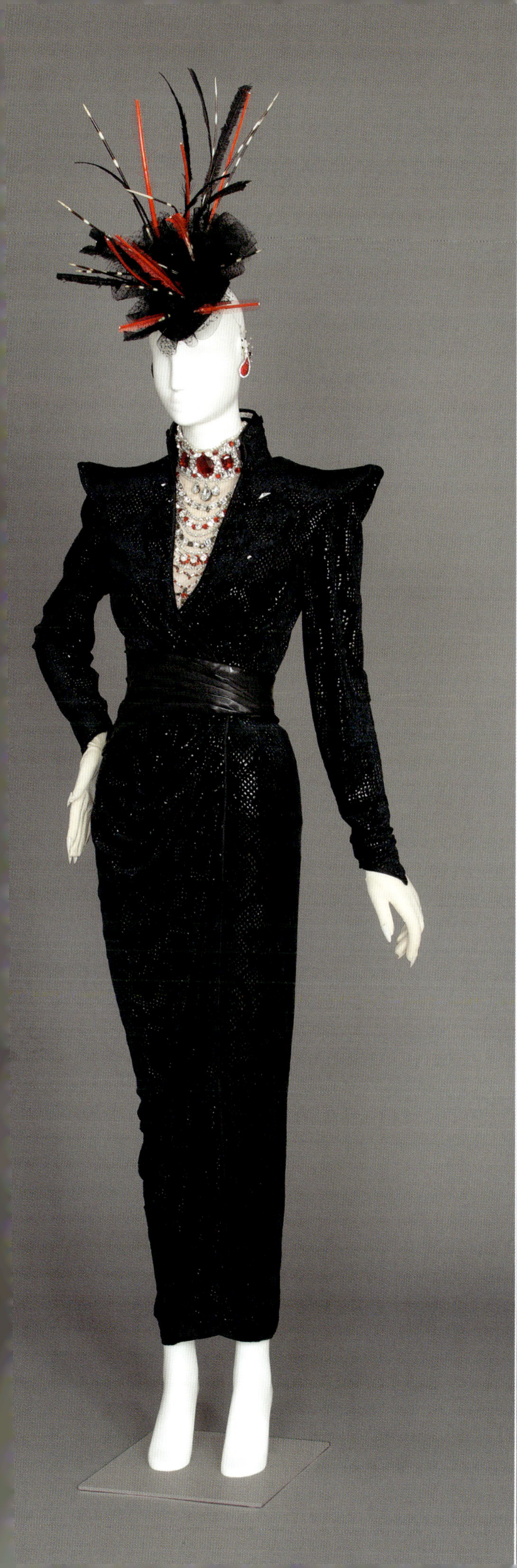

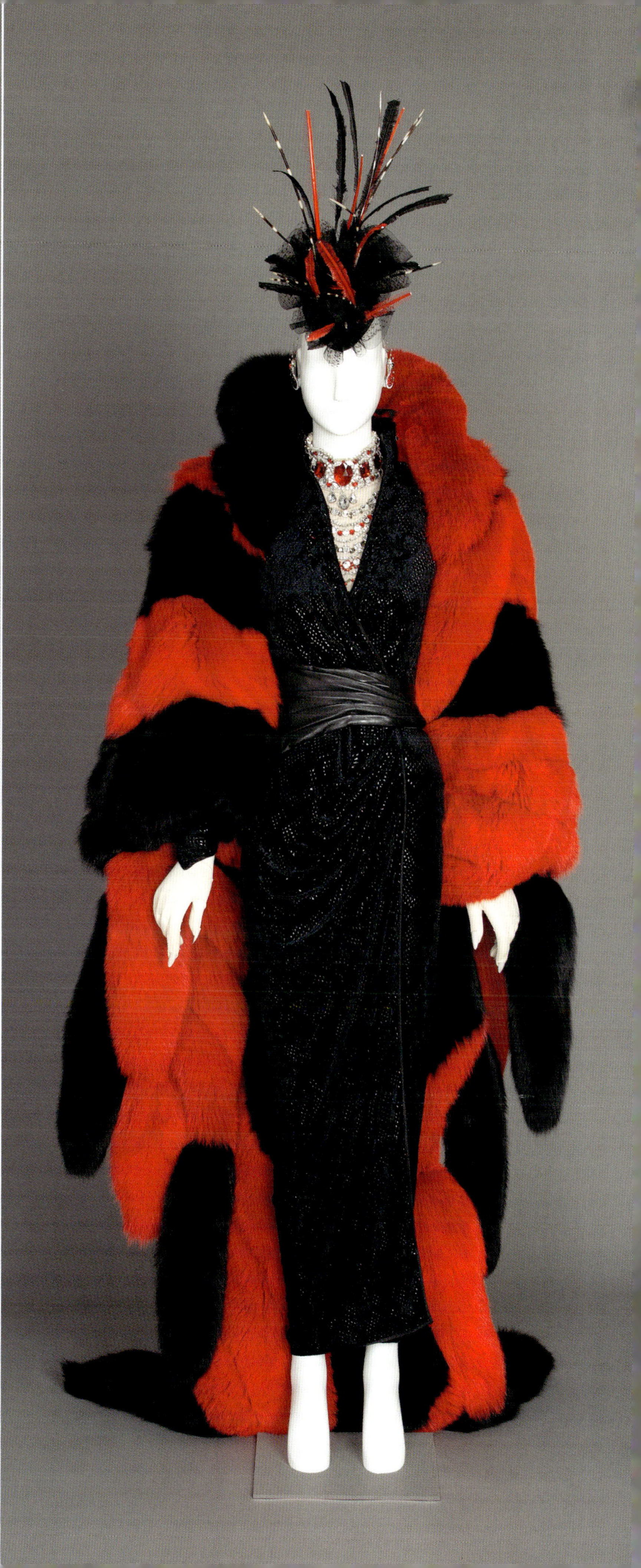

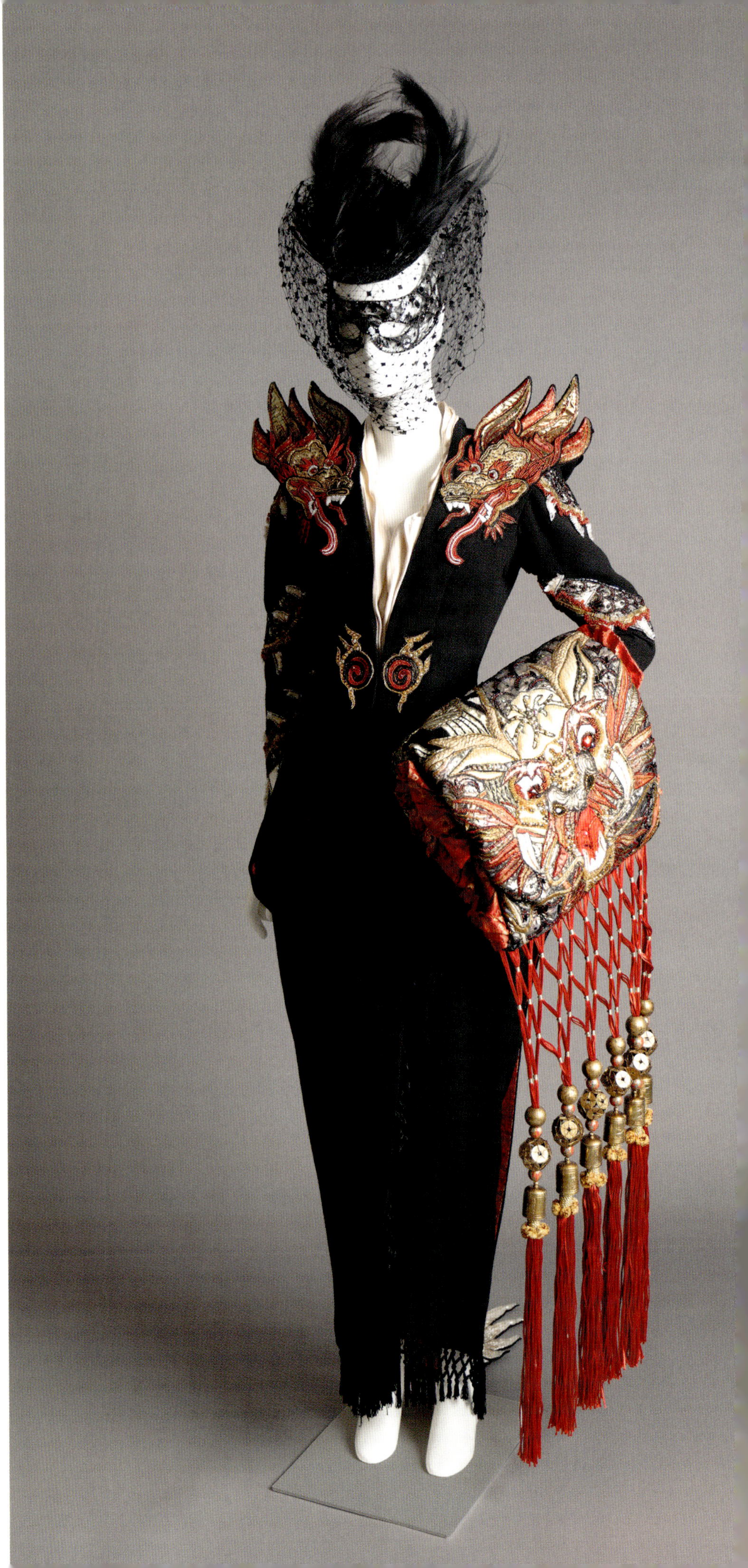

Anthony Powell (English)
Barbara Matera Ltd.
Martin Adams
Woody Shelp
Cruella De Vil/Ella
102 Dalmatians, 2000
Wool, silk, polyester, metallic thread, glass beads, glass stones, plastic sequins, metal, feathers
GC 2017.13.1–.3, .7–.8

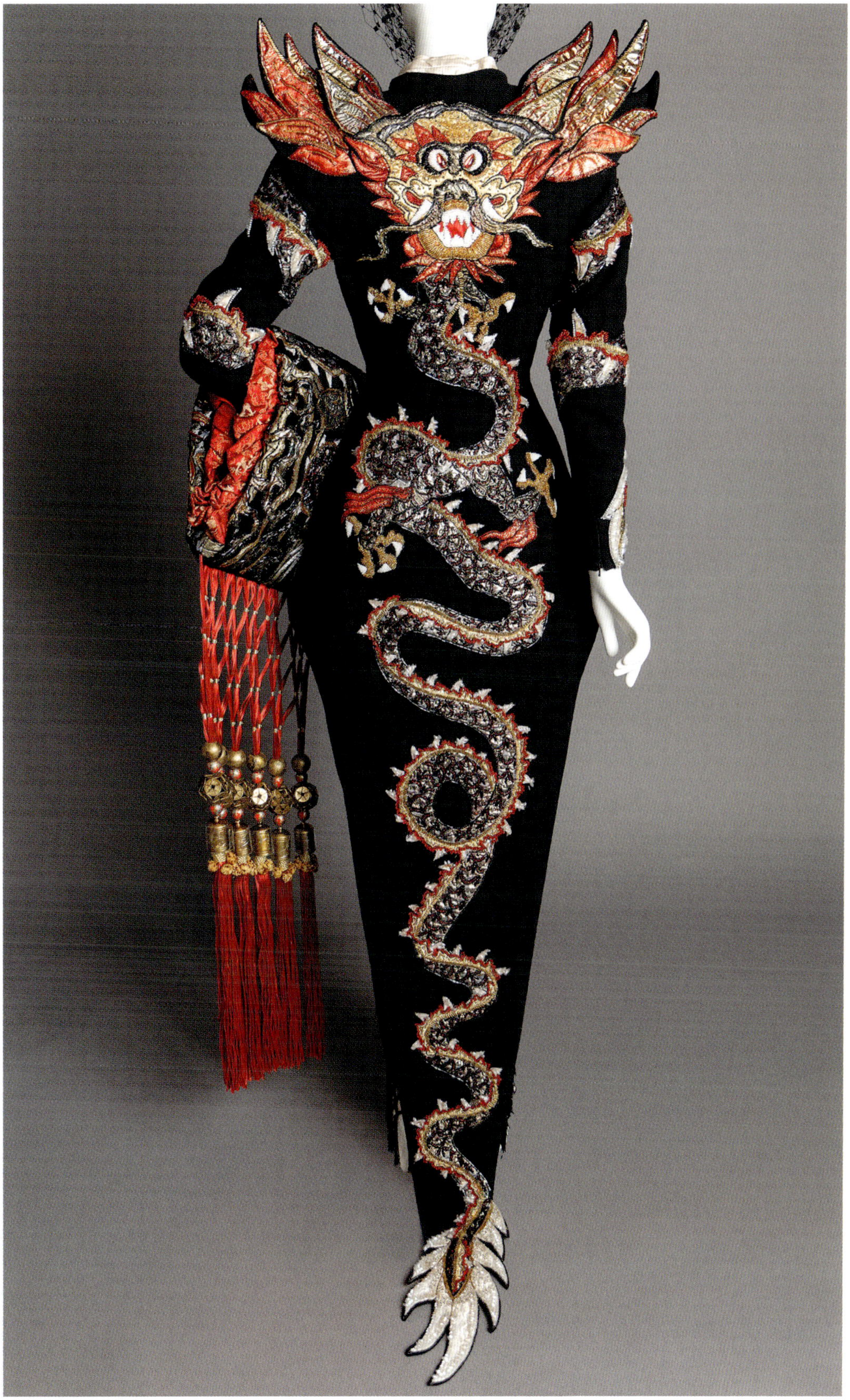

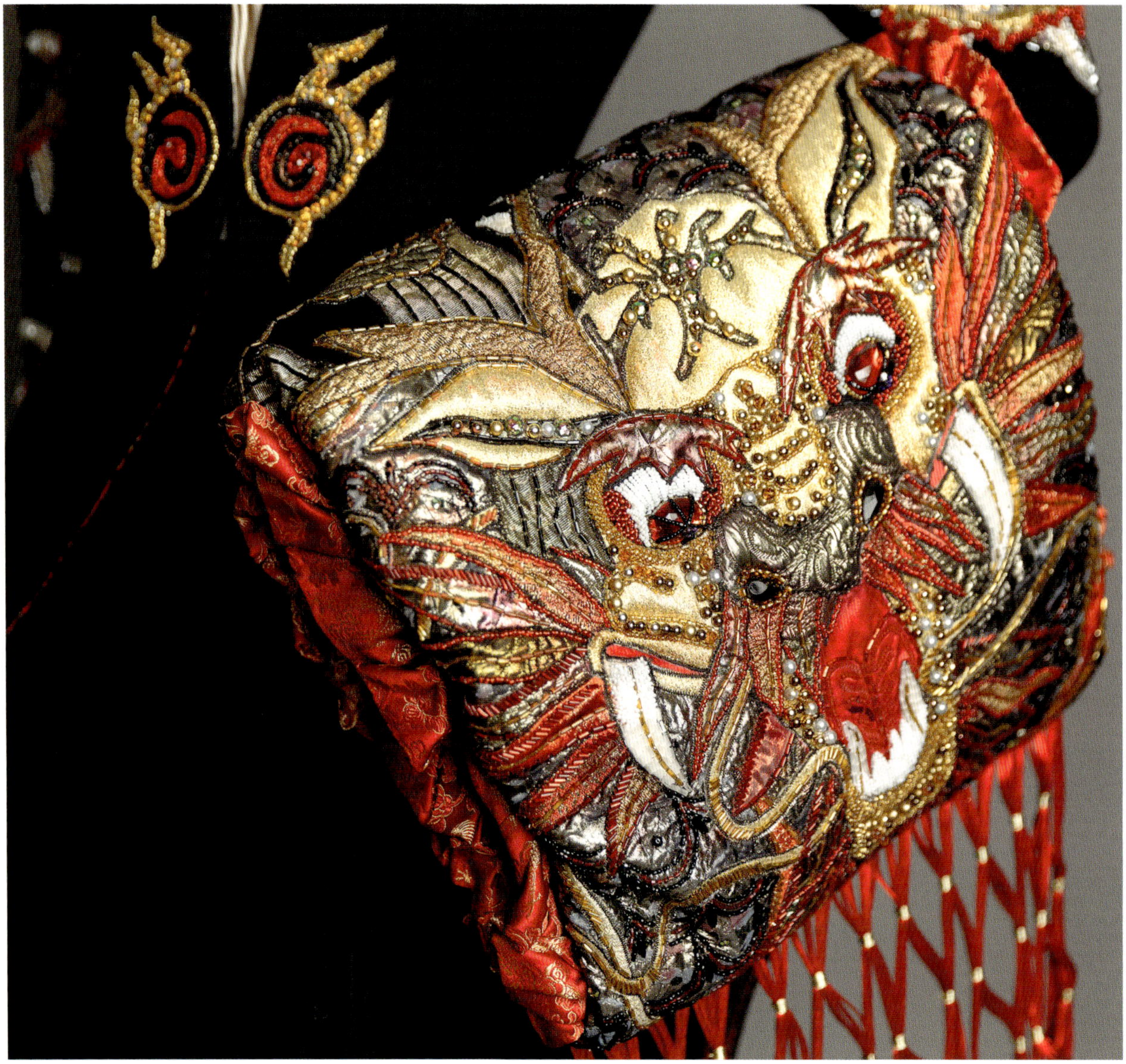

Anthony Powell (English)
Barbara Matera Ltd.
Martin Adams
Woody Shelp
Cruella De Vil/Ella
102 Dalmatians, 2000
Wool, silk, polyester, metallic thread, glass beads, glass stones, plastic sequins, metal, feathers
GC 2017.13.1-.3, .7-.8

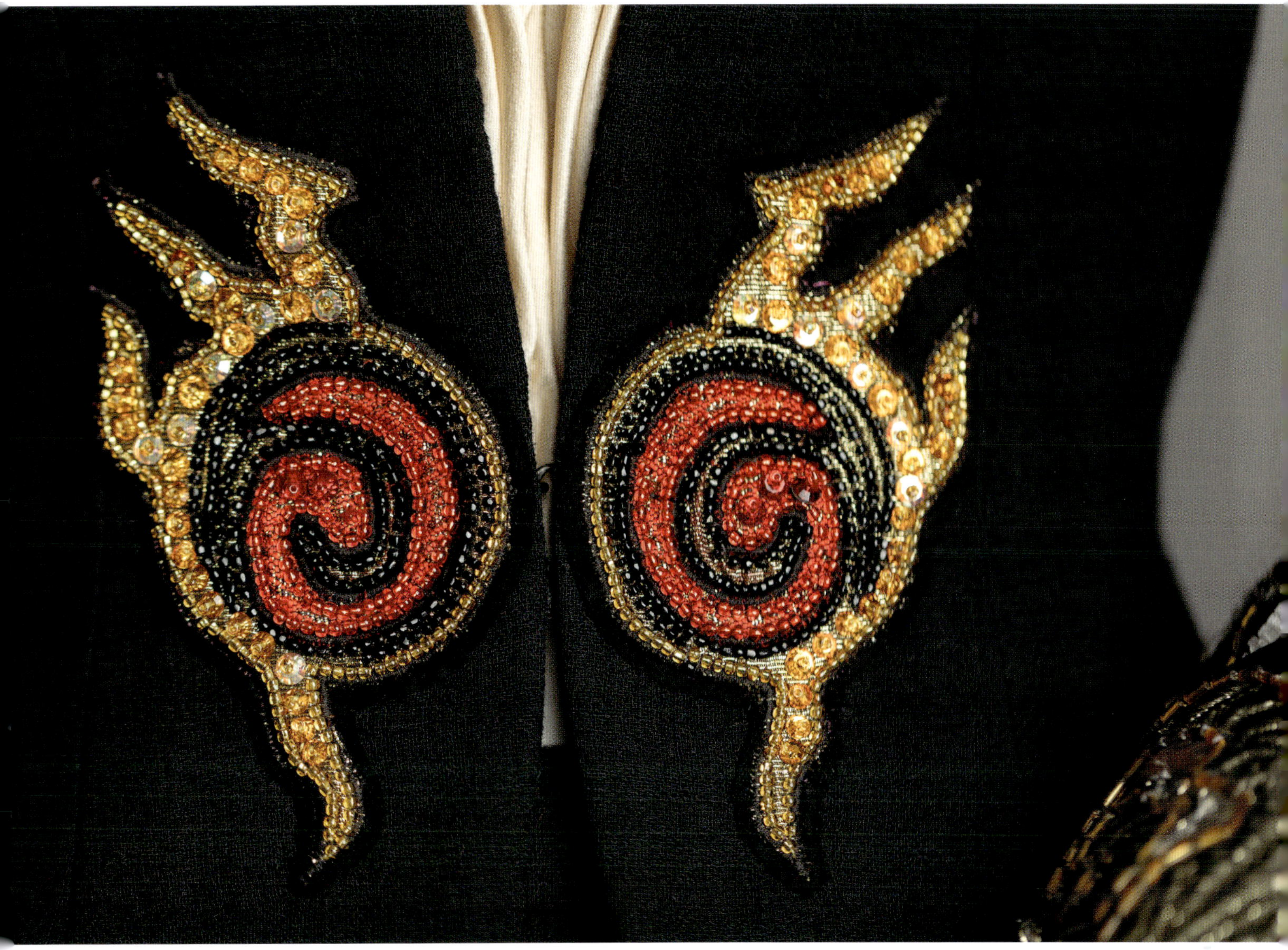

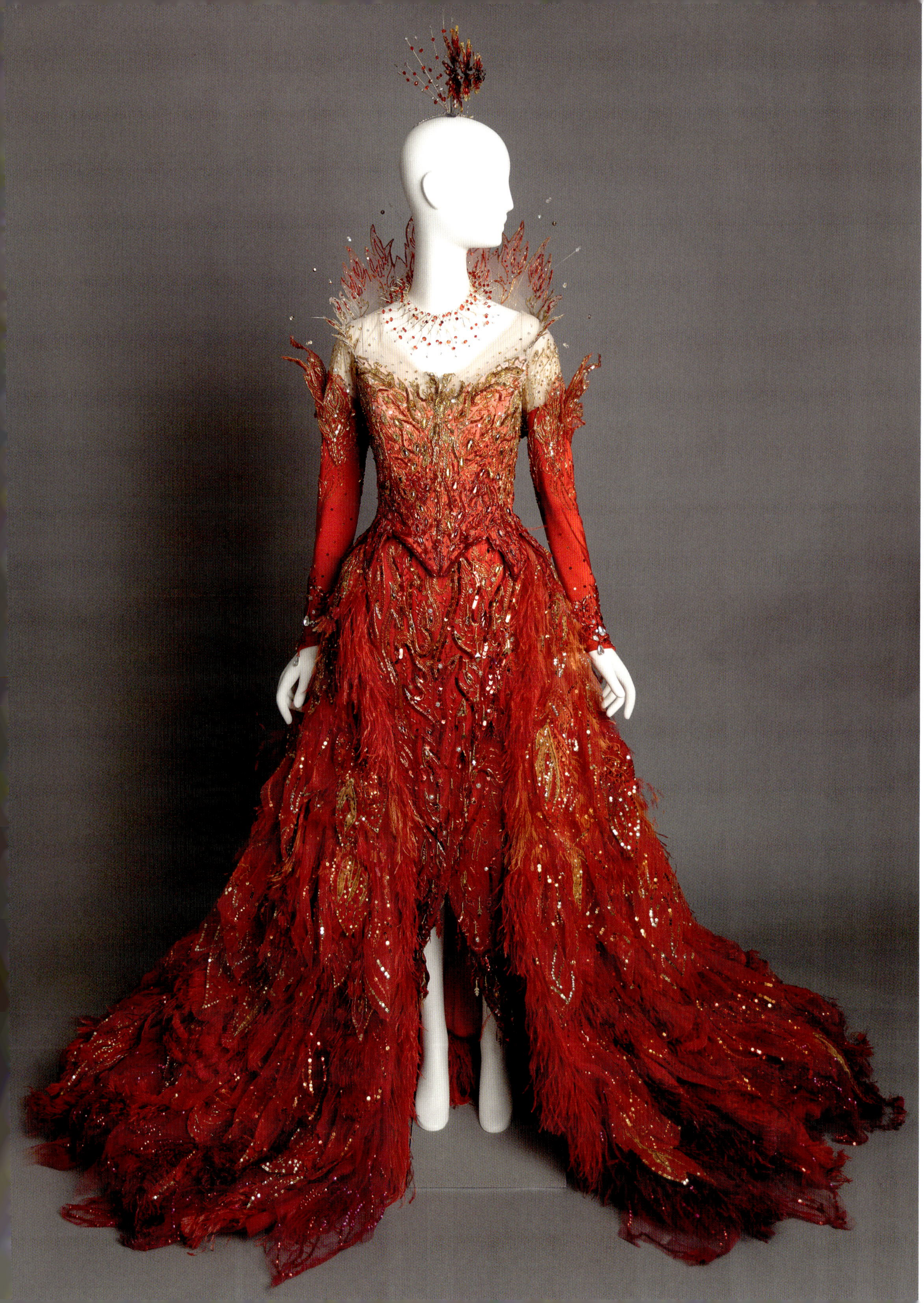

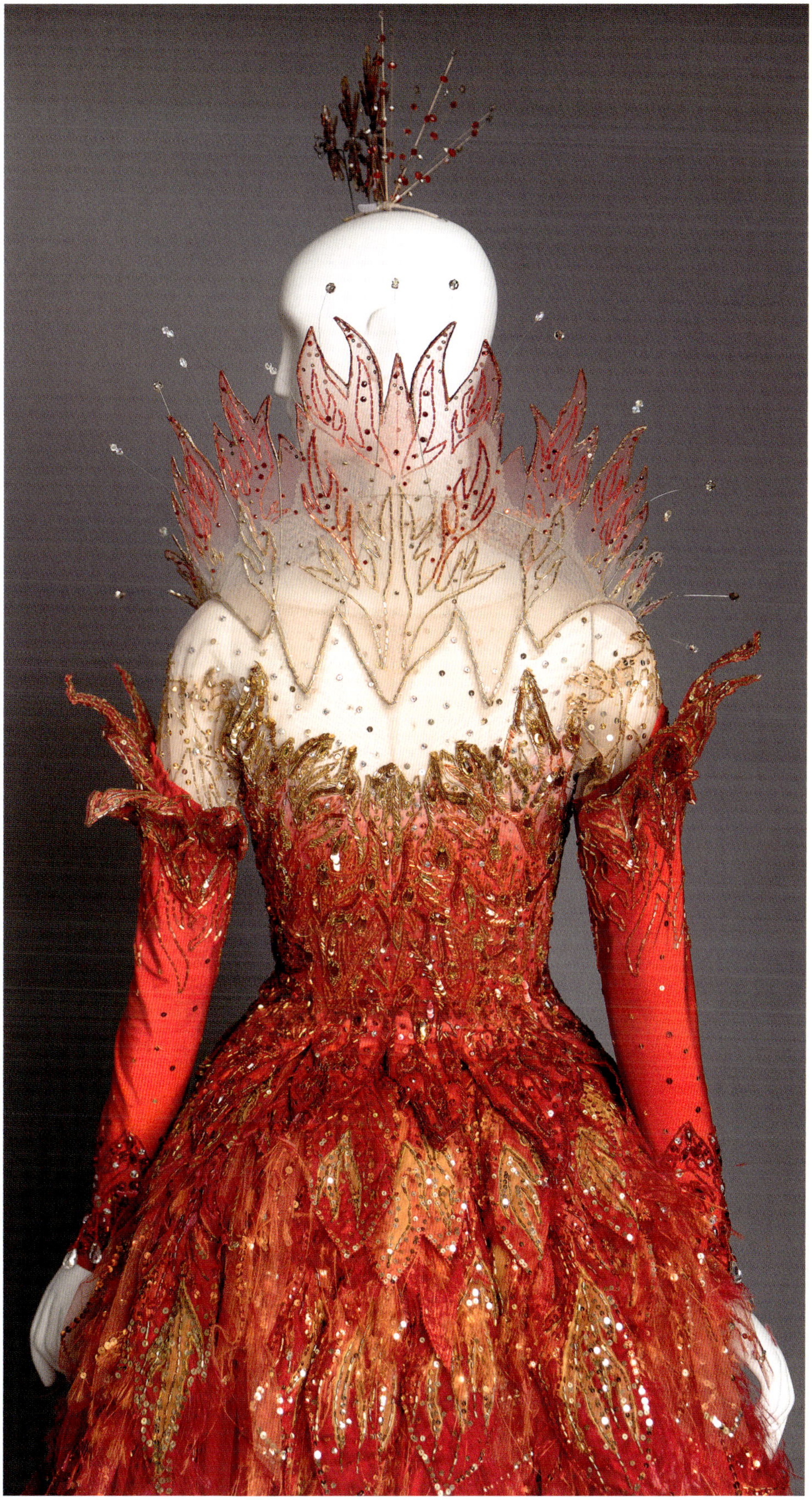

LEFT
Anthony Powell (English)
Barbara Matera Ltd.
Martin Adams
Cruella De Vil/Ella
102 Dalmatians, 2000
Silk, glass beads, glass stones,
plastic sequins, feathers, metal, glass
GC 2017.14.1, .4, .6

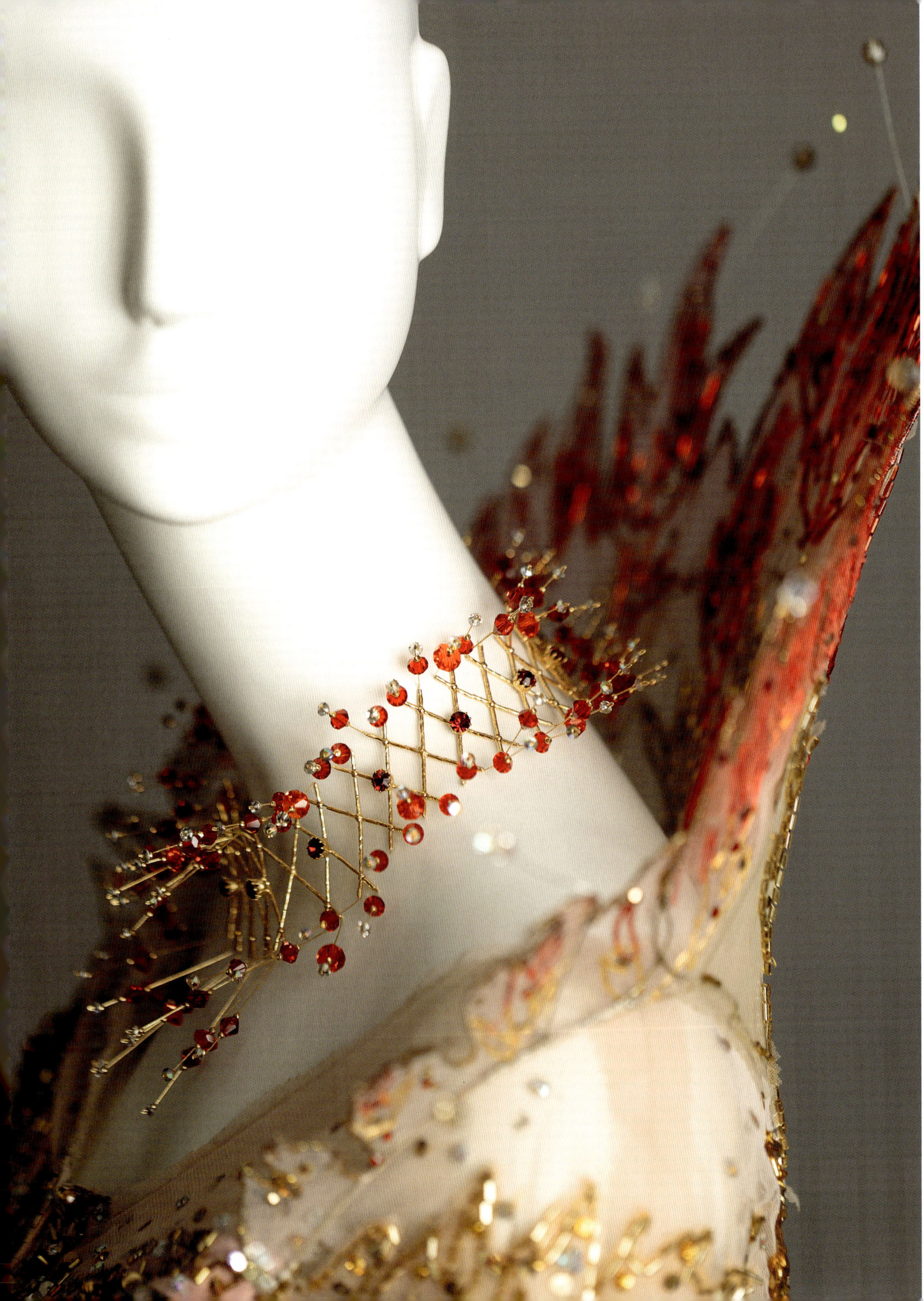

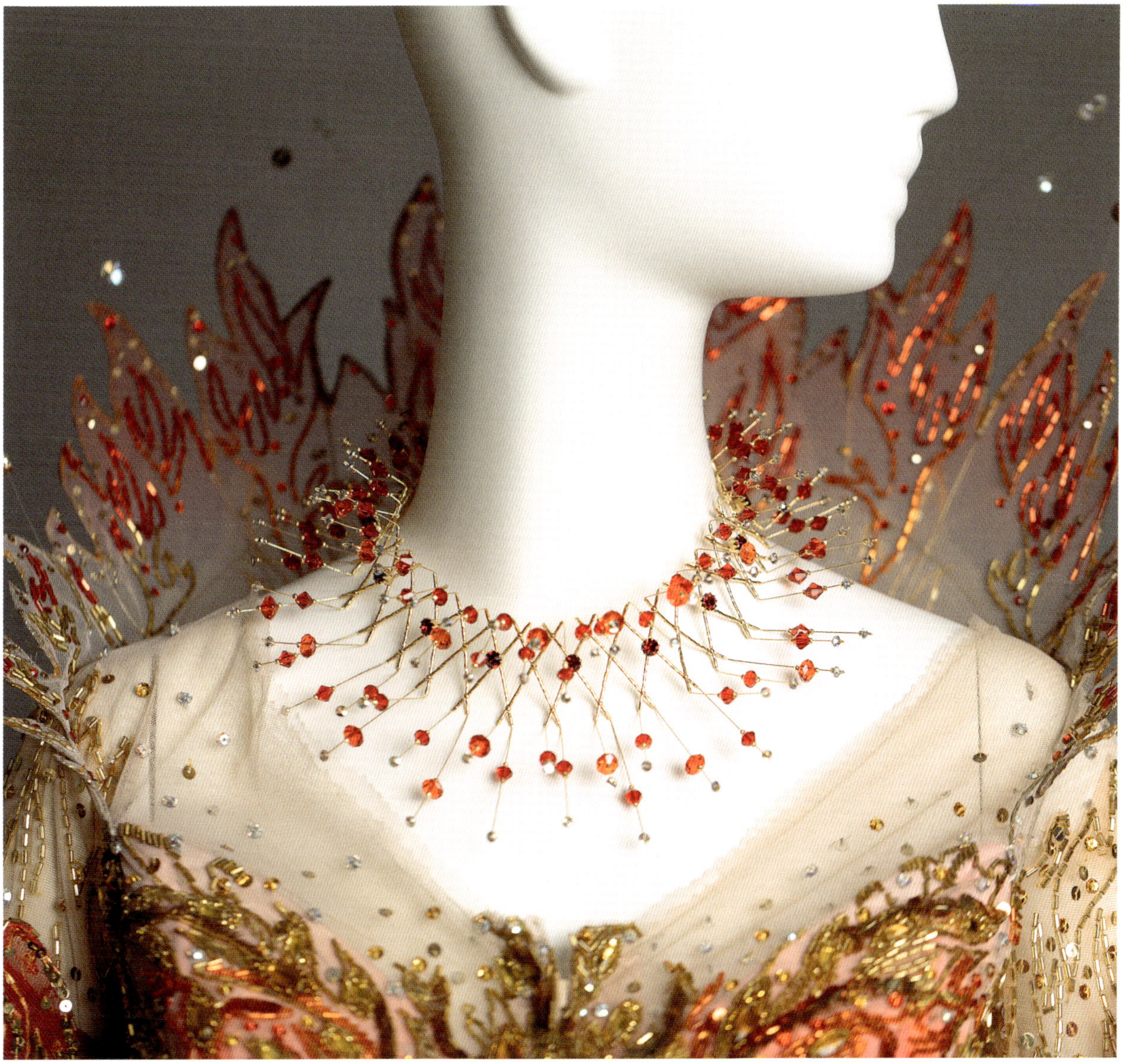

Anthony Powell (English)
Barbara Matera Ltd.
Martin Adams
Cruella De Vil/Ella
102 Dalmatians, 2000
Silk, glass beads, glass stones,
plastic sequins, feathers, metal, glass
GC 2017.14.1, .4, .6

CHARACTER

Nova Prime

Marvel Studios' Guardians of the Galaxy, 2014

GLENN CLOSE ENTERED THE MARVEL CINEMATIC UNIVERSE in 2014 in the role of Commander Irani Rael, the Nova Prime or highest-ranking member of the Nova Corps. The Nova Corps, an intergalactic military and police force charged with keeping the peace in the galaxy, first appeared in Marvel Comics' *Fantastic Four* #205 in 1979 and reappears in other Marvel narratives set in outer space. For the film, Alexandra Byrne created a uniform that communicates Close's belonging to the Nova Corps through the use of shared color, parallel pleating, and yellow-orange insignia bars, while still elevating her as the singular authority and leader. The Nova Corps patch on her right shoulder combines the distinguishing points of the ranks below her into a unique emblem.

Citing her duty to "help the director to tell the story he wants to tell," Byrne designed a range of costumes set in the *Guardians of the Galaxy* universe, dressing imagined species and alien races of different sizes, shapes, and skin tones whose clothing had to reflect the vastly different cultures and environments from which they originated.[8] To realize Nova Prime's look, Byrne fused two layers of neoprene-like fabrics to give the uniform the body, structure, and stretch necessary to support the standaway collar and shoulder flanges, while still providing ease of movement, a close fit, and a sleek, futuristic appearance.

DESIGNER

Alexandra Byrne

Raised in Stratford-upon-Avon, where the Royal Shakespeare Company is based, Alexandra Byrne studied theater design at the English National Opera and trained with the Motley Theatre Design Course. In 1989 she oversaw scenery and costume design for the play *Some Americans Abroad*, earning a Tony Award nomination for Best Scenic Design. She shifted her focus toward costume design in the 1990s, creating the costumes for the four-part television series *The Buddha of Suburbia*, produced by the BBC in 1993. In the years ahead, Byrne worked on a series of period dramas, beginning with the BBC film *Persuasion* (1995). She went on to design the costumes for *Hamlet* (1996); *Elizabeth* (1998), starring Cate Blanchett; *Finding Neverland* (2004); and *Elizabeth: The Golden Age* (2007). She earned Academy Award nominations for Best Costume Design for her work on those four films, winning in 2008 for *Elizabeth: The Golden Age*. She was nominated once again in 2019 for her work on *Mary Queen of Scots* (2018), and has earned seven BAFTA Award nominations, with a win in 1996 for her work on *Persuasion*.

Byrne first worked with Glenn Close on the costuming for her portrayal of Nova Prime in the 2014 film *Marvel Studios' Guardians of the Galaxy*. Since 2011 Byrne's career has included work on a number of films in the Marvel Cinematic Universe, including *Thor* (2011) and *The Avengers* (2012). In addition to her recognition with Academy Award and BAFTA wins, she is a five-time nominee and two-time award winner for Best Costume Design from the Academy of Science Fiction, Fantasy, and Horror Films, and a seven-time nominee at the Costume Designers Guild Awards, winning in 2017 for Excellence in Fantasy Film for her work on *Doctor Strange* (2016). In 2020 she returned to her work on period films, designing the costumes for *Emma*, Autumn de Wilde's adaption of the Jane Austen novel of the same name.

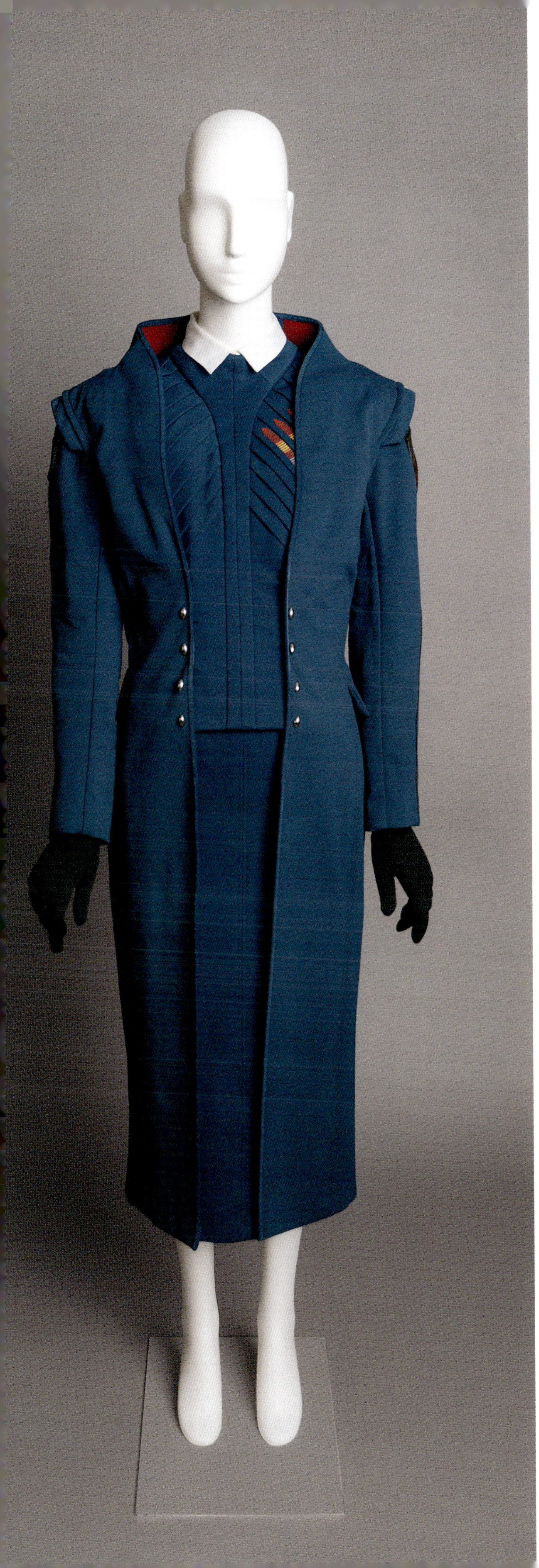

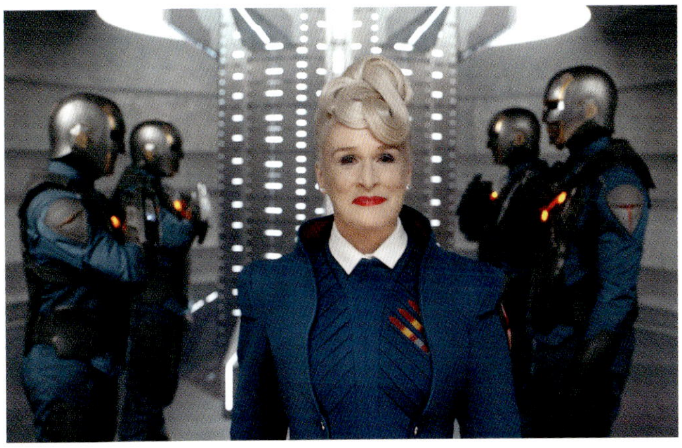

ABOVE
Glenn Close as Nova Prime in *Marvel Studios' Guardians of the Galaxy*, 2014

LEFT
Alexandra Byrne (English)
Nova Prime
Marvel Studios' Guardians of the Galaxy, 2014
Polyester, spandex, rubber, linen, leather
GC 2017.345.1–.4, .6

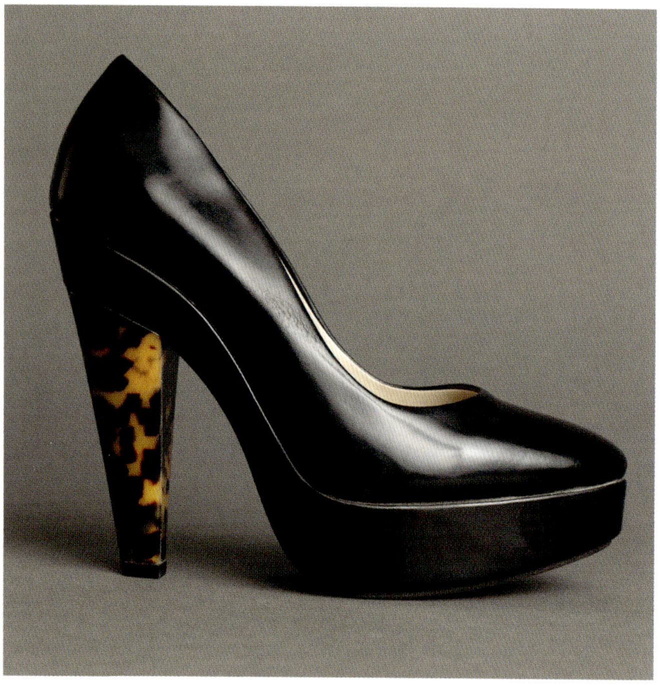

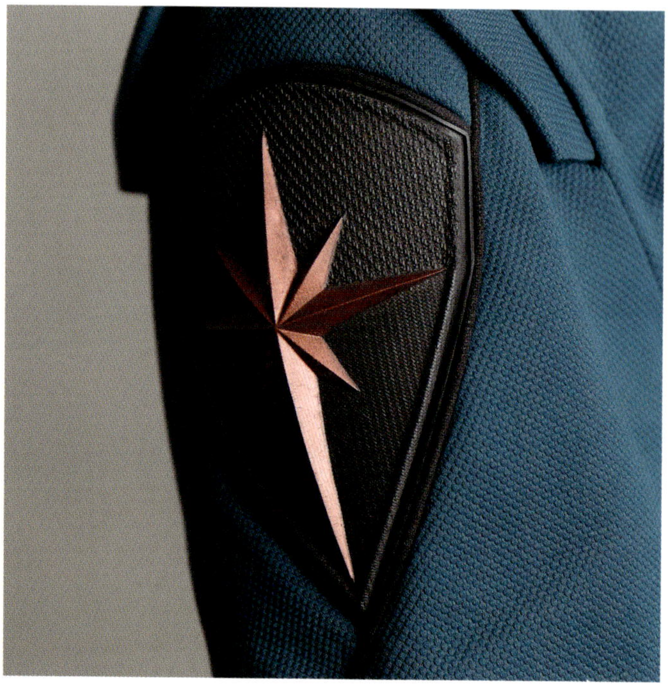

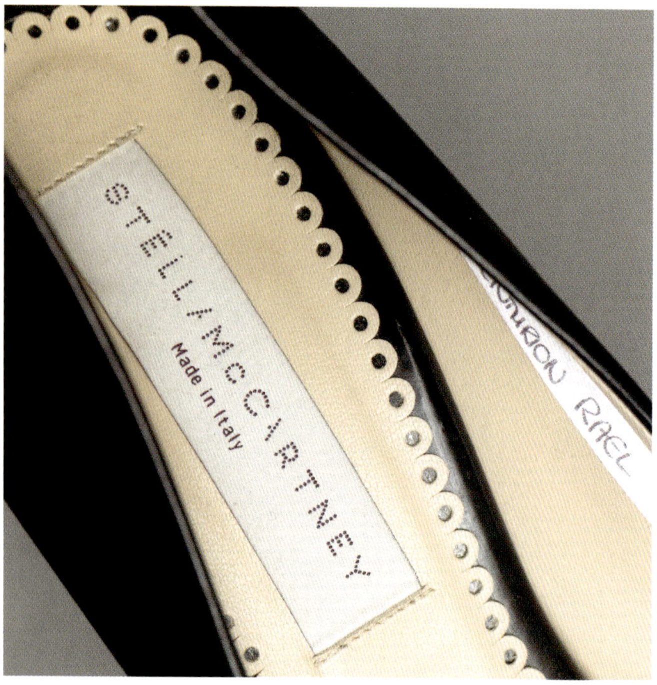

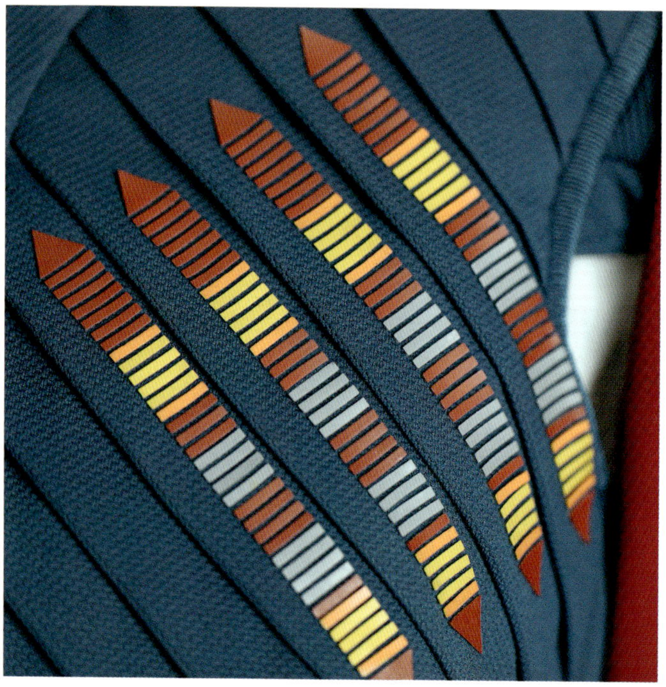

ABOVE LEFT
Alexandra Byrne (English)
Nova Prime
Marvel Studios' Guardians of the Galaxy, 2014
Stella McCartney
Synthetic leather, plastic
GC 2017.345.8 AB

ABOVE RIGHT
Alexandra Byrne (English)
Nova Prime
Marvel Studios' Guardians of the Galaxy, 2014
Polyester, spandex, rubber, linen, leather
GC 2017.345.1–.4, .6

Endnotes

1 Lord Christopher Laverty, "Ellen Mirojnick Explains the Role of Costume Designer," *Clothes on Film*, April 23, 2010, https://clothesonfilm.com/ellen-mirojnick-explains-the-role-of-costume-designer/.

2 Samantha Critchell, "Costumes Become Characters in 'Stepford Wives,'" *The Spokesman-Review*, June 13, 2004, https://www.spokesman.com/stories/2004/jun/13/costumes-become-characters-in-stepford-wives/.

3 Critchell, "Costumes Become Characters."

4 Michelle Paradis, "Contender—Costume Designer Pierre-Yves Gayraud, *Albert Nobbs*," *Below the Line: Voice of the Crew*, January 9, 2012, http://www.btlnews.com/awards/contender-costume-designer-pierre-yves-gayraud-albert-nobbs/.

5 Sara Jablon-Roberts and Eulanda A. Sanders, "The Underlying Definition of Historical Accuracy," *Dress* 45, no. 2 (2019), 107–25.

6 "Movie Preview: Dressed to Kill?: Costume Designer Anthony Powell Talks about His Special Challenge on *102 Dalmatians*—Creating Outfits for the Many Aspects of Wonderfully Outrageous Cruella De Vil," *Guardian*, October 22, 2000.

7 Michael Quintanilla, "It's a Case of Evil Is as Evil Dresses," *Los Angeles Times*, November 12, 2000, https://www.latimes.com/archives/la-xpm-2000-nov-12-ca-50531-story.html.

8 Bryan Abrams, "Costume Designer Alexandra Byrne on Gearing Up the *Guardians*," *Credits*, August 11, 2014, https://www.motionpictures.org/2014/08/costume-designer-alexandra-byrne-on-gearing-up-the-guardians/.

Afterword

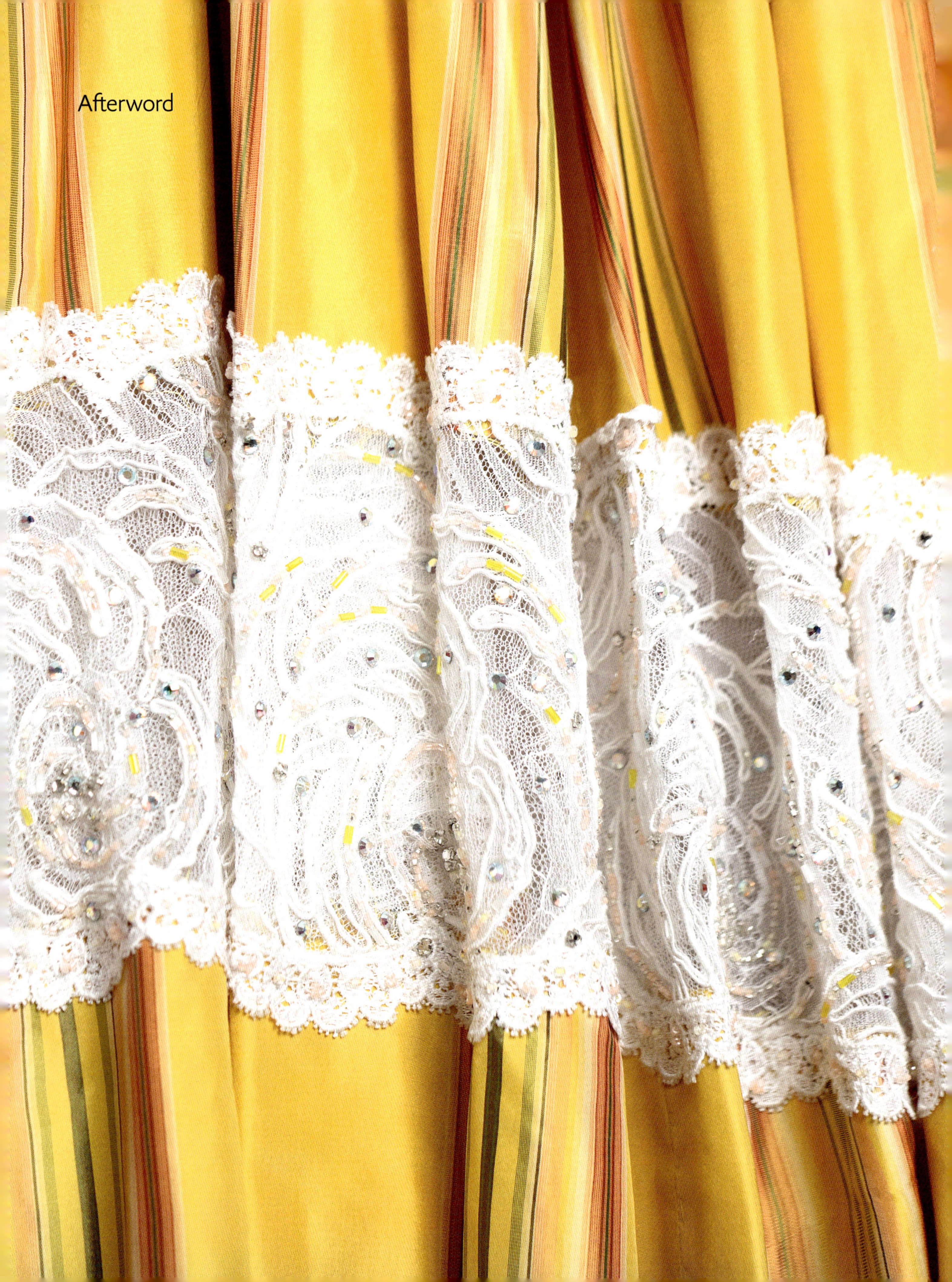

Costume Design and the Discovery of a Character

Ann Roth

Whether one is designing for a leading character or a more minor role, the same questions come to mind. Where do the character's clothes come from? Were they purchased? Were they made-to-order? A thrift shop? A gift? Found in a throwaway bin? Maybe stolen? I once knew a poet who wore a reddish Harris tweed jacket almost every day and it really defined him. When I asked him where it came from, he said a guest at one of his parties had left it. Days later, when he found it, it was still wet and stinking of booze. It was also never retrieved by the original owner and thus, it moved on to a new body.

Glenn Close and I have worked together many times over many years in movies and theater. We both know which questions need to be answered. We may know some of the answers up front, but many of them we discover, or at least confirm, together in the fitting room.

For Jenny Fields in *The World According To Garp*, John Irving was grappling (wrestling pun intended) with, among other things, manifestations of feminism and the feminine in twentieth-century America. To whatever extent he succeeds or fails is not the designer's concern.

The character of Jenny—a nurse, single mother, and feminist-manifesto-writer-turned-icon—is not isolated but surrounded by other representations of the feminine according to Irving and George Roy Hill. They include the virginal wife, the willing coeds, the trans-woman-with-a-heart-of-gold, the Valerie-Solanas-type "rabid" feminists, and the tongue-less rape survivor Ellen James. One is tempted to think that Irving created one woman character whose many aspects are represented by them all.

It is among these that Jenny is situated. Garp is conceived when she rapes his immobile (yet handily erect) father with whose care she is charged. Jenny becomes a nurse at a boys' school and is, in essence, a stand-in mother to them all, Garp just one among many. Later, she takes up writing and immediately overshadows her son's career. Jenny teaches Garp forgiveness and reconciliation in his super-complicated marriage, something with which she has no experience. In short, she is completely independent while Garp is forever dependent. That play of dependence and independence is basis for the nurse fetish that becomes the sexy-nurse trope of vaudeville and beyond. The patient is powerless over the ministrations of the nurse and therefore free from guilt or shame in the encounter. In the reverse, the nurse is subservient to the doctor and that power-play is on display in bits like *Carry On Nurse*.

The level of Glenn's craft allowed her to intuitively understand how to play Jenny's straight-laced nurse uniform as both a rejection of the "sexy nurse" trope and a feminist expansion and inversion of that same trope, while ALWAYS putting the costume first, and foremost, Jenny's actual clothes. Glenn did not need an unbuttoned button, a wisp of hair unloosed, or too much blush/rouge to suggest the vulnerability that lies beneath Jenny's armor. While Irving may not have been aware of or interested in that depth of Jenny, Ms. Close certainly was.

Teddy Barnes in *The Jagged Edge* is a reasonably successful lawyer and single mother living in the San Francisco area. Her courtroom and office clothes are the same. She's a great-looking woman, confident and very capable. I think she buys her suits (as opposed to having them made), which is odd, because at this time such a suit would be quite rare.

Ann Roth, Eric Winterling Inc., (Claire Wellington, *The Stepford Wives*), 2004
Silk, cotton, rhinestones, metal, enamel
GC 2017.301.1-.2, .10

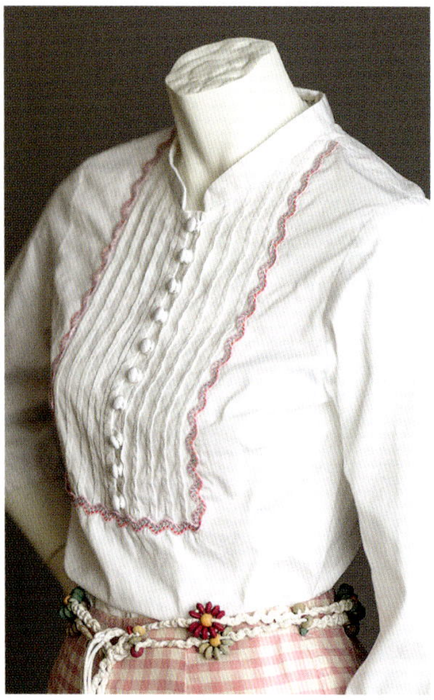

Ann Roth, "Claireobics" costume (Claire Wellington, *The Stepford Wives*, 2004), Cotton, silk, wood, GC 2017.291-.3, .5

In the mid-1980s, Giorgio Armani conquered the fashion world with soft-shouldered, drapey suits for women that involved less construction than office wear had displayed in the past. At that time, women with serious careers and ambitions were all wearing versions of his beautiful clothes.

My purple suit is influenced by the designers Mainbocher and Molyneux, as well as the unnamed labels of French tailors who made clothes for women. I asked Werner Koolevits of Barbara Matera's shop to make it. The suit is unapologetically tailored. I think we made what came to be called a "power suit"—maybe the first. I recall the producer's wife, who visited the set, was quite unhappy. "Too tough! Too strong! Quite unfeminine!" The tan gabardine suit is a bit of a throwback as well, in terms of being highly tailored. But is it not the straight-laced, buttoned-up type that one wants to see come undone?

Claire Wellington in *The Stepford Wives* wants, more than anything, to look like the quintessential, perfect, super-rich, married lady of leisure, the type that lunches as a verb, and whose idea of exercise is an aerobicized celebration of the movements of the household chores she, herself, never does. The type of woman whose entire life is devoted to making her husband happy with her face, form, voice, and movement. In reality, she is an ambitious geneticist and neurosurgeon who is hellbent on creating a perfect world of manicured romance, one white, nuclear family at a time. What bridges the two sides of Claire is her relentless pursuit of a romantic ideal. The woman in Claire just wants to be cherished completely, and if that means that she must be cherished by a robot, well, so be it. Her fantasy world has no gum on the sidewalks and, like Disneyland, you never see a sweat stain, a wrinkled shirtfront, a scuffed shoe, or a troubled brow.

Claire's pink pants and starched cotton shirt with tuxedo front are her idea of "workout" clothes. Since she will not be sweating, she can wear a dozen cotton pleats (set off with pink rickrack) on the front of her blouse. Her macramé belt and straw bag adorned with pink chiffon scarf add to the painstaking care given to her "effortless look."

When she serves as the caller for the Stepford Independence Day square dance, Claire wears a yellow floral skirt and white shirred blouse. The fact that the ultra-conformists of Stepford are celebrating "Independence" is lost on them. As is the fact that they are "squares" dancing. Again, Claire has a white blouse, always a touch of sparkle, so as to be eye-catching while maintaining a modesty that calms the men of Stepford. Her full yellow skirt scattered with roses is Claire's idea of simple country femininity with its voluminous gathers swishing as she moves, the rickrack at the hem, evoking a time with simpler expectations, for ornament. But the shaped yoke from which the skirt hangs, accentuating the waist and rising ever so slightly beneath the bosom, is as a complex a construction as Claire's "guileless country girl" persona. And the ribbon that cinches her waist is clasped with a scarab brooch. In Stepford, even the beetles on the roses are fake.

For the film's finale, the garden party at the Stepford Men's Association, Claire once again is a ray of sunshine in about nine yards of golden plaid silk taffeta. This costume is, again, a heavily constructed fantasy of an extremely rich person's "informal" garden party of another era (think Loretta Young). The skirt is gored and gathered—an honest dirndl (albeit inset with beaded lace)—and the bodice is cut on the bias so that the plaid accentuates Claire's tiny waist. The beaded white lace bolero is her dress version of her white-on-top. A clean, bright, pick-me-up, almost a uniform for a good attitude. Also, like the lab coat of the mad scientist she truly is. Why not both?

Widely considered to be one of the most accomplished costume designers of her generation, Ann Roth is also among the most prolific. She has designed hundreds of productions with unparalleled crossover into film, television, and theater. Her various honors include Tony, Academy, Emmy, and BAFTA awards, as well as the Costume Designers Guild's Career Achievement Award in Film. Throughout her career, Roth has cultivated a talented network of directors, producers, actors, and costume makers. Among these crucial relationships is her nearly forty-year friendship with the actor Glenn Close, who first worked with Roth on The World According to Garp *(1982). The sustained friendship and collaboration between these two Hollywood icons captures the essential role of costuming in the art and craft of character development. The Glenn Close Costume Collection at Indiana University is a testament to the foresight, innovation, and generosity of its benefactor, but it is also an archive of the tremendous artistic and technical accomplishments of designers like Roth. The costumes presented in this catalogue and in its accompanying exhibition are dazzling works of creativity and craftsmanship as well as compelling vehicles for storytelling that will capture the imagination of audiences for generations to come.*

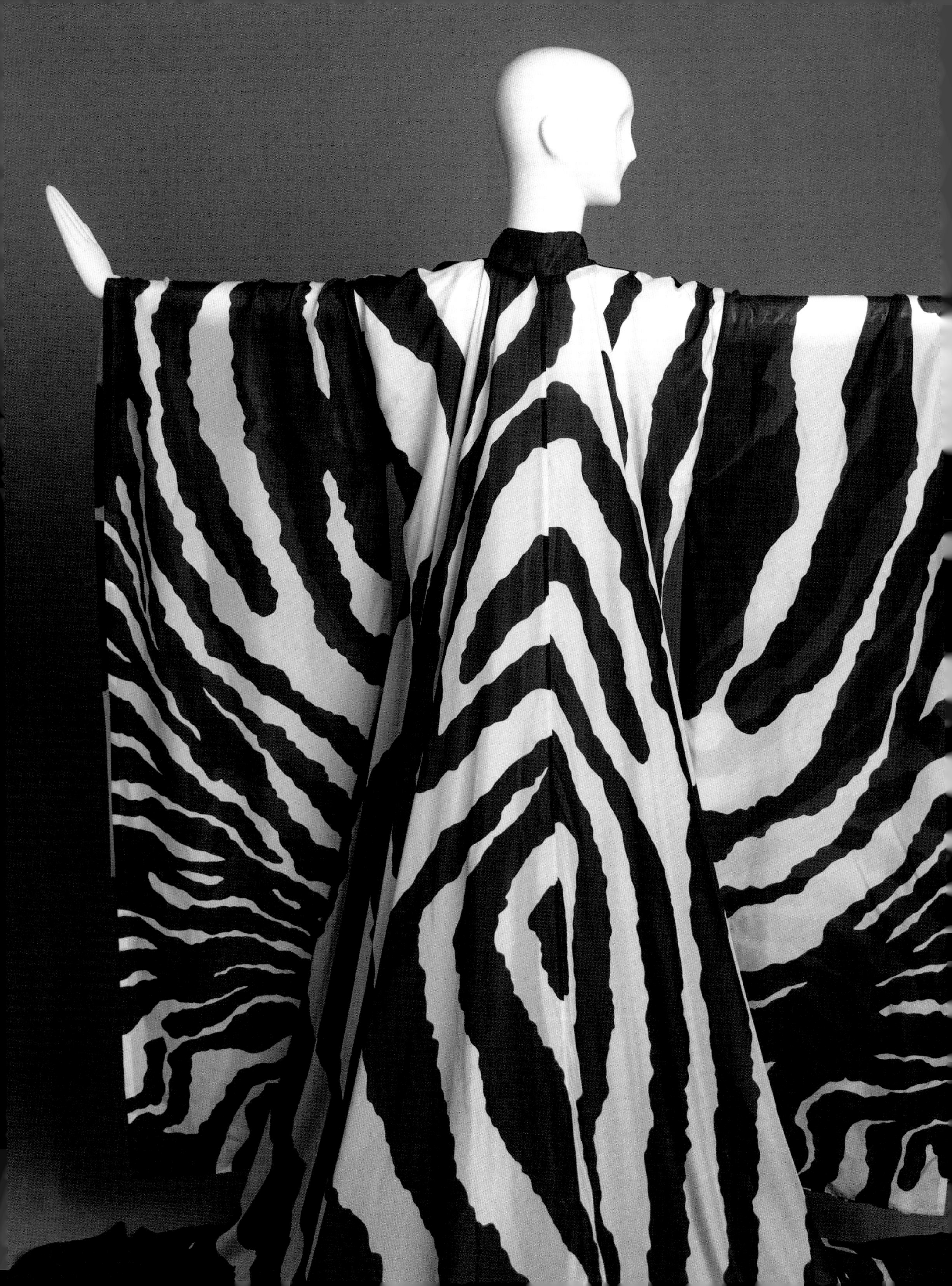

Glenn Close Costume Collection Timeline

Kelly Gallett Richardson

*Costumes for this character are part of the Glenn Close Costume Collection, but worn by a different actor.

The Glenn Close Costume Collection also contains clothing worn by Ms. Close to various awards, events, and personal appearances. See pp. 17 and 29.

Barnum (1980)
Theater

COSTUME DESIGNER:
Raymond Whitney

CHARACTER:
Chairy Barnum (*Tony Award nomination*)

Uncle Vanya (1981)
Theater

COSTUME DESIGNER:
Dunya Ramicova

CHARACTER:
Yelena Andreyevna

The World According to Garp (1982)
Film

COSTUME DESIGNER:
Ann Roth

CHARACTER:
Jenny Fields (*Academy Award nomination*)

The Big Chill (1983)
Film

COSTUME DESIGNER:
April Ferry

CHARACTER:
Sarah Cooper (*Academy Award nomination*)

OPPOSITE
Anthony Powell made by Katherine Marshall and Tricorne, Zebra Kimono (Norma Desmond, *Sunset Boulevard*), 2017, Silk, cotton, GC 2017.353.1

The Real Thing (1983)
Theater

COSTUME DESIGNER:
Anthea Sylbert

CHARACTER:
Annie (*Tony Award*)

Maxie (1985)
Film

COSTUME DESIGNER:
Ann Roth

CHARACTER:
Jan/Maxie (*Golden Globe Award nomination*)

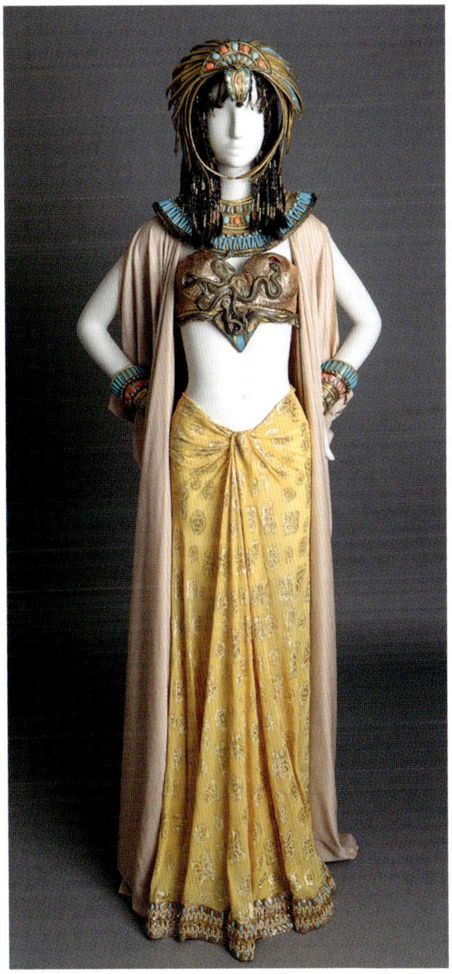

Ann Roth made by Barbara Matera Ltd., Cleopatra Costume (Jan/Maxie, *Maxie*), 1985, Nylon, Lurex, rubber, polyester, spandex, GC 2017.91.1-.5

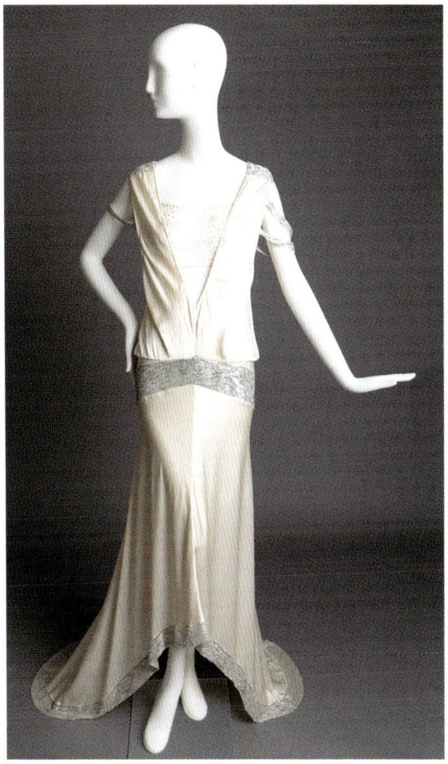

Ann Roth made by Barbara Matera Ltd., Evening Gown (Jan/Maxie, *Maxie*), 1985, Silk, glass beads, plastic sequins, GC 2017.94.1

Jagged Edge (1985)
Film

COSTUME DESIGNER:
Ann Roth

CHARACTER:
Teddy Barnes

Fatal Attraction (1987)
Film

COSTUME DESIGNER:
Ellen Mirojnick

CHARACTER:
Alex Forrest (*Academy Award nomination; Golden Globe Award nomination*)

Dangerous Liaisons (1988)
Film

COSTUME DESIGNER:
James Acheson (*Academy Award*)

CHARACTER:
Marquise de Merteuil (*Academy Award nomination*)

Immediate Family (1989)
Film

COSTUME DESIGNER:
April Ferry

CHARACTER:
Linda Spector

Hamlet (1990)
Film

COSTUME DESIGNER:
Maurizio Millenotti

CHARACTER:
Gertrude

OTHER CHARACTER:
Ophelia*

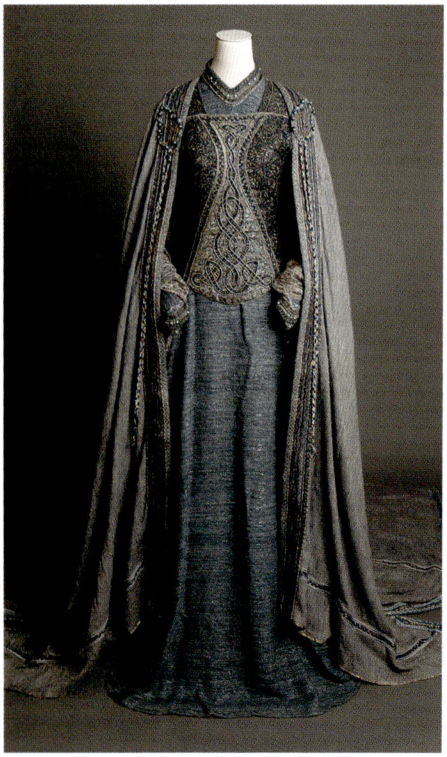

Maurizio Millenotti, Gown, Bodice, and Cape (Queen Gertrude, *Hamlet*), 1990, Silk, Lurex, metallic thread, GC 2017.335.1-.2

Reversal of Fortune (1990)
Film

COSTUME DESIGNER:
Judianna Makovsky

CHARACTER:
Sunny von Bülow

Meeting Venus (1991)
Film

COSTUME DESIGNER:
Catherine Leterrier

CHARACTER:
Karin Anderson

Sarah, Plain and Tall (1991)
Television Film

COSTUME DESIGNER:
Van Broughton Ramsey (*Emmy Award nomination*)

CHARACTER:
Sarah Wheaton Witting (*Golden Globe Award nomination; Emmy Award nomination*)

OTHER CHARACTER:
Anna Witting*

Death and the Maiden (1992)
Theater

COSTUME DESIGNER:
Ann Roth

CHARACTER:
Pauline Salas (*Tony Award*)

The House of the Spirits (1993)
Film

COSTUME DESIGNER:
Barbara Baum

CHARACTER:
Férula Trueba

Skylark (1993)
Television Film

COSTUME DESIGNER:
Van Broughton Ramsey

CHARACTER:
Sarah Wheaton Witting (*Emmy Award nomination*)

OTHER CHARACTERS:
Anna Witting,* Caleb Witting,* Jacob Witting,* Mattie Wheaton,* Harriet Wheaton*

The Paper (1994)
Film

COSTUME DESIGNER:
Rita Ryack

CHARACTER:
Alicia Clark

Sunset Boulevard (1994)
Theater

COSTUME DESIGNER:
Anthony Powell

CHARACTER:
Norma Desmond (*Tony Award*)

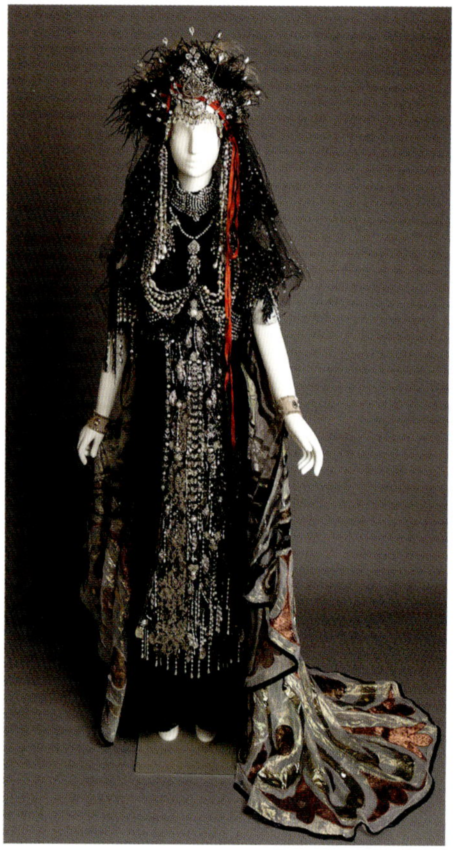

Anthony Powell made by Barbara Matera Ltd. and Woody Shelp, Norma Desmond's Final Look (Norma Desmond, *Sunset Boulevard*), 1994/2017, Silk, glass beads, rhinestones, metal, GC 2017.260.1-.3

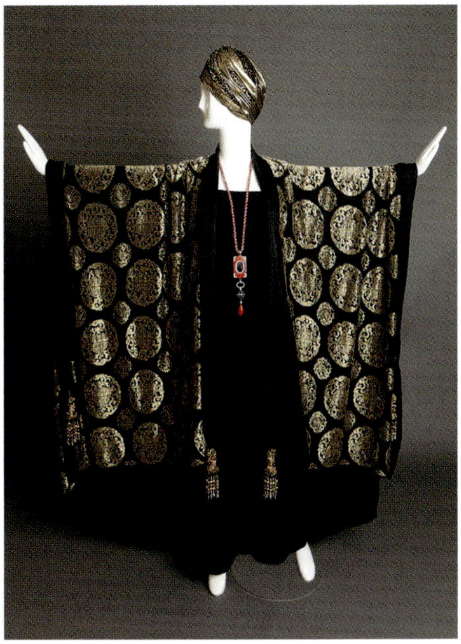

Anthony Powell made by Barbara Matera Ltd., Woody Shelp, and Martin Adams, Gold Medallion Cloak Costume (Norma Desmond, *Sunset Boulevard*), 1994/2017, Silk, metallic thread embroidery, glass beads, rhinestones, resin, GC 2017.260.1–.3

Serving in Silence (1995)
Television Film

COSTUME DESIGNER:
Tish Monaghan

CHARACTER:
Margarethe Cammemeyer (*Golden Globe Award nomination*; *Emmy Award*)

101 Dalmatians (1996)
Film

COSTUME DESIGNER:
Anthony Powell

CHARACTER:
Cruella De Vil (*Golden Globe Award nomination*)

Mary Reilly (1996)
Film

COSTUME DESIGNER:
Consolata Boyle

CHARACTER:
Mrs. Farraday

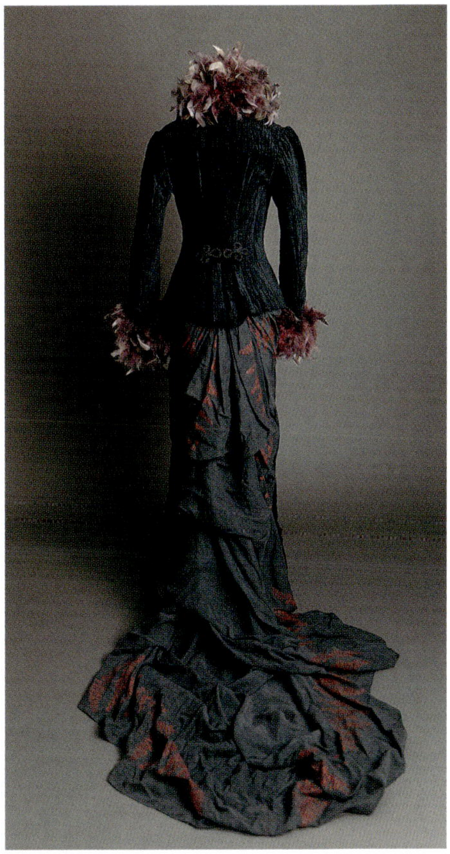

Consolata Boyle, Dress and Jacket (Mrs. Farraday, *Mary Reilly*), 1996, Wool, feathers, silk, rayon, cotton, GC 2017.90.1–.3

In the Gloaming (1997)
Television Film

COSTUME DESIGNER:
Jane Greenwood

CHARACTER:
Janet (*Emmy Award nomination*)

Cookie's Fortune (1999)
Film

COSTUME DESIGNER:
Dona Granata

CHARACTER:
Camille Dixon

Sarah, Plain and Tall: Winter's End (1999)
Television Film

COSTUME DESIGNER:
Van Broughton Ramsey

CHARACTER:
Sarah Wheaton Witting

OTHER CHARACTERS:
Anna Witting,* Caleb Witting,* Cassie Witting,* Jacob Witting,* John Witting*

102 Dalmatians (2000)
Film

COSTUME DESIGNER:
Anthony Powell (*Academy Award nomination*)

CHARACTER:
Cruella De Vil/Ella

South Pacific (2001)
Television Film

COSTUME DESIGNER:
Louise Wakefield

CHARACTER:
Nellie Forbush

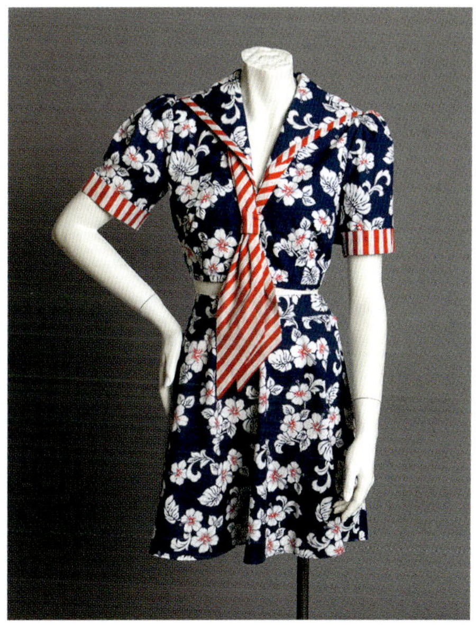

Louise Wakefield, Chorus Girl Costume (Nellie Forbush, *South Pacific*), 2001, Cotton GC 2017.250.1 AB

The Ballad of Lucy Whipple (2001)
Television film

COSTUME DESIGNER:
Van Broughton Ramsey

CHARACTER:
Arvella Whipple

OTHER CHARACTERS:
Lucy Whipple,* Sophie*

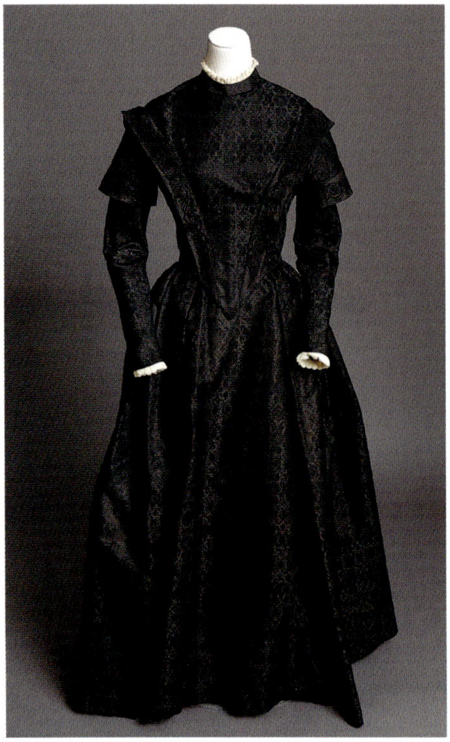

Van Broughton Ramsey made by Barbara Matera Ltd., Mourning Dress (Arvella Whipple, *The Ballad of Lucy Whipple*), 2001, Silk, cotton, GC 2017.279.1-.2

A Streetcar Named Desire (2002)
Theater

COSTUME DESIGNER:
Bunny Christie

CHARACTER:
Blanche DuBois

Le Divorce (2003)
Film

COSTUME DESIGNER:
Carol Ramsey

CHARACTER:
Olivia Pace

The Lion in Winter (2003)
Television Film

COSTUME DESIGNER:
Consolata Boyle (*Emmy Award*)

CHARACTER:
Eleanor of Aquitaine (*Golden Globe Award; Emmy Award nomination*)

The Stepford Wives (2004)
Film

COSTUME DESIGNER:
Ann Roth

CHARACTER:
Claire Wellington

Heights (2005)
Film

COSTUME DESIGNER:
Marina Draghici

CHARACTER:
Diana

The Shield (2005)
Television Series

COSTUME DESIGNER:
Kathryn Morrison

CHARACTER:
Monica Rawling (*Golden Globe Award nomination; Emmy Award nomination*)

Damages (2007–12)
Television Series

COSTUME DESIGNER:
Frank Fleming

CHARACTER:
Patty Hewes (*Golden Globe Award and nominations; Emmy Awards and nominations*)

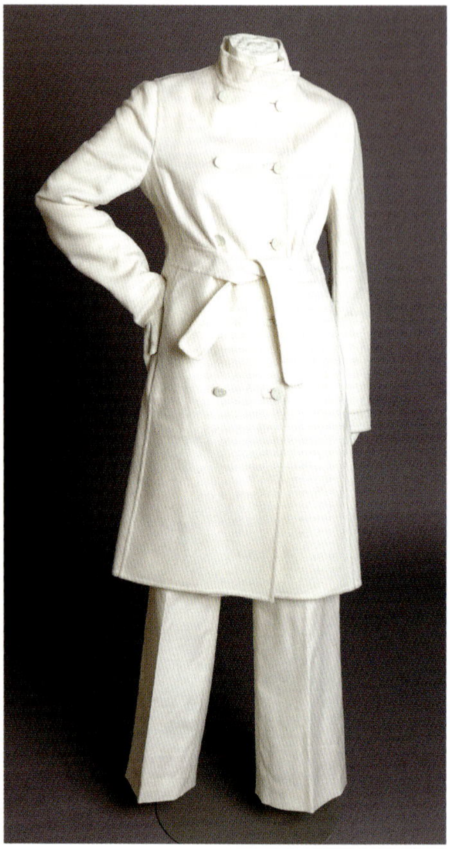

Frank Fleming, Coat and Pants (Patty Hewes, *Damages*), 2007–2012, Valentino, Cashmere, polyester, GC 2017.48.1-.2

Albert Nobbs (2011)
Film

COSTUME DESIGNER:
Pierre-Yves Gayraud

CHARACTER:
Albert Nobbs (*Academy Award nomination; Golden Globe Award nomination*)

A Delicate Balance (2014)
Theater

COSTUME DESIGNER:
Ann Roth

CHARACTER:
Agnes

Marvel Studios' Guardians of the Galaxy (2014)
Film

COSTUME DESIGNER:
Alexandra Byrne

CHARACTER:
Nova Prime

The Girl with All the Gifts (2016)
Film

COSTUME DESIGNER:
Liza Bracey

CHARACTER:
Dr. Caroline Caldwell

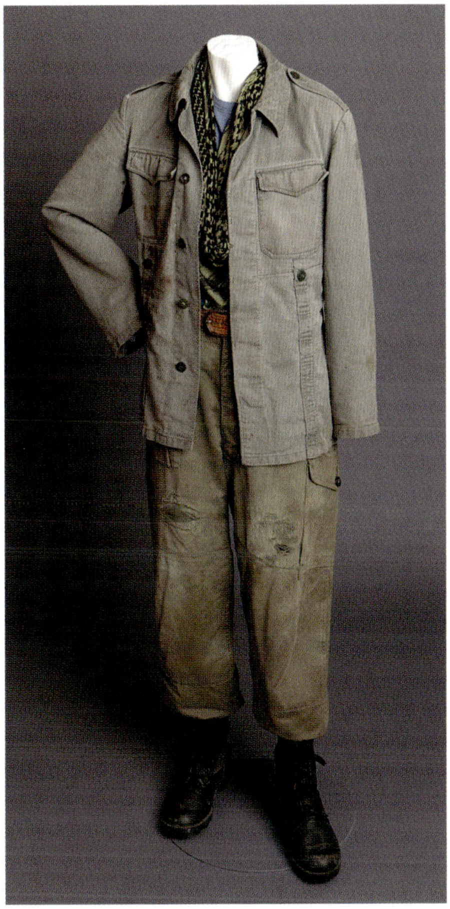

Liza Bracey, Military-Style Ensemble (Dr. Caroline Caldwell, *The Girl with All the Gifts*), 2016, Cotton, leather, GC 2017.347.1-.5

Father Figures (2017)
Film

COSTUME DESIGNER:
Kate Abraham

CHARACTER:
Helen Baxter

Sunset Boulevard (2017)
Theater

COSTUME DESIGNER:
Anthony Powell

CHARACTER:
Norma Desmond

The Wife (2017)
Film

COSTUME DESIGNER:
Trisha Biggar

CHARACTER:
Joan Castleman (*Academy Award nomination; Golden Globe Award*)

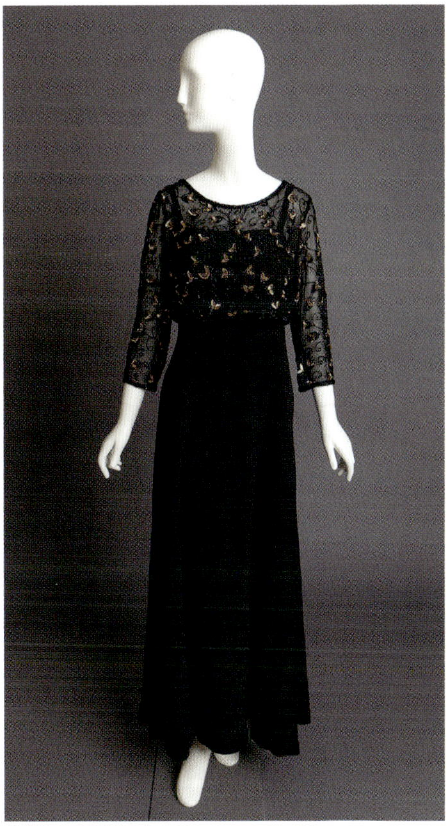

Trisha Biggar, Evening Dress (Joan Castleman, *The Wife*), 2017, Silk, glass beads, GC 2017.356.1-.2

Mother of the Maid (2018)
Theater

COSTUME DESIGNER:
Jane Greenwood

CHARACTER:
Isabelle Arc

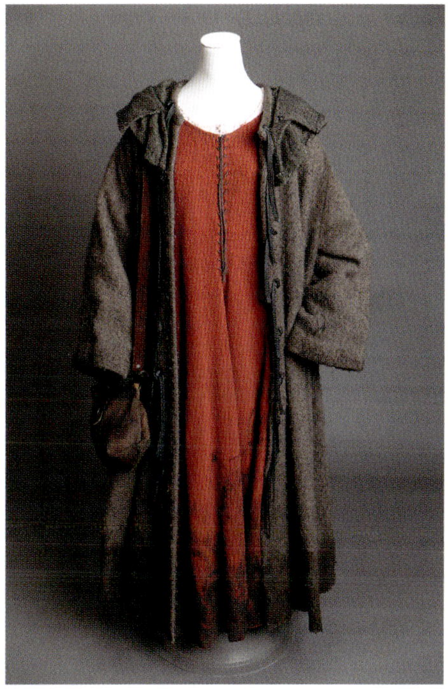

Jane Greenwood, Dress, Chemise, and Coat (Isabelle Arc, *Mother of the Maid*), 2018, Cotton, linen, wool, leather, GC 2019.365.1-.2, .367

Checklist

Kelly Gallett Richardson

All costumes courtesy of the Sage Collection, Sidney and Lois Eskenazi School of Art, Architecture + Design, Indiana University

COSTUMING THE CONTEMPORARY

Sunny von Bülow, *Reversal of Fortune*

Copper Evening Gown
GC 2017.149.1

Pink Cocktail Dress
GC 2017.148.1–.2 AB

Gold and White Evening Dress with Bolero
GC 2017.150.1 AB

Green Bed Jacket and Nightgown
GC 2017.142.1 AB

Pink Bed Jacket and Pewter Nightgown
GC 2017.144.1–.2

Pewter Dressing Gown
GC 2017.141.1

Alex Forrest, *Fatal Attraction*

Navy and Gold Dress
GC 2017.58.1

Black Leather Jacket
GC 2017.66.1 AB

White Dress
GC 2017.57.1

Teddy Barnes, *Jagged Edge*

Navy Blue Suit
GC 2017.76.1–.2

Purple Suit
GC 2017.78.1–.2

Khaki Belted Suit
GC 2017.79.1 AB

Gray Suit
GC 2017.77.1–.2

CRAFTING IDENTITY

Claire Wellington, *The Stepford Wives*

Yellow and White Ladybug Ensemble
GC 2017.300.1–.2 AB

Pink and White "Claireobics" Ensemble
GC 2017.294.1–.3, .5

Shoes
GC 2017.294.4 AB

Blue and White Georgette Dress
GC 2017.296.1–.3, .5

Yellow and White Evening Gown
GC 2017.301.1–.2, .10

Shoes
GC 2017.301.7 AB

Jenny Fields, *The World According to Garp*

Nurse's Uniform and Coat
GC 2017.309.1 B, .310

Robe
GC 2017.308.1 AB

Shoes
GC 2017.309.2 AB

Albert Nobbs, *Albert Nobbs*

Suit
GC 2017.31.1, .3–.8, .10

Silver-Polishing Ensemble
GC 2017 34.1–.4 AB

Corset
GC 2017.32.1

Pocket Watch
GC 2017.31.9

Boots
GC 2017.31.10 AB

Dress
GC 2017.36.1–.2

BRINGING HISTORY TO LIFE

Marquise de Merteuil, *Dangerous Liaisons*

Blue and Pink Dress
GC 2017.50.1, .3

Cape
GC 2017.53.1

White Dress
GC 2017.51.1 AB

Shoes
GC 2017.52.5 AB

Traveling Ensemble
GC 2017.52.1 AB

Corset
GC 2017.50.2

Open Panniers
GC 2017.52.3

Muslin Panniers
GC 2017.52.2

Eleanor of Aquitaine, *The Lion in Winter*

Horseback Ensemble
GC 2017.287.1–.5

Sarah Wheaton Witting, *Sarah, Plain and Tall*

Apron and Blouse
GC 2017.161.1, .162.1

Duster
GC 2017.171.1, .175.1

Dress with Lace Yoke
GC 2017.152.1

Canvas Boots
GC 2017.159.1 AB

Sarah Wheaton Witting, *Skylark*

Birthday Dress
GC 2017.167.1 AB

White Oxfords
GC 2017.189.1 AB

Sarah Wheaton Witting, *Sarah, Plain and Tall: Winter's End*

Ticking Stripe Dress
GC 2017.191.1

Ensemble with Scarf
GC 2017.196.1–.3

Dressing Gown
GC 2017.197.1

Slippers
2017.236.1 AB

Barn Coat
GC 2017.198.1

Leather Boots
GC 2017.235.1 AB

MAKING FANTASY REAL

Cruella De Vil, *101 Dalmatians*

Zebra Coat
GC 2017.6.1–.3, .5

Shoes
GC 2017.2.2 AB

Black Suit
GC 2017.2.1, .5–.7

Tiger Ensemble
GC 2017.3.1–.4, .6 AB

Boots
GC 2017.3.5 AB

Python Dress
GC 2017.7.1

Python Jewelry
GC 2017.7.4 A–D

Shoes
GC 2017.7.2 AB

Arrowhead Jewelry
GC 2017.1.7, .12 AB

Red Dress with Red and Black Fur Coat
GC 2017.1.2, .4–.8

Charm Bracelet
GC 2017.1.8

Cruella De Vil, *102 Dalmatians*

Prison Release Dress
GC 2017.11.1

Prison Coatdress
GC 2017.10.1–.2, .4

Shoes
GC 2017.10.3 AB

Handcuffs and Shackles
GC 2017.10.7, .8

Flower Coatdress
GC 2017.24.1

Bubble Wrap Coatdress
GC 2017.23.1

Dog Bone Dress
GC 2017.12.1, .3–.4

Shoes
GC 2017.12.2 AB

Transformation Suit #1
GC 2017.15.1–.2, .5–.6

Transformation Bracelet #1
GC 2017.15.6

Transformation Suit #2
GC 2017.16.1–.2, .4–.5

Transformation Suit #3
GC 2017.17.1–.2, .6

Transformation Shoes #3
GC 2017.17.3 AB

Black Dress with Red and Black Fur Coat
GC 2017.20.1–.3, .5–.6

Dragon Ensemble
GC 2017.13.1–.3, .7–.8

Flame/Firebird Dress
GC 2017.14.1, .4, .6

Nova Prime, *Marvel Studio's Guardians of the Galaxy*

Nova Prime Uniform
GC 2017.345.1–.4, .6

Shoes
GC 2017.345.8 AB

Index

Italics denote images.
Film characters are listed under the film title.

Photo Credits

All studio photography by Anna Powell Denton, with the exception of the below, by Shanti Carrigan Knight: 20; 22 (below); 61 (left); 62 (below); 81; 85; 89 (left); 90 (right); 91 (left); 104; 105 (top left and top right); 111; 115 (below left); 130; 147; 154; 155; 163 (left).

Courtesy of Joan Marcus: 10; 15; 46 (below); 67.

AF archive/Alamy Stock Photo: 12.

Paul Smith/Alamy Live News: 17.

Photo 12/Alamy Stock Photo: 20.

Allstar Picture Library Ltd./Alamy Stock Photo: 21.

Columbia Pictures/Getty Images: 23.

United Archives GmbH/Alamy Stock Photo: 24.

Francis Specker/Alamy Stock photo; (right) UPI/ Kevin Dietsch/Alamy Stock Photo: 29 (left).

Courtesy of Glenn Close: 25; 26; 59; 63 (top).

Hannah Chiarella: 30.

Courtesy of Indiana University Department of Theatre Drama and Contemporart Dance: 37.

Courtesy of James Nadeaux: 31; 45 (top right); 70 (below).

Columbia/Kobal/Shutterstock: 32.

Courtesy of Heather Milam: 36.

The New York Public Library, Billy Rose Theatre Division: 39 (left).

Kelly Gallett Richardson: 39 (right).

Courtesy of Katherine Marshall: 41.

Courtesy of Eleanor Wolfe: 42; 44; 45 (top left); 47 (top left).

Moviestore Collection Ltd / Alamy Stock Photo: 47 (top right), 51.

© Orion Pictures/ Courtesy: Everett Collection. 52 (top).

World History Archive/Alamy Stock Photo (below): 52 (top).

© Columbia Pictures Collection Christophel/ Alamy Stock Photo: 53.

Snap/Shutterstock: 57.

© Lorimar-Warner Bros/TCD/Prod.DB/Alamy Stock Photo: 58; 115 (top left).

AA Film Archive/Alamy Stock Photo: 60.

© Paramount: TCD/Prod.DB/Alamy Stock Photo: 60.

PARAMOUNT PICTURES/Album: Album/Alamy Stock Photo: 64.

PictureLux/The Hollywood Archive/Alamy Stock Photo: 65.

© 1988 Warner Photo, Credit: Etienne George All Rights Reserved File. PictureLux/The Hollywood Archive/Alamy Stock Photo: 66 (top).

AF archive/Alamy Stock Photo: 66 (below).

AA Film Archive/Alamy Stock Photo: 68 (top).

Photo 12/Alamy Stock Photo: 68 (below left).

Allstar Picture Library Ltd./Alamy Stock Photo: 68 (below left).

Entertainment Pictures/Alamy Stock Photos: 69.

Moviestore Collection Ltd/Alamy Stock Photo 70 (top).

Photo 12/Alamy Stock Photo: 87 (right).

AF archive/Alamy Stock Photo: 90 (left).

Photo by Theo Wargo/Getty Images for DGA: 94.

© Paramount Pictures: TCD/Prod.DB/Alamy Stock Photo: 91 (right).

Kunsthaus Zürich: 102.

Bayerische Staatsgemäldesammlungen - Alte Pinakothek München: 109.

AF archive/Alamy Stock Photo: 117 (top right).

Courtesy the Ramsey's Archive, Texas State University: 123; 128.

Courtesy the Witliff Collections Texas State University: 122.

Collection Christophel © Hallmark Hall of Fame Productions: Collection Christophel / Alamy Stock Photo: 127 (right).

Moviestore Collection Ltd/Alamy Stock Photo: 138 (left).

Photo 12 / Alamy Stock Photo. Photographer Walt Disney Pictures: 142 (left); 144 (left).

Courtesy of Shutterstock: 146 (right).

Photo by Pal Hansen/Contour by Getty Images: 150.

PictureLux/The Hollywood Archive/Alamy Stock Photo. Photographer: PictureLux 153 (top).

Walt Disney Productions/Album/Alamy Stock Photo: 160 (top).

© Marvel Studios: TCD/Prod.DB/Alamy Stock Photo: 173.

Pictorial Press Ltd / Alamy Stock Photo: cover.

Scala Arts Publishers, Inc.
c/o CohnReznick LLP
1301 Avenue of the Americas
10th floor
New York, NY 10019
www.scalapublishers.com
Scala - New York - London

Distributed outside of the Sidney and Lois Eskenazi Museum of Art in the book trade by
ACC Art Books
6 West 18th Street
Suite 4B
New York, NY 10011

In association with the
Sidney and Lois Eskenazi Museum of Art
1133 East 7th Street
Bloomington, IN 47405
artmuseum.indiana.edu/visit

ISBN 978-1-78551-333-6

Edited by Magda Nakassis
Designed by Studio A, Alexandria, VA
Printed in China

10 9 8 7 6 5 4 3 2 1

Captions
Cover: Ann Roth (American), made by Barbara Matera Ltd.,
Evening Gown (Jan/Maxie, *Maxie*), 1985,
Silk, glass beads, plastic sequins,
GC 2017.94.1

Page 2: Judianna Makovsky (American)
Sunny von Bülow
Reversal of Fortune, 1990
Silk, nylon
GC 2017.148.1-.2 AB

Library of Congress Cataloging-in-Publication Data: Names: Sidney and Lois Eskenazi Museum of Art, issuing body. | Richardson, Kelly Gallett, contributor. | Olmsted, Galina K., contributor. | Akou, Heather Marie, contributor. | Maher, Jennifer E., contributor. | Milam, Heather, contributor. | Pisano, Linda, contributor. Title: The art of character : highlights from the Glenn Close costume collection / Kelly Gallett Richardson, Galina Olmsted, Heather Akou, Jennifer E. Maher, Heather Milam, Linda Pisano. Description: Bloomington, Indiana : Eskenazi Museum of Art, Indiana University ; New York, NY : Scala Arts Publishers, Inc., [2021] | Summary: "OSCAR-nominated actor Glenn Close donated her costume collection, comprised of over 800 costumes and accessories, to The Elizabeth Sage Historic Costume Collection—part of the Eskenazi School of Art, Architecture+Design at Indiana University. Costumes from the following films: Fatal Attraction, Dangerous Liaisons, 101 Dalmatians, and Stepford Wives. Designers featured include Anthony Powell, Ann Roth, Ellen Mirojnick, James Acheson and Consolata Boyle. A study of the quality of these outfits and explores how Close considers costume as essential to creating her stage and screen characters"- Provided by publisher. Identifiers: LCCN 2020056112 | ISBN 9781785513336 (hardback) Subjects: LCSH: Close, Glenn, 1947—Clothing-Catalogs. | Sidney and Lois Eskenazi Museum of Art-Catalogs. | Elizabeth Sage Historic Costume Collection-Catalogs. | Costume—United States—Catalogs. Classification: LCC PN2287.C5467 S53 2021 | DDC 391.00973--dc23 LC record available at https://lccn.loc.gov/2020056112

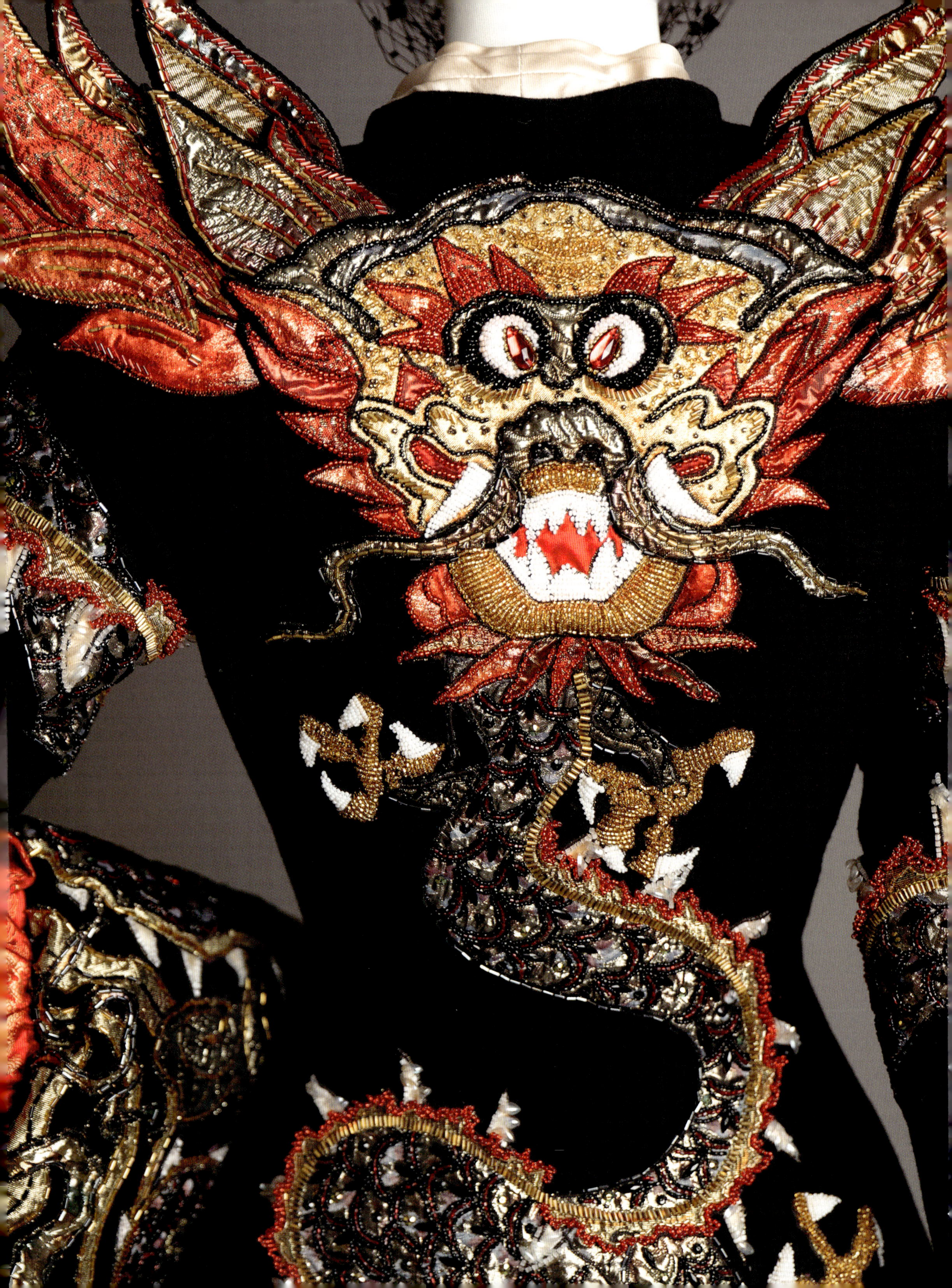